Islamic Interpretive Tradition and Gender Justice

Processes of Canonization, Subversion, and Change

Edited by

NEVIN REDA AND YASMIN AMIN

McGill-Queen's University Press
Montreal & Kingston • Chicago • London

ISBN 978-0-2280-0162-1 (cloth)
ISBN 978-0-2280-0163-8 (paper)
ISBN 978-0-2280-0296-3 (ePDF)

Legal deposit fourth quarter 2020
Bibliothèque nationale du Québec

Printed in Canada on acid-free paper that is 100% ancient forest free (100% post-consumer recycled), processed chlorine free

Funded by the Government of Canada | Financé par le gouvernement du Canada | Canada | Canada Council for the Arts | Conseil des arts du Canada

We acknowledge the support of the Canada Council for the Arts.

Nous remercions le Conseil des arts du Canada de son soutien.

Library and Archives Canada Cataloguing in Publication

Title: Islamic interpretive tradition and gender justice: processes of canonization, subversion, and change / edited by Nevin Reda and Yasmin Amin.

Names: Reda, Nevin, 1965– editor. | Amin, Yasmin, 1962– editor.

Description: Includes bibliographical references and index.

Identifiers: Canadiana (print) 20200224824 | Canadiana (ebook) 20200225057 | ISBN 9780228001621 (cloth) | ISBN 9780228001638 (paper) | ISBN 9780228002963 (ePDF)

Subjects: LCSH: Women in Islam. | LCSH: Women in the Qur'an. | LCSH: Women in the Hadith. | LCSH: Women (Islamic law) | LCSH: Women's rights—Religious aspects—Islam. | LCSH: Feminism—Religious aspects—Islam. | LCSH: Sex role—Religious aspects—Islam. | LCSH: Qur'an—Feminist criticism. | LCSH: Hadith—Feminist criticism.

Classification: LCC BP173.4 .I85 2020 | DDC 297.082—dc23

This book was typeset by Marquis Interscript in 10.5/13 Sabon.

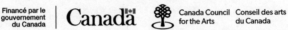

Contents

Acknowledgments

Remember Me and I will remember you; thank Me and do not be ungrateful.

Qur'an 2:152

We are deeply honoured to have worked with all scholars in this volume and to have helped showcase their work. Foremost among them are Omaima Abou-Bakr and Mulki Al-Sharmani, without whose support we may never have embarked on this project and who also helped guide us along the way. The name of the book stems from a panel that Dr Al-Sharmani put together for the International Association for the History of Religions World Congress in Erfurt, Germany, 2015, and that included earlier versions of the essays of Abou-Bakr and Al-Sharmani, Hoda El-Saadi, and our own two. These four essays formed the nucleus around which this book was built. Professor Al-Sharmani also organized a second panel, bearing the same name, in April 2017, which included advanced versions of the four papers, as well as Amira Abou-Taleb's paper. We appreciate the feedback we received from students and faculty at the faculty of theology, University of Helsinki, during the workshop.

We would also like to thank all our contributors – Asma Afsaruddin, Amina Inloes, Aisha Geissinger, Amira Abou-Taleb, Doris Decker, Hoda El-Saadi, and Sarah Eltantawi – for joining this project and enriching the content with their thought-provoking ideas, hard work, and flexibility in accepting the edits, reworks, and numerous suggestions, and for meeting the deadlines. It has been a pleasure working with a group of like-minded, believing scholars.

We are deeply grateful to Emmanuel College of Victoria University of Toronto, led by Principal Michelle Voss-Roberts, for providing a subvention for this project, which allowed the book to be published.

I (Nevin Reda) am indebted to Emmanuel College for the learning opportunities it has provided me and for the spirit of collegiality that permeates the faculty there.

We owe thanks to the McGill-Queen's University Press's editorial team, led by Kyla Madden, and to everyone who was involved in the production of our book. We are deeply appreciative of all their efforts.

Special thanks and gratitude go to Dr Wafya Hamouda for undertaking the gargantuan task of preparing the necessary index for this volume.

Last, but not least, we would like to offer heartfelt thanks to our families, who have supported us during our long years of study and the approximately two years it took to finish the manuscript and get it published: our husbands, Yehia and Haytham, who put up with sometimes being slightly neglected in favour of our work, daughters Naila, Malak, Lenah, and Jasmin, sons, Youssef and Ali, who relinquished some of the time due to them in favour of a worthy cause, and one grandson, Hasan, who will grow up one day and hopefully appreciate his grandma's research, as much as she appreciates the joy he always brings her. A special thought goes to our fathers, Ismail and Ahmed, and our mothers, Zeinab and Brigitte, who were friends for many years and who would be happy to know that their friendship and ours continues in the pursuit of knowledge. We hope to make them proud.

Alhamdulillah (praise and thanks be to God) for the opportunity to edit this collection of essays, which we hope will be thought-provoking and a catalyst for change toward more equitable ends.

Nevin Reda and Yasmin Amin
June 2019

ISLAMIC INTERPRETIVE TRADITION AND GENDER JUSTICE

Introduction

Nevin Reda

"The sharp rocks of old traditions bloody our new-found feet,"[1] wrote May Ziyāda (1886–1941) to Malak Ḥifnī Nāṣif (1886–1918), a pioneer in the first wave of the Muslim women's movement (1900–60),[2] as she expressed the heavy toll that entrenched positions take on women's struggle for gender justice. Since the days of these early Arab trailblazers, Muslim feminists and activists have accomplished much in changing unjust social conditions, particularly in the realms of education, job opportunities, and political participation. As part of a worldwide movement, they have supported the emergence of human rights discourses and large-scale initiatives for the advancement of women, such as the United Nations Convention for the Elimination of Discrimination against Women (CEDAW), and have, in turn, benefited from these developments. Muslim women have also not been silent in the religious realm, producing tomes of new interpretations, leading to the rise of Muslim and Islamic feminism. These two movements embrace discourses and practices of advocacy for women's rights located within an Islamic paradigm and thus sometimes converge. In fact, Islamic feminism is a form of Muslim feminism that is distinguished by its intention to garner change by relying on Islamic sources and working from within the tradition, although both strands of feminism utilize various lines of argumentation that are not all necessarily religious. Since the 1980s, Islamic feminism has become a distinct phenomenon within Muslim feminism, characterized by its grounding in Islamic feminist scholarship and by the sophistication of its scholarly arguments.[3] Global networks have emerged that advocate for Muslim women's equality in law and other realms and that have pioneered knowledge-building programs which are helping disseminate a more egalitarian vision of Islam.[4] Yet despite all of these achievements, women's discourses have not made significant headway in the lived experience of Islam, and traditionalist interpretations remain hegemonic. This lack of headway can be noted, for example, in the area of family law in many Muslim-majority countries, where classical interpretations of *sharīʿa* (Sharia) hold sway. In the Muslim world, men continue to take multiple wives, women do not have equal access to divorce, child marriages (though illegal in most Muslim-majority countries) occur, and segregation is the norm in many religious institutions. No matter how convincing and well-reasoned the new interpretations are or how deeply they are grounded in the sacred texts, unjust authoritarian interpretations continue to find realization and widespread acceptance within Muslim societies. It would seem that what eventually becomes part of the "canon" of accepted interpretations is subject to various processes of authorization in which conformity to the primary sources or even reasonableness may not be the most decisive factor. The entrenchment of tradition that Ziyāda described so vividly continues to thrive in the interpretive realm and is in need of special attention.

The contributors to this book grapple with the problem of fixed interpretations that affect women, the processes by which they become authoritative, and the theoretical foundations upon which they are built. They explore the subtle tensions between processes of canonization, methodological foundations, and living practice within the Islamic interpretive tradition, focusing on the issue of gender justice. The chapters illustrate that in the ongoing struggle for gender equality, oppressive texts, interpretations, and legal formulations – all of these bolstered by canonical processes – are best addressed by marshalling arguments based on strong methodological foundations or by the lived realities that serve to contest their authoritativeness and thus their place within the "canon." This volume thereby raises awareness of the question of canonization in Islam, its connection to gender issues, and its role in communal identity-building, a process that is constantly in flux. It also implicitly argues for new egalitarian, ethical, and gender-conscious engagement with the Qurʾan and with the canons of texts that derive their authority from claims that they interpret it. One should note the centrality of the Islamic interpretive tradition in Muslim identity-building, as one can surmise, for example, from Shahab Ahmed's magnum opus *What Is Islam? The Importance of*

Being Islamic, in which he conceptualizes the phenomenon of Islam as a hermeneutical engagement with various aspects of the revelation to Muḥammad.[5]

Yet can one speak of "canonization" in connection with the Islamic tradition, when Islam's languages, history, cultural presuppositions, and conceptual framework are so different from experiences within the English-speaking world that have forever shaped the meaning of that word? The difficulties with lifting terms and concepts from English-speaking contexts and applying them to Islam have been described at length by Ahmed in his aforementioned work, in which he critiques analytical methods that approach Islam using the categories of "religion" and "culture," among other things.[6] So one can imagine the challenges of using a historically loaded term such as "canonization" in connection with Islam. For example, in the West it evokes meanings that have to do with the Catholic Church and its history of canonizing texts, laws, and saints; when one hears that word in an English-speaking context. However, the Islamic tradition does not have similar centralized authority structures or ordination processes that give authority to its leadership, so the contextual nuances associated with "canonization" are generally absent in Muslim contexts. The Islamic tradition distinguishes itself from other religious traditions by its supposed lack of an institutionalized body, such as a church, or religious authorities, such as priests or rabbis, which the Qur'an mentions critically (Q. 3:64; 9:31). Indeed, that scripture presents its egalitarian approach to religious authority as a cornerstone of its distinctive brand of monotheism.[7] Hence, at least in theory, in Islam there is no formal religious authority that can engage in processes of canonization and authorization and that can privilege some interpretations to the exclusion of others. Even so, "canonization" as a term in English describes phenomena that have significant common ground with various activities in the Muslim world, with the result that using it in connection with Islam facilitates the communication process and describes Islamic phenomena in ways that make sense in an English-speaking context. In fact, using "canonization" also brings an inherent paradox to the forefront, for how can a tradition that prides itself on its egalitarianism and lack of formal structures of religious authority display all the trappings of canonical texts, canonical figures, and canon law? Indeed, the very existence of the phenomenon of canonization in Islam raises to prominence the institutions and religious elites that support it and, by extension, the stark contrast between how they have shaped the tradition and how the Qur'an presents Islamic self-identification. Moreover, the emerging field of canon studies recognizes a variety of similar phenomena in different religious traditions and cultures, including Islam.[8]

Up to this point, five scholars have used the term "canonization" and insights from canon studies to advance the study of Islam, with subtle differences in their usages, ranging from applications that focus purely on text to those within the more practical realm of law. Brannon Wheeler was the earliest to do so, relying on the work of Jonathan Z. Smith and choosing the expression "applying the canon" in connection with the interpretive corpora of the Ḥanafī school of law – the most widespread tradition of legal reasoning in Islam. In his work, he understands "canonization" more or less as "authorization," applying the notion of canon to the repertoire of interpretive choices offered by the Ḥanafī school in any given case and that jurists have at their disposal when issuing rulings. Wheeler's concern is therefore with the realm of law – not necessarily the primary texts of Islam (Qur'an and *Ḥadīth*) – and he highlights the practical aspect of these interpretations, incidentally explaining *sharī'a* as the "definition of practice."[9] Although he relies on sophisticated research in the field of canon studies, his understanding of canonization also recalls the word's etymology – it is derived from the Greek *kanòn*, meaning "measuring stick" and hence "standard,"[10] as well as the Arabic word *qānūn*, meaning "the standard by which everything is measured," which eventually came to mean "law."[11] Wheeler's broad understanding of "canonization" in the sense of "authorization" and his emphasis on the practical dimension is in keeping with how we understand canonization here, although we apply it more broadly than just to the Ḥanafī religious-legal tradition and its hierarchy of interpretive authority.

Instead of to law, Aziz Al-Azmeh and Sylvie Boisliveau apply "canonization" to the Qur'an. Al-Azmeh also examines *ḥadīth* (reports of the Prophet Muḥammad's sayings and actions) and points to *ijmā'* (consensus) as the process by which canonization takes place.[12] *Ijmā'* is an important principle in the Islamic religious-legal tradition, along with the Qur'an, *ḥadīth*, and some forms of legal reasoning (*qiyās*). It is often used to validate existing tradition, so Al-Azmeh is describing well-disseminated discourses. Also, he is implicitly advancing the case for the valorization of the Islamic scripture as an authoritative text through the vehicles of the Islamic legal tradition. Nevertheless, as Boisliveau has pointed out, the Qur'an is self-authorizing in the sense that it is the only book in the Abrahamic tradition to claim for itself the status of divine authorship, gaining its significance from its textual formulations, in contradistinction to *ḥadīth* and to other texts that acquire their authoritative status from the community or religious institution's assertions of divine provenance. To use Boisliveau's terms, the Qur'an is the "cause" of communal authorization, not the "result."[13] Indeed, the text was fixed within decades of the Prophet's passing (if not during his lifetime),[14] which meant it was not subject to the centuries-long processes of selection and elevation that the books of the Bible, for example, had to undergo. The case for the community as the main locus of textual authorization is easier to make for the *ḥadīth* corpus, as aptly demonstrated in the work of Jonathan Brown, who examines the canonization of the collections of Abū ʿAbd Allāh Muḥammad al-Bukhārī (d. 256/870) and Muslim ibn al-Ḥajjāj (d. 261/875). His detailed analysis illustrates the lengthy historical processes of communal acceptance and legitimization that lent the two works their "canonical" status and that brought them continued support by means of a "canonical culture";[15] it also delves into the religious-legal principle of *ijmāʿ*.[16] Like Wheeler, Ahmed El-Shamsy examines canonization in the realm of law, but he focuses on texts and on the community's relationship to these texts and how they came to be viewed as sources of religious norms to the exclusion of other sources. El-Shamsy describes the role of Muḥammad ibn Idrīs al-Shāfiʿī (d. 204/820) and his "canon-centered individualism" in this process[17] in conversation with the locus of authority being communal practice, as in his erstwhile teacher Mālik ibn Anas's (d. 179/795) reliance on the collective practice of his hometown, Medina.[18]

In this volume, we understand canonization to mean non-definitive, non-authoritative "authorization" and large-scale, long-standing communal buy-in, generally led by the predominantly male religious scholarly elite and disseminated in their discourses. We apply "canonization" to a plethora of phenomena in the Islamic tradition, all of which interpret the Qur'an in some form or other, including *tafsīr* (exegesis), *fiqh* (jurisprudence), and also embodied interpretation in the form of exemplary figures or role models. We recognize that the above-mentioned scholars make valuable contributions, but in this volume, for important reasons, we do not apply "canonization" to the Qur'an or equate the phenomenon to *ijmāʿ*. First, as noted earlier, the Qur'an is possibly the only scripture associated with a major religious tradition to self-authorize, and the text was fixed within a short time, so the opportunity for large-scale communal or institutional involvement in selection processes was small. Second, Islamic feminism, upon which some of the chapters in this volume build, is a theologically grounded discourse of believing women[19] who dispute the interpretation of the sacred text, not the *actual* text or its status as divine revelation. Although not all of the contributors identify as Islamic or even Muslim feminists, the history of this movement is such that it makes allowances for dialogue and exchange, as can be noted in the correspondence of May Ziyāda, a Palestinian Christian from Nazareth, and Malak Ḥifnī Nāṣif, an Egyptian Muslim from the al-Fayyūm oasis, which was published in Nāṣif's widely read newspaper column.

With regard to *ijmāʿ*, three reasons prevent us from accepting it as an argument for "canonization." First, ironically, there has been no consensus in Islam as to its constituents. Mālik envisioned it as the consensus of the people of Medina; al-Shāfiʿī strongly disputed this geographically localized *ijmāʿ* and argued for the more inclusive, universal vision of the consensus of the general populace (*ijmāʿ al-ʿawām*);[20] ʿAlī ibn Aḥmad ibn Saʿīd ibn Ḥazm (d. 456/1063) proposed a consensus of scholars (*ijmāʿ al-ʿulamāʾ*) in given cases;[21] Taqī al-Dīn Aḥmad ibn ʿAbd al-Ḥalīm ibn Taymiyya (d. 728/1327) critiqued Ibn Ḥazm's work and demonstrated the impossibility of determining all the scholarly opinions in these cases (except, perhaps, for the first two or three generations of Muslims);[22] and Twelver Shiʿi legal theorists conceptualize an *ijmāʿ* that involves the Imāms and gains its legitimacy from them.[23] Second, all Qurʾanic occurrences of this term – that is, all words that have the same root and form as *ijmāʿ* – point to its use as a tool wielded by powerful majorities to silence the truth in dissenting minority voices: in the case of Noah's people coming to a consensus against him (Q. 10:71); of Joseph's brothers throwing him into a well (Q. 12:15, 102); and of Pharaoh's magicians' opposition to Moses (Q. 20:61–64). In fact, the term does not have a single positive occurrence in the Qurʾan, which makes its usage theologically difficult on the part of believers. Third, in everyday oppressive discourses, this principle is used to silence the ones fighting for justice, which makes the term even more problematic, incidentally recalling the Qurʾanic portrayals.

As one can note with the critique of the notion of *ijmāʿ*, although there are precedents and overlaps in the way we use "canonization" and the work of other scholars, there is one important difference: the degree of charity we are willing to extend canonical interpretations that promulgate and enshrine women's inequality and gendered hierarchies. Brown has noted that a certain amount of "charity" on the part of the interpretive (and scholarly) community is necessary in order to present a text in the best possible light and to smooth over problems in a text's pre-canonical history and inconsistencies with established methodological criteria.[24] Once the texts achieve canonical status, they become part and parcel of communal identity, which is what makes them so difficult to contest. This volume does not approach processes of canonization and their end results descriptively, to explain historical developments, or apologetically, to defend male privilege; rather, the chapters in this collection are decidedly less charitable in their acceptance of the canonicity of unjust interpretations, and even contest those interpretations. Canonization and identity-building are fluid processes that can change over time depending on the various discourses and the traction they find within communities. Women have not had equal opportunity to engage in these processes, with the result that the tradition has been shaped largely by men. For example, al-Azhar, one of the world's oldest and most influential universities, did not accept female students from its founding in 971 until 1961, when it admitted its first female cohort. For almost a thousand years, this institution gave men all the tools and opportunities to shape the tradition and denied them to women. Even today, it is two separate institutions, with women and men segregated during the learning experience. One should, of course, note that although women have not had equal educational opportunities, many did succeed in becoming scholars prior to the twentieth century.[25] This phenomenon is particularly noticeable in *ḥadīth* and in other areas where women functioned largely as passive transmitters of knowledge, participating in the dissemination of books produced by men instead of actively authoring their own compositions. This volume, therefore, provides an opportunity to contest some of the biases that have accrued over the centuries, implicitly arguing for a "decanonization" of unjust texts, interpretations, and laws. As it sheds light on the complexity of the notion of canonization in Islam, it also highlights the historical parallels and the inherent paradox the English term "canonization" brings to the forefront.

Another feature of this collection is its engagement with the problem of methodology. Reformists and Islamic feminists who attempt to introduce change to the tradition are often accused of lacking methodological acumen compared to traditional, male Muslim scholars.

For example, when the controversy surrounding women-led prayers arose in North America in 2005, Hina Azam charitably based her defence of the traditionalist position on its supposed methodological superiority in her response to Nevin Reda, who presented a widely disseminated argument for women-led prayers.[26] For egalitarian discourses to find traction within a broad scholarly constituency, they must grapple with this problem, examining the strengths and weaknesses of traditional methodologies, applying them in cases where they make sense, and exploring new approaches that are better suited to the contemporary era. Accordingly, this volume confronts the myth that exegesis and substantive law are consistently based on sound methodology. As scholars have recognized before us, the *practices* of interpretation and of deriving law existed and thrived prior to the development of the methodological *theories* that attempted to describe – and proscribe – the processes by which such interpretations came into being.[27] Neither exegesis nor law was systematically examined in light of these later methodologies to ascertain whether they adhered to these guidelines and to update them in cases where they did not. By engaging the question of methodology, this volume advances the study of gender justice in Islam one more step.

The third distinctive feature of this volume is its currency, in the sense that it addresses key issues in contemporary feminist discourse that have tangible repercussions for the lived experience of Islam. The collection covers major Islamic categories of knowledge, including *tafsīr*, *fiqh*, and biographical dictionaries. Islamic feminist and other scholarly discourses tease apart the distinctions between *sharīʿa* and *fiqh*. The Arabic word *sharīʿa* literally means the path to the life-giving substance of water and technically refers to the totality of God's will to humankind, that is, the values and principles as revealed to the Prophet Muḥammad in the sacred sources of Islam.[28] In contradistinction, *fiqh* is a human interpretive endeavour of *sharīʿa,* more specifically, the legal aspects and rulings as found in the vast corpus of religious-legal works by Muslim jurists.[29] The chapters in this volume engage key problem areas in contemporary *fiqh*-informed practices, including polygamy, wife-beating, child marriage, interreligious marriage, divorce, segregation, stoning, and slavery. As a collection, they display depth and breadth in their analysis of gender-related issues in the Islamic tradition. More importantly, they link theory with living practice, engaging in thoughtful, deliberate, constructive critique that aims to advance equality for women while proposing appropriate methodologies and new interpretations. Some of the contributors are scholars who are incidentally connected to major Islamic feminist networks and are therefore conversant with the most current issues. This collection thus reflects some of the key concerns of contemporary Islamic feminist discourse, among other gender-related interests.

This volume has ten chapters, organized into three parts, each of which addresses an important issue that has been subject to "canonization" in the Islamic tradition: texts, figures, and laws. The Qur'an is central to Islam. Within the discipline of *fiqh*, it is considered the primary textual source and is generally listed first. Historically, it has been interpreted in diverse ways that have contributed to the process of lawmaking that informs practices pertaining to women. The first section examines the Qur'an and its interpretations, linking text to practice by addressing major issues that have practical implications in the lived experience of women. Each of its three chapters provides important historical background and examines Qur'anic verses through a particular methodological lens.

Omaima Abou-Bakr and Mulki Al-Sharmani's "Islamic Feminist *Tafsīr* and Qur'anic Ethics: Rereading Divorce Verses" leads off this collection. It explores the possibility of a coherent and ethically oriented hermeneutical approach to the gender question in the sacred text. It begins with a brief overview of Islamic feminist scholarship, which will help orient the reader in the field. The chapter also highlights the importance of ethics in contemporary feminist discourses and its emergence as a central question in Islamic feminist scholarship. It takes this concern a step further to present a new methodology for Qur'an interpretation, building upon the work of Muhammad 'Abd Allāh Draz (d. 1958) and Toshihiko Izutsu (d. 1993) among others, in conversation with the "canonical" interpretations of classical Islamic scholarship. The practical case study to which the authors apply this method involves the Qur'anic divorce verses. They systematically examine semantic fields of patterned relations between certain words that constitute the ethico-religious concepts of the Qur'an and, ultimately, the Qur'an's moral code.

The second chapter, Nevin Reda's "*Tafsīr*, Tradition, and Methodological Contestations: The Case of Polygamy," is also concerned with the ethical dimension of the sacred text; this time, though, the focus is on polygamy. It presents an overview and critique of the history of *tafsīr* and the rationale for the fixation of Qur'an interpretation on the "canonical" transmitted traditions of exegetical authorities living in the first and early second centuries of Islam, a method termed *tafsīr bi'l-maʾthūr* (exegesis by transmission). It also revisits the question of methodology and examines the disconnects between this method and classical methodological principles in the case of the polygamy verse (Q. 4:3). Highlighting the importance of language, as well as the literary and historical context, it demonstrates ethical imperatives in the plain meaning of the text and the various strategies employed by classical exegetes to overcome these stipulations.

The third chapter, Asma Afsaruddin's "Reading the Qurʾan through a Gendered, Egalitarian Lens: Revisiting the Concept of *Wilāya* in Q. 9:71," explores a central question that has engaged Islamic feminist exegetes among others and has generated a fair amount of scholarship: *wilāya* (partnership), often interpreted as male guardianship over women. The chapter also examines *wilāya*'s relationship to *qiwāma*, another central issue in Islamic feminist scholarship, which classical exegetes interpret as guardianship or authority. The chapter synthesizes Islamic feminist scholarship, showing how classical and modern exegetes understood this term. Afsaruddin's diachronic reading methodology is another approach to exegesis, one that provides historical insights into how certain interpretations became authoritative to the exclusion of others.

So far, studies of canonization and Islam have focused mainly on texts and laws, specifically Qurʾan, *ḥadīth*, and *fiqh*. But there is another important area that affects women: biographical dictionaries and other texts that depict role models and how pious women are expected to behave. These figures form a kind of "embodied" interpretation of texts and practices, delineating certain hierarchies, limitations, and requirements for pious Muslim women. The four chapters in the second part of the volume address some of these presentations of authoritative figures or typologies, which convey expectations and affect the lived experience of women in Muslim societies.

Amina Inloes's "How Did Eve Get Married? Two Twelver Shiʿi *Ḥadīth* Reports" explores the Shiʿi *ḥadīth* canon and the ontology of gender hierarchy, examining portrayals of the figure of Eve in the story of the marriage of the first human couple. It illustrates that while Shiʿi and Sunni jurisprudence leans toward male authority, when discussing Eve, the Shiʿi *ḥadīth* canon also contains a "counter-narrative," one expressing a world view that does not prescribe a strict gender hierarchy and suggesting that, during the formative era of Islamic thought, belief in a gender hierarchy as an essential Islamic element was not entrenched. Based on the presence and perpetuation of this "counter-narrative," it argues that ideas about the nature and social roles of woman and man were once more fluid than they are often perceived to be, and that male authority does not need to be an essential aspect of Shiʿism, and possibly Islam in general.

Aisha Geissinger's "Female Figures, Marginality, and Qurʾanic Exegesis in Ibn al-Jawzī's *Ṣifat al-ṣafwa*" examines the portrayal of women Qurʾan interpreters in the influential Abū al-Faraj ibn al-Jawzī's (d. 597/1200) *Ṣifat al-ṣafwa* (*Typology of the Elite*),[30] which is unusual among classical texts in its attention to pious and Sufi women, in that it contains a number of depictions of early and medieval Muslim women quoting, reciting, and expounding upon Qurʾanic verses. This chapter examines and critiques textual processes of canonization in relation to women's exegetical authority, using Ibn al-Jawzī's work as a case study. It demonstrates how figures of this type can be memorialized as praiseworthy individuals, even while the knowledge of the Qurʾan that is imputed to them is typically constructed as marginal to the wider community's understandings of the text, and also as reinforcing the notion that interpretive authority is normatively masculine. Two main approaches are taken here to studying these textual processes. First, these texts are read to pinpoint key ways in which these women relate to the Qurʾan, showing how this relationship constructs their image as exemplary individuals even while minimizing their interpretive authority. Second, the portrayals of female figures in the *Ṣifat al-ṣafwa*, interacting in various ways with the Qurʾan, are compared with those for the same individuals found in other surviving classical works. This comparison brings to light the elements in their portrayal that Ibn al-Jawzī chose to emphasize or discard in the construction of his typology.

Amira Abou-Taleb's "Constructing the Image of the Model Muslim Woman: Gender Discourse in Ibn Saʿd's *Kitāb al-ṭabaqāt al-kubrā*" examines segregation and veiling in the oldest extant biographical dictionary of the early Muslim community, which functions as a canon of early exemplary figures and role models for later Muslim generations. This study examines and critiques Muḥammad ibn Saʿd's (d. 230/845) portrayal of the Prophet's wives, comparing and contrasting it with his portrayal of "common" Muslim women in the same dictionary and with the portrayal of the Prophet's wives in the biographical works of other authors. It demonstrates some of his main concerns – segregation and veiling – placing them in their historical context and in the patriarchal culture the ʿAbbāsid imperial project was attempting to promote in its role as guardian of Sunni doctrine at the time.

Doris Decker's "The Love of Prophet Muḥammad for the Jewish Woman Rayḥāna bint Zayd: Transformation and Continuity of Gender Conceptions in Classical Islamic Historiography and *Aḥādīth* Literature" illustrates the processes of canonization of figures in the biographical and historical literature, using interreligious marriage and the love story between Rayḥāna and the Prophet as a case study. It shows how the relationship between them is reconstructed in historical retrospective through the lens of the narrators' specific viewpoints and historical contexts, depicting a unique process of transformation of gender concepts. By comparing the narratives about their relationship in several biographical dictionaries and other historical works, including the compositions of Muḥammad ibn Isḥāq (d. 151/768), Abū ʿAbd Allāh al-Wāqidī (d. 207/823), and Ibn Saʿd, this chapter highlights how depictions of their relationship were reversed over time from a strong, outspoken, and dismissive Rayḥāna, whom the Prophet loved,[31] to a stylized, jealous, and needy Rayḥāna, who loved the Prophet but was ultimately heartbroken. The outcome questions the historical accuracy of historiography and consequently its authoritativeness, showing tensions between the various narratives and the efforts of ancient biographers to bridge those tensions in their construction of an idealized "canonical" version of this interreligious relationship.

The third section of this volume addresses *fiqh* and its applications. *Fiqh* is often translated as "jurisprudence," "positive law," or "substantive law." It denotes the tangible, practical aspect of law derivation or ethical reasoning, in contradistinction to *uṣūl al-fiqh* (legal theory, moral theology), which highlights the theoretical concern with the underlying methodologies. Since the Qurʾan is an important principle and textual source of *uṣūl al-fiqh*, the first part of this volume also falls under this general rubric, particularly since it examines applications in certain cases. What makes this section different from the first is its emphasis on extra-Qurʾanic factors that affect the derivation of ethical-legal judgments. Hoda El-Saadi's "*Fiqh* Rulings and Gendering the Public Space: The Discrepancy between Written Formality and Daily Reality" provides historical perspectives into *siyāsa sharʿiyya*, the ruler's legal prerogative, which affected the application of *fiqh* in Muslim societies. Contrary to popular perception, *fiqh* (or *sharīʿa*) is not synonymous with "Islamic law"; in fact, the two can sometimes differ greatly. "Islamic law" constituted both *fiqh* and *siyāsa sharʿiyya*. Through the juxtaposition of legal and non-legal sources, the chapter demonstrates the interplay of *fiqh*, *siyāsa sharʿiyya*, and women, showing how each reacted and related to the others in the case of juristic attempts to impose seclusion and confine women to the domestic sphere. The chapter thus provides insights into how women resisted these restrictions by ignoring them, thereby contesting their authoritativeness in the living tradition. At the same time, the article disputes the idealized notion that the discourses of jurists were the only source of law in pre-modern Muslim societies.

Sarah Eltantawi's "Mysterious Legislation: ʿUmar ibn al-Khaṭṭāb's Role in the Legalization of the Stoning Punishment in the Sunni Islamic Tradition" highlights another extra-Qurʾanic source that contributed to legal rulings in Islamic history – Islam's second caliph, ʿUmar ibn al-Khaṭṭab (d. 23/644). This charismatic figure almost rivalled the Prophet Muḥammad as lawmaker and was instrumental in the confirmation of stoning as a punishment for *zinā* (illegal sex) in the Sunni canons of *fiqh*, despite the absence of stoning in the Qurʾanic codex and the existence of a different Qurʾan-mandated punishment for the same crime of *zinā*: whipping. The chapter highlights two conclusions that help explain ʿUmar's support for stoning, despite these unusual circumstances. First, ʿUmar was concerned with upholding the patrilineal family structure, an agenda central to ʿUmar both during the Prophet's life and during his own rule as caliph. Second, there is evidence of ʿUmar's general disregard for women, as well as ample evidence that he considered them primarily objects of sexual temptation whose sexuality must be regulated – including by the stoning punishment for married adulterers.

Yasmin Amin's "Revisiting the Issue of Minor Marriages: Multidisciplinary *Ijtihād* on Contemporary Ethical Problems" examines an extra-Qurʾanic textual source that within the classifications of legal theorists comes second after the Qurʾan: *ḥadīth*. It examines reports that represent ʿĀʾisha's age as six at the time of her marriage to the Prophet, and nine when the marriage was consummated in *Ṣaḥīḥ al-Bukhārī*, the most important "authoritative" Sunni *ḥadīth* canon. However, when we examine other Islamic heritage books – for example, history books, *sīra* works, and biographical dictionaries – a different picture emerges. These sources make statements that refute the accuracy of these narrations, suggesting that ʿĀʾisha was at least nineteen years old at the time of consummating her marriage. By critiquing the historicity of al-Bukhārī's depictions and juxtaposing it to exegetical works of verse Q. 65:4 and other verses, this chapter disputes the legal basis for child marriage in Islam. It offers a new *ijtihād* (independent legal reasoning) to challenge the consensus and rulings on the permissibility of child marriage. The aim is to provide an overview of the history and traditional methodologies that canonized the idea of child marriage and to challenge its development from within the tradition, building upon it to develop a way forward.

In light of the above, this collection examines texts, figures, and laws that have been subject to processes of canonization across the ages. It offers thoughtful, deliberate, and constructive critique of these processes, focusing on the gender question and how these traditions affect practice and the lived experiences of women. The chapters highlight the importance of addressing the methodological basis of these discourses and understanding the historical circumstances that led to the elevation of certain traditions over others, which are themselves subject to change.

NOTES

1 *Sukhūr al-taqālīd al-qadīma tudmī aqdāmanā al-jadīda.* Nāsif, *al-Nisā'iyyāt*, 198. All translations from the Arabic are mine, unless otherwise stated.

2 Badran dates the first wave of feminism in Egypt from the 1920s to the 1950s; see Badran, *Feminism in Islam*, 141. Her dating of the start of this wave is likely due to the creation of the Egyptian Feminist Union in 1923, led by Hudā Sha'rāwī (1879–1947). However, the feminist movement was already well under way when this union was created, in part due to the seminal role played by *Al-Madrasa al-Saniyya* (established in 1873) in the education of girls, including many of the early activists, such as Nāṣif. We do not view the creation of this union as the beginning of this activism; rather, we see it as the culmination of the concerted efforts of many women (and men). Our earlier dating of the start of the first wave of Muslim feminists reflects our consideration of their efforts.

3 See Badran, *Feminism in Islam.*

4 See, for example, Mir-Hosseini, "Women in Search of Common Ground."

5 For an alternative translation/conceptualization of Islam as "wholeness making, peacemaking, well-being making, and safety making," see Reda, "What Is Islam?"

6 Ahmed, *What Is Islam?*
7 See, for example, Q. 3:64; 9:31. See also Reda, "From the Canadian Sharia Debates," 80–6.
8 For a brief history of canon studies, see Brown, *Canonization*, 21–31.
9 Wheeler, *Applying the Canon*, 2.
10 Brown, *Canonization*, 21.
11 See *miqyās kull shayʾ* in al-Zabīdī, *Tāj al-ʿarūs*, vol. 18, 466; Wehr, *Arabic-English Dictionary*, 925–6.
12 Al-Azmeh, "Canon and Canonisation"; idem, "Muslim Canon;" Boisliveau, "Canonisation du Coran."
13 Ibid. Translation from the French is mine.
14 Robinson, *Discovering the Qur'an*, 286.
15 Brown, *Canonization*, 262–99.
16 Ibid., 183-93.
17 El-Shamsy, *Canonization*, 6.
18 Ibid., 44–68.
19 Note, for example, Asma Barlas's title of her groundbreaking book *"Believing Women" in Islam: Unreading Patriarchal Interpretations of the Qurʾan*. Here, she styles her exegetical enterprise (and Islamic feminism in general) as the work of "believing women." Although belief is, of course, in the heart, at least one major school of Islamic theology defines belief as "affirmation" (*taṣdīq*), others adding "actions" to "affirmation."
20 Al-Shāfiʿī, *Al-Risāla*, 471–6, 533–55.
21 Ibn Ḥazm, *Marātib al-ijmāʿ*.
22 Ibn Taymiyya, *Naqd marātib al-ijmāʿ*, in Ibn Ḥazm and Ibn Taymiyya, *Marātib al-ijmāʿ wa-yalīh naqd marātib al-ijmāʿ*.
23 Hallaq, *Sharīʿa*, 118-920.
24 Brown, *Canonization*, 262–99.
25 See, for example, Nadwi, *Al-Muḥaddithāt*; Decker, *Frauen als Trägerinnen*; Sayeed, *Women and the Transmission*.
26 See Azam, "Critique"; Reda, "What Would the Prophet Do?"
27 See, for example, Hallaq, *Origins*.
28 See, for example, Musawah, "*Shariʾah, fiqh*, and State Laws."
29 Ibid.
30 This title is often rendered as "Characteristics of the Elite" and sometimes as "The Elite of the Elite." I have chosen "Typology of the Elite" to render the nuances of Ibn al-Jawzī's use of the singular *ṣifa*, when the plural *ṣifāt* or the gerund *waṣf* would have made more sense.
31 In the context of the Prophet Muḥammad's love for Rayḥāna, *wajada fī nafsih* is sometimes rendered "lovesick." I have chosen to translate it as

"love" in accordance with Muḥammad Murtaḍā al-Zabīdī's (d. 1205/1790) entry in *Tāj al-ʿarūs*, one of the most reputable Arabic-language dictionaries. He glosses *wajada* with *yahwāhā* and *yuḥibbuhā* and brings examples of the word's usage in the Arabic language, none of which suggest a nuance of "unrequited love" (although in the case of the Prophet, his love seems to have been initially unrequited). The examples suggest that the word is used in both positive and negative cases, that is, a man loving a woman and also a man not loving his wife, so "love" is a better fit for these diverse usages. See al-Zabīdī, *Tāj al-ʿarūs*, vol. 5, 294.

REFERENCES

Ahmed, Shahab. *What Is Islam? The Importance of Being Islamic.* Princeton: Princeton University Press, 2016.

Al-Azmeh, Aziz. "Canon and Canonisation of the Qurʾān." In *Encyclopaedia of Islam* THREE, ed. Kate Fleet, Gudrun Krämer, Denis Matringe, John Nawas, and Everett Rowson. http://dx.doi.org.myaccess.library.utoronto.ca/10.1163/1573-3912_ei3_COM_24606

– "The Muslim Canon from Late Antiquity to the Era of Modernism." In *The Times of History: Universal Themes in Islamic Historiography*, ed. Aziz Al-Azmeh, 101–35. Budapest: Central European University Press, 2007.

Azam, Hina. "A Critique for the Argument of Women-Led Friday Prayers." 18 March 2005. https://www.islamawareness.net/Deviant/Progressives/critique.html

Badran, Margot. *Feminism in Islam: Secular and Religious Convergences.* Oxford: Oneworld, 2009.

Barlas, Asma. *"Believing Women" in Islam: Unreading Patriarchal Interpretations of the Qurʾan.* Austin: University of Texas Press, 2002.

Boisliveau, Anne-Sylvie. "Canonisation du Coran… par le Coran?" *Revue des Mondes Musulmans et de la Méditerranée* 129 (2011): 153–68.

Brown, Jonathan. *The Canonization of al-Bukhārī and Muslim: The Formation and Function of the Sunnī Ḥadīth Canon.* Leiden: Brill, 2007.

Decker, Doris. *Frauen als Trägerinnen religiösen Wissens. Konzeptionen von Frauenbildern in frühislamischen Überlieferungen bis zum 9. Jahrhundert.* Stuttgart: Kohlhammer Verlag, 2012.

El-Shamsy, Ahmed. *The Canonization of Islamic Law: A Social and Intellectual History.* New York: Cambridge University Press, 2013.

Hallaq, Wael. *The Origins and Evolution of Islamic Law. Cambridge: Cambridge University Press, 2005.*

– *Sharīʿa: Theory, Practice, Transformations*. Cambridge: Cambridge University Press, 2012.

Ibn Ḥazm, ʿAlī ibn Aḥmad ibn Saʿīd and Taqī al-Dīn Aḥmad ibn Taymiyya. *Marātib al-ijmāʿ wa-yalīh naqd marātib al-ijmāʿ*. N.p.: Maktabat al-Qudsī li-Ṣāḥibihā Ḥusām al-Dīn al-Qudsī, 1357 AH.

Mir-Hosseini, Ziba. "Women in Search of Common Ground: Between Islamic and International Human Rights Law." In *Islamic Law and International Human Rights Law*, ed. Anver Emon, Mark Ellis, and Benjamin Glahn, 291–303. Oxford: Oxford University Press, 2012.

Musawah. "*Shariʾah, fiqh*, and State Laws: Clarifying the Terms," Musawah Knowledge Building Briefs—01. N.p.: Musawah, 2016.

Nadwi, Mohammad Akram. *Al-Muḥaddithāt: The Women Scholars in Islam*. Oxford: Interface Publications, 2007.

Nāsif, Malak Ḥifnī [Bāḥithat al-Bādiya]. *Al-Nisāʾiyyāt: majmūʿat maqālāt nushirat fī Al-Jarīda fī mawḍūʿ al-marʾa al-miṣriyyya*, vols. 1–2. Cairo: Woman and Memory Forum, [1910]1998. http://www.wmf.org.eg/mmm/2-11-2017/2-11-2017/nesaeyat.pdf

Reda, Nevin. "From the Canadian Sharia Debates to the Arab World: Developing a Qurʾan-Based Theology of Democracy." In *Religion and Democracy: Islam and Representation*, ed. Ingrid Mattson, Paul Nesbitt-Larking, and Nawaz Tahir, 78–100. Newcastle upon Tyne: Cambridge Scholars Publishing, 2015.

– "What Is Islam? The Importance of Being Islamic in Christian Theological Schools." *Islam and Christian-Muslim Relations* 29, no. 3 (2018): 309–29.

– "What Would the Prophet Do? The Islamic Basis for Female-Led Prayer." http://www.irfi.org/articles/articles_351_400/islamic_basis_for_femaleled.htm. 10 March 2005. http://muslimwakeup.com

Robinson, Neal. *Discovering the Qur'an: A Contemporary Approach to a Veiled Text*. Washington, DC: Georgetown University Press, 2003.

Sayeed, Asma. *Women and the Transmission of Religious Knowledge in Islam*. New York: Cambridge University Press, 2013.

Shāfiʿī, Muḥammad ibn Idrīs al. *Al-Risāla*. Ed. Aḥmad Muḥammad Shākir. Cairo: al-Ḥalabī, 1940.

Wheeler, Brannon M. *Applying the Canon in Islam: The Authorization and Maintenance of Interpretive Reasoning in Ḥanafī Scholarship*. Albany: SUNY Press, 1996.

Zabīdī, Muḥammad Murtaḍā al-. *Tāj al-ʿarūs min jawāhir al-qāmūs. 20 vols. Beirut: Dār al-Fikr, 1994.*

PART ONE

The Qur'an and Its Interpretation

1

Islamic Feminist *Tafsīr* and Qur'anic Ethics

Rereading Divorce Verses

Omaima Abou-Bakr and Mulki Al-Sharmani

Qur'anic *tafsīr* literature holds a central place in the Islamic interpretive tradition. This corpus of knowledge, which took shape in the first and second centuries of Islam, is, in the words of Walid Saleh, the product of a "communal endeavor" of exegetes resulting in a tradition of interpretations transmitted from one generation to subsequent ones over many centuries. Individual exegetes from different eras added interpretations that in some cases diverged from or contested the transmitted traditions, but these processes still took place within shared parameters. Thus, Saleh calls classical *tafsīr* a "genealogical tradition" because it sustains a sense of wholeness and boundedness, while at the same time allowing for internal differences and changes.

This tradition has taken on a significant normative role and over the course of its history has become the central lens through which Muslims understand the Qur'an.[2] In fact, to the extent that *tafsīr* has become an authoritative system of religious meanings and norms inextricably intertwined with the sacred text itself, it has become "canon." The authority of this "canon" is particularly significant in relation to the question of gender. Classical exegetical literature has enshrined distinct constructions of gender norms and rights that sanction hierarchical gender relations, particularly in the family domain, where men and women have unequal rights in marriage, divorce, and parenting. For example, Omaima Abou-Bakr, in a survey of ten centuries of exegesis of Q. 4:34 – starting with the fourth/tenth century Ibn Jarīr al-Ṭabarī (d. 310/923) – has shown that exegetes, through their accumulated layers of individual interpretations in the course of the tradition, constructed *qiwāma* as a multidimensional patriarchal construct sanctioning male superiority and hierarchical spousal relations.[3] And while there were in some cases noteworthy differences between individual exegetes' readings of Q. 4:34, these differences remained within the same broad interpretive framework and system of transmitted meanings, which did not question patriarchal gender norms.[4]

Exegetes' hierarchical construction of gender rights is also mirrored in the authoritative rulings on marriage, divorce, and parenting in classical Islamic jurisprudence (both Sunni and Shiʿi).[5] These rulings, due to their normative and legal hegemony, also form a "canon" in Islamic legal tradition. According to this legal canon, husbands are obligated to provide for their wives in exchange for the latter's obedience (*ṭāʿa)*, frequently defined as the wife's sexual availability to the husband (*tamkīn*) and thus his right to her physical availability in the matrimonial home *(iḥtibās)*.[6] Men have the right to unilaterally repudiate their wives and unilaterally take them back during the waiting period (*ʿidda)*. Women's access to divorce, however, is restricted, and is secured either judicially on limited defined grounds (depending on the juristic school), or in negotiation with the husband, for example through *khulʿ* divorce. Fathers, moreover, have guardianship over their children, whereas mothers' parental rights are limited to custody, which in the case of divorce is temporary until the children reach a certain age (with variations according to the juristic school). Furthermore, the divorced mother's right to custody is conditioned by a number of gendered factors.[7] This construction of spousal and parental roles and rights has been maintained, to varying degrees, in many modern family laws – albeit it has undergone mixing and patching in the processes of lawmaking.[8] Furthermore, the hegemony of this model of marriage and divorce rights not only is reflected in modern Muslim family laws, but also is visible in dominant religious discourses and societal norms and practices in diverse Muslim contexts.[9]

In this chapter, we go back to one of the main sources of this gender construction, the exegetical "canon." We engage with selected classical exegetes' interpretations of divorce verses in the Qurʾan. We argue that while classical exegetes recognized the ethical message of the divine text, they did not consistently and systematically work out how the "ethical" can and should shape the interpretations and rulings they deduced. We ask: How can we reread these Qurʾanic verses using an ethically oriented interpretive approach? How would such an approach work? Can it produce interpretations that reflect coherent Qur'anic ethical principles for gender relations and that fit with the text's broader ethical world view? Can an ethically oriented approach yield interpretations and legal injunctions that make gender justice possible for modern Muslims? We focus on the following classical exegetes: Ibn Jarīr al-Ṭabarī (d. 310/923); Abū al-Qāsim Maḥmūd ibn ʿUmar al-Zamakhsharī (d. 538/1144); Fakhr al-Dīn Muḥammad ibn ʿUmar al-Rāzī (d. 606/1210); and Abū ʿAbd Allāh al-Qurṭubī (d. 671/1273). We have chosen these exegetes because their works are good examples of the classical *tafsīr* corpus, besides presenting different generations. In addition, these exegetes illustrate different and yet interconnected interpretive strands within the exegetical tradition (i.e., *tafsīr bi'l-ma'thur* [exegesis by transmission], exemplified in al-Ṭabarī's commentary; an ethical-legal focus in al-Qurṭubī's *tafsīr*; a linguistic emphasis in al-Zamaksharī's exegesis; and theological attention in the work of al-Rāzī).

In the first section of the chapter, we situate our inquiry within the field of Islamic feminism and explain the nature and goal of our engagement with the Islamic interpretive tradition. We highlight that our critical engagement is from within the tradition, sharing its core beliefs, premises, and goals. In the second section, we explain how our focus on ethics and its relation to Qur'anic injunctions and norms builds on the larger tradition of Islamic ethics. We ponder the rationale behind the need to extend the scope of applied Qur'anic ethical principles to encompass gender. We argue that although ethical issues are discussed and embedded in most of the formal Islamic sciences in classical Islamic writings and modern research studies, a systematic ethical approach applied to specific gender problems is rarely encountered. We outline our hermeneutical framework for realigning Qur'anic ethics with gender justice and equality. We argue that from within Qur'anic logic, considering women as lesser human beings and men as holding a monopoly over privilege or authority is religiously unethical. In the third section, we propose an ethically oriented interpretive approach for engaging with the question of gender in the Qur'anic text. We situate this approach within contemporary and modern Muslim reform debates that address the deeper philosophical dimensions and hermeneutical processes involved in the derivation of meaning. We apply the proposed approach to Qur'anic verses on divorce, reflecting on its interpretive significance and challenges. We conclude with final reflections on how ethically oriented Islamic feminist hermeneutics can lead to deeper insights into the core message and principles of the sacred text; facilitate constructive and dynamic engagement with Islamic interpretive tradition; and create possibilities for legal and religious reform that would enable just and egalitarian gender relations and rights.

ISLAMIC FEMINIST *TAFSĪR*: ENGAGING WITH THE TRADITION FROM WITHIN

This inquiry is situated in Islamic feminist scholarship. We understand Islamic feminism to be a form of scholarship produced by predominantly Muslim women scholars (from different disciplines) who, from a position of believing Muslims, are rereading the Qur'an and critically engaging with the Islamic interpretive tradition. This scholarship has two broad aims – to deconstruct and problematize dominant patriarchal interpretations and their underlying discourses, and to provide egalitarian interpretations that are supported by the Qu'ran and its guiding ethical principles – the goal being to enable legal reform and social transformation.[10]

Islamic feminist scholarship in the English language can be classified into four focus-based categories.[11] The first body of work examines the Qur'an and its exegetical tradition.[12] The second tackles Islamic jurisprudence.[13] The third addresses the *ḥadīth* tradition and tends to be smaller in volume and scope as well as less systematic than the first two categories.[14] The last type focuses on Sufism and its potential role as a theological corrective to religious patriarchy.[15]

An expanding literature has been assessing the scholarship of Islamic feminism since its emergence three decades ago.[16] Some of this literature sees Islamic feminism as an epistemological and political project that can contribute not only to gender-sensitive legal reform but also to hermeneutical reform.[17] But there are also diverse critics of this scholarship. Some question the compatibility of Islam with feminism.[18] Others believe in gender-based reform of the Islamic interpretive tradition but reject feminism, which they associate with a homogenizing, Western-centred liberal framework and Western-based feminist movements, both of which they implicate in past and present colonial history in the Muslim world.[19] Also relevant to this debate has been the politics of labelling scholars as Islamic feminists (i.e., the underlying assumptions of those who do the naming and those who are named).[20]

Some of the critical literature also tackles the hermeneutical approaches of Islamic feminist scholars. Yasmin Moll, for example, argues that Islamic feminist scholars have tenuous methodological affinities to the tradition, in that these scholars use modern theories of hermeneutics and invoke the authority of the tradition without solid knowledge of its methodologies.[21] Two particularly noteworthy critics who have critically examined Islamic feminist scholars' interpretive approaches are Shuruq Naguib and Aysha Hidayatullah. Naguib argues that Islamic feminist scholars' approaches to *tafsīr* seek to dismantle this tradition altogether rather than engage with it constructively and "creatively."[22] One illustration of this approach, Naguib points out, is that these scholars posit the Qurʾan and its exegesis as two opposing poles in that they search for liberation and equality in the former while faulting the latter for its gender oppression and inequality.[23] Naguib attributes the gaps in Islamic feminists' hermeneutics to what she sees as their uncritical espousal of Western rationality and modern notions of gender equality. The result, Naguib concludes, is that Islamic feminist scholars have failed to identify and build on the gender-sensitive interpretations in the exegetical tradition, such as in the example of classical exegetes' interpretation of the Qurʾanic prohibition against marital sex during women's menstruation, which the exegetes explicitly did not read as an affirmation of women's impurity and a call for their isolation during this time, but simply as a form of regulation of marital sexual practices.[24]

Hidayatullah, meanwhile, faults Islamic feminist scholars for adopting a foundational premise that is supported neither by the Qurʾan nor by these scholars' hermeneutical methodologies. She argues that scholars such as Amina Wadud and Asma Barlas (and others) erroneously assume that the notion of gender equality is inherent in the Qurʾan.[25] This reading, Hidayatullah says, is primarily based on the text's notion of ontological and spiritual equality between women and men and its call for mutuality and reciprocity between the sexes.[26] Hidayatullah's counter-argument is that Qurʾanic notions of reciprocity and mutuality between the sexes, whether in spousal relations or in doing good deeds in the public sphere, does not preclude the benevolent patriarchy that seems to be condoned in the text and perhaps even promoted in some of its verses.[27] Nor do reciprocity and mutuality between the sexes necessarily entail an intrinsic Qurʾanic notion of gender equality. Hidayatullah concludes that the gaps she sees in Islamic feminist scholars' hermeneutics arise from their understanding of the text as an authoritative source of norms. What is needed, Hidayatullah contends, is a rethinking of "how we understand what kind of revelatory text the Qur'an is and how God speaks to us through it."[28]

However, what Naguib's and Hidayatullah's critiques fail to take into account is that for Islamic feminist scholars, the gender question is intricately woven into efforts to uncover the Qur'an's ethical world view. Islamic feminists' pursuit of religiously grounded gender equality is first and foremost an endeavour to reclaim and foreground the central ethical principles and messages of the Qur'anic text, which are integral to the Islamic faith. And while there are differences in the hermeneutical methodologies of Islamic feminists' exegesis and in their engagements with the interpretive tradition, they share this concern with the question of Qur'anic ethics and its role in the process of deducing juristic injunctions and modern family laws.

Asma Barlas, for example, adopts a hermeneutical approach that is informed by the Qur'an itself.[29] She argues that since God is one and has ultimate sovereignty, male sovereignty over women through patriarchy transgresses against the notion of *tawḥīd* (oneness of God, monotheism) and God's rule. And since God is just and does not do *ẓulm* (injustice), as the Qur'an instructs, it follows that one should not read *ẓulm* into one's reading of the Qur'anic text. In addition, the Qur'an instructs the reader to privilege the foundational verses over the allegorical verses (Q. 3:7) and warns against atomistic and arbitrary readings (Q. 15:89–93). It also calls upon readers to exercise judgment, to discern, and to hold on to the "best precepts" (Q. 7:145) and the "best of meanings" (Q. 39:18). This signifies that there is no one fixed true interpretation to be arrived at and applied in all contexts and times; rather, there are multiple interpretations. Yet this Qur'anic-based principle of the "best of meanings" does not mean that all readings and interpretations are equal in their ethical significance and moral priority. Instead, the hermeneutical process itself is one that entails "ongoing relationship, engagement, and encounter with divine discourse and with the Divine itself."[30] Barlas also notes that the Qur'an calls on everyone listening to its message to discern and understand its *āyāt* (signs), the implication being that the responsibility and authority to engage actively and ethically with the Qur'an – in order to arrive at its message – is not restricted to a certain group (e.g., male scholars). What is noteworthy in Barlas's hermeneutical approach is that it is guided by a number of Qur'anic ethical and theological principles that are outlined in the text and that the author views as the building blocks of the Qur'anic world view and core message. For her, the "vocation" of Islamic feminist scholars is to uncover the Qur'an's "horizon of ethical possibilities" and how they could apply to contemporary Muslim times.[31] In other words, the hermeneutical process in which Barlas as an Islamic feminist exegete wants to engage is, first and foremost, an ethical process rather than one driven by the pursuit of rights.

Like Barlas, Amina Wadud sees that the hermeneutical process entails a continuous endeavour to arrive at and reclaim the Qur'anic ethical world view. This world view, for Wadud, is premised on overarching theological and ethical principles, namely *taqwā* (God-consciousness, mindfulness of God) and *tawḥīd*.[32] *Taqwā*, which the Qur'an affirms as the only basis for merit among people (Q. 49:13), means exerting moral agency to do God's will of being just, to refrain from injustice, and to fulfill Qur'anic ethical principles.[33] And *tawḥīd*, as social praxis, means reflecting the true meaning of God's oneness and sovereignty through horizontal and egalitarian human-to-human relationships in which no gender or group is marginalized or oppressed.[34] Accordingly, Qur'anic hermeneutics that is informed by this world view adopts a holistic approach that undertakes "analyses of the ethical moral intent" of the sacred text.[35] Wadud stresses that "every local and current application" of the text must "reflect the underlying moral intent as proposed, not the form of their literal articulation."[36] Wadud contends that this kind of Qur'anic hermeneutics is integral to the pursuit of an "intimate experience" with the text,[37] besides being necessary to the work of reforming "the policies and practices that limit Muslim women's access to a full personal, political and spiritual well-being."[38]

Qur'anic ethics is, again, a central guiding interpretive framework in the work of Islamic feminist scholars engaging with *fiqh*. Ziba Mir-Hosseini, for example, highlights the gap between the ethical and the legal in jurists' formulations of marriage and divorce doctrines.[39] She shows how classical jurists' constructions of the legal duties and rights of the spouses are premised on a particular discourse about men's and women's nature and gender roles that diverges from Qur'anic ethics on marriage and divorce. The early jurists' concept of marriage, Mir-Hosseini explains, was based on the notion of sale in which the husband acquired the right to have sexual access to his wife through his payment of dower and his undertaking the responsibility of providing for her.[40] These assumptions and views were the product of the jurists' historical and social contexts. These jurists, however, did not address or resolve the contradiction between the Qur'an's construction of marriage as "tranquility, love, and mercy" (Q. 30:21) on the one hand, and some of their legal rulings on spousal rights on the other. Nor have Qur'anic ethical terms, such as *ma'rūf* (that which is commonly known as good) and *ihsān* (kindness and graciousness), which are used repeatedly in the verses on marriage and divorce, been adequately taken into account by these jurists in their legal constructions of marriage and divorce.

Islamic feminist scholars who write on Sufism also centre the question of Qur'anic ethics in their work. Sa'diyya Shaikh, for instance, provides a corrective to the patriarchy in Muslim legal tradition, employing key Sufi concepts that affirm the equal worth and potential of all human beings. She highlights the existential and spiritual equality of women and men, as well as their equal potential for spiritual striving and advancement.[41] This means, as Shaikh points out, the ethical and theological incompatibility of patriarchy with the striving of men or women toward the spiritual realization of the latent divine attributes (*al-insān al-kāmil*) that God has placed in their nature. Shaikh concludes that revisiting Islamic legal tradition through the lens of Sufism has important implications for interpretations of and injunctions on gender roles and rights.

Like the Islamic feminist scholars discussed above, the present inquiry foregrounds Qur'anic ethics. Similarly, we see the gender issue in the Qur'an as integrally linked to the text's ethical world view and principles. Our work is an endeavour to unearth this world view and these principles and shed light on how they function as a guide for gender relations. Our starting point, like that of the community of classical exegetes and jurists, is our shared belief that the Qur'an is God's revelation to guide its followers to the divine path and a spiritually nourishing and happy life. From this starting point, we undertake a holistic and ethically oriented hermeneutical reading of Qur'anic verses on divorce. Our reading is informed by the exegetical tradition while at the same time critically engaging with it.[42] In the process of our hermeneutical reading, we identify the ethical directives proposed in the specific verses (and their larger thematic units of verses), as well as the possibilities for legal injunctions that would be true to these ethical directives in different Muslim contexts. Our aim is not to jettison the exegetical tradition in its entirety but rather to question its infallibility and offer alternatives with the aim of rendering this tradition theologically and ethically meaningful and relevant to present-day Muslim realities. It is precisely because of its imperfections and perceived failings that our present engagement and revisiting can be productive. Scrutinizing past understandings of Qur'anic verses from a critical perspective allows – even inspires – a reformed and more interactive ethical reasoning. In the next section, we situate our inquiry within the tradition of Islamic ethics in general.

ISLAMIC ETHICS AND ISLAMIC FEMINIST HERMENEUTICS

Ethics in Islamic thought is referred to as *ʿilm al-akhlāq*. *Akhlāq* (also related to *khuluq*) means the disposition or moral character of the person that guides her/his actions. *Akhlāq*, in other words, relates both to the inner self and to its ethical moorings, as well as to the actions undertaken by that self which result from these ethical principles. The centrality of ethics in both the Qur'an and the Sunnah, the two main sources of Islamic teachings and law, is attested by numerous Qur'anic verses and Prophetic reports. When ʿĀ'isha, the wife of the Prophet Muḥammad, was asked about his character, she described it as being that of the Qur'an.[43] This statement highlights two important points: first, the Qur'an is the main source of Islamic ethics, and second, the Prophet in his character and actions exemplified Qur'anic ethics. The Qur'an also affirms the ethical goal of the Prophetic mission of Muḥammad: "We sent you not but as a mercy for all creatures" (Q. 21:107).[44] And in a *ḥadīth* narrated from the Prophet, he emphasizes the ethical nature of his mission: "But I have been sent to perfect good morals."[45]

In a review article, Abdul Haq Ansari argues that Islamic ethics has never developed into a systematic field.[46] Instead, ethical issues and questions were tackled in a dispersed way in four subfields of Islamic sciences: philosophy, jurisprudential writings (*uṣūl al-fiqh*), theology (*ʿilm al-kalām*), and Sufism.[47] In the field of Islamic philosophy, early works on ethics began with the writings of Muslim philosophers such as Abū Naṣr al-Farābī (d. 329/950) and Abū ʿAlī ibn Miskawayh (d. 421/1030). Al-Farābī and Ibn Miskawayh both perceived ethics as the science concerned with the human soul. Influenced by Greek philosophy, these early philosophers were concerned with the question of the good and its goal, happiness. Human nature, which was believed to be rational in its essence, could pursue the good through seeking knowledge and moral virtue. Ibn Miskawayh, in particular, authored a number of works that attempted to systematically tackle the question of good. In his best-known work, *Tahdhib al-akhlāq* (*The Refinement of Morals*), Ibn Miskawayh was concerned with this question: How do we acquire the right disposition to act morally? Ibn Miskawayh ties the acquisition of virtue to the human soul's capacity to reason. According to him, the more we reason and deliberate, the more we can cultivate virtue. Ibn Miskawayh is often described as a humanist, one whose writings do not necessarily privilege religion, and at times he explains religious rituals, such as communal prayers, in utilitarian terms. This latter point was critiqued by Abū Ḥāmid al-Ghazālī, the twelfth-century jurist and Sufi (d. 505/1111).[48]

Ansari views the works of al-Ghazālī as exemplifying the ethical debates in jurisprudential writings. At the centre of al-Ghazālī's writings was *sharīʿa,* being the framework delineating the duties of a Muslim toward God and toward other human beings. The key question for al-Ghazālī was the objective of *sharīʿa.* He sought to bring to the fore the inseparable relationship between law and ethics. He was critical of legalistic juristic discourse that was preoccupied with external rulings and that lost sight of the intricate link between *fiqh* rulings (*aḥkām*) and "inner discernment [*fiqh al-nafs*]," as he called it. The goal of *fiqh*, according to him, was to enable Muslims to cultivate *taqwā.*[49]

The fourteenth-century jurist Abū Isḥāq al-Shāṭibī (d. 790/1388) built on al-Ghazālī's ideas and developed a theory for the objectives of *sharīʿa* (*maqāsid al- sharīʿa*). He argued that those objectives can be viewed as three concentric circles of ethical objectives: compelling necessity (*darūriyyāt*), needs (*ḥājiyyāt*), and improvements (*taḥsīniyyāt*). Under the first concentric circle, five universal objectives are to be fulfilled: the protection and preservation of religion, life, offspring, reason, and property. The category of needs encourages flexibility to eliminate challenges that may be generated by new contexts, whereas the third category seeks refinement and further improvement. The *maqāsid* theory, notably, has become one of the main religious frameworks guiding contemporary Islamic ethical deliberations, for example, in the field of biomedical ethics.[50] On a more general level, the jurisprudential writings of al-Ghazālī and al-Shāṭibī also raise broad ethical issues, such as the nature of religious obligation, its levels, the factors that determine its priority, the motivation behind actions and rulings, and so on.

Ethical issues and questions were also tackled in classical Islamic theology (*'ilm al-kalām*). An illustrative example was the debates between the Muʿtazilī and the Ashʿarī theologians.[51] This debate tackled key theological issues that had direct and important ethical implications, such as human will, God's power, and the relationship between reason and revelation, among other things. The Muʿtazila emphasized God's justice and maintained the position that human beings enjoyed free will; that the good could be known through reason; and that things were good in and of themselves, without necessarily needing to be assessed as such through revelation (objectivist). The Ashʿarī theologians emphasized God's omnipotence and acknowledged free will to the extent that it was linked to human responsibility and to divine justice (voluntarist). But in their view, revelation was the main path through which the good and the right could be ascertained. That is, reason could not, on its own, know the good.

The question of ethics was also pertinent in Sufism.[52] The life goal of the Sufi, being the pursuit of the Divine through the path of self-knowledge and spiritual advancement, by its nature was an ethical one as much as it was theological. In Saʿdiyya Shaikh's words, the focus of Sufism was "ethical and spiritual cultivation." What is particularly noteworthy about Sufism is that in its pursuit of the underlying ethical and spiritual essence of Islam, it foregrounded the ontological and spiritual equality of men and women. As Shaikh shows, this notion is best argued and illustrated in the work of the thirteen-century Sufi scholar and jurist Muḥyī al-Dīn ibn ʿArabī (d. 638/1240).

The concern with the interwoven relationship between the theological, the ethical, and the legal as illustrated in the above-mentioned medieval Islamic fields illuminates the long historical trajectory of ethics as central to the Islamic intellectual tradition, even if has not been systematically developed as a separate field. Furthermore, the linkage between gender equality and the ontological and spiritual equality of men and women, put forward in some of the works of notable medieval Sufi scholars, paves the way for contemporary Islamic feminist scholars' efforts to centre the ethical once more as they reread the sacred text and engage with its interpretive tradition. It is in this aspect that the work presented in this chapter also situates itself within the tradition of Islamic ethics.

With regard to modern scholarship on Islamic ethics, we draw on four scholars whose hermeneutical approaches to the Qur'an are informative in relation to the goal of a coherent, ethically oriented reading of the sacred text. These scholars are Muḥammad ʿAbd Allāh Drāz (d. 1958), Fazlur Raḥman (d. 1988), Toshihiko Izutsu (d. 1993), and Khaled Abou El Fadl. Drāz is known for his pioneering and influential work *The Moral World of Qurʾan*, in which he takes a philosophical as well as comparative perspective.[53] This landmark book outlines and develops in great detail the ethical theory emerging from the Qurʾanic text. Drāz presents a comprehensive investigation of the Qurʾan's general ethical principles; upon these, he builds and formulates practical rules, thus arriving at a unified ethical system. He contends that the Qurʾan's basic ethical concerns underpin the most direct divine commandments/law in the text. Drāz also demonstrates how these Qurʾanic verses with commandments always attach the moral precept or value that justifies each resolution of the law. Every slightest recommendation for a certain conduct is usually supported with an aphorism toward the end of the verse to establish the moral value, not just a mindless following of duties:

> Divine reason does not hold the form of its verdict as the primary principle of moral obligation any more than human reason. It too claims reference to another criterion. It directs us back to the very essence of duty, to the quality of the action [itself], to its intrinsic value. It is in its accord with this objective truth that the commandment justifies itself in our eyes; it is through this that it solicits our adherence, and it is upon this that it establishes its moral command.[54]

Drāz's book dissects the foundations of ethical theory and the sources and conditions of moral law, engaging mostly with Kant and Bergson, but focusing on a probing examination of ethical concepts within the Qurʾanic text. Analyses of obligation, responsibility, sanction, intention, effort, human will, conscience, and reason in the Qurʾan prove certain underlying principles. Human beings are endowed with an embedded moral awareness, but it can be activated and refined only through the "reflective activity of the soul,"[55] that is, the individual rational conscience. The Qurʾan provides us with a moral framework within which we exercise our intellectual search for righteous duties to the extent of our capabilities. Drāz repeatedly emphasizes that the Qurʾan is not just a religious text of doctrine, law, and spirituality; it also operates on a higher level, for it is an *ethical* book that establishes moral notions as ultimate reference and source, even of divine injunction itself. As he writes, "the Qur'an does not present … divine commandment as absolute power, sufficient in itself to establish the realm of duty for us," but often "tries to attach its justification to each resolution of the law, and to each precept the moral value which constitutes the established benefit"[56] as the true source of obligation. Hence, in examining the system of Qur'anic exhortations, he shows that commands are rarely given without a moral rationalization to make them acceptable to our conscience: "We are urged to morality by and for morality."[57] In conclusion, the Qur'an clearly and strongly cultivates a sense of moral obligation linked to legal imperatives; it presupposes the existence of human conscience, nurtures it, refines it, and carries it further, then refers to it anew in order to establish its own realm.

In the first half of the book, Drāz thoroughly examines this complex Qur'anic world view and how it forms a unified applicable system, giving useful textual examples. However, in the second half of the book, he only outlines domains of practical ethics and includes textual extracts from the Qu'ran without further interpretation. Verses related to women, marriage, and divorce are listed and grouped under the rubric "family ethics" without providing new hermeneutical applications to specific related issues. Hence, more work could be done to identify and apply some of his moral analysis relevant to gender relations (as is attempted hereunder) – a noticeable gap in the work of most modern Muslim reformists in the area of Islamic ethics.

Writing a few years later, Izutsu identifies three layers of ethical discourse in the Qur'an.[58] The first is related to the nature of God; the second to the nature of humanity's relationship to God; the third to the socio-ethical relations between individuals. Izutsu focuses on the second layer of this discourse, but of course the second is also intrinsically related to the third, and both derive from the first. For how we relate to others, how we treat them and they treat us, and how we organize our rights and duties vis-à-vis others arises from the ethical self that we strive to cultivate in our relationship with God. As Jerusha Tanner Lamptey points out, there are notable linkages between the work of Islamic feminist exegetes and that of Izutsu. Like Izutsu, Islamic feminist exegetes see the Qu'ran as a unified whole with a coherent ethical world view. In addition, they, like him, engage with

Qur'anic terms as part of a semantic field, interpreting parts of the Qur'an with other parts. And similarly, Islamic feminist scholars seek the relational meanings of Qur'anic terms and concepts.[59]

But it is Fazlur Rahman's work that is perhaps the most relevant to Islamic feminist scholars, for he has greatly influenced many Islamic feminist exegetes in their formulation of hermeneutical approaches and methodologies.[60] According to Rahman:

> Muslim scholars have never attempted an ethics of the Qur'an systematically or otherwise. Yet the ethics of the Qur'an is its essence and it is also the necessary link between theology and law. It is true that the Qur'an tends to concretize the ethical, to clothe the general in a particular paradigm, and to translate the ethical into legal or quasi-legal commands. But it is precisely a sign of moral favour that it is not content only with generalizable ethical propositions, but is keen on translating them into actual paradigms. The Muslims' failure to make a clear distinction between Qur'anic ethics and law has resulted in confusion between the two.[61]

In the above quotation, Rahman highlights the dialectic relationship between the ethical and the legal in the Qur'an. On the one hand, the ethical in itself is not significant unless it is translated into concrete injunctions and rulings to organize social relations and rights; at the same time, though, every legal injunction is grounded in ethical objective(s). Yet the process of discerning the relationship between the two (without collapsing the two into one entity) is an open, unfolding, and dynamic process influenced by the contexts of interpretation and application. This explains why Rahman stresses that "certainty belongs not to the meanings of particular verses and their content, but to the Qur'an as a whole."[62] Rahman also laments that the "Islamic legal system, though in the main unsystematically linked with the Qur'an and Sunna, was not founded on a systematic intellectual working out of the socio-moral values of the Qur'an."[63] Following the suit of Rahman, Islamic feminist scholars also hold that there is "ongoing dialectic between doctrine and ethics," and they locate the universality of the Qur'an in its "ongoing capacity" to "provide the foundations for contextually responsive and ethical doctrinal possibilities."[64] Rahman's work on Qur'anic ethics also foregrounds ethico-theological principles derived from key terms in the Qur'anic text, which he sees as the foundation for a Qur'anic ethical world view. Three of these central Qur'anic terms are *imān*, *islām*, and *taqwā*. This is again an approach that Islamic feminist scholars adopt. A good example is Rahman's analysis of *taqwā* as a Qur'anic concept that functions as a "moral x-ray" by which the individual agent makes decisions, acts, and judges his or her intentions and deeds. Similarly, Wadud's work focuses on *taqwā* as a central ethical principle that serves as the normative guide for individual praxis.

Khaled Abou El Fadl has made a rich contribution to the issues of moral inquiry and the ultimate value of beauty within *sharīʿa* since *The Search for Beauty in Islam* (2006). His most recent work, *Reasoning with God*, is especially relevant to our attempts at identifying a specific ethical approach to gender, for it can yield a systematic hermeneutical methodology. This study of *sharīʿa* – its epistemology and legal determinations, questions of historicity, interpretive tradition, hermeneutics, ethics, relation between reason and revelation, literalism and human contingencies, and so on – does not centralize gender issues or feminist analysis. It does, however, provide significant insights into methodology. To his previous determination that beauty and the moral imperative are the ultimate objectives of *sharīʿa*, Abou El Fadl adds *another* criterion – reasonableness. At the risk of simplifying a very sophisticated discussion, it is sufficient to state that he outlines the three evaluative categories by which reasonableness can be measured: proportionality between means and ends; balance between valid interests and roles; and "measuredness" to preserve reciprocity between agents acting in a social setting.[65] He sees that each can be a "methodological tool that helps ascertain whether a legal judgment, decision, or interpretation is balanced, fair, and relevant."[66]

Abou El Fadl argues that an ethical investigation must be grounded in an approach that involves the reader or the interpreter in "the process of ethical instruction and learning by analytically investigating the normative dynamics and trajectory of the Qur'an."[67] A Qur'anic ethical principle should be viewed as setting a "normative potential in motion that is realizable in different ways and extents within varying time and space contingencies."[68] Qur'anic instructions must be interpreted in terms of the moral purpose and trajectory that caused this revelation in the first place. Hence, to understand this moral instructional thrust, interpreters should first analyze the "historical circumstances and epistemological parameters in which specific Qur'anic ethical norms were negotiated."[69] Abou El Fadl outlines three methodological steps for applying this ethical and beautiful potential of the divine text to different times and places: first, understand the epistemological paradigm at the time of the revelation; second, position these problems and issues raised by the divine commandment in the contemporary context and circumstances; and third, understand and apply the moral objectives being set in motion and direction by the original commandment in its context.[70]

Abou El Fadl illustrates his proposed ethical approach to *sharī'a* by considering its ramifications for a number of controversial gender laws. The idea is to investigate to what extent this basic Qur'anic discourse of what is ethical, fair, and just can shape the law in a way that completes the pursuit of moral objectives. For example, several well-known Qur'anic verses clearly respond to specific abusive situations that existed at the time of revelation, concerning women, and instruct change for immediate rectification and fairness. The idea is to read the verses not just as instructions to be applied *only literally*, but also as an illustration and an ethical methodology for addressing similar abusive situations. Such verses/texts are not final destinations, but rather directions toward a course and toward further heights of fulfilling the *amāna* (trust) that God assigned to Muslims, meaning the ultimate *sharī'a* objectives and eternal laws of goodness, justice, fairness, and beauty. Since jurisprudence is the human effort to achieve and concretize these ideals, its task is to seek consistent legal application. With regard to inheritance laws, for instance, Abou El Fadl actually argues for the possibility of change in accordance with *sharī'a*'s moral guidance and the changing social dynamics of women's situation in the modern age.[71]

Do these interpretive notions of "potential," "moral trajectory," "setting an ethical principle in motion," "not stopping where a text concludes, but proceeding to travel along that path," and "moral growth of individuals and communities"[72] eventually raise questions about the actual relevance of the Qur'anic text? This is the point behind Hidayatullah's claim that feminist demands for justice and equality are imposed modern projections that are not supported by the text. Does this also mean we ought to leave the Qur'an behind as it can no longer be normatively sufficient or binding? Or is this an easy way out of trying to prove authentic normativity/referentiality of the tradition, thus moving closer to the Western liberal position critiqued by Saba Mahmoud and Laila Abu Lughod?[73]

To the contrary, the power of the aforementioned argument and of the hermeneutical stance we adopt lies specifically in how it counters such critiques. The Qurʾanic text continues to be valid, normative, and living, and it is actually positioned in front of us – not transcended – as a continuous reminder (*tadhkira*) of goodness, and we are to strive to fulfill it in various ways and applications. What we leave behind are humanity's old mis/understandings and cultural practices – on the path to the ultimate *ḥaqq* (truth), *iḥsān* (the doing of beautiful deeds), *ḥikma* (wisdom), *birr* (kindness), *qisṭ* (fairness), *khuluq* (ethics of goodness), and other Qurʾanic principles that in the end constitute *sharīʿa*. In the following section, we propose and apply an interpretive approach that exemplifies the above-mentioned ethical framework to selected Qurʾanic verses on divorce.

AN ETHICALLY ORIENTED INTERPRETIVE APPROACH TO SELECTED QURʾANIC VERSES

Our proposed approach builds partly on the basic notions and themes of Islamic feminists; it also fills some of the gaps (regarding gender issues) in the philosophical and theological work of classical and modern male ethicists. By gendering ethical inquiry and applying close textual hermeneutics, we seek to bring the *sharīʿa* principles of justice and fairness – already embedded in the divine text – to more fruition in our times. We have selected a number of representative verses on divorce – an issue given to either abuse or magnanimity – as an example to illustrate an ethically oriented hermeneutical reading that should have been the focus of traditional legal deductions.

We examine from Surat al-Baqara a group of nine verses (Q. 2:227–32, 236–37, 241), complemented by two from Surat al-Ṭalāq (Q. 65:1–2) and one from *Sūrat al-Aḥzāb* (Q. 33:49), that form a distinct unit on divorce procedures and injunctions, excluding the verses specific to the Prophet's wives. We also consider the four above-mentioned traditional *tafsīr* commentaries: those of al-Tabarī, al-Zamakhsharī, al-Rāzī, and al-Qurtubī. The goal is to assess within this accumulation the presence or lack of a consistent ethical interpretive outlook that impacts legal rulings.

Our analysis of the selected string of verses as a whole will demonstrate an intertextual pattern of the following running threads: (1) emphasis on consciousness of God and God's boundaries,

(2) specific moral virtues, and (3) women's partnership in moral agency. The overarching message one distills from these verses is fairness (both financial and in conduct). Indeed, it is this basic principle that the Qur'anic text instructs the addressees to follow as the ethical criterion for specific legal and procedural deductions. However, the socio-cultural patriarchal context, which occasioned the revelation of these verses in the first place to edify and reform the practices of marriage and divorce in the early community, was clearly far from fairness or belief in the equal humanity of women. Hence, implicit in the details and steps mentioned in the verses are moral provisions that are part of the underlying divine intent. In other words, the pursuit of moral virtues is intricately tied to God-consciousness. In what follows, we present our ethically oriented reading of these verses and their exegesis.

The al-Baqara verses begin with verse 227, which signals God's direct oversight of the decision and process of divorce: "But if they are resolved on divorce – behold, God is all-hearing, all knowing." It is noteworthy that the particular divine attribute of "all-knowing" (*'alīm*) is used more than once in this unit (Q. 2:227–32). But other attributes and direct references to God also recur to complement the essential meaning and message of each verse: "almighty, wise" (Q. 2:228); "God's bounds" (mentioned four times in Q. 2:229 and twice in Q. 2:230); "messages of God," "God's blessings," "conscious of God," "God's full knowledge [*'alīm*] of everything" (Q. 2:231); "who believes in God and the Last Day," "God knows" (Q. 2:232); "God-consciousness," "God sees all that you do" (Q. 2:237); "God's bounds" (Q.65:1); "be conscious of God" (Q. 65:1); "who believe in God and the Last Day," "he who is conscious of God" (Q. 65:2). Noticeable are the repeated terms of *taqwā* toward God and God's *ḥudūd* (limits, boundaries), seen here as God's ethical limits or restraints to be observed and followed as an essential part of faith. All of these terms establish the first theme – that God's consciousness is the ultimate source and incentive of moral behaviour.

At the same time, the selected verses enumerate the second theme of moral virtues: "fairness" (Q. 2:228, 229, 231, 241, 232, 241, and 65:2); "goodness" (Q. 2:229); "those who would do good" (Q. 2:236); "the most virtuous [way] and the cleanest" (Q. 2:232); "forgo," "grace" (Q. 2:237); "a beautiful release" (Q. 33:49). The third theme is the theme of women's shared responsibility in making moral decisions related to the different stages of separation: the appeal to their conscience in the same manner as to the husbands, and introducing a principle of mutuality or exchange during divorce procedures (Q. 2:228); woman's partnership in determining the failure of a marital union and incumbent financial repercussions (Q. 2:229); women's inclusion in the decision to return following the triple divorce and in the willingness of *both* partners "to keep within God's bounds" (Q. 2:230); respecting women's "consent" in cases of returning to previous husbands (Q. 2:232); women's moral agency in willingly making concessions and forgoing entitlements (Q. 2:237). Hence, considered as a whole, the passage appears as a coherent network in terms of its value system, which can be applied on the smaller level of verse units as well.

Now we examine each verse individually. Q. 2:228 mainly addresses the issue of the right behaviour, on the part of both spouses, during the waiting period following the divorce:

> And the divorced women shall undergo, without remarrying, a waiting-period of three monthly courses: for it is not lawful for them to conceal what God may have created in their wombs, if they believe in God and the Last Day. And during this period their husbands are fully entitled to take them back, if they desire reconciliation; but, in accordance with justice, the rights of the wives [with regard to their husbands] are equal to the [husbands'] rights with regard to them, although men have precedence over them [in this respect]. And God is almighty, wise.

Given the original context of the revelation that exegetes mention (that of the husband revoking a divorce with the intention of harming the wife and then divorcing her again to repeat the process), the ethical focus of the verse is a moral commitment not to harm the other partner, to reform one's intentions, and to exchange rights and duties. The ending phrase "And God is almighty, wise," is not superfluous, but on the contrary should be viewed – in a backward reading – as the governing precept. Abiding by the guiding spirit of divine wisdom necessitates the pursuit of egalitarian praxis in this situation.

The verse's prohibition of the unethical behaviour of a divorced woman hiding her pregnancy is followed by a commandment that the husband be allowed to revoke the divorce *if* he pursues reform and reconciliation, not for further abuse or out of spite. In other words, the verse puts this intention to reform as a *condition* to the husband's right to take a wife back during the waiting period. One of the earliest second/tenth[th] century exegetes, al-Ṭabarī (d. 310/922), clearly understood this clause as a condition: "*unless* he wants by the return reforming his and her ways."[74] However, the discussion that follows demonstrates a typically traditional method of deducing a legal ruling without considering ethical stipulations, and of separating the technical correctness of a ruling according to the apparent textual level from its underlying and complementing moral message. Al-Ṭabarī differentiates between the "ruling" (*ḥukm*) that allows the return to happen and intent or conscience that is "between God and him." Thus, if the husband wants to harm her by revoking the divorce and does not want to reform or reconcile, then this is not sanctioned (*ghayr jā'iz murāja'atihā*). Yet as a legal determination to be implemented, it is considered formally correct, even if he has sinned by having bad intentions: "If he wants to harm the wife by this return, he can obtain this ruling, though he is sinful [*āthim*] in this deed, undertaking to do what God does not permit him to do, and so God is in charge of punishing him for that."[75]

Subsequent exegetes also acknowledged the divine urging (*taḥrīḍ*) to reform and to cease harm and did not see this as a condition or legal stipulation that can invalidate revocation (e.g., al-Zamakhsharī, al-Rāzī, and al-Qurṭubī). Al-Rāzī, for example, argues:

> If it is said that the word *in* (if) is conditional and that the condition invalidates the ruling when it is absent, meaning that if the will to reform or reconcile is absent then the right of revocation cannot be set, the reply is: human will is an inner motive that is not discerned, so the *shar'* does not hinge the validity of revocation on it. Its correctness between God and him is dependent upon this inner will, so that if he returns her with the intention of harm, he commits a sin.[76]

Al-Qurṭubī (d. 672/1273) calls the revocation *ṣaḥīḥa* (legally correct) even though he uses a stronger word in describing a husband's behaviour in elongating the waiting period/s and depriving the wife of her freedom (*muḥarram*/forbidden).[77] Still, he does spell out the legal implications of this forbidden act when it is committed by the husband.

It is noteworthy that most exegetes interpreted the *they* in "if they desire reconciliation" as a masculine plural pronoun referring to husbands; it is *their* will or intention to reform and seek reconciliation.

Perhaps this reflected the assumption that it was the husband who initiated the separation in the first place, so it was his responsibility to rectify the situation. Yet another possibility is that the Qur'anic text calls upon *both* (grammatically the masculine pronoun being inclusive of both genders) to want and strive for reform as a condition for resuming the marriage. In other words, and in keeping with the egalitarian spirit of the verse, the wife's will and intention are also part of the process. We will see later how Q. 2:232 admonishes men for attempting to ignore the woman's wish to resume a previous marriage, or to contract a new marriage; it follows that the principle of recognizing women's will and desire should be generalized throughout all related/similar steps or stages. This subtle point was set aside by jurists during the lawmaking process.

The egalitarian and ethical purpose of Q. 2:228 is clear in the basic idea of exchange of entitlements vis-à-vis each other, which al-Ṭabarī recognized in his interpretation of the passage "the rights of the wives [with regard to their husbands] are equal to the [husbands'] rights with regard to them" as forbidding harmful and dishonest behaviour: he exhorted the husband not to retract the divorce and return to his wife unless he intended to reform his ways, and he exhorted the wife not to conceal a pregnancy. Al-Ṭabarī emphasizes this aspect of reciprocity in the need to prevent harm to either party (*tark al-maḍār*). As for the second part of the verse, which contains the term "degree," al-Ṭabarī clearly states that what is meant by degree "in this situation or context" is "man's tolerance or lenience towards his wife concerning her duty to him, while fully performing all of *his* duties to her."[78] The verse is to be understood as urging a husband to earn this degree of advantage or moral excellence through exemplary virtuous conduct and the exercise of magnanimity – that is, by waiving some of the rights to which he may be entitled. Al-Ṭabarī then adds a significant comment: "Though the apparent meaning appears to be a statement of fact, it really means urging men to aspire to reach this level of extra virtue."[79] In other words, this is an earned moral state conditioned by a certain behaviour, not an inherent privilege of men.

Al-Ṭabarī's subtle interpretation of *daraja* (degree, precedence) was never considered, discussed, or recycled by later exegetes, who have continued – up to modern times – to treat it as a generalized statement by the Qur'an that men are entitled to more rights, are naturally superior, and are entitled to a given degree of preference. Though most of the exegetes who followed him continued to recognize spousal "common rights" in that "each should heed the other's rights" (al-Rāzī) as well as the divine injunction not to harm the wife (al-Qurṭubī), they gradually lost sight of the verse's ethico-egalitarian intentions as their focus came to centre on justifications for a hierarchal understanding of the term *daraja* and on the concept of mutual rights itself – of rights being different in nature and exchanged between two unequal beings. However, since the Qurʾanic text does not flesh out the nature of this degree of precedence and the verse's ethical assumption centres on fairness (*bi'l-maʿrūf*) and moral reciprocity – in addition to reminding us of God's wisdom – al-Ṭabarī's view that it is an extra demand upon husbands to improve themselves (given the prevailing oppressive practices at the time of revelation) is a kind of acceptable ethical reasoning.

To build further on this: Since the context of the verse is the moral imperative even in the situation of divorce, could it mean there is an extra degree of *taklīf* (an ethical obligation) upon men to exert more effort and work harder to reform themselves? We have seen how al-Ṭabarī said something close to this when he maintained that this degree urges (*nadb*) men to acquire this higher level of magnanimity and conscientiousness (for example, by not seeking revenge or acting out of spite when retracting divorce). Again, God mostly addressed men in matters like this, not to ignore women, but because men in the context of revelation (based on our knowledge of the marriage and divorce practices of those times) were more prone to abuse of authority and so more in need of reform.[80]

Moving to Q. 2:229–30, we find that they too foreground the repetition of God's moral limits, ethical terms/concepts, and women's involvement in decisions of separation and resumption of the marital relationship:

> A divorce may be [revoked] twice, whereupon the marriage must either be resumed in fairness or dissolved in a goodly manner. And it is not lawful for you to take back anything of what you have ever given to your wives unless both [partners] have cause to fear that they may not be able to keep within the bounds set by God: hence, if you have cause to fear that the two may not be able to keep within the bounds set by God, there shall be no sin upon either of them for what the wife may give up [to her husband] in order to free herself. These are the bounds set by God; do not, then, transgress them: for they who transgress the bounds set by God – it is they, they who are evildoers!

The beginning of Q. 2:229 contains the primary ethical injunctions of *maʿrūf* (fairness) and *iḥsān* (good deeds, goodly manner), and the expression God's *ḥudūd* occurs six times in both verses. The main thrust here, as related to the historical context, was to limit the number of divorces and retractions (in comparison to the unlimited number practised by men with the intention of prolonging the duration of waiting periods) and to institute the possibility of the woman-initiated divorce (*khulʿ*). In other words, divine intent centred on the moral education of abusive husbands for the purpose of encouraging them to conduct themselves during divorce in a fair and goodly manner, and on pointing out women's agency in this situation. Women's feelings and wishes were to be considered: *both* were to take the decision of terminating or resuming the marriage, and *both* were expected to uphold the "bounds" set by God for an equitable relationship.

Al-Ṭabarī's understanding of the nuanced ethical implications here is again relevant to our analysis and focus. The first significant point in his discussion is that he uses the term *nushūz* to describe a wife's showing hatred and rejection as a condition of the *khulʿ* because for her to reach this point will inevitably violate the egalitarian ethics of the marriage – that each is entitled to good treatment and companionship from the other. Second, he attributes the procedure of the husband accepting a financial settlement when the woman initiates the separation to the primary requirement of upholding God's moral limits, meaning that her rejection of him will lead him to respond by neglecting his own duties toward her and, hence, going against God's *ḥudūd*. Third, al-Ṭabarī is interestingly aware that this settlement should not turn into a bribe in cases where the rejection originates with the husband and he is harming the wife with the intention of obtaining a certain settlement. He emphasizes that this provision must be given willingly (*ʿan ṭīb nafs*) for her own and her partner's avoidance of "guilt and sin" and only if the *nushūz* is on her part. Al-Zamakhsharī and al-Rāzī both also recognize the factors of good companionship and fulfilling marital duties on both sides as manifestations of upholding God's commandments, and both emphasize the prohibition of harm through repeated unconscionable divorces. Al-Rāzī explains the *iḥsān* in divorce – "if he leaves her, he should pay all her financial rights, not speak ill of her, or drive people away from her"[81] – and he understands divorces/revocations as trial separations, meant for both partners to review the relationship. One can discern an awareness on the part of early exegetes of the subtle ethical implications of such verses in the way they identified certain debates about intention (*qaṣd*), conscience, and correct behaviour. However, by the time we reach al-Qurṭubī or ʿImād al-Dīn Ismāʿīl ibn ʿUmar ibn Kathīr (d. 775/1373), interest in such discussions has waned and is reduced either to reiterating previously established positions or to detailed explanations of intricate legal technicalities and rulings.

However, what was naturally left unarticulated in the context of the times, but is to be highlighted through a gender lens, is the persistent use of the dual form in the two verses.[82] Q. 2:229–30 refers to the role, sentiments, and conscience of both partners in this situation:

> And if he divorces her, she shall thereafter not be lawful unto him unless she first takes another man for husband; then, if the latter divorces her, there shall be no sin upon either of the two if they return to one another – provided that both of them think that they will be able to keep within the bounds set by God: for these are the bounds of God which He makes clear unto people of [innate] knowledge. (Q. 2:230)

This inclusion of women's agency seems a logical consequence of the initial establishment of the principle of mutuality in the first verse of the passage (Q. 2:228). Also worth noting here is the reference to people "who know" (*qawm yaʿlamūn*, Q. 2:230) as an echo of the reference to God the "All-Knowing" in the initial verse 227. These people of knowledge, who uphold God's moral criteria, are contrasted with those who transgress those criteria – *al-ẓālimūn* (Q. 2:229). It is such textual and intertextual signs in the sequence of verses that create the Qurʾanic network of interrelated ethical meanings as applied to gender and marital relations.

The following verse in this sequence is extremely significant in consolidating further the above-mentioned themes and principles in emphatic terms:

> And so, when you divorce women and they are about to reach the end of their waiting-term, then either retain them in a fair manner or let them go in a fair manner. But do not retain them against their will in order to hurt [them]: for he who does so sins indeed against himself. And do not take [these] messages of God in a frivolous spirit; and remember the blessings with which God has graced you, and all the revelation and the wisdom which He

> has bestowed on you from on high in order to admonish you thereby; and remain conscious of God, and know that God has full knowledge of everything (Q. 2:231).

Both the prohibition against hurting women by holding them in marriage against their will and the injunction to conduct the marital relationship or separation in a "fair manner" are repeated, again applying *ma'rūf*. The rest of the verse reiterates the moral justification of this divine commandment by describing those who do not follow this virtuous path as "sinning against themselves" (using the term *ẓalam*, which links with verse 229) and once again connecting to *taqwā* and God as the *'alīm* (all-knowing). The verse warns strongly against against abuse and unethical behaviour, as it directly addresses men/husbands and unequivocally places the act deep within the core of revelation and its wisdom (*al-kitāb wa'l-ḥikmah*), which God specifically admonishes and advises them about.

With regard to the exegetical discourse for verse Q. 2:231, it was mostly al-Ṭabarī and al-Rāzī who noted the emphasis on the magnitude of this kind of harm and the consequent seriousness of this sin (that is, repeating the revocation just before the end of the three-month period to subject the woman to a nine-month waiting period). Al-Ṭabarī especially lingers on the significance of associating marital and divorce practices directly with God's *āyāt* (messages or injunctions), blessings, and wisdom: God has made divorce a means of "exit" or "deliverance" from a bad union and the retraction an opportunity for what "affection" or inclination might call for.[83] So these blessings should not be abused or taken lightly, for this would in effect subvert the original divine intent of ceasing harm to and ill-treatment of women. In the manner noted by Drāz in his analysis of the final exhortations in the verses, al-Ṭabarī ends this segment with a passage on religious ethics as a comment on the last portion of the verse ("remain conscious of God and know that God has full knowledge of everything"):

> O people, know that God who drew for you these boundaries, legislated for you these laws, and prescribed for you these injunctions in his Book and revelation to the Prophet Muhammad knows everything that you do – good or evil, fair or bad, obedience or sin – and nothing is unknown to Him, whether apparent or hidden, secret or declared; and so He will repay you good for

> good and bad for bad, except if He forgives, so don't expose yourself to His punishment or do injustice to yourselves.[84]

Al-Rāzī also explains why verse 231 seems to repeat the ruling of the two revocations in verse 229 by commenting that verse 231 highlights what he calls "the greatest kind of harmful acts" (elongating the waiting period to nine months) and by describing such deliberate acts as "the greatest kind of sins."[85] According to his understanding, this seriousness merits the repetition and emphasis.

Q. 2:232 continues the ethical outlook developed from the beginning by highlighting women's consent in these situations:

> And when you divorce women, and they have come to the end of their waiting-term, hinder them not from marrying other men if they have agreed with each other in a fair manner. This is an admonishment unto every one of you who believes in God and the Last Day; it is the most virtuous [way] for you, and the cleanest. And God knows, whereas you do not know.

In the *tafsīr* literature, the general consensus is that the occasion of this revelation is a response to this situation: a man whose sister he had previously married to a cousin, and who was divorced and not returned during the waiting period, then approached again by the husband for a new proposal; though his sister wanted to return to her former husband, the brother refused and prevented this remarriage. Hence, the verse prohibits such brothers, fathers, or uncles from practising this *'aḍl* (preventing, holding back, hindering), when women reach the end of the waiting term and they wish to remarry their former husbands, "if they have agreed with each other in a fair manner." Then, as previously mentioned, following the general pattern of most gender verses that gave rise to legal rulings, the verse moves to the level of moral edification, which is actually the underlying objective: "This is an admonishment unto every one of you who believes in God and the Last Day." Once again, the particular context of the revelation, though initially addressed to this man and others in similar situations, also conveys a general principle of curbing patriarchal autocratic control, especially when the notion of *mutual consent* between the couple is clearly introduced here. The verse signals the existence of a separate individual will – the woman's – and thus charts a new path toward change of conduct and social practices for this highly patriarchal community to pursue and fulfill. Lastly, the verse ends with the customary ethical justification or reasoning behind this prohibition: "That is more virtuous and pure for you." This hermeneutical approach that foregrounds and emphasizes ethical and egalitarian nuances to be followed to their logical fruition ought to have legal ramifications, adjustments, or revisions.

Interestingly, however, instead of focusing on the possibility of deducing – from this very verse (v. 232) – a law or legal stipulations that would guarantee women's choices and free will in all marriage and divorce decisions, or that would eventually limit and weaken autocratic control in the social practice of male legal guardianship, exegetes and jurists focused their attention on what they saw as the need for the *walī* (male guardian) to play a role in their female wards' marriages – albeit acknowledging the Qur'an's call to the guardian not to prevent his ward from marrying if she wished it.[86] The logic of interpretation and deduction as we find in al-Ṭabarī, for example, is as follows: this divine prohibition against holding back a woman actually confirms a guardian's rightful responsibility for her marital state to begin with; otherwise, that prohibition would not have been needed in the first place. This means that a guardian *does* possess the means and the decision-making authority as a premise. Hence, "this verse contains the clear proof of the correctness of what was said – no marrying without a guardian of the tribe."[87] Although according to this representative exegetical discussion al-Ṭabarī at least managed to stress forbidding "injustice" and "harm" to the woman, as well as the element of the couple's consent, he still did not see the full implication of this general ethical address. His time-bound partial application of Qur'anic egalitarian gender ethics led him only as far as a progress from spiteful patriarchy to a benevolent paternalism – albeit one without legal ramifications.

Al-Qurṭubī agrees with al-Ṭabarī that the verse's address is to the *walī* on account of the specific occasion of its revelation, being an address to this man, Ma'qal bin Yasār, as a guardian to his sister. He also deduces that even with the woman's "consent," marriage without a guardian is not legal.[88] And al-Rāzī considers another factor in determining the address, that being, the coherent logic of the whole unit's arrangement (*naẓm* or *tartīb*) – the fact that all the divorce verses so far address husbands. However, the focus here is on the legal technicalities pertaining to the dower as the object of agreement in marriage between the two parties, without considering women's consent, which is what the verse highlights.[89] Al-Zamakhsharī presents both possibilities, focusing on explaining the act of *'aḍl* (hindering) itself, whether by husbands or guardians. Overall, then, most exegetes focused on ensuring the correct legal procedures, reasoning that formal correctness was the only or most important purpose of these verses, naturally on account of their patriarchal milieu, and ignoring these verses' call to consider women's wishes and consent during different steps. A hermeneutics of ethics hopes to uncover and apply these verses' egalitarian spirit.

Q. 2:236–7 regulates an aspect of the financial settlement in a divorce situation when the marriage was not consummated, with or without determining a dower for the wife:

> You will incur no sin if you divorce women while you have not yet touched them nor settled a dower upon them; but [even in such a case] make provision for them – the affluent according to his means, and the straitened according to his means – a provision in an equitable manner: this is a duty upon all who would do good. And if you divorce them before having touched them, but after having settled a dower upon them, then [give them] half of what you have settled – unless it be that they forgo their claim or he in whose hand is the marriage-tie forgoes his claim [to half of the dower]: and to forgo what is due to you is more in accord with God-consciousness. And forget not [that you are to act with] grace towards one another: verily, God sees all that you do.

Naturally, the verses provide an important basis for specific legal determinations regarding what each divorced party is entitled to in these cases, such as the husband bestowing a suitable gift as compensation – if there was no dower – or forgoing half the fixed dower to the divorced wife. The central legal ruling this revelation conveys is infused with two equally important levels of meaning in the text: one related to the social context that occasioned the verses, and the other related to the moral justification or value the verses attach to the law. A prevalent practice at the time among men upon divorce was to take back the money or property they gave to their wives, or they would, at their will, refuse to pay any divorce settlement. Basically, the Qur'an prohibited taking money back and prescribed fair provision/alimony for divorced women. First, it is noteworthy that in addressing a social problem at the time of revelation and rectifying an unfair situation for women, the Qur'an removed the element of unchecked, arbitrary, autocratic will from husbands and balanced the situation with a guarantee of monetary compensation as a safety net for women – a group kept dependent and disempowered in society. Both verses end by clearly outlining particular moral virtues that justify these prescribed acts: verse 236 declares that bestowing on the divorced wife (in the case of an unconsummated legal bond) a gift of a suitable, reasonable amount is a fitting, true imperative (*ḥaqq*) upon those who want to do the right thing (*'alā al-muḥsinīn*), those who want to be generous and pursuant of goodness and the beautiful. The second verse (v. 237) urges men to give women half the fixed dower, unless either the woman or the husband renounces or waives (using the term *'afw* three times, which originally connoted pardon and the effacement of grievances or sins). Two more phrases in the latter part of the verse emphasize ethics: this magnanimous exemption (forgoing what is legally due to you) is the closest to God-consciousness (*taqwā*); additionally, God commands both separating parties not to forget mutual graciousness (*al-faḍl baynakum*). As Drāz notes, and as we saw in the previous analysis, the pattern in the Qur'an does not merely convey a divine commandment as sufficient in itself to be obeyed and implemented, but "it is edifying to see with what care the Book often tries to attach its justification to each resolution of the law, and to each precept the moral value which constitutes the established benefit."[90] A divine commandment is very often supported and validated by referral to a moral, humane criterion.

Once again, the matter of the guardian's role and authority is raised by the exegetes in determining whether the address in Q. 2:237 ("he in whose hand is the marriage-tie") is to the husband or the *walī*. Al-Ṭabarī argues that it is directed at the husband, highlighting mutual tolerance and magnanimity on the part of both partners. He further explains how this behaviour is a manifestation of *taqwā*: when a man hastens to what God urges him to do, preferring this to his own whim or self-interest, even though this particular act is not legally prescribed. Al-Ṭabarī distinguishes between what is *farḍ* and what is *nadb* and judges that pursuing what was only *mandūb* (recommended) is a virtuous, commendable act; he even implies its ethical superiority. He also lingers on the virtue of *faḍl* (grace toward one another), which he interprets as a form of magnanimity, and he uses the word *tafaḍḍul* on the part of both the man and the woman toward each other. In other words, he recommends that each partner "surpass the other in being gracious and waiving entitlements."[91] Typical also of al-Ṭabarī's hermeneutical discourse is his attention to the last phrase of a verse; here, he attempts to link its final exhortation or the mention of a divine attribute to the principal meaning. In explaining that "God sees all that you do," he again highlights the fact that "God sees and knows the graciousness and virtuous behaviour that He urged you to follow, or its contrary, so that He can repay you either for your kindness or hurtfulness."[92] In other words, the virtuous, moral path is indeed rewarding and worth pursuing.

As for the following three exegetes, al-Zamakhsharī, al-Rāzī, and al-Qurṭubī, the discussions mostly centre on reporting the jurisprudential arguments concerning the legality of this act of forgoing half the fixed dower, as well as on the debate over whether the addressed is the husband or the *walī*. However, all agree that this part of the verse – "to forgo what is due to you is more in accord with God-consciousness; and forget not grace towards one another" – addresses both men and women in general, urging tolerance and kindness. Al-Rāzī comments that this act would lead one to abandon "*ẓulm*" (injustice), which is in reality *taqwā*, "because he who waives his due right out of closeness to God will be most unlikely to do injustice to another by taking what's not his right."[93] Furthermore, the reason for the recommendation to both partners at the same time that they forgo the full dower is the "urging to each one to do what removes hurt from the other's heart/self,"[94] and the verse closes "with the accustomed threat: God sees all that you do."[95]

Finally, reading the two verses holistically, we can see that this revelation presents a particular case of ethical edification: support for a weakened, disempowered group (what Abou El Fadl calls the condition of *istiḍʿāf* mentioned in the Qurʾan) to redress the balance, as well as affirmation of certain ethical principles that can have a broad application to similar oppressive situations. In Abou El Fadl's words, "In many ways, ethical and moral objectives being the same, the Qurʾan does not explicate unwavering rules that are applicable to women; rather, the Qurʾan illustrates an ethical methodology on how to deal with situations that were abusive to women."[96] In other words, if such verses are read *only* literally as definite textual stopping points, we are bound to miss the Qurʾanic moral message and path that it instructs us to follow and fulfill. It is noted, for example, that almost all similar verses addressed to men (as husbands, fathers, brothers) aim at modifying the customary patriarchal inclination towards arbitrary and autocratic will and at the ethical rehabilitation of this early community, besides sending a message for all Muslims (men in particular) to continue to grow and evolve morally until all abuses and inequalities are eliminated.

The final verse in Surat al-Baqara mentioning divorce is 2:241: "And the divorced women, too, shall have [a right to] maintenance in a goodly manner: this is a duty for all who are conscious of God." This verse enforces the commandment that the divorce monetary compensation (*mut'a*) be a "duty for all who are conscious of God"; this reflects the previous "duty upon all who would do good" in Q. 2:236.

The two verses in Surat al-Ṭalāq (Q. 65:1–2) also reiterate the noted ethical terms and consolidate the pursuit of moral and virtuous behaviour as a divine imperative:

> O Prophet! When you [intend to divorce women, divorce them with a view to the waiting period appointed for them, and reckon the period [carefully], and be conscious of God, your Sustainer. Do not expel them from their homes; and neither shall they [be made to] leave, unless they become openly guilty of immoral conduct. These, then, are the bounds set by God – and he who transgresses the bounds set by God does indeed sin against himself: [for, O man, although] thou knowest it not, after that [first breach] God may well cause something new to come about. And so, when they are about to reach the end of their waiting-term, either retain them in a fair manner or part with them in a fair manner. And let two persons of [known] probity from among your own community witness [what you have decided]; and do yourselves bear true witness before God, He [always] grants a way out [of unhappiness].

In general, they contain more specific injunctions concerning the time of divorcing and observing, and they call for the careful spacing of waiting periods so that any hasty act can be reconsidered, so as to resume the marital relationship or to ensure parting "in a fair manner" to avoid abuse. The two new regulations in these verses state that divorced women are not to be expelled from their homes during the waiting period and that two upright persons are to be invited as witnesses to the process. In fact, the rest of this passage (Q. 65:3–7) continues to outline certain procedures and stipulations to ensure provision, housing, and dignity for divorced women.

Then the final part of al-Aḥzāb (Q. 33:49), which commands men when divorcing to "release them in a becoming manner," condenses the whole Qur'anic ethical thrust to be observed and applied in divorce and separation situations; the terms "release" and "becoming/beautiful" highlight the principles of freedom and goodness: "O You who have attained to faith! If you marry believing women and then divorce them ere you have touched them, you have no reason to expect, and to calculate, any waiting-period on their part: hence, make [at once] provision for them, and release them in a becoming manner."

We can here recall the kind of linguistic analysis approach that Izutsu undertakes, in which he systematically examines the connotative system of Qur'anic ethical terms to arrive at the particular world view it represents and embodies, and ultimately the Qur'an's moral code. Having examined what he calls the "semantic fields" of patterned relations between certain words, thus forming a significant group or combination, he illustrates how this method classifies and explains the "ethico-religious concepts"[97] of the Qur'an. In the Qur'anic context, every term has a connotative meaning in relation to other words and concepts; these multiple relations between concepts result in several semantic areas or fields, each composed of a cluster of key terms that denote positive moral properties. Considered holistically, this network forms the Qur'an's total ethical discourse or criteria. For example, we have noted the consistent occurrence of *ma'rūf*, *iḥsān*, *taqwā*, and *ḥudūd* in marriage and divorce verses; these create a patterned cluster of moral virtues that are almost always mentioned in situations or legal prescriptions that concern women. One can conclude that the repeated use of these ethical terms is not haphazard or redundant; rather, they create clear semantic fields to be considered in the production of law as conditions or measures.

The preceding textual and hermeneutical analysis has, therefore, shown that the positive and negative mixed bag of the tradition is attributed to the tension between the recognition of the ethical, egalitarian dimension of the revelation and the exegetes' own patriarchal cultural systems. This ambivalence led to difficulties in lawmaking and implementation, and in the separation (as we have seen) between the ethical and the legal, between inner unknowable conscience and formal discernable correctness.

This question arises next: What have been the implications of this ethically oriented reading of divorce verses in contemporary Muslim contexts? How can they be illustrated through norms or possible legal rulings? When we foreground the ethical messages in these verses, it becomes necessary to revisit the religious permissibility of the following: men's right to unilaterally divorce their wives and to revoke that divorce during the waiting period; the negation of the wife's will in the revocation process; women's restricted access to divorce; and the inability of a woman to conclude a marriage without a guardian. An ethical reading of these divorce verses points toward the need for substantive reform of hierarchical divorce rights that privilege men and discriminate against women and that go against the Qur'an's notion of the reciprocity of doing good by one another that is demanded of both spouses. This would mean delinking the tie between *qiwāma*, understood as the man's authority or guardianship over his spouse, and hierarchical divorce rights that privilege husbands.[98]

The harms that befall women in different lived realities in Muslim contexts as result of these hierarchical divorce rulings have been well-documented and have helped drive some of the reforms introduced (inconsistently) in contemporary Muslim family law.[99] For instance, the legal requirement that male-initiated divorces be registered – at times poorly implemented – has been the first step in regulating men's right to unilateral repudiation.[100] Furthermore, in some countries, the husband's exercise of divorce and the ensuing financial settlement are now administered by the courts, as a further step toward regulating and thereby minimizing the abuse of men's unilateral right to divorce. However, this does not mean that courts have the authority to reject a man's petition for divorce (unlike the case for women). As for women's access to divorce, different reforms have been introduced in various Muslim contexts to expand the claims women can make when seeking judicial divorce and to improve the legal process and courtroom procedures regarding existing divorce laws. For example, in Morocco since the new family law was introducted in 2004 (*al-mudawwana*), women, like men, can petition the court for *shiqāq* divorce, which they are guaranteed after a judicial process in the course of which the monies owed by each party to the other are worked out.[101] In Egypt, judicial *khul'* divorce was legislated in 2000 allowing a woman to secure divorce from the court without the consent of her husband, provided that she relinquished her financial rights.[102]

Notwithstanding these legal reforms introduced (unevenly) to address some of the injustices arising from hierarchical divorce (and marriage) rulings, what remains elusive is the promotion and spread – in communities and among religious actors, legislators, and individual Muslims – of an understanding of the integral link between the ethics of the Qur'an on marriage and divorce on the one hand, and the need for egalitarian gender norms and family law on the other. We believe that such an understanding, once widely shared, could play a transformative role in a multilayered reform that does not stop at regulating and safeguarding rights but could also enable the formation of Muslim subjectivities that enact the Qur'anic ethos.

CONCLUSION

In this chapter we have proposed and applied an ethically oriented reading to the principal divorce verses in the Qur'an. Our aim has been to undertake a hermeneutical process guided by the Qur'anic ethical world view and message. Thus with regard to the divorce verses in question, we have sought to make explicit the central Qur'anic ethical principles that underlie these verses; to highlight key terms in the verses that provide a guiding framework for ethical directives; and to explore the range of context-appropriate legal possibilities that can be derived from these directives.

As part of our reading, we engaged with classical exegesis and some of its main interpretations of the verses in question. We shed light on how classical exegetes understood the ethical message conveyed in the verses and whether they brought it to bear on the process of deriving legal injunctions from these verses. We noted the inconsistency and the unfinished work of exegetes such as al-Ṭabarī in foregrounding the ethical messages in the process of deducing legal interpretations. This is not to say that classical interpreters and jurists were unconcerned with virtues or were not conscientious in their efforts to understand and explain God's *sharīʿa*. Indeed, numerous scholarly debates and intricate discussions about the "correct" way to address Qur'anic injunctions permeate the tradition. In some instances, these scholars were able to take steps in the right direction. However, those steps did not go far enough to work out the implications of the ethical directives in the divine texts for the exegetical process and the related task of deducing rulings. This was an interpretive choice by these exegetes – albeit one shaped by their particular cultural and historical contexts. Hence, in these other instances, exegetes' contingent mis/understandings or oversights prevailed. The consequence of this lack of systematic and consistent attention to Qur'anic ethics in the hermeneutical process was grave: patriarchal interpretations transmitted and reinforced over generations resulted in the hegemonic construction of gender relations and rights in the exegetical corpus. This gender construction became even more dominant (and detrimental) as the exegetical corpus itself, over the course of its history, evolved into an authoritative "canon" through which the meanings of the sacred text were accessed. Furthermore, this religiously sanctioned gender inequality and injustice took hold in the legal tradition as a "canon" of juristic rulings on marriage and divorce rights also developed. Today this juristic model of spousal rights is sustained in many contemporary Muslim family laws. It follows that a systematic and coherent ethical hermeneutics must be viewed as an integral step in a multidimensional reform endeavour.

To sum up, as an Islamic feminist inquiry, this chapter argues that one cannot adequately understand and evaluate the hermeneutical work of Islamic feminist scholars on the Qur'an and the interpretive tradition without taking into account these scholars' engagement with Qur'anic ethics, both as a guiding framework for legal injunctions on gender and as methodological principles guiding the interpretive process. By centring the ethical in our interpretive approach toward the Qur'anic text, we are not undermining the normative significance of the text. Rather, we are seeking the knowledge of all the ethico-legal potentialities suggested by and embedded in the text to fulfill its universal objectives that apply to humanity in different times and contexts.

NOTES

1 Saleh, *Formation*, 14.
2 Saleh, "Quranic Commentaries," 1657.
3 Abou-Bakr, "Interpretive Legacy."
4 For example, Abou Bakr notes the difference between Muhammad ʿAbduh's patriarchal interpretation of *qiwāma* and that of classical exegetes such as al-Tabari. ʿAbduh's interpretation added the notions of innate female domesticity and male rationality as the basis for a gendered division of the private and public spheres. While this difference between modern and pre-modern patriarchy is noteworthy, still the hierarchical notion of marriage and spousal roles is maintained throughout the exegetical tradition. See Abou-Bakr, "The Interpretive Legacy," 55.
5 Stowasser, *Women in the Qur'an*; Wadud, *Qur'an and Woman*; Ali, "Marriage"; Barlas, *Believing Women;* Abou-Bakr, "Interpretive Legacy."
6 Mir-Hosseini, "Construction of Gender," 1–25; Ali, "Progressive Muslims."

7 For example, according to all four Sunni schools, a mother loses the custody of her children if she marries a man who is not blood related to the children. See al-Jazīrī, *al-Fiqh ʿala al-madhāhib al-arbaʿa*. Shiʿi Jurisprudence applies the same ruling. See al-Ḥillī, *Mukhtalaf al-shīʿa*.

8 Welchman, "A Husband's Authority," 1–23; Mir-Hosseini, "Justice, Equality," 7–34.

9 Al-Sharmani and Rumminger, "Understanding *Qiwamah* and *Wilayah*."

10 Al-Sharmani, "Islamic Feminism: Transnational," 83.

11 For scholarship on Islamic feminism in the Arab World, see Aboud, "Annotated Bibliography"; and Al-Sharmani, "Contemporary Egyptian Islamic Feminism."

12 Scholars who work in this area include Riffat Hassan, Azizah al-Hibri, Amina Wadud, Asma Barlas, Omaima Abou-Bakr, Asma Lamrabet, Masyam al-Faruqi, Nevin Reda, and to a lesser degree Kecia Ali, who focuses more on Islamic jurisprudence.

13 Islamic feminist scholarship on Islamic jurisprudence is spearheaded by Ziba Mir-Hosseini and Kecia Ali. Azizah al-Hibri has also contributed to this area.

14 Scholars who have produced work in this category include Ayesha Chaudhry, Faqihuddin Abdul Kodir, Nimat Hafez Barazangi, Kecia Ali, Amina Inloes, and Yasmin Amin, among others.

15 The work of Saʿdiyya Shaikh leads this scholarship. Laury Silvers and Maria Massi Dakake have also contributed to this area.

16 Abou-Bakr, "Islamic Feminism"; Badran, "Islamic Feminism"; idem, "Between Secular and Islamic"; idem, "From Islamic Feminism"; Cooke, *Women Claim Islam*; Fernea, *In Search of Islamic*; Hidayatullah, *Feminist Edges*; Karam, *Women, Islamism, and the State*; Moll, "People Like Us"; Mir-Hosseini, "Muslim Women's Quest"; Mir-Hosseini, "Beyond Islam vs. Feminism"; Tohidi, "Women's Rights."

17 Shaikh, "Transforming Feminism"; Mir-Hosseini, "Muslim Women's Quest"; Al-Sharmani, "Islamic Feminism"; Abou-Bakr, "Why Do We Need."

18 Moghissi, *Feminism and Islamic Fundamentalism*; Moghadam, "Islamic Feminism and Its Discontents," 1135–71.

19 Barlas, "Engaging Islamic Feminism"; Seedat, "Islam, Feminism."

20 Abou-Bakr, "Islamic Feminism."

21 Moll, "People Like Us."

22 Naguib, "Horizons and Limitations," 1–23.

23 Ibid., 4.

24 Ibid., 7–11.

25 Hidayatullah, *Feminist Edges*.

26 Ibid., 160.
27 Ibid.
28 Hidayatullah, "Claims to the Sacred," 137.
29 Barlas, "Reading the Qur'an."
30 Lamptey, *Never Wholly Other*, 85.
31 Barlas, "Secular and Feminist Critiques," 119.
32 Wadud, "Islam beyond Patriarchy"; Wadud, "Ethics of Tawhid."
33 Wadud, "Islam beyond Patriarchy," 98–9.
34 Wadud, "Ethics of Tawhid," 267.
35 Wadud, "Qur'an, Gender," 330.
36 Ibid.
37 Wadud, "Can One Critique," 132.
38 Ibid., 131.
39 Mir-Hosseini, "Construction of Gender."
40 Mir-Hosseini, "Classical Fiqh"; idem, "Justice, Equality and Muslim."
41 Shaikh, "Islamic Law."
42 We view our critical engagement as "internal intervention" within the tradition. We draw this notion from Asad, *Idea of Anthropology*; and Amir-Moazami and Salvatore, "Gender, Generation."
43 Muslim ibn al-Ḥajjāj, *Ṣaḥīḥ Muslim: Kitāb al-tahajjud*, no. 746.
44 Muhammad Asad's translation of the Qur'an is used throughout. See Asad, *Message of the Qur'an*. All other translations from the Arabic are ours, unless otherwise stated.
45 Al-Bukhārī, *Kitāb al-adab al-mufrad: bāb ḥusn al-khuluq*, no. 269. Authors' translation. This *ḥadīth* is generally classified as *ḥasan* (good). For more sources and different versions of this *ḥadīth*, see *Takhrīj al-ḥadīth* [*bu'ithtu li-utammim ṣāliḥ al-akhlāq*]. http://library.islamweb.net/hadith/hadithServices.php?type=1&cid=2226&sid=4396
46 Ansari, "Islamic Ethics," 81.
47 Ibid., 81.
48 Leaman, "Ibn Miskawayh," 472.
49 Moosa, "Muslim Ethics?," 239.
50 Ghaly, *Islamic Perspectives*.
51 Ansari, "Islamic Ethics," 86.
52 Ibid., 90.
53 Drāz's book was first published in French as Draz, *La Morale du Koran* (1951), and translated into Arabic in 1972. For this chapter, we are using the English translation of the book, published in 1982.
54 Draz, *Moral World*, 27.
55 Ibid., 15.

56 Ibid., 26.
57 Ibid., 135.
58 Izutsu, *Structure.*
59 Lamptey, *Never Wholly Other,* 131.
60 For example, Wadud's and Barlas' methods of applying historical and holistic readings to the Qur'an build on Rahman's methodology of the "double movement" and distinguishing the universal from the particular verses.
61 Rahman, *Islam and Modernity,* 154.
62 Ibid., 20.
63 Ibid., 29
64 Lamptey, *Never Wholly Other*, 120.
65 Abou El Fadl, *Reasoning with God*, 346.
66 Ibid., 347.
67 Ibid., 374.
68 Ibid., 31.
69 Ibid.
70 Ibid., 373.
71 Ibid., 380–1.
72 Ibid., Chapter 8. The words between single quotes are the authors' paraphrases of terms and concepts used by Abu El Fadl in different parts of the chapter.
73 Mahmood, "Secularism, Hermeneutics, and Empire," 323–47; Abou Lughod, *Do Muslim Women Need Saving?*
74 Al-Ṭabarī, *Jāmiʿ al-bayān,* vol. 2, 614.
75 Ibid., 614.
76 Al-Rāzī, *al-Tafsīr al-kabīr,* vol. 6, 81.
77 Al-Qurṭubī, *al-Jāmiʿ li-aḥkām al-Qurʾān,* vol. 3, 123.
78 Al-Ṭabari, *Jāmiʿ al-bayān,* vol. 2, 617.
79 Ibid.
80 See for example Stern, *Marriage in Early Islam.*
81 Al-Rāzī, *al-Tafsīr al-kabīr,* vol. 6, 85.
82 Nevin Reda also notes the use of the dual form and how the story introduces women as equal partners in *taklīf* and the shared responsibility for wrongdoing, as opposed to laying the traditional blame only on Eve. See Reda, *al-Baqara Crescendo*, 143.
83 Al-Ṭabarī, *Jāmiʿ al-bayān*, vol. 2, 654
84 Ibid., 656.
85 Al-Rāzī, *al-Tafsīr al-kabīr,* vol. 6, 452–3.
86 Masud, "Gender Equality," 127–52.

87 Al-Ṭabarī, *Jāmi' al-bayān*, vol. 2, 662.
88 Al-Qurṭubī, *al-Jāmi' li-aḥkām al-Qur'ān*, vol. 3, 159.
89 Al-Rāzī, *al-Tafsīr al-kabīr*, vol. 6, 455.
90 Draz, *Moral World*, 26.
91 Al-Ṭabarī, *Jāmi' al-bayān*, vol. 2, 748.
92 Ibid., 749–50.
93 Al-Rāzī, *al-Tafsir al-kabir*, vol. 6, 481.
94 Ibid.
95 Ibid.
96 Abou El Fadl, *Reasoning with God*, 378.
97 Izutsu, *Ethico-Religious Concepts*, 17.
98 Mir-Hosseini, Al-Sharmani, and Rumminger, *Men in Charge?*
99 Welchman, *Women and Muslim*; Yassari, *Changing God's Law.*
100 Welchman, *Women and Muslim,* 108.
101 El Hajjami, "Religious Arguments," 81–106.
102 Al-Sharmani, *Gender Justice and Legal.*

REFERENCES

Abou-Bakr, Omaima. "The Interpretive Legacy of Qiwamah as an Exegetical Construct." In *Men in Charge? Rethinking Authority in Muslim Legal Tradition,* ed. Ziba Mir-Hosseini, Mulki Al-Sharmani, and Jana Rumminger, 44–64. Oxford: Oneworld, 2015.

– "Islamic Feminism? What's in a Name? Preliminary Reflections." *Association for Middle East Women's Studies* 15 (2001): 1–2.

– "Why Do We Need Feminism from an Islamic Perspective?" In *Feminist and Islamic Perspectives: New Horizons of Knowledge and Reform,* ed. Omaima Abou-Bakr, 4–9. Cairo: Women and Memory Forum.

Aboud, Hosn. "Annotated Bibliography: General and Foundational Trends in 'Islamic Feminism' in the Arab World." In *Feminist and Islamic Perspectives: New Horizons of Knowledge and Reform,* ed. Omaima Abou-Bakr, 194–219. Cairo: Women and Memory Forum and KVINFO, 2013.

Abou El Fadl, Khaled. *Reasoning with God: Reclaiming Shari'ah in the Modern Age*. Lanham: Rowman and Littlefield, 2014.

Abu Lughod, Lila. *Do Muslim Women Need Saving?* Cambridge, MA: Harvard University Press, 2013.

Ali, Kecia. "Marriage in Classical Islamic Jurisprudence: A Survey of Doctrines." In *The Islamic Marriage Contract: Case Studies in Islamic Family Law,* ed. Asifah Qureshi and Frank Vogel, 11–36. Cambridge, MA: Harvard University Press, 2008.

– "Progressive Muslims and Islamic Jurisprudence: The Necessity for Critical Engagement with Marriage and Divorce Law." In *Progressive Muslims on Justice, Gender, and Pluralism*, ed. Omid Safi, 164–89. Oxford: Oneworld, 2003.

Al-Sharmani, Mulki. "Contemporary Egyptian Islamic Feminism: Possibilities and Challenges." *Afriche e Orienti* 18, no. 1 (2016): 58–77.

– "Islamic Feminism and Reforming Muslim Family Laws." European University Institute working paper RSCAS 2011/29, Robert Schuman Centre for Advanced Studies, Mediterranean Programme. 1–24.

– "Islamic Feminism: Transnational and National Reflections." *Approaching Religion* 4, no. 2 (2014): 83–94.

Al-Sharmani, Mulki, and Jana Rumminger. "Understanding *Qiwamah* and *Wilayah* through Life Stories." In *Men in Charge? Rethinking Authority in Muslim Legal Tradition,* ed. Ziba Mir-Hosseini, Mulki Al-Sharmani, and Jana Rumminger, 219–55. Oxford: Oneworld, 2015.

Amir-Moazami, Schirin, and Armando Salvatore. "Gender, Generation, and the Reform of Tradition: From Muslim Majority to Western Europe." In *Muslim Networks and Transnational Communities in and across Europe,* ed. S. Allievi and J. Nielsen, 309–30. Leiden: Brill, 2003.

Ansari, Abdul-Haq. "Islamic Ethics: Concept and Prospect." *American Journal of Islamic Social Science* 6, no. 1 (1989): 81–91.

Asad, Muhammad. *The Message of the Qur'an*. Gibraltar: Dar Al-Andalus, 1980.

Asad, Talal. *The Idea of an Anthropology of Islam.* Washington, DC: Center for Contemporary Arab Studies, Georgetown University, 1986.

Badran, Margot. "Between Secular and Islamic Feminism/s: Reflections on the Middle East and Beyond." *Journal of Middle East Women's Studies* 1, no. 1 (2005): 6–26.

– "From Islamic Feminism to a Muslim Holistic Feminism." *IDS Bulletin* 42, no. 1 (2011): 78–87.

– "Islamic Feminism: What Is in a Name?" *Al-Ahram Weekly* 569 (17–23 January 2002), 1–8.

Barlas, Asma. *Believing Women in Islam: Un-reading Patriarchal Interpretations of the Qur'an*. Austin: University of Texas Press, 2004.

– "Engaging Islamic Feminism: Provincializing Feminism as Master Narrative." In *Islamic Feminism: Current Perspectives,* ed. Anitta Kynsilheto, 15–24. Tampere: Tampere Peace Research Institute, 2008.

– "Reading the Qur'an: Challenges and Possibilities for Muslim Women." Paper presented at Symposium on Gender, Race, and Islam, and the War on Terror, Simon Fraser University, 11–13 May 2006.

– "Secular and Feminist Critiques of the Qur'an: Anti-Hermeneutics as Liberation?" *Journal of Feminist Studies in Religion* 32, no. 2 (2016): 111–21.

Bukhārī, Muḥammad ibn Ismāʿīl al-. *Kitāb al-adab al-mufrad*. http://library.islamweb.net/hadith/display_hbook.php?bk_no=141&hid=269&pid=96629

Cooke, Miriam. *Women Claim Islam: Creating Islamic Feminism through Literature*. London: Routledge, 2004.

Draz, M[uḥammad] A[bd Allāh]. *La Morale du Koran. Étude Comparée de la Morale Théorique du Koran*. Paris: Presses Universitaires de France, 1951.

– *The Moral World of the Qur'an*. Trans. Danielle Robinson and Rebecca Masterton. London: I.B. Taurus, 2008.

Fernea, Elizabeth. *In Search of Islamic Feminism: One Woman's Global Journey*. New York: First Anchor Books, 1998.

Ghaly, Mohammad, ed. *Islamic Perspectives on the Principles of Biomedical Ethics: Muslim Religious Scholars and Biomedical Scientists Face to Face Dialogue with Western Ethicists*. London: World Scientific, 2016.

Hajjami, Aïcha El. "The Religious Arguments in the Debate on the Reform of the Moroccan Family Code." In *Gender and Equality in Muslim Family Law*, ed. Ziba Mir-Hosseini, Kari Vogt, Lena Larsen, and Christian Moe, 81–106. London: I.B. Taurus, 2013.

Hidayatullah, Aysha. "Claims to the Sacred." *Journal of Feminist Studies in Religion* 32, no. 2 (2016): 134–8.

– *Feminist Edges of the Qur'an*. Oxford: Oxford University Press, 2014.

Ḥillī, al-Ḥasan ibn Yūsuf al-Muṭahhar al-. *Mukhtalaf al-shīʿa fīaḥkām al-sharīʿa*. 10 vols. Qom: Islamic Sciences Research Center, 1991.

Karam, Azza. *Women, Islamism, and the State*. New York: St. Martin's Press, 1998.

Izutsu, Toshihiku. *Ethico-Religious Concepts in the Qur'an*. Montreal and Kingston: McGill–Queen's University Press, 1966.

– *The Structure of the Ethical Terms in the Qur'an*. Tokyo: Keio Institute for Philological Studies, 1959.

Jazīrī, ʿAbd al-Raḥmān al-. *Al-fiqh ʿala al-madhāhib al-arbaʿa: al-nikāh wa'l-ṭalāq*, vol. 3. Cairo: Dār al-Taqwā.

Lamptey, Jerusha Tanner. *Never Wholly Other: A Muslima Theology of Religious Pluralism*. Oxford: Oxford University Press, 2014.

Leaman, Oliver. "Ibn Misakawayh." In *History of Islamic Philosophy*, ed. Seyyed Hossein Nasr and Oliver Leaman, 466–76. London and New York: Routledge, 2008.

Mahmood, Saba. "Secularism, Hermeneutics, and Empire: The Politics of Islamic Reformation." *Public Culture* 18, no. 2 (2006): 323–47.

Masud, Muhammad Khalid. "Gender Equality and the Doctrine of Wilaya." In *Gender and Equality in Muslim Family Law: Justice and Ethics in Muslim Legal Tradition,* ed. Ziba Mir-Hosseini, Kari Vogt, Lena Larsen, and Christian Moe, 127–52. London: I.B. Taurus, 2013.

Mir-Hosseini, Ziba. "Beyond Islam vs. Feminism." *IDS Bulletin* 42, no. 1(2011): 67–77.

– "Classical Fiqh, Contemporary Ethics, and Gender Justice." In *New Directions in Islamic Thought: Exploring Reform and Muslim Tradition*, ed. Kari Vogt, Lena Larsen, and Christian Moe, 77–88. London: I.B. Tauris, 2010.

– "The Construction of Gender in Islamic Legal Thought and Strategies for Reform." *Hawwa* 1, no. 1 (2003): 1–25.

– "Justice, Equality, and Muslim Family Laws: New Ideas, New Prospects." In *Gender and Equality in Muslim Family Law: Justice and Ethics in the Islamic Legal Tradition*, ed. Ziba Mir-Hosseini, Kari Vogt, Lena Larsen, and Christian Moe, 7–34. London: I.B. Tauris, 2013.

– "Muslim Women's Quest for Equality: Between Islamic Law and Feminism." *Critical Inquiry* 32, no. 4 (2006): 629–45.

Mir-Hosseini, Ziba, Mulki Al-Sharmani, and Jana Rumminger, eds. *Men in Charge? Rethinking Authority in Muslim Legal Tradition.* Oxford: Oneworld, 2015.

Moghadam, Valentine. "Islamic Feminism and Its Discontents: Towards a Resolution of the Debate." *Signs: Journal of Women in Culture and Society* 27, no. 4 (2002): 1135–71.

Moghissi, Haideh. *Feminism and Islamic Fundamentalism: The Limits of Postmodern Analysis*. New York: Zed Books, 1999.

Moll, Yasmin. "People Like Us in Pursuit of God and Rights: Islamic Discourse and Sisters in Islam in Malaysia." *Journal of Women's Studies* 11, no. 1 (2009): 40–55.

Moosa, Ebrahim. "Muslim Ethics?" In *The Blackwell Companion to Religious Ethics*, ed. William Schweiker, 237–43. Victoria, Australia: Blackwell, 2005.

Muslim ibn Hajjāj. *Sahīh Muslim.* Beirut: Dār al-Kutub al-ʿIlmiyya, 1994.

Naguib, Shuruq. "Horizons and Limitations of Muslim Feminist Hermeneutics: Reflections on the Menstruation Verse." In *New Topics in Feminist Philosophy of Religion,* ed. Pamela Sue Anderson, 33–49. Dordrecht: Springer, 2009.

Qurṭubī, Abū ʿAbd Allāh Muḥammad ibn Aḥmad al-Anṣārī al-. *Al-Jāmiʿ li-aḥkām al-Qurʾān*. 20 vols. Cairo: Dār al-Kutub al-Miṣriyya, 1964.

Rahman, Fazlur. *Islam and Modernity: Transformation of Intellectual Tradition*. Chicago: University of Chicago Press, 1982.

Rāzī, Fakhr al-Dīn Muḥammad ibn ʿUmar al-. .*Al-Tafsīr al-kabīr*. 16 vols. Beirut: Dār al-Kutub al-ʿIlmiyya, 2004.

Reda, Nevin. *The al-Baqara Crescendo: Understanding the Qurʾan's Style, Narrative Structure, and Running Themes*. Montreal and Kingston: McGil-Queens University Press, 2017.

Saleh, Walid. *The Formation of the Classical* Tafsīr *Tradition: The Qurʾān Commentary of al-Thaʿlābī (d. 427/1035)*. Leiden: Brill, 2004.

– "Quranic Commentaries." In *The Study of Quran: A New Translation and Commentary*, ed. Seyyed Hussein Nasr et al., 1679–95. New York: Harper One, 2015.

Seedat, Fatima. "Islam, Feminism, and Islamic Feminism: Between Inadequacy and Inevitability." *Journal of Feminist Studies in Religion* 29, no. 2 (2013): 25–45.

– "Islamic Law, Sufism, and Gender: Rethinking the Terms of the Debate." In *Men in Charge? Rethinking Authority in Muslim Legal Tradition*, ed. Ziba Mir-Hosseini, Mulki Al-Sharmani, and Jana Rumminger, 106–31. Oxford: Oneworld, 2015.

– "Transforming Feminism: Islam, Women, and Gender Justice." In *Progressive Muslims: On Justice, Gender, and Pluralism*, ed. Omid Safi, 147–62. Oxford: Oneworld, 2003.

Stowasser, Barbara. *Women in the Qurʾan, Traditions, and Interpretation*. Oxford: Oxford University Press, 1994.

Ṭabarī, Abū Jaʿfar Muḥammad ibn Jarīr al-. *Jāmiʿ al-bayān ʿan taʾwīl āy al-Qurʾān*, ed. Sidqī al-ʿAṭṭār. 15 vols. Beirut: Dār al-Fikr, 1998.

Tohidi, Nayereh. "Women's Rights in the Muslim World: The Universal-Particular Interplay." *Hawwa* 1, no. 2 (2003): 152–88.

Wadud, Amina. "Can One Critique Cancel All Past Efforts?" *Journal of Feminist Studies in Religion* 32, no. 2 (2016): 130–4.

– "The Ethics of *Tawhid* over the Ethics of *Qiwamah*." In *Men in Charge? Rethinking Authority in Muslim Legal Tradition*, ed. Ziba Mir-Hosseini, Mulki Al-Sharmani, and Jana Rumminger, 256–74. Oxford: Oneworld, 2015.

– "Islam beyond Patriarchy through Gender Inclusive Qur'anic Analysis." In *Wanted: Equality and Justice in the Muslim Family*, ed. Zainah Anwar, 95–112. Kuala Lumpur: Musawah/Sisters in Islam, 2009.

– *Qur'an and Woman: Reading the Sacred Text from a Women's Perspective*. New York and Oxford: Oxford University Press, 1999.
Welchman, Lynn. "A Husband's Authority: Emerging Formulations in Muslim Family Laws." *International Journal of Law, Policy, and Family* 25, no. 1 (2011): 1–23.
– *Women and Muslim Family Law in Arab States: A Comparative Overview of Textual Development and Advocacy*. Amsterdam: Amsterdam University Press, 2007.
– *Women's Rights and Islamic Family Law: Perspectives on Reform*. London: Zed Books, 2004.
Yassari, Nadjma, ed. *Changing God's Law: The Dynamics of Middle Eastern Family Law*. London: Routledge, 2016.

2

Tafsīr, Tradition, and Methodological Contestations

The Case of Polygamy

Nevin Reda

Polygamy is a contentious issue that arises in a variety of discourses with competing ethical claims and social and legal ramifications. In Canada, for example, Parliament has passed the Zero Tolerance for Barbaric Cultural Practices Act (2015), which frames polygamy as a foreign practice that threatens Canadian national identity.[1] At the global level, the UN Convention on the Elimination of All Forms of Discrimination against Women (CEDAW) has concluded that polygamous marriages ought to be discouraged and prohibited.[2] Regulatory measures like these are usually informed by considerations of gender equality and the prevention of harm, since evidence-based studies have demonstrated polygamy's adverse effects on women, children, and societies as a whole.[3] However, scholars and activists have also pointed to the fear-mongering, Islamophobia, and harm to Muslim identities that often accompany discourses that target polygamy.[4] Moreover, the legalization of same-sex marriage has brought hitherto unforeseen perspectives on polygamous and polyamorous unions. Queer theorists have constructed arguments against mono-normativity and legal theorists have suggested that the vulnerabilities of children of plural parentage require the recognition of alternative forms of marriage, among other things.[5] As one can see, ideas about gender equality, prevention of harm, vulnerability, LGBT rights, religious freedom, and Islamophobia all add layers of complexity to the topic of polygamy and hint at its importance in the contemporary context. They also underscore the need for present-day Muslims to re-examine polygamy's textual basis in the Qur'an, the sacred scripture that lies at the heart of the Islamic tradition and its ethical deliberations.

However, there are obstacles that Islamic feminists and reformists and other interested parties face whenever they attempt any new exploration of the Qur'an, particularly exegetical endeavours that are concerned with the question of gender justice. For feminists working within the tradition, it is often not enough to present a cogent argument with a sound basis in the primary texts – they inevitably stumble across the problem of methodology. For centuries, traditionalist scholars have taught that a closed canon of interpretations inherited from exegetical authorities living in the first two centuries of Islam are linguistically more accurate and methodologically superior, so that anything else must be erroneous, even whimsical, and hence undesirable. Feminists and other reformists must therefore tackle the methodological assumptions of the patriarchal interpretations they challenge in order for their discourses to make headway in dominant traditionalist circles.

This chapter examines the problems of the traditionalist method of Qur'an interpretation, known as ***tafsīr bi'l-ma'thūr*** (exegesis by transmission), and its closed canon of interpretive choices, using the Qur'anic verse that regulates polygamy as a case study (Q. 4:3). It argues that contrary to both classical and modern claims, such interpretations are neither literal nor methodologically transparent, but rely on hermeneutical processes of "canonization" in order to gain widespread recognition. The paper has two parts. The first part provides an overview of the process of canonization of the corpus of traditionalist interpretations, focusing on the work of two important scholars: Ibn Jarīr al-Ṭabarī (d. 310/923), who collected them, and Taqī al-Dīn Aḥmad ibn Taymiyya (d. 728/1328), who provided the most current rationale for their "canonical" status in his hermeneutical theory. The second part focuses on the case study. It distills some of al-Ṭabarī's and Ibn Taymiyya's methodological principles and uses them to critique al-Ṭabarī's collection of interpretations and to develop a new interpretation and translation that is more reflective of these methodological guidelines. It illustrates how traditionalist exegesis normalizes polygamy, whereas by contrast a close textual reading promotes monogamy and places restrictions on polygamy that can help provide ethical guidance in the contemporary context. My location within this study is that of a scholar and activist within the Islamic feminist movement.

1. CANONIZATION OF THE EXEGETICAL ĀTHĀR

In his valuable work on the history and contribution of the Shāfiʿī ethical-legal school, Ahmed El-Shamsy recognizes two applications of the term "canonization" in the Islamic tradition. One is in relation to the fixing of a definitive body of texts: the Qur'an and *ḥadīth*. The second is in relation to how these sacred texts came to be conceptualized and employed as sources of religious norms in the Muslim community. It is this second kind of transformation that concerns El-Shamsy; his book demonstrates Muḥammad ibn Idrīs al-Shāfiʿī's (d. 204/820) foundational role in the formation of Sunni ethical-legal theory and his influence on *tafsīr* and other realms of Islamic thought.[6]

Here I employ "canonization" in both these meanings, but in relation to the fixing of exegetical traditions (*āthār*) that enshrined how the first two generations of Muslims interpreted the Qur'an. As Jonathan Brown has demonstrated in connection with *ḥadīth*, it is not enough to collect such reports for them to become a canon. Rather, canons are formed at the "nexus of text, authority and communal identity," since without a process of communal authorization such traditions would not have gained their normative status and widespread acceptance.[7] Accordingly, canonization here refers to the establishment of an authoritative set of interpretations and the process whereby they came to set the standard in Qur'anic exegesis. Phrased differently, it refers to the process whereby the meaning of the sacred text came to be restricted to a select number of interpretative options, reduced to its reception by certain individuals living in the first and early second centuries of Islam, as transmitted by later generations. Of course, it would be simplistic to suggest that the Muslim community stopped interpreting the Qur'an after the first two generations of Muslims. Rather, these *āthār* formed a core of exegetical material that was continuously cited, reshuffled, deselected, expanded, and otherwise refined, contributing to what Walid Saleh has termed the "genealogical" character of the *tafsīr* tradition.[8] Today there are different trends in modern Qur'an exegesis, including scientific, feminist, political, literary, and holistic interpretations, with traditionalist exegesis being dominant.[9] Their positions are bolstered in part by Ibn Taymiyya's interpretive methodology, which places the exegetical *āthār* front and centre, and in which, unsurprisingly, al-Shāfiʿī is cited,[10] whose influence incidentally extends to both the collection and the normalization of the corpus. It is the dominance of these traditions in the realm of exegesis that feminists and other reformists are trying to change.[11]

Ibn Taymiyya's Hermeneutics

Ibn Taymiyya's *Muqaddima fī uṣūl al-tafsīr* (*Introduction to the Principles of Exegesis*) stands out not only for its articulation of a Sunni hermeneutical theory but also for its reach, for it was taken up and promoted by no less than Badr al-Dīn al-Zarkashī (d. 794/1391) and Jalāl al-Dīn al-Suyūṭī (d. 911/1505) in their seminal works on the exegetical sciences,[12] as well as by the influential modern thinkers Muḥammad ʿAbduh (d. 1905) and Muḥammad Ḥusayn al-Dhahabī (d. 1977), among others. While few pre-modern scholars applied this theory to their exegetical compositions, its spread among contemporary traditionalists and reformists alike and the dearth of competing works of similar stature suggest that it is worthy of being termed "classical" hermeneutics. A brief summary of its main highlights is in order. To put it concisely, Ibn Taymiyya classifies exegesis into two kinds: opinion-based (*raʾy*) and knowledge-based (*ʿilm*), where knowledge derives either from clear proofs of reason or from revelation, for which he identifies four epistemological categories. The first and highest-ranked in Ibn Taymiyya's view is the Qurʾan; thus, interpreting the Qurʾan intertextually by means of other verses and passages is the best method for interpreting the Qurʾan. However, Ibn Taymiyya does not seem to be convinced of the practicalities of this method; instead he advises the budding exegete to use traditional interpretations if this category should prove too tiresome (*fa-ʾin aʿyāka dhālik*).[13] The remaining three methods are tradition-based, bolstered by chains of transmission going all the way back to the Prophet Muḥammad himself for the second epistemological category, or to his companions (*ṣaḥāba*) and their immediate successors (*tābiʿūn*) for the third and fourth epistemological categories. The scarcity of exegetical traditions that contain the Prophet Muḥammad's explanations for distinct verses and the prevalence of traditions of the third and fourth categories – technically known as *āthār* (plural of *athar*, meaning trace, trail, record) – led to this particular tradition-based method being termed *tafsīr bi'l-ma'thūr* (exegesis by transmission). The ones who followed and preserved this particular method were termed *ahl al-athar* (the record folk). Anything else belongs to the generally blameworthy "opinion"-based category, known as *tafsīr bi'l-ra'y* (exegesis by opinion, personal judgment, reason).

To be sure, Ibn Taymiyya did not come up with a new method of interpreting the Qur'an since these exegetical traditions were already in use and widely circulated. Rather, what he did was produce a new way of framing an already widespread method of interpreting the Qur'an, one that has been a mainstay of the Islamic exegetical tradition since the early centuries. In effectively shutting the door to new interpretations with his characterization of "opinion-based" exegesis, he inadvertently opened the arena for such readings by introducing the notion of "interpreting the Qur'an by means of the Qur'an" into his hermeneutical framework and, more importantly, by ranking this method as superior. It is this feature that has made his theory so versatile and popular among various constituencies today, from modernist to traditionalist. This ability to combine the seemingly irreconcilable – innovation and tradition – within a single framework is what has allowed his hermeneutical framework to survive and thrive even in the twenty-first century.

Al-Ṭabarī's Language-Based Argument

So what is it that Ibn Taymiyya introduced into the conversation about hermeneutics? To answer this question, one must go back in time to Ibn Jarīr al-Ṭabarī, another well-known figure in the Sunni exegetical tradition. He was the first prominent exegete to collect the exegetical traditions, in his encyclopedic *Jāmi' al-bayān* (*The Comprehensive Exposition*), and also to offer a rationale for the *tafsīr bi'l-ma'thūr* method. One can note his significance in the way both Ibn Taymiyya and al-Suyūṭī heap praises on his commentary, calling it "the most sublime and the greatest of exegetical works" (*ajall al-tafāsīr wa-a'ẓamuhā*).[14] Of all of al-Shāfi'ī's second-generation students, al-Ṭabarī is the only one to leave us his commentary in its entirety, although Ibn Abī Ḥātim al-Rāzī's (d. 327/938) *tafsīr* is extant in part.[15] More importantly, al-Ṭabarī's influence extends to modernity, as can be noted, for example, in the work of the reformer Muḥammad 'Abduh, who continuously cites him.[16] To be sure, other major exegetes, such as al-Tha'labī (d. 427/1035), also collected the early exegetical material and produced far more sophisticated commentaries; however, al-Tha'labī's *tafsīr* is no longer in vogue, no doubt partly due to Ibn Taymiyya's critique of his indiscriminate use of *ḥadīth*.[17] One would have expected the influence of al-Ṭabarī's exegetical *āthār* to wane in the realm of exegesis that emphasizes linguistic analysis;[18] however, a careful perusal of Jār Allāh al-Zamakhsharī's (d. 538/1144) *Kashshāf* and Abū Ḥayyān al-Andalusī's (d. 754/1353) *al-Baḥr al-muḥīṭ* demonstrates that, despite their preoccupation with language, they selectively regurgitated al-Ṭabarī's interpretive options and did not stray outside these general boundaries, at least in relation to verse Q. 4:3 below.[19] As one can see, al-Ṭabarī's influence – at least, the discourse and exegetical direction his work represents – has been pervasive and long-lasting.

Like al-Shāfiʿī, al-Ṭabarī was ultimately interested in law, his Qurʾan commentary serving to convince his intellectual milieu of the alignment of his *madhhab* (law school) – the short-lived Jarīriyya – with scripture among other things, as Ulrika Mårtensson has convincingly argued.[20] Moreover, this *tafsīr* expounds al-Ṭabarī's traditionalist theological doctrines, as Mustafa Shah has demonstrated, even if it is best-known for its collection of exegetical *āthār*.[21] Like al-Shāfiʿī, he bolsters the interpretive authority of the first two generations of exegetes, resting his claim on their being the Qurʾan's primary audience and on their superior knowledge of the Arabic language.[22] Seemingly highly conscious of his own Persian-speaking origins and therefore non-native Arabic-speaking roots (which one would not know from the excellence of his writing), he was also sensitive to the cultural distortions that can occur in language when it is adopted by non-Arabs. It seems that this scholar emphasized the importance of the early linguistic context; he viewed meaning as something that is acquired in specific communicative contexts. Moreover, he contended that uncovering the meaning of the Qurʾan required re-creating these early speech contexts.[23] For al-Ṭabarī, the Qurʾan was clear and eloquent (*mubīn*); thus, the first two generations of Muslims must have understood it in the way it should have been understood.[24] Due to their unassailable knowledge of the Arabic idiom and modes of expression when it came to language, the Qurʾan was clear only to them; for everyone else it was ambiguous and confusing.[25] Of course, these superior qualifications were held only by a select number of individuals of the first two generations, who together with their transmitters became *ahl al-taʾwīl* (the interpretation folk).26 For them, the Qurʾan's clarity was the link between authorial intent and the text's interpretation; it was what made the text more or less equivalent to its interpretation and what removed the barrier between the divine word and its reception. Needless to say, this argument stands in opposition to those who would use the Qurʾan's clarity to make its meanings accessible to a wider range of people and to downplay the importance of *ḥadīth* and *āthār* in explaining the Qurʾan. This phenomenon is not restricted to present-day critics; it also existed in the past, as one can surmise from al-Shāfiʿī's interlocutor in the first part of *Jimāʿ al-ʿilm*, in which he responds to such ideas.[27] Thus the basic assumptions of *tafsīr biʾl-maʾthūr* did not go unchallenged in their heyday, even if this method holds sway today.

From a contemporary perspective, some of al-Shāfiʿī's and al-Ṭabarī's presuppositions are difficult to digest. Literary theorists have come to recognize the distinction between author-oriented approaches and reader-oriented approaches, with the latter gaining increasingly widespread acceptance. Whereas author-oriented approaches are based on the assumption that meaning lies with the author and that the reader's job is to uncover the intended meaning of the author, reader-oriented approaches are based on the assumption that the reader plays a role in the creation of meaning. Furthermore, readers bring ideas into the text based on their own predispositions, cultural biases, personal subjectivity, reading history, and other factors from their own lived experience and context. Based on the individuality of each reader, there can be as many interpretations as there are readers.[28] Linguistic accuracy cannot be the only factor at play when interpreting texts; as al-Shāfiʿī and his followers correctly claimed, other cultural and personal factors have an impact. One must therefore wonder at the underlying theological assumptions of the *tafsīr biʾl-maʾthūr* method. Did God really intend the Qurʾan to speak only to the first two generations of Muslims? Are Muslims today not also the intended recipients of the text, and is the text not clear for them too? Are they too not entitled to read the Qurʾan and interpret it in their own contexts and in accordance with the needs of their time? No reading is devoid of contextual and subjective factors, so should one then assume that the cultural biases and personal whims of the first two generations of Muslims (and their transmitters) form part of the intended communique by God? For example, in the exegesis of Q. 4:3, all of the tradents are men with one notable exception, ʿĀʾisha bint Abī Bakr (d. 58/678), but even her thoughts are filtered through later male transmitters in the chains of transmission of the exegetical *āthār*. This overwhelming gender imbalance may well be reflected in the interpretive process. If all of these men were predisposed toward polygamy, is it not possible that their personal whims may have influenced the way they read the verse, wittingly or not? Are male scholars exempt from "whim" when it comes to legislating polygamy, or is "whim" an accusation to be levelled only against women and other reformists? These questions highlight the elevated position of *ahl al-taʾwīl* vis-à-vis the contemporary reader and the way their subjective understandings have shaped the tradition. In the *tafsīr bi'l-maʾthūr* method of interpretation, these interlocutors become intermediaries to the revelation, despite the basic understanding of monotheism in the Qur'an, which entails that there be no intermediaries between a person and God, a feature that sets Islam apart from other forms of monotheism, as Amina Wadud and others have expounded.[29] Canonization of these exegetical authorities' interpretations thereby makes them go-betweens, blocking later readers' direct access to the divine word.

Al-Ṭabarī's preoccupation with language shows itself in other ways. For the purposes of hermeneutics, he is often associated with the rule of thumb *al-iʿtibār bi-ʿumūm al-lafẓ lā bi-khuṣūṣ al-sabab* (abiding by the generality of the Qur'anic wording, not the specificity of the occasion), since he applies it in his exegesis of verse Q. 4:24. This approach entails favouring the Qur'anic text over and above a type of exegetical *āthār* known as occasions of revelation, reasons of revelation, or contexts of revelation (*āsbāb al-nuzūl*), which describe circumstances surrounding the revelation of certain verses and which later developed into a separate genre. Thus al-Ṭabarī recognized the possibility of the exegetical traditions conflicting with the literal meaning of the Qur'anic text and privileged the literal meaning over tradition. Unlike Ibn Taymiyya, al-Ṭabarī had good reason to be familiar with the discrepancies between *lafẓ* (articulation, literal text) and interpretation. After all, he was heavily engaged in exegesis, producing a monumental verse-by-verse commentary on the entire Qur'an, something that Ibn Taymiyya, despite his many accomplishments, never managed to carry out.

In contemporary exegetical theory, the *tafsīr bi'l-maʾthūr* method is often described as "literal" and those who adhere to this method as "literalists" or "textualists," perhaps due to claims that the exegetical *āthār* are linguistically accurate. For example, in his valuable work on Qur'an interpretation, Abdullah Saeed classifies contemporary exegesis into textualist, semi-textualist, and contextualist, depending on the extent of their dependence on linguistic criteria vis-à-vis their attention to the Qur'an's early socio-historical and modern-day contexts; he argues for the contextualist approach.[30] In this helpful contribution, he describes as "textualists" a rigid subset of followers of the *tafsīr bi'l-ma'thūr* method who do not make allowances for changing contexts and who approach interpretation from a narrow, linguistic perspective.[31] It is my contention here that "literalism" and a rigid adherence to exegetical *āthār* do not go hand in hand, since these traditions often diverge in significant ways from the linguistic sense of the text, as I demonstrate with regard to the exegetical traditions that are marshalled for verse Q. 4:3. Rather, these traditions reflect the early reception of the text during which the readers' subjectivity and cultural circumstances (and those of their transmitters) came into play. Moreover, although "textualist" is an attractive term and has value, it too suggests literalism. Textualism is best-known from the realm of statutory law, where it is used to distinguish between those who follow the letter of the law and those who would try to ascertain its intentions and interrogate its spirit. Although there are different expressions of textualism that are complicated by political and ideological factors, textualism is an "interpretive program that privileges plain, textual meaning."[32] Because of the existence of these intermediate texts and their complicated relationships to the source Qur'anic text, it is difficult to describe the *tafsīr bi'l-ma'thūr* method as either "literalist" or "texualist." Rather, "traditionalist" is the best description for this method, or as Abdullah Saeed has phrased it, "tradition-based" exegesis.[33]

The Legal Dimension

What Ibn Taymiyya contributed to the already well-established *tafsīr bi'l-ma'thūr* method was a shift in the argument away from language toward a more legalistic perspective in keeping with his distinctive understanding of Islamic legal theory. For Ibn Taymiyya, the crux of the matter was not language. After all, by his time, Arabic was widely spoken in many parts of the Muslim world, certainly in what is contemporary Egypt, Iraq, the Levant, and of course Saudi Arabia – that is to say, anywhere Ibn Taymiyya may have had occasion to live and work. Thus, for Ibn Taymiyya, al-Ṭabarī's argument may not have held as much sway – not unlike the situation in many Arabic-speaking countries today. Moreover, the norms of legal theory had become quite well-established within the Muslim psyche, so an exchange between exegesis and legal theory was not difficult to imagine. As Walid Saleh has convincingly demonstrated, Ibn Taymiyya's four-tiered classification recalls the four principles of Islamic legal theory, with the first two comprising practically the same two bodies of text as the hermeneutical taxonomy: the Qur'an and the Sunna.[34] However, Ibn Taymiyya also made allowances for the last two religious-legal principles, reasoning (by analogy) (*ʿaql* or *qiyās*)[35] and consensus (*ijmāʿ*). *Qiyās* recalls Ibn Taymiyya's non-revealed category of knowledge: reason, which he describes as "a statement that can be defended by an accepted [logical] proof."[36] *Ijmāʿ* he incorporates into the third and four categories of his hermeneutical framework, since for Ibn Taymiyya, this principle seems to have been restricted to these early generations. Unlike many of his contemporaries and his predecessors – many of whom varied greatly in their definition and understanding of this religious-legal principle – Ibn Taymiyya considered only the first generations to comprise the consensus of the Muslim community for religious-legal purposes.[37] In fact, he stands out for his critique of Ibn Ḥazm's (d. 456/1064) *Marātib al-ijmāʿ* (*Categories of Consensus*), in which he lists the various cases that are governed by *ijmāʿ* and in which he opts for the consensus of scholars (*al-ʿulamāʾ*). Ibn Taymiyya's critique points to the impossibility of knowing the positions of all the later scholarly authorities on any given issue in theory and in practice, demonstrating divergent scholarly positions in several of Ibn Ḥazm's cases.[38] Ibn Taymiyya's notion of consensus does not allow for later occurrences of consensus, and the same can be said of his understanding of exegesis; in both cases, paradigmatic authority is reserved for the early generations. Therefore, Ibn Taymiyya's hermeneutical framework resonates strongly with his vision and interpretation of legal theory, a feature that highlights the interconnections and interplay between exegesis and the Islamic juridical disciplines.

Ibn Taymiyya's rationale for his exegetical restrictions also recalls developments in Islamic law. By Ibn Taymiyya's time, the juridical authority of the Qur'an was virtually indistinguishable from that of the Sunna, since both were generally deemed divine revelation (*waḥy*); hence, it was considered perfectly acceptable to abrogate the Qur'an on the basis of the Sunna.[39] In a like manner, Ibn Taymiyya assumes that the interpretations of the first two generations of Muslims were not based on their own individual efforts and use of personal judgment, but rather had acquired these interpretations from the Prophet Muḥammad himself. Hence, they too had the authority of revealed knowledge. This assumption is probably the biggest weakness in his hermeneutical framework, since it is unsupported by al-Ṭabarī and earlier generations of traditionists, who did not connect the bulk of these traditions to the Prophet in their chains of transmission (*isnād*). Had these traditions been connected (*marfūʿ*), these exegetes would not have had to resort to the language argument. These traditions would not have been termed *āthār* – and hence *tafsīr bi'l-maʾthūr* – but rather *ḥadīth*, for which there is no substantiation in al-Ṭabarī's magnum opus. For example, in the case study below, none of the interpretations of verse Q. 4:3 are traced back to the Prophet Muḥammad, but stop at his companions.

Canonization and Ibn Taymiyya

Ibn Taymiyya had no formal religious authority by which he could declare the exegetical *āthār* "canonical." In fact, the Islamic tradition does not recognize priests, rabbis, or other ordained clergy-like figures of authority, so in theory no one has that power (Q. 3:64; 9:31). How then did Ibn Taymiyya reconceptualize these traditions in ways that affirmed their status as a normative canon in *tafsīr*? It is my contention that he did this in two steps: first, through the "ḥadīthification" of the *āthār*, and second, through the "legalization" of the exegetical process. By "ḥadīthification" of the *āthār* I mean lending them quasi-*ḥadīth* status. Ibn Taymiyya blurred the boundaries between them and *ḥadīth* by professing that the Prophet *explained* the Qurʾanic verses to his companions and that these *āthār* constitute nothing more than a record of these explanations, a claim that would have been unthinkable in early Shāfiʿī circles. One should note that although Ibn Taymiyya almost elevated the *āthār* into *ḥadīth* in terms of weight and function, he stopped short of calling them *ḥadīth*.

By "legalization" of exegesis, I mean the way Ibn Taymiyya embedded legal undertones in his four-tiered exegetical taxonomy, in which the last two categories recall his rather unusual notion of consensus. Aziz al-Azmeh has noted the important role of consensus in Islamic processes of canonization, suggesting that processes of canonization are "accompanied and sustained by scholarly and institutional traditions and sanctions, called consensus [*ijmāʿ*]."[40] In the area of *ḥadīth*, Jonathan Brown has also demonstrated the importance of the discourses of legal theory and the notion of *ijmāʿ* in the canonization of *ḥadīth*.[41] As one can see, Ibn Taymiyya affirmed the pre-eminence of the traditionalist canon by recasting the *āthār* as *ḥadīth*-like and by re-envisioning their authority in ways that recall his conceptualization of the principle of *ijmāʿ*. These two processes form the basis for the canonization of the corpus of exegetical *āthār* that had been collected and transmitted by earlier generations.

2. POLYGAMY AS A CASE STUDY

How does "canonization" play out in the exegesis of Q. 4:3, the polygamy verse? As a case study, Q. 4:3 demonstrates some of the linguistic gaps between the Qurʾanic text and its interpretation in the canon of exegetical *āthār*. It thereby illustrates the problems with the *tafsīr bi'l-maʾthūr* method, particularly the assumption that the exegetical *āthār* are linguistically consistent with the Qurʾanic text and do not diverge from the literal meaning. Rather, these interpretations harmonize between certain presuppositions and the Qurʾanic text, glossing over the inconsistencies between the two and reading meanings into the Qurʾan that are just not there. These presuppositions, which may be related to custom and cultural practice, find expression in scholarly consensus – the notion of *ijmāʿ* that is reflected in Ibn Taymiyya's hermeneutics and that is central to processes of canonization. Ibn Ḥazm, in his *Marātib al-ijmāʿ*, summarizes the scholarly consensus as follows: "They have agreed that the marriage of a free, mature, chaste, unflawed, legally competent, Muslim man to four or less free, unflawed, not fornicating Muslim women is permissible (*ḥalāl*)."[42] Although he reiterates the more general marriage conditions (which also exist for monogamous marriages), he does not place restraints on polygamy, apart from limiting it to four women.

As I show below, the Qurʾanic text presents monogamy as the ontological norm and polygamy as the exception, to be engaged in only under certain clear-cut conditions that include the women's consent and a fear for the well-being of widows and orphans that outweighs the inequality inherent in polygamous unions. None of these conditions are reproduced in Ibn Ḥazm's rendition of the scholarly consensus or in al-Ṭabarī's exegetical glosses. Moreover, Ibn Taymiyya does not include polygamy in his critique of Ibn Ḥazm's book, which seems only to affirm the general consensus and scholars' avoidance of placing ethical-legal restraints on polygamy. Despite Ibn Taymiyya's and al-Ṭabarī's insistence on the *āthār*'s linguistic acumen and their elaborate methodological vision, their basic assumptions are not in evidence in the "canonical" *āthār* of Q. 4:3. In fact, their works allow for a sound, methodologically based contestation of the "canonical" interpretations and, by extension, the "canon law" that is derived from these verses. Moreover, the discrepancies between text and *āthār* contest claims that traditionalist interpretations are "literal" readings or that early authorities used linguistic criteria alone to determine meaning and to interpret the ethico-legal content.[43]

I begin by briefly reiterating pertinent methodological considerations that derive from the works of al-Tabarī and Ibn Taymiyya and that form the basis of my contestation of the "canonical" interpretations. I then introduce Q. 4:3 and the verses in its immediate vicinity by means of a new translation and a brief explanation of relevant linguistic features and their historical context. I then follow with al-Ṭabarī's exegetical *āthār*, demonstrating how they diverge from these methodological principles. I conclude with some observations on the ethical imperatives of Q. 4:3 and their relevance in the contemporary context.

Methodological Considerations

At first glance, a reader will note profound differences between my translation of Q. 4:34 (below) and al-Ṭabarī's interpretation, which informs many contemporary translations and interpretations. No doubt, every translation is inherently an interpretation, so placing these very different interpretations in close proximity brings the edges into sharp relief. There are three methodological underpinnings that make my translation very different from others and that I incidentally derive from the works of al-Ṭabarī and that of Ibn Taymiyya. They are briefly listed as follows:

1. I follow the above-mentioned rule of thumb of "abiding by the generality of the Qur'anic wording, not the specificity of the occasion." Although al-Ṭabarī supports it, it is not evident in some of the exegetical *āthār* below.
2. I follow semantic equivalence, ensuring that the translation/interpretation is a close linguistic fit with the wording of the Qur'anic text. In contrast, some of the *āthār* rely on changing the linguistic and grammatical gist of Qur'anic words and replacing them with others. This feature recalls the Qur'anic notion of *taḥrīf al-kalim ʿan mawāḍiʿih* (distorting the meanings of words

and taking them out of their context), which is a very harsh Qur'anic critique levelled against the People of the Book (Jews and Christians) for altering the meaning of their scripture (Q. 4:46; 5:13, 41). This critique underscores the importance of linguistic accuracy in any interpretation of the Qur'an, including the exegetical *āthār*. It may also explain al-Ṭabarī's and Ibn Taymiyya's emphasis on the linguistic competence of *ahl al-ta'wīl* and their abiding by the semantics of the Qur'anic text despite evidence to the contrary.

3. I follow Ibn Taymiyya's method of "interpreting the Qur'an by means of the Qur'an" in the sense of interpreting unclear words intertextually and taking into account the verse's immediate context of preceding and subsequent verses. In contrast, the exegetical *āthār* are atomistic, generally examining verses or parts thereof in isolation from their literary context. In modernity, the "interpreting the Qur'an by means of the Qur'an" method has become widespread and in its most developed permutation takes the form of holistic approaches, which treat suras as whole units and sometimes even the Qur'an as a whole.[44] Some modernists rely on another Qur'anic critique to support this method, a critique that is levelled more generally against people who fragment scripture and cut it up into bite-sized pieces, presumably in order to follow some of it and discard other portions (Q. 15:90–3). I also take into consideration the historical context of the verses, not by trying to impose the occasions of revelation onto the text in order to compel certain meanings, but by using these occasions to point to surrounding historical circumstances in the early Islamic environment. Taking into account both the verse's textual context and its historical context recalls Abdullah Saeed's description of the "Contextualist" approach.[45]

Introducing Verse Q. 4:3

In accordance with the above principles, I translate Q. 4:1-4 as follows:

1. O humankind, be mindful of your Lord, who created you from a single self, and from it created its mate, and from the pair of them spread forth many men and women; be mindful of God,

in whose name you make requests of one another, as well as your kinship responsibilities, for God is always watching you.
2. Give widows and orphans their property; do not replace good things with bad, and do not devour their property into your own, for that is a grave sin.
3. If you fear that you will not do social justice to widows and orphans, then marry whoever is favourably disposed toward you from among the women: two, three or four at the same time;[46] however, if you fear that you will not uphold equality, marry one woman or what your right hands possess. This will bring you closer to not committing grave injustice.
4. Give women their marriage gift free of constraints, though if they are favourably disposed to give you some of it, then you may enjoy it with a clear conscience.

Linguistic Features

Q. 4:3 displays certain linguistic features that deserve special attention. It consists of two conditional sentences, joined by the conjunction *fa-*, translated as "however" above. Both sentences speak of a fear of failing to do justice, but they use two different words for it: *tuqsiṭū* from the word *qisṭ*, and *ta'dilū* from the word *'adl*. I have translated the first as "social justice," since it has societal connotations and denotes justice in the sense of equity, not as a charity but as a right.[47] It is therefore well-suited to vulnerable members of society – widows and orphans – since they may require more resources than others in order to reach their full potential. I have translated the second as "equality" (or "fairness" below), since it denotes justice in the sense of parity and is therefore well suited to equality between co-wives or even between husband and wife. These words are well-circulated in the contemporary English-speaking context and have similar ethical connotations.

In the above, I have translated the word *yatāmā* as "widows and orphans," instead of the more common "orphans."[48] In Arabic, the word applies only to those who have lost their father, not the ones who have lost both father and mother (singular: *laṭīm*, plural: *luṭamā'*). It also includes the widow of the deceased, for example, as can be noted in Q. 4:127 (below), which explains *yatāmā* as including women and young children. The application of *yatāmā* to widows can also be noted in ancient Arabic poetry: "The graves have marital relations with the single ones: the widowed *yatāmā* women."[49] Exegetes generally acknowledge that this word applies linguistically to adults as well, but they restrict its meaning to young children based on Islamic law. Thus they generally replace the linguistic meaning this word had at the time of the Prophet with the religious-legal meaning the word acquired in subsequent centuries. It is noteworthy that in verse Q. 4:3, exegetes sometimes go a step further and limit the meaning of the word to young girls, even though the term *yatāma* appears as a masculine plural and not as a feminine plural in the passage. In the Arabic language, the masculine plural is used to refer to groups that have at least one male among them, that is, they can be all male or a mix of males and females with a minimum of one male. In contrast, the feminine plural is used in connection with groups that are exclusively female. The meaning of "young fatherless girls" therefore is not a good grammatical fit for *yatāma* as it appears in its immediate context and in the Qur'an in general.

I have translated *mā ṭāba lakum min al-nisāʾ* as "women who are favourably disposed toward you." While there is generally no disagreement that the subject of the verb *ṭāba* refers to the women,[50] it is more commonly interpreted as meaning "women to whom you are favourably disposed" or "women who seem good to you," highlighting the importance of the men's consent and disregarding women. The semantic range of the word includes both that the women are pleasing to the men and that they are pleased with the men. However, from an intertextual methodological perspective, the subsequent verse (Q. 4:4) contains the very same verb, which in this case highlights the women as the ones who are favourably disposed; thus, "women who are favourably disposed toward you" is a better fit for Q. 4:3. Just in case someone has missed this nuance in Q. 4:3, Q. 4:4 picks up the same wording, emphasizes it through repetition, and highlights the importance of women's agreement by using the feminine plural, which is restricted to the female gender in the Arabic language. As one can see, when read as a continuous, interconnected passage, there can be no doubt of the need for women's consent to polygamous unions and their good pleasure in Q. 4:3.

It has been suggested that the word *taʿūlū*, which I have translated as "committing grave injustice," can also mean "have numerous children" from *taʿīlū*. However, commentators before me have pointed out that even though the two words may sound very similar, they are not synonymous or interchangeable, since they have two different root letters: *ta'ūlū* has a *wāw* and *ta'īlū* has a *yā'*.[51] Therefore, "committing grave injustice" is linguistically more accurate than "have numerous children."

In light of the above, the immediate literary context of the polygamy verse (i.e., the surrounding verses), and the special features of its phrasing in the Arabic language, suggest certain norms and special conditions that place limitations on polygamy. Q. 4:1 confirms monogamy as the ontological norm established at the time of the creation of humanity, thereby framing polygamy as an exception. Q. 4:2 introduces the general context as that of vulnerable populations, specifically widows and orphans. Q. 4:3, which introduces polygamy, sets out three conditions that have ethical undertones. The first is "If you fear that you will not do social justice to widows and orphans," introduced by the conditional "if"/*in*. The second is contained in "favourably disposed toward you from among the women," which implies consent of the women, the choice of the verb *ṭāba* signalling that the women (and men) need to feel good about this arrangement. The third condition is implied in the second conditional, also introduced by "if"/*in*, "if you fear that you will not uphold equality, marry one woman or what your right hands possess." The dual conditional implies two sets of fears with which a conscientious individual has to contend: fear of injustice toward widows and orphans, and fear of the inequality inherent in polygamous unions. If the first fear prevails, then individuals may engage in polygamous unions, but if the second fear prevails, then they may marry only one wife. Therefore, the third condition is that the fear of social injustice toward widows and orphans exceed the fear of inequality between co-wives or between husband and wife/wives. The wording of the Qur'anic text and the way it sets apart the third condition highlights equality as an ethical imperative that needs to be taken into consideration in the process of ethical reasoning and decision-making in the context of marriage. As one can see, there are three conditions for polygamy in the text of Q. 4:3 that are not reproduced in Ibn Ḥazm's presentation of the scholarly consensus, but are ignored.

Historical Context

The polygamy verse's general historical context helps illustrate the special circumstances that surround the practice. Sūrat al-Nisā', in which the verse is located, is generally acknowledged to be a Medinan sura, revealed shortly after the Battle of Uḥud (3/625), which took place between the nascent Muslim polity in Medina and the polytheists of Mecca and which resulted in several losses, such as that of Abū Salama, who died leaving a widow and children behind. In pre-Islamic times, tribal solidarity entailed that the deceased's clan or tribe take care of his family; however, since the Meccan immigrants had left their tribal support network behind when moving to Medina, their welfare was precarious. In this context, Surat al-Nisā' is in conversation with tribal solidarity, its opening verse extending the kinship ties of tribe and clan to all of humanity by virtue of their descent from a single ancestor. As a result, the responsibility, care, and support that were known to the ancient Arabs through their strong sense of tribal solidarity expand to encompass all of humanity, including the immigrant families from Mecca.

There is one genre of texts that is used in the Islamic exegetical tradition to historicize verses and to provide an immediate context for them: the previously mentioned occasions of revelation (*asbāb al-nuzūl*). With regard to the polygamy verse, there are two such traditions, both of which go back to 'Ā'isha, the Prophet Muḥammad's wife, via her nephew 'Urwa ibn al-Zubayr (d. 94/712–13).[52] One of them is reported by Ibn Shihāb al-Zuhrī (d. 124/741–42), 'Urwa's eminent student, and the other by his son, Hishām ibn 'Urwa (d. 146/763). The two narrations are reported from the same source, but they differ in content, which is not unusual in this genre of literature and more generally in traditions that have an oral history. Whereas Hishām's narration revolves around an orphaned girl whose guardian kept her unmarried in order to retain control of her inheritance, Ibn Shihāb's narration is about a girl whose guardian wished to marry her for her wealth and beauty without paying her a bridal gift in accordance with her station. Both stories involve a fatherless girl with an unjust guardian; however, the events differ. There is also some confusion with regard to the verse in question, since the stories are a better linguistic fit for verse Q. 4:127, which, unlike verse Q. 4:3, distinctly mentions *women* who have lost either fathers or husbands or both and who have been denied their due in the context of marriage, urging social justice: "They seek a ruling from you about women, say: 'God gives you a ruling about them and what is recited to you in the book regarding women who have lost their husbands and/or fathers [*yatāma al-nisā'*] and whom you have not given their due and yet wish to marry, and also helpless young children [*al-mustaḍ'afīn min al-wildān*], that you stand up for social justice for widows and orphans. God is well-aware of whatever good you may do.'"

When read in conjunction with verse Q. 4:3 (and also Q. 4:127), the two *asbāb al-nuzūl* reports provide a narrative context for the verses and reflect a general concern for the welfare of fatherless girls when it comes to marriage. So in the context of ancient Arabia, these reports can be read very narrowly to reflect the plight of young minor girls to the exclusion of widows and orphan boys. However, they can also be read more broadly to reflect general social conditions in ancient Arabia, where widows and orphans were in need of support. The vulnerabilities of widows and orphans in many parts of the ancient world are well-known; those who were unable to find protection were at risk of enslavement, prostitution, or other misfortune.[53] As one can see, interpreting occasions of revelation and their relationship to a verse requires weighing options and exercising interpretive choice.

Al-Tabari's Exegetical Choices

Al-Ṭabarī presents five different interpretations for Q. 4:3, but none reproduce the three above-mentioned conditions for polygamy; rather, they do away with them. They are as follows:

> 1. O guardians of orphans, if you fear that you are unable to do social justice to them with regard to their bridal gift and deal with it fairly [*fa-ta'dilū*] by giving them a bridal gift that is equal to their station, then do not marry them, but marry other women "strangers," i.e. women who are not closely related to you, whom God has made legally permissible [*aḥallahunna*] and good for you [*tayyibahunna*], from one up to four. However, if you fear to commit injustice, i.e. if you marry more than one woman "stranger," by not upholding equality, then marry one woman, or what your right hands possess.
> 2. This is the injunction against marrying more than four out of fear that their guardians will deplete the funds of orphans [*yatāmā*]. This is because, in the tribe of Quraysh, men used to marry ten women, or more, or less, and when they became penniless, they would turn to the funds of the orphan under their guardianship, spending it or using it to marry again. So they were prohibited from doing that, and it was said to them: "If you fear spending the funds of your orphans [*aytāmakum*] – and in this

way not uphold fairness [*ta'dilū*] concerning these [funds] – because of your need for them due to your responsibility to provide for your women, then do not exceed four women. Again, if you fear that four women will not allow you to deal fairly with regard to the orphan's funds, then limit yourselves to one, or what your right hands possess."

3. People used to fear dealing unfairly with regard to the funds of orphans [*yatāmā*], but not fear dealing unfairly with women. So they were told: "Just as you fear not to deal fairly with orphans, then likewise, fear dealing unfairly with women and do not marry except from one up to four, and do not exceed this number. Again, if you fear that you will not deal fairly with more than one, then do not marry except where you have no fear of committing injustice toward women: one or what your right hands possess."

4. Just as you fear with regard to orphans, likewise also fear with regard to women that you commit adultery with them, so marry whomever you are favourably disposed toward from among women.

5. If you fear that you are unable to do justice to the female orphans who are under your guardianship, then do not marry them, but marry of them what is legally permissible for you.

All of al-Ṭabarī's exegetical selections normalize polygamy and fail to uphold the three conditions mentioned above: fear for social justice vis-à-vis vulnerable women and children, the women's agreement, and that the fear of committing injustice to these vulnerable populations exceed the fear of committing injustice due to the inequality between spouses. Moreover, they deal with favourable disposition from a distinct male perspective, implying that in order for a man to enter into a polygamous union, the arrangement need be pleasing only to him. There is nothing mentioned of the consent and favourable disposition of women. To read al-Ṭabarī, one would think that a wife has no right to expect a monogamous marriage or that her husband may need her consent if he wants to take a second wife. This exegetical lapse is largely due to three features: (1) privileging the occasion over and above the wording of the Qur'anic text; (2) using replacement words or expressions that are not linguistically accurate; and (3) atomism. These three features are methodologically opposed to the three principles that I mention above and that are at work in my interpretation.

In all five of al-Ṭabarī's interpretive options, atomism is evident in his failure to relate these verses to Q. 4:1, which draws upon the story of Adam and Eve and describes the creation of humanity in pairs, suggesting that monogamy is the ontological norm. Reading the above *āthār* one would imagine that polygamy is the norm and monogamy the exception and then only for men who fear they will be unfair to their wives. Discarding Qur'anic narrative material when discussing the legal implications of verses is not unusual. The Islamic legal tradition has often approached the Qur'an in an atomistic fashion, differentiating between verses that have legal significance [*āyāt al-aḥkām*] and those that do not, and generally discarding the latter in their legal musings. Out of the Qur'an's 6,235 verses, only about 350 are considered to have legal significance.[54] Narratives generally fall into the non-legal category, which incidentally forms approximately 95 percent of the Qur'an. Given this history, it is not unusual for exegetes to ignore the story of Adam and Eve and other narrative material in their ethical-legal deliberations, even when it occurs in the immediate vicinity of the "legal" verses.

In all of al-Ṭabarī's five interpretive options above, atomism and semantic poverty are also evident in the removal of the second condition of polygamy, that is, that all the women be in accord with this arrangement. Semantic poverty is evident in the way this condition has been glossed as women who are "legally permissible to you," such as women "strangers" who are not closely related. This piece of information seems self-evident since the Islamic tradition does not allow incestuous marriages to mothers, daughters, sisters, nieces, and aunts (Q. 4:23). Moreover, "legally permissible to you" does not reproduce the full semantic range of the word *ṭāba*, and restricts it to something that is banal rather than giving meaning to the phrase. Fakhr al-Dīn al-Rāzī (d. 606/1209) in particular has commented on this linguistic poverty, arguing that it "renders the verse without benefit" and that it removes its legal thrust. In his analysis, the command "then marry" entails legal permissibility, which would make "legally permissible to you" redundant as a description for prospective wives. He suggests, therefore, that the meaning of *ṭāba* has to do with good pleasure and seeking consent (*istiṭābat al-nafs*) and the inclination of the heart (*mayl al-qalb*), although he does not specify whether this refers to the men, the women, or both.[55] Al-Razī is one of few commentators whose interpretation makes sense when one takes into account the reoccurrence of this phrasing in Q. 4:4, which similarly mentions women being "favourably disposed" to giving up something precious to them: their marriage gift. Like polygamy, giving up some of this gift runs contrary to their best interests and requires a generosity of spirit (*ṭīb al-nafs*). The text suggests that both the marriage gift and a monogamous marriage are a woman's undisputed right, but one that she can opt out of if she so chooses. The need for consent of not only later wives but also the first one is historically supported in the *ḥadīth* literature, which portrays the Prophet Muḥammad's daughter Fāṭima not allowing her husband ʿĀlī to take a second wife and her father supporting her decision and announcing as much from the pulpit.[56] As one can see, atomism is evident in the separation of verse Q. 4:4 from verse Q. 4:3 in discerning the meaning of "favourably disposed" when interpreting the second condition for polygamy. It allows for the dismissal of the women's consent in polygamous unions so that men may engage in them unhindered by such considerations.

Privileging the occasion of revelation over and above the wording of the Qurʾanic text is evident in numbers 1 and 5 above, which interpret the first condition for polygamy in the context of marriage to young, fatherless girls. This interpretation does not fit the grammatical sense of the word *yatāmā*, which is treated as a masculine plural in the verse's immediate context and in the entirety of the Qurʾan. Perhaps the exegetes were not interested in marrying widows and caring for their offspring, but only in younger women? Moreover, in order to fit the general wording of the Qurʾan to the specificity of the occasion literature, al-Ṭabarī added the number "one" to the number of wives that men may marry. It would not make sense for men who fear injustice to young orphan girls not to have the option of marrying only one other woman but would have to marry two, three or four. It seems that al-Ṭabarī noticed the difficulties of reconciling the text of the occasion of revelation to the Qurʾanic wording, so his insertion of "one" is an attempt to harmonize between them, by making this verse about the bridal gifts of young, fatherless girls and not about polygamy. Including the option of marrying "one" woman to the numbers two, three, and four changes the meaning of the text away from polygamy, lumping polygamy with monogamy as something to be taken for granted and thereby removing the distinctions between the two. Finally, al-Ṭabarī has not paid attention to the finer nuances of meaning between the words *tuqsiṭū* and *taʿdilū*, both of which mean doing justice, and has glossed *tuqsiṭū* with *taʿdilū*.

Al-Ṭabarī's remaining three selections (numbers 2 to 4 above) are distinctive in that they do not uphold the force of the conditional "if"/*in* but rather gloss it as "just as"/*kamā*. The first part of the verse therefore is no longer a condition for polygamy but is given new meanings: a restriction on polygamy from an open-ended number to just four women, an exhortation to dealing with co-wives with equality, and a counter-measure against unbridled adultery. This minute change in wording from "if" to "just as" therefore has substantive implications. Other minute changes that harmonize between this imposed meaning and the wording of the Qur'anic text – such as glossing social justice/*qisṭ* with equality/*ʿadl* and the addition of "one" to the number of concurrent wives in the first half of the verse, thereby extending polygamy to include monogamy – recall al-Ṭabarī's first interpretation. These minute changes shift the meaning of the sentence so that it is no longer about setting conditions for polygamy (except for the limit to four women) but about something else – bridal gifts, equality between co-wives, or adultery.

It is noteworthy that though al-Ṭabarī does not set restraints on polygamy, he seems to encourage monogamy in three of his interpretations, either for fear of treating the women unequally (1 and 3) or for fear that more than one wife will deplete the funds of orphans under a guardian's care (2). Contemporary discourses that discourage or prohibit polygamy usually draw on the fear of treating co-wives unequally. For example, Muḥammad ʿAbduh explicitly states, "Thereby it is known that a plurality of wives is unequivocally forbidden [*muḥarram qaṭʿan*] when there is fear of inequality."[57] The notion that equal treatment of co-wives is a condition for polygamy is well-disseminated in modernity and finds an additional basis in Q. 4:129, "You will never be able to uphold equality between your wives, even should you be careful, so do not neglect one altogether leaving her hanging. If you make amends and are mindful of God, then He is most forgiving, merciful." However, this verse suggests that equality between co-wives is impossible, so this notion is difficult to reconcile with the text of Q. 4:129. Indeed, the directives of "do not neglect one altogether" and "make amends" are at odds with equality between co-wives. Rather, the verse supports the notion of an ever-present fear of unequal treatment of co-wives that can only be mitigated by an even greater fear for the welfare of widows and orphans. As one can see, the interpretation of Q. 4:3 as stipulating equality between co-wives as a precondition for polygamy is not supported by Q. 4:129 and does not fit the text. Equality (*ʿadl*) is a general ethical imperative for dealing with other people, an expectation for humanity that informs practice,[58] one that cannot find realization in polygamous unions, either between husband and wife or even between co-wives.

In light of the above, none of the interpretations that al-Ṭabarī has included in his collection fit the literal meaning of the text and immediate literary context. Rather, they employ a variety of strategies that lead to a dismissal of three important conditions for polygamy – fear of social injustice to widows and orphans, agreement of all parties involved, and that the first fear exceed the ever-present fear of injustice in polygamous unions. These strategies include harmonizing between the text and the *asbāb al-nuzūl* literature, glossing words with others that do not reproduce the force of the conditional and other nuances of meanings, and engaging in atomism. Although the *asbāb al-nuzūl* provide important historical and contextual information, they can be read in different ways, some of which can support the conditions contained in the text and others that veer away from it. Although al-Ṭabarī's exegetical canon incorporates a plurality of interpretations, none of them are favourable to women, clearly restrict polygamy (except for limiting the number to four), or uphold a woman's right to a monogamous marriage.

The Ethical Dimension

In light of the above, the canon of exegetical *āthār* reflects a concern for orphans, equal bridal gifts for orphan girls, equality between co-wives, a fear of adultery, an encouragement of monogamy, and a general desire for justice. All these are ethical concerns that reflect the cultural norms and world views of individuals living in the first and second centuries of Islam as expressed by later generations. However, this canon of interpretations also limits the interpretive options in ways that normalize polygamy and that remove three Qur'anic conditions that have an ethical dimension: (1) fear of failing to provide social justice to some of the most vulnerable members of society: widows and orphans; (2) the unequivocal consent of the women involved in polygamy; and (3) that the fear for social justice to the vulnerable populations exceed the fear of inequality that is always present in polygamous unions. These exegetical lacunae do no justice to the Qur'anic text and hinder its meanings from reaching their full potential in the contemporary context. Removing these cultural filters and distilling the text to its bare linguistic sense, while taking the literary and general historical context into account, allows for a re-exploration of the text and for uncovering the ontological norm of monogamy. It also allows for uncovering important ethical directives when regulating for non-normative marriages: (1) social justice to vulnerable populations, (2) unequivocal consent, and (3) equality. All of these notions are relevant in the modern-day context, even if they may not have been as relevant in al-Ṭabarī's day and age. Ethical reasoning is generally context-specific and involves weighing between competing norms, principles, and concerns on a case-by-case basis (as reflected in the double conditional of Q. 4:3, which teaches weighing between different vulnerabilities, fears, and needs for justice). In the contemporary context, in order for Muslims to rejuvenate their thinking in regard to polygamy and perhaps other forms of non-normative marriage, they must deal with these competing ethical imperatives in their different social, geographic, and political contexts. They must carefully consider how they are going to uphold mono-normativity on the one hand, and social justice, consent, and equality on the other.

CONCLUSION

This chapter has discussed two competing paradigms for interpreting the Qur'an in general and Q. 4:3 in particular. The first is the *tafsīr bi'l-ma'thūr* method, which is prevalent in traditionalist circles today. Based on the assumption that God spoke primarily to the first two generations of Muslims, who were best qualified to interpret the Qur'an due to their linguistic and cultural acumen, it restricts interpretation to a limited number of canonical possibilities that act as intermediaries to the revelation. Ibn Taymiyya's classical hermeneutical framework contributed the last piece in the canonization project by claiming that these exegetical *āthār* were in fact records of explanations that led back to the Prophet Muḥammad, thereby lending them *ḥadīth*-like status. In this paradigm, polygamy is a man's God-given right, with few limitations other than restriction of the number to four and some vague instructions to treat co-wives equally. The second paradigm is an Islamic feminist one. It is based on the assumption that God speaks to all equally and that the revelation is well-suited to every time and place, not tailor-made to fit the cultural presuppositions of the first two centuries of Islam alone. In this paradigm, monogamy is the norm and polygamy the exception, subject to ethical imperatives that include social justice to vulnerable populations, the consent of all parties, and considerations of equality. Methodologically it draws on classical exegesis by emphasizing language and historical context, but it differs in its direct application of these suppositions onto the Qur'anic text and thus leads to a more linguistically and historically accurate interpretation. Moreover, it draws on Ibn Taymiyya's hermeneutics, locating itself within his intra-textual "interpreting the Qur'an by means of the Qur'an" method. This framing is useful in conversation with traditionalists since it allows feminists to subvert the classical system and claim methodological superiority, using the very same hermeneutical framework with which traditionalists are familiar.

NOTES

This chapter is based in part on a paper titled "*Al-Niswiyya al-islāmiyya wa-uṣūl al-fiqh: ru'ya mu'āṣira li'l-ijmā' min khilāl mas'alat ta'addud al-zawjāt*" (Islamic Feminism and Legal Theory: A Contemporary Perspective on the Principle of Consensus in Light of the Question of Polygamy), presented at the conference "Women's Issues: Toward a Contemporary *Ijtihad* (Islamic Reasoning)," Bibliotheca Alexandrina, Alexandria, 10 March 2014. The conference gave Islamic feminists from the Arab world the opportunity to present their work to (male) traditionalist and other scholars. It also launched the Alexandria Declaration of Women's Rights in Islam and the Islamic feminist network *shaqā'iq* (Sisters) in the Arabic-speaking world, with grassroots connections to several civil-society organizations working for women's advancement. This initiative was spearheaded by the Egyptian Mada foundation (www.madafoundation.net) and the chairman of its board of trustees, Dr Hesham Gaafar. It was supported by one of Mada's projects, Markaz Nūn li-Qaḍāyā al-Mar'a wa'l-Usra (Nūn Centre for Women and Family Issues), Bibliotheca Alexandrina, and the Swedish Institute in Alexandria. After two years of energetic activity, at a time of political unrest, this promising network came to an end and the organization's work was frozen; Dr Hesham Gaafar was arrested and detained for reasons that are not entirely clear and subjected to prolonged imprisonment without trial despite deteriorating health https://www.amnesty.org/en/latest/news/2017/10/egypt-end-two-year-arbitrary-detention-of-human-rights-defender-hisham-gaafar.

1 Gaucher, "Monogamous Canadian Citizenship," 533. In Canada, polygamy is considered a criminal offence under Section 293 of the Criminal Code, and those found guilty are liable to imprisonment for a term not exceeding five years. It was upheld as recently as November 2011 by the Supreme Court of British Columbia in connection with a case against Winston Blackmore and James Oler, two religious leaders of the Mormon community in Bountiful, BC, where polygamy has been practised for generations and where it is considered a "religious obligation" by this fundamentalist minority within the Mormon faith tradition. See also Allard and Geadah, *Polygamy.*

2 CEDAW, General Recommendation No. 21.

3 See, for example, al-Krenawi, Graham, and al Gharaibeh, "Comparison Study"; Campbell, Bala, and Duvall-Antonacopoulos, *Polygamy in Canada.*

4 See, for example, Kutty, "Canada Not Immune"; Sadek, "Islamophobia, Shame."

5 Fowler, "Queer Critique"; Otter, "Three May Not Be a Crowd"; Marvel, "Evolution of Plural Parentage"; Fineman, "Vulnerability and the Institution of Marriage."

6 El-Shamsy, *Canonization*, 4, 2012–16.

7 Brown, *Canonization*, 20.

8 Saleh, *Formation*, 14–16; idem, "Preliminary Remarks," 18. See also Karen Bauer, *Gender Hierarchy.*

9 Campanini, *Qur'an*, 1.

10 Ibn Taymiyya, *Muqaddima*, 93–4.

11 For a history of the term *tafsīr bi'l-ma'thūr*, see Saleh, "Preliminary Remarks," 21–37.

12 Al-Zarkashī, *al-Burhān*; al-Suyūṭī, *al-Itqān.*

13 Ibn Taymiyya, *Muqaddima*, 93.

14 Al-Suyūṭī, *al-Itqān*, vol. 4, 212. He reiterates ibn Taymiyya's wording: "*ajall al-tafāsīr al-ma'thūra wa-a'ẓamuhā*"; see Ibn Taymiyya, *Muqaddima*, 90.

15 El-Shamsy, *Canonization*, 212–16.

16 See, for example, his exegesis of Q. 4:3, 'Abduh and Riḍā, *Tafsīr al-manār*, vol. 4, 283–5.

17 Saleh, *Formation.* See also Ibn Taymiyya, *Muqaddima*, 76. For more on the shift to the use of sound *ḥadīth*, see Bauer, *Gender Hierarchy*, 273–5; and Tottoli, "Methods and Contexts."

18 Saleh, "Preliminary Remarks."

19 Al-Zamakhsharī reproduces al-Ṭabarī's options 3, 4, and 1 (see below) in this order and al-Andalusī options 1, 2, 3, and 4. See al-Zamakhsharī, *Kashshāf*, vol. 1, 409; al-Andalusī, *al-Baḥr al-Muḥīṭ*, vol. 3, 503.

20 Mårtensson, "Al-Ṭabarī's Concept," 20; see also Stewart, Muḥammad b. Jarīr al-Ṭabarī's al-Bayān."
21 Shah, "Al-Ṭabarī and the Dynamics."
22 El-Shamsy, *Canonization*, 71–84; al-Shāfiʿī, *Risāla*; idem, *Umm*, 1:22 (paras. 173–7); al-Ṭabarī, *Jāmiʿ al-bayān*, 75–6. According to al-Ṭabarī, some knowledge is the purview of God alone or the Prophet, such as knowledge of the timing of the Anti-Christ (*dajjāl*). See ibid., 73–5.
23 See also Mårtensson, "Al-Ṭabarī's Concept," 24. See also al-Ṭabarī, *Jāmiʿ al-bayān*, 82–3. For more on how these early contexts were constructed, see also Rippin, "The Construction."
24 See al-Ṭabarī, *Jāmiʿ al-bayān*, 8–12, 80–3. See also Q. 11:6; 15:1; 16:89.
25 See al-Ṭabarī, *Jāmiʿ al-bayān*, 77–83, 90–3. Compare al-Shāfiʿī in El-Shamsy's analysis, El-Shamsy, *Canonization*, 73–5.
26 See al-Ṭabarī, *Jāmiʿ al-bayān*, 80–3. For a more detailed understanding of al-Ṭabarī's notion of exegetical authority, see Devin Stewart, "Consensus, Authority."
27 El-Shamsy, *Canonization*, 73n18. See also Musa, *Ḥadīth as Scripture.*
28 See Reda, *al-Baqara Crescendo*, 29–33.
29 The notion of monotheism is not new to Islamic feminist hermeneutics, as can be noted in Amina Wadud's deployment of the term *tawḥīd* (monotheism, the worship of one God) in her exposition of the Tawhidic paradigm. See Wadud, "Islam Beyond Patriarchy." Aysha Hidayatullah has applied this term more broadly to encompass more than just Wadud's work in her critique of Islamic feminist exegesis. See Hidayatullah, *Feminist Edges*, 110–23. Her critique has generated a lively debate. For more on this debate, see Ali, "On Critique and Careful Reading"; Barlas, "Secular and Feminist Critiques"; Hidayatullah, "Claims to the Sacred"; Wadud, "Can One Critique."
30 Saeed, *Interpreting the Qurʾan*, 3. For an application of Saeed's approach in the study of polygamy, see Nurmila, *Women, Islam.*
31 Saeed, *Interpreting the Qurʾan*, 50.
32 Tutt, "Fifty Shades of Textualism," 309.
33 Saeed, *Interpreting the Qurʾan*, 42.
34 Saleh, "Ibn Taymiyya and the Rise," 145.
35 *ʿAql* is the term more commonly used for this principle within Shiʿi circles, but it also occurs in prominent Sunni works, for example, in Abū Ḥāmid al-Ghazālī's *al-Mustaṣfā min ʿilm al-uṣūl.*
36 Translation by Saleh, "Ibn Taymiyya and the Rise," 126.
37 Rapoport, "Ibn Taymiyya's Radical Legal Thought," 204–6.

38 Ibn Taymiyya, *Naqd marātib al-ijmāʿ* in Ibn Ḥazm and Ibn Taymiyya, *Marātib al-ijmāʿ wa-yalīh naqd marātib al-ijmāʿ*, 285-308.
39 See, for example, al-Dārimī, *Sunan*, #586–90; al-Ghazālī, *al-Mustasfā*, 1:80–1.
40 Al-Azmeh, "Canon and Canonisation."
41 Brown, *Canonization*, 183–96.
42 Ibn Ḥazm, *Marātib al-ijmāʿ*, 115.
43 See, for example, Saeed, *Reading the Qurʾan*, 3; idem, *Interpreting the Qurʾan*, 1.
44 See, Reda, "Holistic Approaches."
45 Saeed, *Reading the Qurʾan*, 58–9.
46 Not all translations include "at the same time." The Arabic words *mathnā*, *thulāth*, and *rubāʿ* convey this nuance, differing from *ithnayn, thalātha*, and *arbaʿa* (two, three, and four).
47 Harvey, who has presented an in-depth study of the notion of justice in the Qurʾan, also highlights the social aspect of *qisṭ*, translating it as "societal justice." See Ramon, *Qurʾan and the Just Society.*
48 Giladi, "Orphans," 603–4. Al-Zamakhsharī also offers a good linguistic discussion of the word; see *Al-Kashshāf*, vol. 1, 407.
49 Ibn Abī Ṭāhir Ṭayfūr (d. 280/893), *Balāghāt al-nisāʾ*, 103.
50 For the various meanings of the relative pronoun *mā*, see al-Andalusī, *al-Baḥr al-muḥīṭ*, vol. 3, 504–5. *Mā* may also refer back to the gerund "marriage."
51 See, for example, al-Fakhr al-Rāzī, *Tafsīr*, 9:176–9.
52 For the two narrations, See Muslim ibn al-Ḥajjāj, *Ṣaḥīḥ Muslim, Kitāb al-tafsīr*, nos. 6–9.
53 See, for example, Hübner, "Callirhoe's Dilemma," 63; Galpaz-Feller, "Widow in the Bible," 231–53.
54 Kamali, *Shariʿah Law*, 19.
55 Al-Rāzī, *Tafsīr*, 9:173.
56 Muslim ibn al-Ḥajjāj, *Ṣaḥīḥ Muslim, kitāb faḍāʾil al-ṣāḥāba, bāb faḍāʾil Fāṭima bint al-nabī*, no. 2449.
57 ʿAbduh and Riḍā, *Tafsīr al-manār*, vol. 4, 287.
58 See, for example, Q. 2:48, 123.

REFERENCES

Abdel Haleem, M.A.S. *The Qurʾan.* Oxford: Oxford University Press, 2008.

ʿAbduh, Muḥammad, and Muḥammad Rashīd Riḍā. *Tafsīr al-manār*, vol. 4. Cairo: Al-Hayʾa al-Miṣriyya al-ʿĀmma liʾl-Kitāb, 1973.

Ali, Kecia. "On Critique and Careful Reading," *Journal of Feminist Studies in Religion* 32, no. 2 (2016): 121–6.

Allard, Marie-Andrée (Research and Analysis Director) and Yolande Geadah (research and writing). *Polygamy and the Rights of Women*. Québec: Conseil du statut de la femme, 2010.

Andalusī, Abū Ḥayyān Muḥammad ibn Yūsuf al-Gharnāṭī al-. *Al-Baḥr al-muḥīṭ fī al-tafsīr*. 11 vols. Beirut: Dār al-Fikr, 2005.

Azmeh, Aziz, al-. "Canon and Canonisation of the Qurʾān." In *Encyclopaedia of Islam*, THREE, ed. Kate Fleet, Gudrun Krämer, Denis Matringe, John Nawas, and Everett Rowson. Leiden: Brill, 2013. http://dx.doi.org.myaccess.library.utoronto.ca/10.1163/1573-3912_ei3_COM_24606

Barlas, Asma. "Secular and Feminist Critiques of the Qurʾan: Anti-Hermeneutics as Liberation?" *Journal of Feminist Studies in Religion* 32, no. 2 (2016): 111–21.

Bauer, Karen. *Gender Hierarchy in the Qurʾān: Medieval Interpretations, Modern Responses*. Cambridge: Cambridge University Press, 2015.

Brown, Jonathan. *The Canonization of al-Bukhārī and Muslim: The Formation and Function of the Sunnī Ḥadīth Canon*. Leiden: Brill, 2007.

Campanini, Massimo. *The Qurʾan: Modern Muslim Interpretations*. Trans. Caroline Higgitt. London: Routledge, 2011.

Campbell, Angela, Nicholas Bala, and Katherine Duvall-Antonacopoulos. *Polygamy in Canada: Legal and Social Implications for Women and Children: A Collection of Policy Research*. Ottawa: Status of Women, 2005.

CEDAW (Convention on the Elimination of All Forms of Discrimination against Women). "General Recommendations Made by the Committee on the Elimination of Discrimination against Women. General Recommendation no. 21." 13th session, 1994. http://www.un.org/womenwatch/daw/cedaw/recommendations/recomm.htm

Dārimī, ʿAbd Allāh ibn ʿAbd al-Raḥmān al-. *Sunan al-Dārimī*. Beirut: Dār al-Kitāb al-ʿArabī, 1987.

El-Shamsy, Ahmed. *The Canonization of Islamic Law: A Social and Intellectual History*. New York: Cambridge University Press, 2013.

Fineman, Martha Albertson. "Vulnerability and the Institution of Marriage." *Emory Law Journal* 64, no. 6 (2015): 2089–92.

Fowler, Erin. "A Queer Critique on the Polygamy Debate in Canada: Law, Culture, and Diversity." *Dalhousie Journal of Legal Studies* 21 (2012): 93–126.

Galpaz-Feller, Pnina. "The Widow in the Bible and in Ancient Egypt." *Zeitschrift für die alttestamentliche Wissenschaft* 120, no. 2 (2008): 231–53.

Gaucher, Megan. "Monogamous Canadian Citizenship, Constructing Foreignness, and the Limits of Harm Discourse." *Canadian Journal of Political Science* 49, no. 3 (2016): 519–38.

Ghazālī, Abū Ḥāmid Muḥammad ibn Muḥammad al-. *Al-Mustaṣfā min ʿilm al-uṣūl*. [Cairo]: al-Maktaba al-Tujāriyya al-Kubrā, 1937.

Giladi, Avner. "Orphans." In *Encyclopaedia of the Qurʾan*, vol. 3, ed. Jane Dammen McAuliffe, 603–4. Leiden: Brill Academic, 2003.

Harvey, Ramon. *The Qurʾan and the Just Society*. Edinburgh: Edinburgh University Press, 2018.

Hidayatullah. Aysha A. "Claims to the Sacred." *Journal of Feminist Studies in Religion* 32, no. 2 (2016): 134–8.

– *Feminist Edges of the Qurʾan*. New York: Oxford University Press, 2014.

Hübner, Sabine R. "Callirhoe's Dilemma: Remarriage and Stepfathers in the Greco-Roman East." In *Growing up Fatherless in Antiquity*, ed. Sabine R. Hübner and David M. Ratzan, 61–82. Cambridge: Cambridge University Press, 2009.

Ibn Abī Ṭāhir Ṭayfūr and Abū al-Faḍl Aḥmad. *Balāghāt al-nisāʾ*. Ed. Aḥmad al-Alfī. Cairo: Maṭbaʿat Madrasat Wālidat ʿAbbās al-Awwal, 1326 AH/1908 CE.

Ibn al-Ḥajjāj al-Qushayrī, Muslim. *Ṣaḥīḥ Muslim*. 5 vols. Beirut: Dār al-Fikr, 1999.

Ibn Ḥazm, ʿAlī ibn Aḥmad ibn Saʿīd and Taqī al-Dīn Aḥmad ibn Taymmiyya. *Marātib al-ijmāʿ wa-yalīh naqd marātib al-ijmāʿ*. N.p: Maktabat al-Qudsī li-Ṣāḥibihā Ḥusām al-Dīn al-Qudsī, 1357 AH.

– *Marātib al-ijmāʿ wa-yalīh naqd marātib al-ijmāʿ*. N.p.: Maktabat al-Qudsī li-Ṣāḥibihā Ḥusām al-Dīn al-Qudsī, 1357 AH.

Ibn Taymiyya, Ṭaqī al-Dīn Aḥmad ibn ʿAbd al-Ḥalīm. *Muqaddima fī uṣūl al-tafsīr*. Cairo: Maktabat al-Turāth al-Islāmī, 1988.

Kamali, Mohammad Hashim. *Shariʿah Law: An Introduction*. Oxford: Oneworld, 2008.

Krenawi, Alean Al-, John Graham, and Fakir Al Gharaibeh. "A Comparison Study of Psychological, Family Function Marital and Life Satisfactions of Polygamous and Monogamous Women in Jordan." *Community Mental Health Journal* 47, no. 5 (2011): 595–602.

Kutty, Faisal. "Canada Not Immune from a Legacy of Fear-Mongering." *Washington Report on Middle East Affairs* 36, no. 2 (2017): 40–1.

Marvel, Stu. "The Evolution of Plural Parentage: Applying Vulnerability Theory to Polygamy and Same-Sex Marriage." *Emory Law Journal* 64, no. 6 (2015), 2046-88.

Mårtensson, Ulrika. "Al-Ṭabarī's Concept of the Qur'an: A Systematic Analysis." *Journal of Qur'anic Studies* 18, no. 2 (2016): 9–57.

Musa, Aisha Y. *Hadīth as Scripture: Discussions on the Authority of Prophetic Traditions in Islam.* New York: Palgrave Macmillan, 2008.

Nurmila, Nina. *Women, Islam, and Everyday Life: Renegotiating Polygamy in Indonesia.* London: Routledge, 2009.

Otter, Ronald C. Den. "Three May not Be a Crowd: The Case for a Constitutional Right to Plural Marriage." *Emory Law Journal* 64, no. 6 (2015): 1977–2045.

Rapoport, Yossef. "Ibn Taymiyya's Radical Legal Thought: Rationalism, Pluralism, and the Primacy of Intention." In *Ibn Taymiyya and His Times*, ed. Yossef Rapoport and Shahab Ahmed, 191-228. Oxford: Oxford University Press, 2010.

Rāzī, Fakhr al-Dīn Muḥammad ibn ʿUmar al-. *Al-Tafsīr al-kabīr.* 32 vols. in 16. Cairo: al-Maṭbaʿa al-Bahiyya al-Miṣriya, n.d.

Reda, Nevin. *The al-Baqara Crescendo: Understanding the Qur'an's Style, Narrative Structure, and Running Themes. Montreal and Kingston: McGill-Queen's University Press, 2017.*

– "Holistic Approaches to the Qur'an: A Historical Background." *Religion Compass* 4, no. 8 (2010): 495–506.

Rippin, Andrew. "The Construction of the Arabian Historical Context in Muslim Interpretation of the Qur'an." In *Aims, Methods, and Contexts of Qur'anic Exegesis (2nd/8*th*–9th/15th c.)*, ed. Karen Bauer, 173–98. Oxford: Oxford University Press in association with Instituite of Ismaili Studies, 2013.

Sadek, Noha. "Islamophobia, Shame, and the Collapse of Muslim Identities." *International Journal of Applied Psychoanalytic Studies* 14, no. 3 (2017): 200–21.

Saeed, Abdullah. *Interpreting the Qur'ān: Towards a Contemporary Approach.* London: Routledge, 2006.

– *Reading the Qur'an in the Twenty-First Century: A Contextualist Approach.* London: Routledge, 2014.

Saleh, Walid. *The Formation of the Classical* Tafsīr *Tradition: The Qur'ān Commentary of al-Thaʿlabī (d. 427/1035).* Leiden: Brill, 2004.

Saleh, Walid A. "Ibn Taymiyya and the Rise of Radical Hermeneutics: An Analysis of *An Introduction to the Foundations of Qur'ānic Exegesis*." In *Ibn Taymiyya and His Times*, ed. Yossef Rapoport and Shahab Ahmed, 123–62. Oxford: Oxford University Press, 2010.

– "Preliminary Remarks on the Historiography of *tafsīr* in Arabic: A History of the Book Approach." *Journal of Qur'anic Studies* 12 (2010): 6–40.

Shāfiʿī, Muḥammad ibn Idrīs al. *Al-Risāla*. Ed. Aḥmad Muḥammad Shākir. Cairo: al-Ḥalabī, 1940.

– *Al-Umm*, edited by M. Z. al-Najjār. 8 vols. Beirut: Dār al-Maʿrifa, n.d.

Shah, Mustafa. "Al-Ṭabarī and the Dynamics of *tafsīr*: Theological Dimensions of a Legacy." *Journal of Qur'anic Studies* 15, no. 2 (2013): 83–139.

Stewart, Devin J. "Consensus, Authority, and the Interpretive Community in the Thought of Muḥammad b. Jarīr al-Ṭabarī." *Journal of Qur'anic Studies* 18, no. 2 (2016): 130–79.

– "Muḥammad b. Jarīr al-Ṭabarī's al-Bayān ʿan uṣūl al-aḥkām and the Genre of Uṣūl al-fiqh in Ninth Century Baghdād." In *ʿAbbasid Studies: Occasional Papers of the School of ʿAbbasid Studies, Cambridge 6–10 July 2002*, ed. J.E. Montgomery,321–49. Orientalia Lovaniensia Analecta 135, 2004.

Suyūṭī, Jalāl al-Dīn ʿAbd al-Raḥmān al-. *Al-Itqān fī ʿulūm al-Qurʾān*. Ed. Muḥammad Abū al-Faḍl Ibrāhīm. 4 vols. Cairo: Dār al-Turāth, n.d.

Ṭabarī, Abū Jaʿfar Muḥammad ibn Jarīr al-. *Jāmiʿ al-bayān ʿan taʾwīl āy al-Qurʾān*. Ed. Maḥmūd Muḥammad Shākir. 16 vols. Cairo: Dār al-Maʿārif, 1958.

Tottoli, Roberto. "Methods and Contexts in the Use of Hadiths in Classical *Tafsīr* Literature: The Exegesis of Q. 21:85 and Q. 17:1." In *Aims, Methods and Contexts of Qur'anic Exegesis (2nd/8th—9th/15th c.)*, ed. Karen Bauer, 173–98. Oxford: Oxford University Press in association with Institute of Ismaili Studies, 2013.

Tutt, Andrew. "Fifty Shades of Textualism." *Journal of Law and Politics* 29, no. 2 (2014): 309–51.

Wadud, Amina. "Can One Critique Cancel All Previous Efforts?" *Journal of Feminist Studies in Religion* 32, no. 2 (2016): 130–4.

– "Islam Beyond Patriarchy through Gender Inclusive Qur'anic Analysis." In *Wanted: Equality and Justice in the Muslim Family*, ed. Zainah Anwar, 95–112. Petaling Jaya: Musawah, 2009.Zamakhsharī, Abū al-Qāsim Jār Allāh Maḥmūd ibn ʿUmar al-. *Al-Kashshāf ʿan ḥaqāʾiq al-tanzīl wa-ʿuyūn al-aqāwīl fī wujūh al-taʾwīl*. Ed. Yūsuf al-Ḥammādī. 4 vols. Al-Fajjāla, Cairo: Maktabat Miṣr, n.d.

Zarkashī, Badr al-Dīn Muḥammad ibn ʿAbd Allāh al-. *Al-burhān fī ʿulūm al-Qurʾān*. Ed. Muḥammad Abū al-Faḍl Ibrāhīm. 4 vols. Cairo: Dār al-Turāth, n.d.

3

Reading the Qur'an through a Gendered, Egalitarian Lens

Revisiting the Concept of *Wilāya* in Q. 9:71

Asma Afsaruddin

In roughly the third or fourth year of the Islamic era (corresponding to 625–26 CE), the Medinan woman Companion Umm ʿUmāra from the first generation of Muslims remarked to the Prophet Muḥammad in connection with the Qurʾanic revelations he had received up to that point, "I see that everything pertains to men; I do not see the mention of women."[1] Umm ʿUmāra (Nusayba bint Kaʿb al-Anṣāriyya, d. 13/634) was commenting on the fact that Qurʾanic verses that had come down so far primarily referred to men and their good deeds and the rewards they were consequently promised in the hereafter. Were women believers not to be recognized as equal participants in this grand unfolding drama of human agency, fulfillment, and salvation? Subsequently, this particular verse was revealed:

> Those who have surrendered to God among males and females; those who believe among males and females; those who are sincere among males and females; those who are truthful among males and females; those who are patient among males and females; those who fear God among males and females; those who give in charity among males and females; those who fast among males and females; those who remember God often among males and females – God has prepared for them forgiveness and great reward. (Q. 33:35)[2]

The Qur'an had settled the question once and for all: women and men had equal moral agency in their quest for the good and righteous life in this world, for which they would reap identical rewards in the afterlife. Gender thus had no role to play in the otherworldly, salvific efficacy offered by the Qur'an through its prescription for a well-ordered moral existence on Earth. Muslim feminist scholars often point to this verse (and others like it) to underscore the gender egalitarianism inherent in the Qur'an.

The question of the Qur'anic ascription of equal moral agency to men and women is further explored in this chapter through a discussion of the exegeses of two additional verses – Q. 9:71 and Q. 4:34 – by select pre-modern and modern male exegetes. These exegeses are contrasted to those generated by Muslim feminist scholars in the modern period, who offer critiques of traditional methodologies of engaging the Qur'an and posit instead a holistic reading of the Qur'an. Such a hermeneutic enterprise allows these women exegetes to develop "alternative" readings of verses that deal specifically with gendered relations and to question the "canonical" status of a body of exegetical literature generated by influential male exegetes. The chapter concludes by offering an analysis of such feminist rereadings of particularly Q. 9:71 and Q. 4:34 and briefly assesses their potential efficacy in challenging the normativity of masculinist interpretations of the Qur'an.

The diachronic nature of this survey helps us plot the exegetical shifts that have occurred over time as conceptions of women's status and roles in society changed in variegated socio-historical circumstances. These sorts of diachronic shifts have not received adequate attention in previous literature. Such an approach is vital, however, for identifying the provenance and historical development of androcentric interpretations that are considered problematic today and thereby allowing such interpretations to be credibly challenged and potentially changed in contemporary contexts. From the perspective of the larger goals of this volume, this diachronic approach furthermore offers a glimpse into the living processes of canonization and decanonization in the past and in the present.

RETRIEVING GENDER EGALITARIANISM FROM WITHIN THE QUR'AN

Women's readings and perspectives on the Qur'an have not been copiously preserved for us through the centuries. When feminine voices can be retrieved from the early, pre-modern extra-Qur'anic sources, they are sometimes heard to argue for justice and equitable treatment for women. We have documented instances of women in our sources occasionally pleading for the proper implementation of Qur'anic and prophetic injunctions that would guarantee their social and economic rights after the death of the Prophet.[3] Muḥammad's youngest widow ʿĀʾisha (bint Abī Bakr, d. 58/678) is often heard remonstrating with some male Companions after they purvey misogynist reports they have carelessly and mendaciously attributed to him.[4]

Such vignettes provide fascinating glimpses into the Muslim past, into times when an alternatively conceptualized society, in which the gifts and contributions of men and women were deemed equally valuable, was possible. Early biographical works, such as *al-Ṭabaqāt al-kubrā* of Ibn Saʿd (d. 230/845), document that the details of the lives of first-generation Muslim women, when available, provide instructive examples of women's lives lived in service to their community and religion, largely unhampered by later socio-political constructions of restrictive, gendered identities.[5] The memory of these inspirational women, however, begins to dim in subsequent centuries. As historians have shown, critical changes that crept into Muslim societies from the outside considerably reshaped their orientations and substantially attenuated the gender egalitarianism of the early period. Persian, Greek, and Byzantine notions of social hierarchies and gendered privileges progressively shaped societal and juridical conceptions of women's socio-economic rights and led to their eventual circumscription.[6]

These striking societal and cultural transformations left a broad imprint on the way certain Qur'anic verses that deal with human agency and male–female relations, particularly within the family, were read and interpreted by male scholars through the centuries. Their interpretations provide a valuable window onto the gradual "patriarchalization" of Muslim society and the elaborate arguments constructed to support this world view – all couched in a legitimizing religious idiom. Such patriarchal perspectives became "canonized" so to speak by the male scholarly elite, so that by the later medieval period (after the fourth/tenth century) such views became widely accepted as orthodox and normative.

Going back to the foundational texts of Islam – particularly the Qur'an – however, disabuses us of many of these "canonical" notions that promoted the gender inequality and discrimination that became so deeply entrenched in Islamic societies over time.[7] For example, if we refer to verses that describe the creation of Adam and his wife before their earthly existence, we observe that the Qur'an either (a) blames Adam exclusively for the "Fall" or (b) blames Adam and his wife equally for giving in to the blandishments of Satan.

Western readers from a Judeo-Christian background will be struck by the fact that Adam's wife (named Ḥawwāʾ [Eve] in the exegetical literature) is not singled out for exclusive blame in the Qur'an, in contrast to the principal Biblical creation account contained in the Book of Genesis, which makes Eve the sole cause of the banishment of humans from Paradise. On balance, Adam in the Qur'an is the one who is morally culpable for failing to heed God's injunctions and succumbing to wrongdoing. He is, however, forgiven by God, and he and his wife are given an equal opportunity to redeem themselves by establishing a righteous and God-fearing community on earth. In its creation accounts (Q. 2:30–9; 7:11–27; 15:26–43; 20: 115–24; and 38:71–85), the Qur'an does not assign any kind of ontological moral failing to the woman companion of Adam and thus, by extension, to womankind in general.[8]

This point has been underscored by Muslim feminists in particular as they argue from within the Islamic tradition for gender egalitarianism. Recuperation of the meanings of the original Qur'anic verses concerning Adam and Eve is highly important in feminist discourses as a corrective to a very different story that emerges from the prolific exegetical literature (*tafsīr*) on this topic. Qur'an commentaries from after the third/ninth century reveal that the Qur'anic exoneration of Adam's wife proved unpalatable to a number of later Muslim male exegetes, such as al-Zamakhsharī (d. 538/1144) and Fakhr al-Dīn al-Rāzī (d. 606/1210), and that they deliberately imported the Biblical creation story into their interpretations to reassign the blame to her. Earlier commentators, including Ibn Jarīr al-Ṭabarī (d. 310/923), stayed closer to the Qur'anic text and noted that Adam in the Qur'an bore the brunt of the blame for having caused the Fall. Later exegetes – roughly after the fourth/tenth century – however, began to show a marked preference for the Biblical version, which mandates the wife's subjugation to her husband as a result of her sin, an interpretation that was more in line with the increasingly patriarchal nature of society. Not surprisingly, the well-known exegete from the late sixth/twelfth century al-Rāzī embellishes his narrative with the story of woman's creation from Adam's rib to drive home the point that the female is secondary to the male as a human being, and that that Biblical literary motif had by his time taken deep root in Muslim exegeses.[9]

Such construals are markedly in contrast to what the Qur'an actually says concerning the creation of humankind. One such verse states, "O humankind! Be careful of your duty to your Lord Who created you from a single soul [*nafs wāḥida*] and from it created its mate and from them the two has spread abroad a multitude of men and women" (Q. 4:1). As feminist exegetes stress, simultaneous creation from the *nafs wāḥida* (one soul) negates the possibility of man being granted an ontologically superior status by virtue of having been created first and from whose body is then derived the woman's. Interpreted through this gendered, egalitarian lens, the Qur'an clearly undermines the notion of a hierarchical relationship between man and woman.

WOMEN'S MORAL AGENCY IN THE QUR'AN

Feminist exegetes typically emphasize the influence of socio-political and historical contexts in the reading of the Qur'anic text by male exegetes in the pre-modern period. They also insist that a holistic reading of the Qur'an – that is to say, by considering the Qur'an's message as a whole so that verses are read cross-referentially when referring to the same topic or theme[10] – prevents us from falling into the trap of reading certain verses that deal with women's issues in an atomistic, decontextualized manner. They point out that culturally derived attitudes that progressively undermined women's equal status in society in the formative period of Islam and that became enshrined in *fiqh* are belied by several passages in the Qur'an that affirm gender equality in various contexts. One such critical verse is Q. 9:71, which establishes equal and complementary moral agency for men and women. The verse states, "[Male] believers [*al-mu'minūn*] and [female] believers [*al-mu'mināt*] are the natural partners [*awliyā'*] of one another; they command the good and forbid wrong and they perform prayer, give the obligatory alms, and obey God and His messenger. They are those upon whom God has mercy; indeed, God is Almighty, Wise." The obvious intent of the verse is to establish complete parity between men and women as partners in the common venture to promote the good, righteous society on Earth and in the fulfillment of their individual and communal obligations toward God.[11] As obvious as this meaning may seem to us today, male interpreters from the pre-modern and modern periods have understood this verse in ways that more often than not are consonant with their own particularist views of proper male–female relations and, particularly for the later period, subversive of its egalitarian thrust. A sampling of the perspectives of a number of influential exegetes is provided below to offer a glimpse into the conceptualization of such gendered identities in variegated historical circumstances in the pre-modern period, a conceptualization that persists to this day.

Pre-Modern Exegeses of Q. 9:71

From the first half of the second/eighth century during the Umayyad period, the exegete Muqātil ibn Sulaymān (d. 150/767) asserts the full and equal partnership of female and male believers in matters of religion (*fī al-dīn*) and highlights their mutually reinforcing obedience to God in Q. 9:71.[12] The celebrated late-ninth-century exegete al-Ṭabarī from the ʿAbbāsid period similarly emphasizes that righteous men and women "who believe in God, His messenger and the verses of His book" are each other's allies (*anṣār*) and supporters (*aʿwān*). Their fundamental duty to promote what is right and prevent what is wrong consists in inviting people to monotheism, to abandon the worship of idols, and to carry out their fundamental religious obligations, such as offering prayers and paying alms.[13]

The fifth/eleventh-century exegete Abū al-Ḥasan al-Wāḥidī (d. 468/1076) similarly underscores that the complementarity of men and women's religious and familial roles is indicated in this verse. He quotes from the famous Companion ʿAbd Allāh ibn ʿAbbās (d. 68/687), who stated that believing women and men were allies of each other "in regard to mercy and affection" (*fī al-raḥma wa'l-maḥabba*). Al-Wāḥidī understands this statement to mean that they were like "one hand in supporting [one another]" and, like al-Ṭabarī, stresses that they were called on in particular to invite people to worship the one God and to themselves observe the fundamental tenets of Islam.[14] Very similar views are expressed by the well-known Andalusian exegete Muḥammad ibn Aḥmad al-Qurṭubī (d. 671/1273), who, on the basis of this verse, characterizes the relationship between men and women as one of "hearts united in mutual affection, love, and empathy."[15]

Interestingly, al-Qurṭubī's predecessor, the famous Fakhr al-Dīn al-Rāzī, who is otherwise generally quite prolix in his commentary on individual verses, does not comment at all on the nature of this partnership (*wilāya*) between women and men as indicated in Q. 9:71.[16]

The influential Mamluk exegete Ismāʿīl ibn ʿUmar ibn Kathīr (d. 774/1373) in the eighth/fourteenth century does comment on this special bond existing among believers, men and women, and invokes the *ḥadīth* in which the Prophet describes the faithful as constituting "a [single] edifice in which each strengthens the other" in this context.[17] Worthy of note, however, is that Ibn Kathīr uses only the masculine noun for believers (*al-muʾminīn*) in his commentary, in stark contrast to our earlier commentators, who repeated in their exegeses the masculine and the feminine plural nouns occurring in Q. 9:71 that refer explicitly to believers of both sexes.

Modern Exegeses of Q. 9:71

In the nineteenth century, the prominent Egyptian scholar and reformer Muḥammad ʿAbduh (d. 1905) and his loyal student Rashīd Riḍā (d. 1935) collaborated on a Qurʾan commentary project titled *Tafsīr al-manār*, which remains influential to this day. Since Riḍā continued with this project after ʿAbduh's death, it is his voice that we hear from the exegesis of Qurʾanic chapter 5 onwards, and therefore we are referring to him alone in our continued discussion of Q. 9:71.

It is in the *Tafsīr al-manār* that we finally obtain a more detailed explanation of the nature of *wilāya*[18] (partnership) understood to be indicated in the verse and how that applies to men and women, both equally and differentially. As far as their fundamental relationship is concerned, Riḍā states, the *wilāya* that exists, according to this verse, between believing women and men has to do "in general with mutual support, solidarity and affection" (*taʿumm wilāyat al-nuṣra wa-wilāyat al-ikhwa wa'l-mawadda*). He also invokes *aḥādīth* as proof-texts, including one in which Muḥammad describes the community of Muslims as "one body" (*al-jasad al-wāḥid*) and another (previously quoted by Ibn Kathīr) in which the *umma* constitutes a "single edifice in which each strengthens the other." The alliance of support (*wilāyat al-nuṣra*) is specifically constituted so that all may collaborate in defending truth, justice, the religious community, and the nation.[19]

Where gender does make a difference is in the realm of military defence of the polity. Here, says Riḍā, women offer their help and efforts in everything short of actual combat. He points to the example of the women Companions during the lifetime of the Prophet who provided water for thirsty combatants, prepared food, and tended to the wounded on the battlefield.[20] Aside from this difference, Riḍā appears to consider men and women to be equally engaged in their efforts to promote what is right and prevent what is wrong and, therefore, in working together for the common good.

Analysis and Critique of Exegeses of Q. 9:71

The fairly brief comments on the whole recorded by pre-modern male exegetes regarding what otherwise strikes us today as a revolutionary verse with potentially striking socio-political implications are perhaps telling. They underscore for us that the medieval male imaginary was not capable of extrapolating from this verse a larger scriptural mandate for men and women to work together companionably and on an equal footing in all spheres of life. They restrict the *wilāya* indicated in Q. 9:71 to essentially the religious sphere, and they do not (and perhaps could not) derive a broader empowerment of men and women equally in reforming both themselves and the larger society around them.

Riḍā in the twentieth century has a more capacious understanding of *wilāya* in connection with both men and women. However, he places one restriction on the purview of the *wilāya* of women – that it does not extend to fighting on the battlefield, which remains a male preserve. By default, all other activities that aid in the promotion of truth, justice, and righteousness appear to be open equally to women and men by virtue of the Qur'anic mandate to serve as "allies of one another."

MALE GUARDIANSHIP OVER WOMEN?

Whereas Q. 9:71 has typically not been the focus of masculine attention, another verse – Q. 4:34 – has been, and continues to be, the subject of prolific exegeses. In fact, one may view this verse, in many ways, as casting a long shadow over other Qur'anic verses dealing with gender and as having influenced the reading of *wilāya* in Q. 9:71. We will note that compared to this verse, Q. 4:34 received disproportionate exegetical attention, since it allowed pre-modern commentators to develop their notions of gendered identities and roles during its explication. The verse states:

> Men are *qawwāmūn* over women because God has preferred some of them over others and because of what they spend of their wealth. Virtuous women are devout, preserving that which

> is hidden according to what God has preserved. As for those women whose recalcitrance may be feared, reprimand them, banish them to their beds, and strike/avoid them. And if they obey you, then do not misbehave towards them at all; indeed, God is majestic and great.

The predicate adjective *qawwāmūn* that occurs in the verse is deliberately left untranslated here because of its contested meanings, as we will be discussing shortly. The later verbal imperative in the verse, which can be read either as *wa-'dribūhunna* (majority pre-modern and modern reading) or as *wa-ʾadribūhunna* (minority modern feminist reading), is translated to reflect both possible meanings. A sampling of pre-modern and modern exegeses is offered below to establish a range of common interpretations, which have been questioned and revisited by contemporary Muslim feminists.[21]

Pre-Modern Exegeses of Q. 4:34

The Umayyad exegete Muqātil ibn Sulayman preserves an early exegetical report on the occasion of revelation for the verse. According to this report, the verse concerns one of the eminent Anṣār, Saʿd ibn al-Rabīʿ ibn ʿAmr, who struck his wife Ḥabība bint Zayd ibn Abī Zuhayr. Ḥabība and her father came to Muḥammad to register a complaint about Saʿd's behaviour. The Prophet said that she was entitled to hit him back in retaliation (*qiṣāṣ*) for his behaviour. But then Q. 4:34 was revealed and the Prophet retracted his opinion and deferred to the divine judgment pronounced in the verse. Muqātil's construal of the implications of this divine judgment is highly revealing of the social mores of his time – the late Umayyad period. He proceeds to explain that *qawwāmūn* in this verse means that men have been granted authority over women (*musallaṭūn ʿalā al-nisāʾ*) and that men have been granted greater rights over women by virtue of the fact that they pay the bridal gift (*mahr*) to them. Men also exercise their authority in regard to general discipline and power over women. A wife cannot seek financial compensation or retribution (*qiṣāṣ*) against her husband except in cases of injury or loss of life. The rest of the verse refers to virtuous women who are obedient (*qānitāt*) to God and *to their husbands* (emphasis added) and who guard their private parts and their wealth in the absence of their husbands. As for those who manifest disobedience (*nushūz*) to their husbands like Saʿd's wife, comments Muqātil, they should first of all be given a warning, followed by abstention from intercourse with them. If these two measures do not achieve the desired result, then the wife may be struck in a way that does not cause any agony or disfigurement (*ghayr mubarriḥ yaʿnī ghayr shāʾin*). Once she has returned to proper wifely obedience, she should not be burdened with showing affection to her husband "more than she is capable of."[22]

Muqātil's exegesis became very influential and has been reproduced in many commentaries after him. Al-Ṭabarī in the late third (ninth–early tenth) century refers to the occasion of revelation listed by Muqātil and provides it with several chains of transmission, thus documenting its widespread dissemination. Interestingly, the couple's names are not given in the versions listed by al-Ṭabarī.[23] It is worth noting that both Muqātil and al-Ṭabarī clearly understand the verse as referring to the relationship between a husband and wife; therefore, the husband's *qiwāma* (verbal noun derived from the same root as *qawwāmūn* and roughly meaning "guardianship/authority") is primarily a functional one, emanating from his position as financial provider for the family, to which a certain moral authority is appended.[24] Only one report, cited from the late second/eighth century scholar Ibn al-Mubārak (d. 181/797) (and attributed to the pious Medinan jurist Sufyān al-Thawrī [d. 161/778]), does not provide the larger marital context and suggests that the verse be generally understood as referring to "God's preference for men over women."[25]

In reference to the Arabic word *qānitāt* that occurs in the verse, al-Ṭabarī cites several authorities who understand it to mean women who are obedient to both God and their husbands. The same Ibn al-Mubārak referred to above is cited as voicing the opinion that the word refers solely to "women who are obedient to their husbands." Once again, the ultimate authority for this point of view is Sufyān al-Thawrī, for which al-Ṭabarī proceeds to express a clear preference.[26] As for the *nushūz* of the women, it consists of their haughtiness towards their husbands, "rising up from their [husbands'] beds in disobedience" and contradicting their husbands in matters in which they should be obedient. This understanding, al-Ṭabarī notes, is consistent with the etymology of the Arabic word *nushūz*, which has to do with "elevation."[27] Other authorities cited by al-Ṭabarī offer similar meanings. One source – the Medinan Successor ʿAṭāʾ ibn Abī Rabāḥ (d. 114/732 or 115/733) – maintained, significantly, that *nushūz* applied equally to the wife and husband and referred to the desire of each to separate from the other.[28]

Al-Ṭabarī then elaborates upon what he understands to be the distinctive steps recommended by the Qur'an for dealing with a recalcitrant wife. Since this section is fairly long, only a synopsis of the broader points he makes is given here. The first step for the husband is to counsel the wife to remember God and return to the marital bed. According to Mujāhid ibn Jabr (d. ~104/722), the husband should plead with the wife to "Fear God and return to your bed!" When the wife does so, no further action should be taken toward her.[29]

If the wife should fail to heed this counsel, the next step is for the husband to desist from having sexual relations with her and sleep apart from her; this was the view of Ibn ʿAbbās, Saʿīd ibn Jubayr (d. 95/714) and many others. A few authorities, such as ʿIkrima (d. 105/723), were of the opinion that the husband should also avoid speaking to his wife.[30]

Should these first two steps not suffice, then the husband may lightly beat her (*ḍarabahā ghayr mubarriḥ*), so as to leave no marks on the body (*ghayr mu'aththir*), until she returns to a state of wifely obedience; this was the predominant interpretation attributed to Ibn ʿAbbās and others.[31] A more detailed commentary from Ibn ʿAbbās warns against striking the wife to the extent of breaking her bones, whether she acquiesces to her husband's entreaties or not. If she is physically hurt, then the husband must pay a compensation (*fidya*) for her injuries.[32] Ibn ʿAbbās is also the main source for the view that a "light beating" amounted to a more or less symbolic tapping with the equivalent of a toothbrush (*al-siwāk*).[33] Al-Ṭabarī concludes by asserting that once the wife has returned to obedience, the husband is obligated to fulfill his duties toward her and may not seek to cause her any kind of physical or emotional harm.[34]

In his brief remarks on this verse, al-Wāḥidī (d. 468/1075) in the fifth/eleventh century indicates to us that certain specific interpretations of Q. 4:34 had gained hold and were subsequently disseminated as authoritative understandings of key terms in the verse. Thus, he understands the "preference" that God has shown for "some of them over others" as a specific reference to the "superiority, as decreed by God, of men over women, by virtue of their intelligence, their body, knowledge, resolve, martial ability, status as legal witness, and greater rights in inheritance."[35] What for the earlier exegetes constituted primarily the functional superiority of men over women in a domestic context has now been rendered in al-Wāḥidī's understanding as both an ontological and functional superiority.

Al-Wāḥidī further glosses the term *qānitāt* as exclusively a reference to women who are "obedient to their husbands." Significantly, unlike al-Ṭabarī, he does not mention that there were earlier authorities who understood the term to refer to women who are obedient to God and their husbands. *Nushūz* is defined by him specifically and solely as the wife's "disobedience of [her] husband" and her defiant disagreement with him. Should verbal reprimand followed by abstinence from intercourse with her fail to achieve the desired result, the husband may gently strike her without causing physical harm (*ghayr mubarriḥ*).[36]

Very similar interpretations are recorded by al-Rāzī in the sixth/twelfth century.[37] He too understands the superiority attributed to men over women in both ontological and functional terms, as in al-Wāḥidī's commentary, but the list of reasons why men *qua* men are to be understood as superior to women has grown longer. Thus, in addition to the reasons cited by al-Wāḥidī, al-Rāzī lists, for example, the man's ability to work harder, to write, his horsemanship, and his skill in spear-throwing. Furthermore, he reminds us that through time the prophets and scholars have all been men, as have been political rulers, prayer leaders, callers to prayer, orators, and many others.[38]

This ontological sense of male superiority over the female, in addition to the functional one, now becomes pervasive in the exegetical literature, as affirmed by al-Qurṭubī in the seventh/thirteenth century.[39] Al-Qurṭubī indicates on the authority of unnamed sources that by his time it had become customary to believe in the inherent differences in the natures of men and women that are also complementary so that the nature (*ṭabʿ*) of man is assumed to be defined by "heat and dryness, in which there is force and strength" while the nature of woman is governed by "moistness and cold, in which there is the essence of tenderness and weakness."[40] Like a number of his predecessors, al-Qurṭubī understands the virtuous *qānitāt* to refer specifically to women who obey their husbands while fulfilling the rights of their husbands over them.[41] Unlike the other exegetes surveyed above, al-Qurṭubī references the farewell sermon of Muḥammad in which the Prophet cites Q. 4:34 and reminds his audience that men and women have specific rights in relation to each other. In this version of the farewell speech, Muḥammad refers to "overt wrongdoing" (*fāḥisha mubayyina*) as the reason for banishing women to their beds, followed by non-injurious beating if the first course of action fails to rectify her behaviour. Al-Qurṭubī is careful to point out that this does not refer to adultery, since that would incur the *ḥadd* punishment. According to him, the overall meaning of this part of the farewell speech in regard to the ideal domestic relationship, which serves as commentary on Q. 4:34, is that wives are exhorted not to anger their husbands and that they are to concede to their husbands the right to determine, for example, who visits their household, while husbands are required to feed and clothe them.[42]

In the commentary of the seventh/thirteenth-century exegete al-Bayḍāwī (d. 685/1286), men now possess "perfection of intelligence" (*kamāl al-ʿaql*) and "excellence of deliberation" (*ḥusn al-tadbīr*), on account of which, and many other distinctive traits, they enjoy an unqualified guardianship over women. Significantly, however, the virtuous *qānitāt* are glossed as those who are obedient *to God* while cognizant of the rights their husbands enjoy over them – a commentary that is in striking contrast to that of most of al-Bayḍāwī's predecessors, who showed a marked preference for glossing *qānitāt* as women who owed obedience either exclusively to their husbands or to God and their husbands together.[43]

Ibn Kathīr (d. 774/1373) in the eighth/fourteenth century leaves no doubt that the guardianship men are understood to enjoy over women, based on his reading of Q. 4:34, is one of unassailable authority over every aspect of the latter's existence and conduct. The words he uses – largely unprecedented in comparison with previous exegeses – in describing this aggrandized hierarchical relationship are revealing of the extent to which the marital bond between man and woman has been reconfigured as one of essential domination and subjugation. Thus the man has become the woman's "head" (*raʾīsuhā*); her "elder" (*kabīruhā*), her "ruler/judge" *(al-ḥākim ʿalayhā*), and her "discipliner [*muʾaddibuhā*] if she should stray." He adduces as an authoritative proof-text the solitary report recorded by al-Bukhārī (d. 256/870) in which the Prophet warns that a nation governed by a woman will not prosper. This is a new proof-text that we encounter in Ibn Kathīr's commentary in the context of this verse, which is clearly being deployed to warn against the consequences of letting women get "the upper hand" in any manner or form (not just in the domestic sphere) in relation to men. It is also in his commentary that we see the clearest iteration of the absolute nature of man's superiority over woman by virtue of being male (*fa'l-rajul afḍal min al-marʾa fī nafsih*).[44]

Not surprisingly, Ibn Kathīr glosses the *qānitāt* solely as women who are obedient to their husbands, citing Ibn ʿAbbās "and others" as his source. The nature of this unconditional obedience of wives to their husbands is driven home by the purported *ḥadīth* in which Muḥammad declares, "If I were to command anyone to prostrate himself before another [person], it would be the wife before her husband on account of the rights he enjoys in relation to her." Again, we had not encountered this *ḥadīth* previously as proof-text in the exegetical discussions of Ibn Kathīr's predecessors, which proves to us once again that male authoritarian attitudes toward women in the later period were progressively projected back to the time of the Prophet in the form of *aḥādīth* attributed to him, creating a powerful legitimizing source for such changed sensibilities.[45]

Like his predecessors, Ibn Kathīr expounds further on the various ways in which a wife can be coaxed back into the desired state of obedience; he similarly emphasizes that the last step can only be a gentle and non-pain-inducing beating. Once she has returned to compliance, she cannot be subjected to further discipline or harsh behaviour because that would constitute wrongdoing toward her. Men are explicitly warned against oppressing wives in this manner in the latter part of the verse.[46]

Analysis and Critique of Exegeses of Q. 4:34

The earliest exegetes in our survey, Muqātil ibn Sulaymān and al-Ṭabarī, clearly understand Q. 4:34 to be applicable exclusively in the domestic context, so that the husband enjoys his preferential status by virtue of his role as economic provider. *Qānitāt* is understood by both of them to refer to women who are obedient to God *and* their husbands. Ibn al-Mubārak emerges as the sole authority in both these early exegetical works who tries to promote a highly patriarchal understanding of Q. 4:34. In Muqātil's *tafsīr*, he extrapolates a general divine preference for men over women from this verse, while in al-Ṭabarī's commentary, he is cited as interpreting *qānitāt* as women who are primarily obedient to their husbands. It is telling that al-Ṭabarī expresses his approval of this latter commentary by Ibn al-Mubārak, for it indicates to us that by the early fourth/tenth century, such masculinist interpretations had started to take deep root. Significantly, al-Ṭabarī notes the more egalitarian understanding of a very early authority – the early second/eighth-century pious Successor ʿAṭāʾ ibn Abī Rabāḥ – who notes that *nushūz* applies equally to the husband and wife and was a basic reference to the desire of either party to separate from the other. It is however an interpretation that does not find favour with al-Ṭabarī.

Ibn al-Mubārak's perspective clearly proved to be the more enduring one throughout the vicissitudes of Islamic history. It is evident that by al-Wāḥidī's time in the fifth/eleventh century, male exegetes had made up their minds that a generic male superiority over women is to be assumed on the basis of this verse, rather than a more limited, functional one restricted to the domestic sphere. To this end, al-Wāḥidī compiles a long list of the superior essential attributes that men enjoy *qua* men and the weighty socio-political roles they play that are denied to women. Significantly, and not at all unexpectedly, al-Wāḥidī glosses *qanitāt only* as women who are obedient to their husbands and *nushūz* as applying only to women, ignoring Q. 4:128, where it is mentioned in relation to husbands. Al-Rāzī in the sixth/twelfth century adds even more laudable traits to the list produced by al-Wāḥidī to underscore the male's intrinsic superiority over the female. It is clear that by this time man's superiority over woman is primarily assumed to be ontological and is taken to be self-evident. This conviction is now projected back to the Prophet's time, as we see in the exegesis of al-Qurṭubī, who invokes Muḥammad's farewell speech as a proof-text. Even though that sermon refers to the reciprocal, and potentially equal, rights of wives and husbands, al-Qurṭubī puts a hierarchical spin on it and makes wives subordinate to the will of their husbands in adjudicating household matters in particular.

Although al-Bayḍāwī in the seventh/thirteenth century similarly endorses men's "guardianship" over women, he notably glosses *qānitāt* as a reference to virtuous women who owe their obedience *only to God*, unlike most of his predecessors. His seems to be a lone, dissenting voice in the late medieval period, by which time an overwhelming majority of male exegetes had convinced themselves and their readers that the Arabic root *qnt* in relation to women referred either to obedience on their part to both God and their husbands or exclusively to their husbands, while the same root in relation to men referred to their obedience to God alone.

GOING BACK TO THE BASICS: WOMEN SCHOLARS' REREADING THE QURʾAN

A slim volume published by an American Muslim scholar, Amina Wadud, in 1992 by a little-known Malaysian publisher under the title of *Qur'ān and Woman* quickly gained the recognition it deserved. Written from the perspective of a female scholar of Islam, and reissued by Oxford University Press in 1999, it was the first monograph-length treatment of specifically "the woman question" in Islam's holiest text.[47] Most traditionalist male authors writing on the "woman question" in the modern period adopted a didactic tone, seeking to instruct Muslim women on how to comport themselves properly.[48] When they invoked the Qur'an to discuss normative gendered behaviour, they frequently reproduced the commentaries of the classical exegetes, adding very little that was original to the discussion. Exceptions are sometimes to be found among modernist male thinkers like Muḥammad ʿAbduh and Rashid Riḍā, but their influence was not as extensive as that of the more traditionalist male exegetes. Wadud's work proved to be groundbreaking, not only because she was a female scholar, but also because it insisted on going back to the actual wording of the original Qurʾanic verses – bypassing, as it were, the learned but highly gendered exegeses of the classical male commentators – in order to retrieve a "woman-friendly" perspective. In her book, she comments on her rationale for writing it:

> If the way we view the text has been predominantly articulated on the basis of male experiences and through the male psyche, then visions that respond to the male-center of being would have been considered in greatest detail, over and above any differences, inherent or contrived, in the female-center of experience. The extent to which women are seen as distinct from men, therefore, implies the necessity for a female-centered consideration of the Qur'ān as the only means by which that distinctiveness will be justly considered in the formulas of basic Islamic identity.[49]

Wadud suggests adopting a "hermeneutics of *tawḥīd*," referring to a holistic method of reading the Qur'an that specifically challenges the line-by-line atomistic method of interpretation that was so popular among medieval exegetes (and remains so to this day). If the Qurʾanic claim of establishing a "universal basis for moral guidance" is to be taken seriously, asserts Wadud, then Muslim exegetes must develop a hermeneutical framework that leads to "a systematic rationale for making correlations [among Qurʾanic verses] and [which] sufficiently exemplifies the full impact of Qurʾanic coherence."[50] Universals and particulars must be distinguished from each other; time- and place-bound interpretations must be recognized as such and their limited applicability recognized. Wadud's interpretive venture is thus fundamentally concerned with retrieving an unending "trajectory of social, political, and moral possibilities" that remain consistent with the overall "Qur'anic ethos of equity, justice, and human dignity" across changing historical and socio-political circumstances.[51]

Another prominent feminist scholar, Asma Barlas, similarly emphasizes the development of a new Qur'anic hermeneutics that would effectively challenge and undermine traditional understandings of key Qur'anic verses related to gender and women's roles in society. Barlas says:

> Even though a Qur'ānic hermeneutics cannot by itself put an end to patriarchal, authoritarian, and undemocratic regimes and practices, it nonetheless remains crucial for various reasons. First, hermeneutic and existential questions are ineluctably *connected* [emphasis in text]. As the concept of sexual/textual oppression suggests, there is a relationship between what we read texts to be saying and how we think about and treat real women. This insight, though associated with feminists because of their work on reading and representation, is at the core of revelation albeit in the form of the reverse premise: that there is a relationship between reading [sacred texts] and liberation ... Accordingly, if we wish to ensure Muslim women their rights, we not only need to contest readings of the Qur'ān that justify the abuse and degradation of women, we also need to establish the legitimacy of liberatory readings. Even if such readings do not succeed in effecting a radical change in Muslim societies. It is safe to say that no meaningful change can occur in these societies that does not derive its legitimacy from the Qur'ān's teachings, a lesson secular Muslims everywhere are having to learn to their own detriment.[52]

This emphasis on a holistic reading of the Qur'anic text is a hallmark of modernist and feminist exegeses. By this approach, single verses, especially those that appear to be promoting gender inequity, are read in conjunction with other verses that are thematically and semantically related, allowing for the emergence of other interpretive possibilities. A classic example of this is the term *nushūz*, which, as it occurs in Q. 4:34, was understood exclusively as a reference to a woman's arrogant demeanour and behaviour towards her husband. Only one very early source – ʿAṭāʾ ibn Abī Rabāḥ – is quoted by al-Ṭabarī as understanding *nushūz* to refer to a constellation of negative traits in *both* men and women.

ʿAṭāʾ may have been among the very early feminist readers of the Qurʾan who preferred to read the text cross-referentially, for the Qurʾan does in fact refer to *nushūz* on the part of both men and women. The corresponding verse in regard to men is Q. 4:128, which states, "If a woman fears *nushūz* or rejection [*iʿrāḍ*] from her husband, there is no blame on them if they reach a settlement, and settlement is better, even though people's souls are miserly." Al-Ṭabarī understands *nushūz* on part of the husband to be similar to *nushūz* on the part of the wife – that it is an attitude of haughtiness and pride toward one's spouse and an expression of distaste toward her, whether because of her lack of comeliness, her advancing years, or other reasons. *Iʿrāḍ* consists of turning away from her with his face or withholding certain benefits she is accustomed to receiving from him. In such cases, the couple is exhorted to seek arbitration and reconciliation, which, he comments, is better than separation and/or divorce.[53] It is highly noteworthy that even though the same term is used in both verses and may be understood to imply the same basic meaning in relation to the husband and wife, none of the male exegetes mentioned above referred to Q. 4:128 in connection with Q. 4:34. Instead, they showed a clear preference for explaining the term solely as it occurs in the latter verse to sharply demarcate gendered differences, with the earliest commentators delineating these differences within the domestic sphere, progressing to al-Ṭabarī and his successors, who extrapolated broad ontological differences between the male and the female. The result was a highly patriarchal family, with *nushūz* implying primarily wifely disobedience to her husband, who wielded considerable authority over her physical and emotional well-being. Reading the two verses that contain the term *nushūz* together allows one to retrieve a more egalitarian and reciprocal concept of marital rights and duties. This kind of cross-referential reading has become the hallmark of feminist exegeses that seek thereby to question and revise the more predominant androcentric conceptions of marriage and family.[54]

Feminist exegetes will furthermore argue that a fuller sense of the equal, complementary roles that men and women are expected to assume within an Islamic marriage emerges when other Qurʾanic verses that are relevant to this discussion are brought in. Prominent among them is Q. 2:187, which reads, "[wives] are your garments and you [husbands] are their garments" (with "garments" here a metaphor for mutual comfort and joy and the equal rights shared by wives and husbands vis-à-vis each other in the marital relationship). Another equally relevant verse is Q. 30:21, which states, "And among His signs is this, that He has created for you mates from among yourselves, that you may dwell in tranquility with them; and He has put love and mercy between you."

When we import into this discussion the Qur'anic assertion that men and women enjoy fundamental equal rights as human beings (Q. 33:35) and that they are expected to play complementary roles as partners in establishing a good and just society (Q. 9:71), the patriarchal conceptions of marriage and family, which had spilled over into the socio-economic sphere, are logically rendered untenable within the Islamic milieu.[55] This did not of course prevent some male scholars from promoting the patriarchal model of familial and marital relations as worthy of adoption, as we saw, no doubt because it was in conformity with the prevailing cultural notions and sensibilities of their day.[56]

A few feminist scholars continue to express discomfort, however, with the specific wording of Q. 4:34 and have concluded that the verse either should ultimately give us pause[57] or invite us to reconsider the modernist position that the Qur'an actually undermines the concept of a patriarchal family.[58] I propose that this anxiety is engendered by our inability to take seriously the profound semantic difference between the description of women as *qānitāt* in the verse and the verb *aṭaʿna* (meaning "they [feminine] obey") in the latter part of the verse. The usual conflation of the two lexemes allows for the interpretation that first, women should be obedient to men *in general*, and second, wives should be obedient to their husbands *in general* (as is the case with most of our male exegetes). But this conflation elides the fact that the verse specifically uses the verb *aṭaʿna* only in connection with the *nāshizāt*, who are clearly guilty of some flagrant form of wrongdoing, and not with women in general. If marriage is a partnership, as is certainly indicated in Q. 2:187, and if men and women in general are equal partners in promoting what is good and preventing what is wrong (Q. 9:71), then a wife's failure to uphold her end of marital responsibilities must invite censure, as it would for the husband. In other words, the wife's obedience to her husband in this specific instance is not contingent on her gender but is a consequence of her grievous misconduct, for which she is morally accountable.[59]

Q. 4:34 furthermore indicates that the Qur'an prefers that such instances of marital discord be first resolved by the couple themselves.

The protocol that is outlined for the husband to correct the erring wife's behaviour in such cases is geared toward this end. When these efforts at cajoling the wife into recognizing and amending her errant ways fail, the next verse 4:35 counsels the couple to seek arbitration. Although the imperative *fa-'ḍribū* in Q. 4:34 when understood to mean "strike" or "beat" understandably continues to generate feminist anxiety, we must be willing to consider the potential multiple meanings of this verb, which would accord better with the overall tenor of the Qur'ān, which is otherwise very protective of a woman's rights within a marriage as well as in larger social contexts; the very polyvalence of the lexeme's root invites us to do so. Neglecting to do so would constitute a failure of our moral imagination in this case and an inability to find the "best meaning" from its text, as the Qur'an invites its reader to do.[60]

Husbands described as guilty of *nushūz* in Q. 4:128 are similarly directed to seek arbitration. Wives are not told to directly censure such behavioural infractions on the part of their husbands because of their obvious vulnerability in such situations, especially if these husbands are already abusive toward them. This kind of cross-referential reading of relevant verses allows the non-gendered nature of a human being's moral standing and accountability to emerge from within the Qur'an and allows us to avoid the trap of superimposing culturally mediated notions of gendered hierarchical roles on the language of the Qur'an.[61]

CONCLUSION

My discussion above, based on a diachronic treatment of male exegetical discussions of Qur'anic verses relevant to gender issues, clearly establishes that modern Muslim feminist hermeneutics is predicated on the critical premise that pre-modern exegetical and juridical discourses – often regarded as "canonical" – must be seen as specific products of their time and milieu. This process of historicization allows feminist exegetes to question the implicit "canonicity" of such discourses and to posit instead the argument that the normativity of scriptural interpretation rests on whether or not they conform to the fundamental Qur'anic ethos of justice and equality with respect to gender. As our notions of justice and equality change and evolve, so can our readings of scripture, which is polysemous to begin with; this very polysemy allows for the generation of multiple meanings in variegated contexts. When traditional exegeses fail to meet the criteria of being just and egalitarian, they can be understood to forfeit their so-called canonical status. Instead, "alternative" readings can be generated in variegated historical contexts that align with these criteria, which are deemed indispensable in the Islamic milieu. This perspective continues to be the driving force behind Muslim feminist hermeneutics.

As Margot Badran has stated, Islamic feminism rooted in this kind of hermeneutics has the potential to be more radical than secular feminism, since the former calls for comprehensive equal rights for women in all spheres of life, public and private.[62] The positive results of this new feminist consciousness that takes seriously the Qur'an's proclamation of the equal partnership of men and women in all walks of life is becoming slowly but surely evident.

NOTES

1 Ibn Ḥajar, *Al-Iṣāba*, vol. 8, 262. In other sources, Umm Salama or Asmāʾ bint ʿUmays is mentioned instead.
2 All translations of the Qurʾan are mine, although I have freely consulted published English translations.
3 For one such encounter of a woman chastising the second caliph ʿUmar for unilaterally attempting to impose a ceiling on the value of the bride-gift (*mahr*), see al-Shawkānī, *Fatḥ al-qadīr*, vol. 1, 563; Afsaruddin, *First Muslims*, 40.
4 See, for example, Mernissi, *Veil and the Male Elite*, 51ff.
5 See Afsaruddin, "Early Women Exemplars," 23–48.
6 Ahmed, *Women and Gender*; Marlow, *Hierarchy and Egalitarianism*.
7 Ahmed, *Women and Gender*, 39–124.
8 Stowasser, "The Chapter of Eve," 25–38.
9 Hassan, "'Made from Adam's Rib,'" 124–55; Stowasser, "Chapter of Eve," 28–37.
10 Reda, "Holistic Approaches," 495–506.
11 Al-Hibri, "Study of Islamic Herstory?," 207–19. See also the more recent comprehensive treatment of this verse as well as of Q. 4:34 in Mir-Hosseini, al-Sharmani, and Rumminger (eds.), *Men in Charge?*
12 Muqātil, *Tafsīr*, vol. 2, 181.
13 Al-Ṭabarī, *Jāmiʿ al-bayān*, vol. 6, 415.
14 Al-Wāḥidī, *Al-Wasīṭ*, vol. 2, 509.
15 Al-Qurṭubī, *Jāmiʿ*, vol. 8, 186.

16 Al-Rāzī, *al-Tafsīr al-kabīr*, vol. 6, 101–3.
17 Ibn Kathīr, *Tafsīr*, vol. 2, 353.
18 *Wilāya* is the verbal noun derived from the same verbal root as *awliyā'* ("partners/allies").
19 Riḍā, *Tafsīr*, vol. 10, 471.
20 Ibid.
21 For a recent monograph-length study of this verse, particularly from a legal perspective, see Chaudhry, *Domestic Violence*.
22 Muqātil, *Tafsīr*, vol. 1, 370–1.
23 Al-Ṭabarī, *Jāmi' al-bayān*, vol. 4, 60–1.
24 For a discussion of various interpretations of *qiwāma*, see Omaima Abou-Bakr's excellent chapter "Interpretive Legacy."
25 Al-Ṭabarī, *Jāmi' al-bayān*, vol. 4, 60.
26 Ibid., vol. 4, 62.
27 Ibid., vol. 4, 64.
28 Ibid.
29 Other authorities are cited for similar interpretations; see the full discussion in ibid., vol. 4, 65.
30 See this extensive discussion in ibid., vol. 4, 67–69.
31 Ibid., vol. 4, 69–71.
32 Ibid., vol. 4, 70.
33 Ibid., vol. 4, 71.
34 Ibid.
35 Al-Wāḥidī, *Al-Wasīṭ*, vol. 2, 45.
36 Ibid., vol. 2, 46–7.
37 Al-Rāzī, *Al-Tafsīr*, vol. 4, 70–3.
38 Ibid., vol. 4, 70.
39 Al-Qurṭubī, *Al-Jāmi'*, vol. 5, 161–7.
40 Ibid., vol. 5, 162.
41 Ibid.
42 Ibid., vol. 5, 166.
43 Al-Bayḍāwī, *Tafsīr*, vol. 1, 213.
44 Ibn Kathīr, *Tafsīr*, vol. 1, 465.
45 Ibid., vol. 1, 466.
46 Ibid., vol. 1, 466–7.
47 Wadud, *Qur'an and Woman*.
48 One such example is the Urdu publication *Bihishti Zewar* (Heavenly Ornaments) written by the Indian Deobandi scholar Ashraf 'Ali Thanawi (d. 1943). For a partial translation of this work, see Metcalf, *Perfecting Women*.

49 Wadud, *Qur'an and Woman*, xv.
50 Ibid., xii.
51 Ibid., xii–xiii. See also her subsequent book *Inside the Gender Jihad*, which builds on her first book in pushing forward a hermeneutical schema for emphasizing gender equality in the Qurʾanic context.
52 Barlas, "*Believing Women*."
53 Al-Ṭabarī, *Jāmiʿ al-bayān*, vol. 4, 304ff.
54 See further discussion of *nushūz* by feminist scholars in Mahmoud, "To Beat or Not to Beat," 546–9; see also Chaudhry, *Domestic Violence*, 62–8.
55 Al-Hibri, "Study of Islamic Herstory," 218.
56 This development is well-illustrated by Sadeghi, *Logic of Law Making*.
57 Wadud, *Inside the Gender Jihad*, 200.
58 Hidayatullah, *Feminist Edges,* passim.
59 In her critique of feminist exegeses of Q. 4;34, Hidayatullah misses this fundamental point, which leads her to postulate that the verse as a whole mandates female obedience to males; see her *Feminist Edges,* 162. Her misconstrual of this verse offers us an opportunity to reflect on our own socio-cultural biases and preconceptions about normative gendered roles that allow us to automatically read not just wives' but women's general obedience to men into this verse (as did a majority of the pre-modern male exegetes) – when such obedience in a general sense is not only *not* explicitly stated in this verse but is clearly undermined by the usage of a word (*qānitāt*) that in the Qur'anic milieu signals women's direct obedience to God on an equal footing with that of men. Lexemes derived from the root *qnt* are never used in the Qurʾan to describe in general women's obedience to men or that of humans to other humans. When Q. 4:34 in its latter part switches to the verb *aṭaʿna*, only the *nāshizāt,* that is to say, only specific erring wives are indicated, not women or wives in general.
60 This is emphasized by Barlas, "*Believing Women*," 7, 25–7.
61 Besides the Prophet, the only human beings to whom believing men and women owe their obedience in the Qur'an are the *ulū 'l-amr* (Q. 4:59); obedience in such instances is indicated by the use of verbal derivatives specifically from the root *twʿ*. Since we are not told differently, and since Q. 9:71 describes men and women as being endowed with equal moral agency, the *ulū 'l-amr* would include both men and women who have the requisite qualifications for holding positions of authority. This would explain why so many men were willing to follow Ā'isha, the Prophet's widow, onto the battlefield and obey her commands. Obedience in the Qurʾan, it should be noted, is never blind and unquestioning, nor is obedience due to humans based on their social status and gender; rather,

it is contingent on the proper and righteous behaviour of the principals involved and their attendant moral authority grounded in knowledge and understanding. See my discussion of the term *ulū al-amr* and its various interpretations in "Obedience to Political Authority," 37–60.

62 Badran, *Feminism in Islam*.

REFERENCES

Abou-Bakr, Omaima. "The Interpretive Legacy of Qiwamah as an Exegetical Construct." In *Men in Charge? Rethinking Authority in Muslim Legal Tradition*, ed. Ziba Mir-Hosseini, Mulki al-Sharmani, and Jana Rumminger, 44–64. Oxford: Oneworld, 2015.

Afsaruddin, Asma. "Early Women Exemplars and the Construction of Gendered Space: (Re-)Defining Feminine Moral Excellence." In *Harem Histories: Envisioning Places and Living Spaces*, ed. Marilyn Booth. Durham: Duke University Press, 2010.

– *The First Muslims: History and Memory*. Oxford: Oneworld, 2008.

– "Obedience to Political Authority: An Evolutionary Concept." In *Islamic Democratic Discourse: Theory, Debates, and Directions*, ed. Muqtedar Khan. Lanham: Lexington Books, 2006.

Ahmed, Leila. *Women and Gender in Islam: Historical Roots of a Modern Debate*. New Haven: Yale University Press, 1993.

Badran, Margot. *Feminism in Islam: Secular and Religious Convergences*. Oxford: Oneworld, 2009.

Barlas, Asma. *"Believing Women" in Islam: Unreading Patriarchal Interpretations of the Qur'an*. Austin: University of Texas Press, 2004.

Bayḍāwī, ʿAbd Allāh ibn ʿUmar al-. *Tafsīr al-Bayḍāwī*. Beirut: Dār al-Kutub al-ʿIlmiyya, 1988.

Chaudhry, Ayesha. *Domestic Violence in the Islamic Tradition*. Oxford: Oxford University Press, 2016.

Hassan, Riffat. "'Made from Adam's Rib': The Woman's Creation Question." *Al-Mushir* 27, no. 3 (1985): 124–55.

Hibri, Azizah al-. "A Study of Islamic Herstory?" *Women's Studies International Forum*. Special Issue: *Women and Islam* 5 (1982): 207–19.

Hidayatullah, Aysha. *The Feminist Edges of the Qur'an*. Oxford: Oxford University Press, 2014.

Ibn Ḥajar al-ʿAsqalānī, Shihāb al-Dīn. *Al-Iṣāba fī tamyīz al-ṣaḥāba*. Beirut: Dār Iḥyāʾ al-Turāth al-ʿArabī, n.d.

Ibn Kathīr, Ismāʿīl ibn ʿUmar. *Tafsīr al-Qurʾān al-ʿaẓīm*. Beirut: Dār al-Jīl, 1990.

Mahmoud, Mohamed. "To Beat or Not to Beat: On the Exegetical Dilemmas over Qur'ān, 4:34." *Journal of the American Oriental Society* 126, no. 4 (2006): 537–50.

Marlow, Louise. *Hierarchy and Egalitarianism in Islam*. Cambridge: Cambridge University Press, 2002.

Mernissi, Fatima. *The Veil and the Male Elite: A Feminist Interpretation of Women's Rights in Islam*. Trans. Mary Jo Lakeland. Reading: Addison-Wesley, 1991.

Metcalf, Barbara. *Perfecting Women: Maulana Ashraf Ali Thanawi's Bihishti Zewar*. Berkeley: University of California Press, 1992.

Mir-Hosseini, Ziba, Mulki al-Sharmani, and Jana Rumminger, eds. *Men in Charge? Rethinking Authority in Muslim Legal Tradition*. Oxford: Oneworld, 2015.

Muqātil ibn Sulaymān. *Tafsīr Muqātil ibn Sulaymān*. Cairo: Mu'assasat al-Ḥalabī wa-Shurakā'uh, 1969.

Qurṭubī, Abū 'Abd Allāh Muḥammad ibn Aḥmad al-. *Al-Jāmi' li-aḥkām al-Qur'ān*. Ed. 'Abd al-Razzāq al-Mahdī. Beirut: Dār al-Kitāb al-'Arabī, 2001.

Rāzī, Fakhr al-Dīn al-. *Al-Tafsīr al-kabīr*. Beirut: Dār Iḥyā' al-Turāth al-'Arabī, 1999.

Reda, Nevin. "Holistic Approaches to the Qur'an: A Historical Background," *Religion Compass* 4, no. 8 (2010): 495–506.

Riḍā, Rashīd. *Tafsīr al-manār*. Beirut: Dār al-Kutub al-'Ilmiyya, 1999.

Sadeghi, Behnam. *The Logic of Law Making in Islam: Women and Prayer in the Legal Tradition*. Cambridge: Cambridge University Press, 2013.

Shawkānī, Muḥammad ibn 'Alī al-. *Fatḥ al-qadīr: al-jāmi' bayna fannay al-riwāya wa-'l-dirāya min 'ilm al-tafsīr*. Beirut: Dār al-Ma'rifa, 1996.

Stowasser, Barbara. "The Chapter of Eve." In *Women in the Qur'an, Traditions, and Interpretation*, 25–38. Oxford: Oxford University Press, 1994.

Ṭabarī, Muḥammad ibn Jarīr al-. *Jāmi' al-bayān fī tafsīr al-Qur'ān*. Beirut: Dār al-Kutub al-'Ilmiyya, 1997.

Wadud, Amina. *Inside the Gender Jihad: Women's Reform in Islam*. Oxford: Oneworld, 2006.

– *Qur'an and Woman: Rereading the Sacred Text from a Woman's Perspective*. New York: Oxford University Press, 1999.

Wāḥidī, 'Alī ibn Aḥmad al-. *Al-Wasīṭ fī tafsīr al-Qur'ān*. Ed. 'Ādil Aḥmad 'Abd al-Mawjūd. Beirut: Dār al-Kutub al-'Ilmiyya, 1994.

PART TWO

Figurative Representation: *Ḥadīth* and Biographical Dictionaries

4

How Did Eve Get Married? Two Twelver Shiʿi *Ḥadīth* Reports

Amina Inloes

How did Eve and Adam get married? As is often the case with sacred narrative, accounts of their wedding say more about the world view of the speakers than about Eve and Adam themselves. This chapter explores two structurally similar but thematically different Twelver Shiʿi *aḥādīth* telling the story of the marriage of Eve and Adam. Since, unlike the Qurʾan, *ḥadīth* tend to present Eve and Adam as archetypes of female and male, these *aḥādīth* reflect religious and cultural ideals about the nature and relationship between male and female. While some of these messages are implicit, others are explicit. All in all, these two *aḥādīth* convey conflicting expectations about spousal obedience, male guardianship, and female agency; about the relationship between marriage and slavery; and about the inclusion of women in sacred cosmology – all issues that are still relevant today. Quite a heavy burden to put on Eve's shoulders!

Both *aḥādīth* are taken from Twelver Shiʿi *ḥadīth* collections and are attributed to Imam Jaʿfar al-Ṣādiq (d. 148/765). Twelver Shiʿis consider Imam al-Ṣādiq to be sixth in the line of Imams, or divinely appointed and divinely guided successors to Prophet Muḥammad; he is also a prominent figure in many Sufi orders, and he interacted with founding members of the Sunni juristic schools. In the Twelver Shiʿi tradition, *aḥādīth* from the twelve Imams and Fāṭima al-Zahrāʾ (d. 11/632), the daughter of the Prophet Muḥammad, are accepted due to the belief that they had a perfect understanding of the Prophetic teachings; thus, the Twelver Shiʿi collections include *aḥādīth* that emerged over a period of two hundred years after the Prophet's death (d. 11/632), and in several geographical regions, thereby preserving a variety of snapshots of peoples and cultures across the Muslim empire. (Additionally – as will be seen here – Shiʿi *aḥādīth* can be quite lengthy.) For this reason, Twelver Shiʿi *ḥadīth* can be valuable not only to students of Shiʿism but also to those interested in the religious and cultural diversity of the classical Near East. These two particular *aḥādīth* were selected not only for the sake of contrast but also because they provide lengthy discussions about Eve's marriage. The main goal of this chapter is not to examine the authenticity of these *aḥādīth*, but rather to explore how they, intentionally or not, through being recorded, canonized conflicting ideals regarding gender roles. However, I would like to note from the outset that, due to the thematic disagreement of the *aḥādīth*, at least one of them must be (in whole or in part) inauthentic, since it is unlikely that two such conflicting world views would have issued forth from a single person. Also, while *aḥādīth* are traditionally seen as irreconcilable only if they have clashing content, I would like to put forward the methodological suggestion that *aḥādīth* should also be seen as irreconcilable if they have clashing subtexts, and that re-evaluating *aḥādīth* on the basis of their subtexts can shed new light on *aḥādīth*.

Before discussing these two *aḥādīth*, a few words on canonization and what it means in the Shiʿi tradition are in order. "Canonization" itself as a concept is, of course, situated in the Christian and Latinate tradition and as such may not be a complete match with Islamic texts. Nonetheless, the concept is applied today to Shiʿi *aḥādīth* as with Sunni *aḥādīth*. Unlike in the Sunni tradition, in the Shiʿi tradition there was no major trend of compiling "authentic" (*ṣaḥīḥ*) books of *aḥādīth* – that is to say, *aḥādīth* that meet specific technical standards of authenticity. As a result, there is no Shiʿi equivalent of the Sunni "six books." Nonetheless, four early Shiʿi *ḥadīth* collections acquired a prominent status and are today referred to as the "Four Books." (In fact, they are said to have originally been five books, but one was lost.) The Four Books are *al-Kāfī* (The Sufficient) by Muḥammad ibn Yaʿqūb al-Kulaynī (d. 329/940-41), *Man lā yaḥḍuruh al-faqīh* (He Who Lacks a Jurist) by Shaykh al-Ṣadūq (also known as Ibn Bābāwayh, d. 381/991), and *Tahdhīb al-aḥkām* (Refinement of Laws) and *al-Istibṣār fī mā ikhtulif min al-akhbār* (Insight into Differing Reports) by Muḥammad ibn al-Ḥasan al-Ṭūsī (d. 460/1068). The *aḥādīth* recorded in these books do not all match the technical criteria for "authentic" or *ṣaḥīḥ ḥadīth* with respect to their chains of narration. They are neither the earliest nor the only books of Shiʿi *ḥadīth*;

they simply are given a special position. These books are also selective rather than inclusive, and focus heavily on jurisprudence. The reasons why these books became prominent, and when, is debated; traditionally trained Shiʿi scholars argue that these books gained prominence early on simply due to their style of organization and usefulness, whereas other thinkers have advanced the view that they did not gain this status until the Safavid Empire (1501-1736) and the government sponsorship of Shiʿi scholarship. In any case, they are prominent today and can be treated as a sort of "canon," particularly since part of the impetus behind compiling these books was to sift through a diverse amount of *ḥadīth* material and codify "orthodox" views, especially regarding theology and jurisprudence.[1]

Centuries later, a second significant wave of *ḥadīth* compilation occurred during the Safavid empire. The Safavid empire is best-known for converting Iran to Shiʿism; as a by-product, the rulers encouraged, sponsored, and provided a safe space for Shiʿi scholarship. This resulted in the compilation of mega-collections, the most commonly cited of which is the 110-volume *Biḥār al-anwār al-jāmiʿa li-durar akhbār al-aʾimma al-aṭhār* (The Oceans of Lights: A Compendium of the Pearls of the Narrations of the Pure Imāms), compiled by ʿAllāma Muḥammad Bāqir al-Majlisī (d. 1110/1698). Encyclopaedic in nature, *Biḥār* favours the preservation rather than selective inclusion of *aḥādīth*, and features *aḥādīth* from known books, including the Four Books, as well as from obscure sources; the compiler himself is said to have tasked himself with finding rare manuscripts at risk of destruction.[2] As a result, *Biḥār* includes many Twelver Shiʿi *ḥadīth* in existence today and often functions as a *de facto* reference work, despite not having the quasi-"canonical" status of the Four Books. While al-Majlisī was, in theory, merely replicating the material of earlier scholars, the compilation of his work in a different milieu from the previous works – namely, Safavid Iran, in which Shiʿism was state-sponsored rather than persecuted – does raise the question of whether his socio-cultural environment affected the final product. With respect to questions regarding women in Shiʿism, on the one hand, women in Iran are generally considered to have had a more active public social role than in Muslim-ruled Iraq; it has also been argued that al-Majlisī sought to codify a more restrictive set of values regarding women on the grounds that it was more "Islamic."[3] On the other hand, he was also compiling it during a time in Islamic history when the mediaeval romance had become a popular genre and when stories of human love had become common metaphors in Islamic mystical circles for divine love; this may have influenced his decision to include elaborate narratives such as those celebrating Zulaykha's love for the prophet Yūsuf. In short, while the Four Books represent selectiveness and differentiation, these later collections represent inclusiveness. Due to their broader span of included material, as well as the later time in which these mega-collections were compiled, they almost certainly contain more spurious material; nonetheless, due to their comprehensiveness and ease of use, these collections are frequently consulted and thus enjoy a quasi-canonical status in practice, even if not in theory.

These two *aḥādīth* represent both sets of sources: one is from the Four Books, and one is found only in *Biḥār.* Whether or not one wishes to consider the thematic difference between the *aḥādīth* as indicative of thematic differences between the two sets of sources, the thematic difference between these two *aḥādīth* is particularly compelling since they share the same story framework. Both describe Eve's creation and marriage to Adam. Both versions of the marriage inform the audience how an idealized *sharīʿa* marriage should be solemnized. In both accounts, Adam seeks Eve's hand from Allah, who acts as Eve's male guardian; Allah specifies the *mahr* (bride-price) and performs the marriage. While these facets are not specific to Shiʿism, both *aḥādīth* are distinctly Shiʿi. The two *aḥādīth* do differ on one theological point – that is, whether or not Eve was created from Adam's rib. However, as demonstrated below, this difference is of minimal importance here, since, ironically, the *ḥadīth* that says that Eve was created from Adam's rib is far more equitable to women than the one that says she wasn't. This difference shows that the real issue is not whether Eve was created from Adam's rib, but rather what ramifications one assigns to that belief.

THE FIRST NARRATION: EVE, THE SLAVE-GIRL[4]

The first *ḥadīth* is related from Imām Jaʿfar al-Ṣādiq by Zurāra ibn Aʿyān (d. c. 150/767), a prolific Shiʿi narrator as well as a jurist, exegete, and theologian, who lived and died in Kufa.[5] When reading the *ḥadīth*, two biographical points about Zurāra are noteworthy. First, Zurāra is said to have been the son of a Byzantine Christian monk (alternatively, a Persian) who was captured, brought to Iraq, and sold as a slave to a member of the Shaybān tribe, who taught him the Qurʾan.[6] Zurāra himself is identified as a *mawlā* – freed slave or client of the Shaybān tribe, meaning that while he enjoyed some social protection, it was as a member of the underclass. Second, while Zurāra's father was the one to convert to Islam, it was Zurāra's sister who first adopted Shiʿism; the rest of the family, including Zurāra, followed her.[7] The *ḥadīth* itself was recorded by al-Shaykh al-Ṣadūq, in *Man lā yaḥḍuruh al-faqīh*, a jurisprudential self-help book. Whether or not the *ḥadīth* is authentic (i.e., whether or not Imām al-Ṣādiq actually said it, and whether or not Zurāra actually transmitted it), given the range of dates, it can be inferred that it reflects the cultural and religious ideals of Arab Muslim Iraq between 767 and 991 CE – that is, between the time Zurāra actually lived (if it indeed was transmitted from him and was not merely attributed to him) and the time it was recorded. This latter point is critical, insofar as it supports the hypothesis, popularized in the past few decades, that restrictive ideals toward women became normalized during the ʿAbbāsid era.[8] Conversely, the canonization of this *ḥadīth* in such a prominent collection incidentally led to the canonization of its subtexts about gender as "orthodox"; these subtexts still inform Shiʿi interpretations of *sharīʿa* and portrayals of sacred history.

The first part of the *ḥadīth* reads as follows:

> Abū ʿAbd Allāh [Imām al-Ṣādiq] was asked about Eve's creation. It was said to him, "Some people among us are saying that Allah – the Mighty and Glorious – created Eve from Adam's shortest left rib."
>
> He said, "Glory be to Allah, and far exalted be He above that! Does the person who says this say that Allah – the Blessed and Exalted – did not have the ability to create a wife for Adam from anything other than his rib? He makes a way for a disgraceful theological opponent to argue that one part of Adam married another part of himself – if she was created from his rib! What is wrong with them? May Allah judge between us and them."[9]

Here, the main issue at hand is how Eve was created. By arguing that Eve was *not* created from Adam's rib, the *ḥadīth* is letting the audience know that Muslims in Kufa tended to believe that Eve *was* created from Adam's rib and that some were resistant to letting go of this belief. Other Shiʿi *ḥadīth* do not agree on whether Eve was created from Adam's rib: some say she was, and others say she was created independently, although this one treats the matter polemically. The Qur'an itself does not specify how she was created, and the relevant *āya* (Q. 4:1) can be interpreted to mean that Eve was created *from* Adam, or that Eve was created *of the same type* as Adam. However, perhaps because of this *ḥadīth*, the dominant Shiʿi view tends to be that Eve was not created from Adam's rib, although al-Majlisī and al-Ṣadūq attempted to reconcile these *aḥādīth* by proffering that Eve could have been created from the clay that was left over after Adam was created – hardly a flattering view, but one that does solve the technical problem.[10]

With its legalistic approach, this theological argument has the distinct flavour of classical Islamic scholarship.[11] Theoretical and implausible scenarios are often employed in jurisprudence to define boundaries. Here, the argument is technically correct: Eve could not have been created from Adam, or else the marriage would have, as a boundary condition (marrying yourself), been *ḥarām* (impermissible). By extension, the use of a legalistic approach sends the message that jurisprudence and/or dialectic theology should be the central focus of Islam, as well as the central arbiter of Islamic debates. In essence, one could describe this as a "left-brained *ḥadīth*" – one that is analytic, juristic, and rational. Of course, the question of whether or not the Prophet himself intended Islam to be primarily a legalistic tradition is still debated today.

At this point in the *ḥadīth*, there is a subtle break. In part, this is indicated by the repetition of the speaker (i.e., it is reintroduced by "then he [al-Ṣādiq] said"). While this, in and of itself, is not unusual, the real difference between the first section and the second section is stylistic. While the first section consists of a question and answer followed by a theological argument, the subsequent section consists of a narrative, with an allusion to Genesis and the conflation of marriage with slavery. Therefore, it is possible that the *ḥadīth* is actually comprised of material from two separate sources, which were later appended together as one *ḥadīth*.

In any case, the *ḥadīth* continues with Imām al-Ṣādiq saying:

> When Allah, the Blessed and Exalted, created Adam, peace be upon him, from clay, and ordered the angels to prostrate to him, he cast a slumber over him. Then he fashioned Eve for him, and placed her in the small of his back between his hipbones; this was so that the woman would follow the man. So she began

> to move, and he awoke to her movement. When he awoke, [a voice] called out, "Move away from him!"
>
> When he looked at her, he saw a handsome creation, resembling his own face, except that it was female. He spoke to her, and she spoke back to him in his own language. He asked her, "Who are you?"
>
> She said, "A creation. Allah created me as you see."

The Qurʾan does not say that Allah cast a slumber over Adam before creating Eve; it also does not draw conclusions about the nature of women or from where and how woman was created. However, Genesis 2:21–4 does. Some Muslims might argue that this poses no theological problem, since the Qurʾan and the Hebrew Bible have many commonalities. However, despite these similarities, the *ḥadīth* offers its own take on Genesis. While Genesis 2:24 concludes that, because Eve was created from Adam, "that is why a man leaves his father and mother is united to his wife, and they become one flesh,"[12] here, the conclusion is that the woman follows the man. In fact, given the prevalence of polygyny among the elite in ʿAbbāsid Iraq, it would have been difficult to idealize marriage as the union of "one flesh." Thus, this comes across more as an example of intertextuality; that is, the back-projection of a pre-existing scripture to fit later beliefs and customs. The text also comes across as confused: while the first part of the *ḥadīth* ardently refutes that Eve was created from Adam's rib, this second part takes pains to make her creation as close to that as possible. According to Osman, knowledge is a central component of the position of the human being as the vicegerent of Allah; therefore, women and men are equally bound by the duty to seek knowledge, in order to reach full personhood. When Adam is associated with knowledge, it is because he is symbolic of the human, not specifically the male.[13] To me, these are signs that this second part of this *ḥadīth* comes from a different source than the first part of the *ḥadīth*, although it is enlightening to see how the text attempts to reconcile different types of material under the aegis of "Islamic norms."

The *ḥadīth* then launches into an ʿAbbāsid-style slave-wife barter, and the divine ordination of a gender hierarchy:

> Upon that, Adam, peace be upon him, said, "O Lord! What is this handsome creation? When I am near it and look upon it, it eases my loneliness."

> Allah – the Blessed and Exalted – said, "O Adam! This is my slave-girl, Eve. Do you wish her to be with you, to ease your loneliness and speak to you, and for her to obey your command?"
>
> He said, "Yes! O Lord, praise and thanks be to You as long as I am alive!"
>
> Allah, the Mighty and Glorious, said, "So seek her hand from me. For she is My slave, and she is also good for you as a wife, because of your desires." And Allah, the Mighty and Glorious, cast carnal desires upon him, although He had already taught him knowledge of all things.
>
> He said, "O Lord! I seek her hand in marriage from you. What will be satisfactory to you?" [i.e., as a *mahr*, or bride-price.]
>
> He, the Mighty and Glorious, said, "I will be satisfied if you teach her knowledge of My religion."
>
> He said, "Yes, I will do that for You, O Lord, if You will me to."
>
> He, the Mighty and Glorious, said, "I have willed that. I have now married her to you, so take her to yourself."
>
> So Adam, peace be upon him, told her, "Come to me."
>
> She told him, "No, you come to me."
>
> So Allah, the Mighty and Glorious, ordered Adam to be in charge of her [*yaqūm*]; and, were it not for that, women would go to men and seek their hands in marriage for themselves. This is the story of Eve, blessings be upon her.

What stands out here is the portrayal of Eve as a slave. While in the classical Islamic tradition, the word "slave" (*ʿabd*) is used as a synonym for "human being" to denote the position of the human being as a slave of Allah, the dialogue here suggests that the characterization of Eve as Allah's "slave" is meant in a more earthly sense, particularly since Adam is not also referred to as a slave. Allah acts not only as Eve's male guardian but also as close to being a "merchant," advertising Eve's merits, urging Adam to "buy" her, and offering him a price. It has been argued that the Islamic jurisprudential paradigm of marriage was heavily influenced by the prevalence of marrying slave-girls in Arab Muslim Iraq, to the degree that wifehood began to be seen as parallel to slavery, and husbandhood as ownership, even though neither of these are indicated by the Qur'an.[14] For instance, Kecia Ali writes:

> But slavery was … central to the jurists' conceptual world. In particular, it affected how marriage and gender were thought about. There was a vital relationship between enslavement and femaleness as legal disabilities, and between slave ownership and marriage as legal institutions. Slaves and women were overlapping categories of legally inferior persons constructed against one another and in relation to one another … Slavery was frequently analogized to marriage: both were forms of control or domination exercised by one person over another. The contracting of marriage was parallel to the purchase of a slave, and divorce parallel to freeing a slave.[15]

By treating Eve as a commodity, this *ḥadīth* idealizes that paradigm on a creational level.

Additionally, the portrayal of marriage is overwhelmingly androcentric. The *ḥadīth* only looks at Adam's wishes. Eve's preferences are not considered: Eve exists to serve him and has been pre-programmed to obey him. (This also calls to mind I Corinthians 11:8–9: "For the man is not of the woman; but the woman of the man. Neither was the man created for the woman; but the woman for the man"; however, the evidence of this being an influence seems less strong here.) The marriage is portrayed as a "marriage-for-sex" arrangement – which is also part of the dominant jurisprudential paradigm – and physical desires are ascribed only to the man. Although, in theory, in Shiʿi jurisprudence, a bride must consent to a marriage, not once is Eve asked whether she consents to the marriage or whether she has any opinion about it at all; Adam, however, is extremely enthusiastic. Eve's absence and voicelessness in this *ḥadīth* gives substance and "canonical" status to a cultural norm of marriage being an arrangement contracted between male actors; even though, again, this is not mandated by Shiʿi law, as in Shiʿi law, a virgin girl (or, according to some interpretations, an immature or dependent girl) must usually obtain the permission of her father or paternal grandfather – or, lacking that, a jurist – before marriage but may not be married off without being consulted; the involvement of a male guardian is not required for other women, nor are other relatives given any formal role. Of course, theory and practice often differ; this text is pointing to the latter. The astute reader will also notice that this particular marriage does not involve witnesses; according to Shiʿi law, witnesses for a marriage are recommended but not required. The wedding portrayed in the next *ḥadīth* does include witnesses. That being said, it is particularly curious that the narration concludes with an explanation of why men approach women for marriage, rather than vice versa, given that a number of women offered to marry the Prophet (Q. 33:50).

This *ḥadīth* can also be taken as an implicit exegesis of Q. 4:34 ("Men are guardians (*qawwāmūn*) over women because of how Allah has favoured some over others, and because of what they spend out of their wealth. So the righteous women are humble/obedient [*qānitāt*] ..."). While the word *qānitāt* has been interpreted to mean either "humble toward Allah" or "obedient to a husband," this *ḥadīth* mandates that it is the latter.[16] A broader discussion of whether or not, in the Shiʿi world view, a woman is expected to obey her husband is outside the scope of this chapter. In any case, legalistic discussions centre on a wife's obligation to fulfill her conjugal duties – as, indeed, Eve is expected to do here – as opposed to formally assigning the husband any spiritual or ethical authority.

On a subtler level, this *ḥadīth* presents Adam as the source of knowledge, and Eve as the learner; Eve, here, does not even seem to know her own name. Since Eve – according to this narrative – had just been created, it would be reasonable to assume that Adam did in fact know more than her. However, since this narrative presents itself as a paradigm for male–female relations, it conveys the assumption that knowledge is under the control of men. This particular *ḥadīth* also, incidentally, echoes 1 Corinthians 14:35, which advises women to learn from their husbands. In doing that, it puts forward a psychologically uncomfortable power dynamic whereby a husband controls his wife's awareness of and access to the divine, thereby setting up the man as a sort of demigod. The term "demigod" here is being borrowed from Saʿdiyya Shaikh and Khalid Abou El Fadl, who use it to refer to the tacit assumption that what redeems women is their relationship with their husbands, not with God.[17] The idea that men are the gatekeepers of knowledge recurs in other *aḥādīth*, both Sunni and Shiʿi, but differs from what is related about the practice of the Prophet and the tradition of educated women in classical Islamic civilization. For instance, a *ḥadīth* found in several variants in both Sunni and Shiʿi collections advises men to teach girls Surat al-Nūr but not Surat Yūsuf, not to teach them to read or write, and to confine them to chambers away from the road in order to protect their chastity. Al-Ḥākim al-Naysābūrī, who relates it from ʿĀʾisha, calls this a *ṣaḥīḥ ḥadīth*, although it should be observed that ʿĀʾisha was not unlearned, nor did she confine herself to chambers away from the road.[18] It also differs from the belief that Fāṭima al-Zahrā' had direct access to spiritual knowledge, culminating in her receiving knowledge of the past and future and related subjects from the angels, which was then recorded in *Muṣḥaf Fāṭima* or "the scrolls of Fāṭima."[19]

Although the goal of this section is not to compare this *ḥadīth* with the Qur'an, it is worth examining how it stands up against the Qur'an, thematically. While the first part employs Qur'anic phraseology (such as "Glory be to Allah, and far exalted be He above that [*subḥāna Allāhu wa-ta'ālā 'an dhālika 'uluwwan kabīran*]!" cf. Q. 17:43), the second part diverges from the Qur'an. One of the most obvious differences is that the Qur'an does not use Eve or Adam to convey archetypal messages about the nature of man or woman, or gender roles. Additionally, there is the possibility of adaptation from Genesis (and, perhaps, I Corinthians). On a theological level, the anthropomorphic approach – especially in how the *ḥadīth* implicitly genders Allah by employing Him as Eve's male guardian – is at odds with the Qur'anic portrayal of divine transcendence. Furthermore, while here, Adam stands between Eve and Allah, in the Qur'an (for instance, Q. 4:32 and 33:35), men and women are independently responsible towards Allah, regardless of the piety (or lack thereof) of their spouse.

In her study on women in Shi'i *ḥadīth* and exegesis, Osman also notes three ways in which this *ḥadīth* diverges from the Qur'an. First, it presents lust as being introduced to Adam first, whereas the Qur'an (Q. 7:22) says that Adam and Eve both came to understand their nakedness after they ate from the forbidden tree. Second, it places Adam in the garden first, whereas the Qur'an tells Adam and Eve together to dwell in the garden (Q. 7:19). Third, it conflicts with the interpretation of humanity being created from a "single self" (*nafs wāḥida*) in Q. 4:1 in that it sets up a hierarchy and mandates intrinsic differences between Adam and Eve.[20] This is apart from the fact that none of the above points – such as Allah creating the man to teach the woman, or the woman to follow the man – are indicated by the Qur'an. With these points in mind, it can be said that the second part of the *ḥadīth* does not agree with the Qur'an; and that, by extension, perhaps the cultural norms it is modelling also do not sit well with the Qur'an, even though they persist today.

In sum, this *ḥadīth* sends strong messages – both stated and unstated – about the nature and role of women. It sends the messages that (a) women lack agency, (b) men control knowledge, (c) only men experience physical desires, (d) women must obey their husbands, and (e) marriage, for women, is akin to slavery. It also (f) portrays a gender hierarchy, in which man stands between the woman and the divine, and (g) puts divine sanction on a stylized model of courtship consisting of negotiation between male agents.[21] Since the provenance of this *ḥadīth* situates it in ʿAbbāsid Iraq, it most likely records the customs or ideals popular in that era; and, certainly, it supports the thesis that a strong patriarchy and restrictive attitudes toward women were integrated into Islam during that time.

Lastly, it is worth returning to what is recorded about the life of the primary narrator, Zurāra. While in theory, a *ḥadīth* narrator should report what she or he hears verbatim, without subjecting it to her or his personal views, it can be eye-opening to consider how this *ḥadīth* both fits into and conflicts with his personal circumstances. As a child of a foreign slave, Zurāra might have found the paradigm of slavery natural. He and Eve would have shared something in common – being socially marginalized, and having limited personal agency. As the child of a convert, Zurāra may have felt an implicit pressure to express distinctly Islamic beliefs – in this case, the belief that Eve was not created from a rib. At the same time, as the child of a former Christian monk, it is likely that he would have been exposed to the subtler aspects of the Christian heritage – as, indeed, other Muslims were in the mediaeval Near East. Thus, the integration of Biblical material might have seemed natural. On the other hand, the idea that it was Zurāra's sister who introduced him and his clan to Shiʿism does not fit with the idea that man instructs woman about religion, or that woman follows the man. None of this, necessarily, has any bearing on the authenticity of the *ḥadīth* – which may have had nothing at all to do with him – but it does humanize the text.

THE SECOND NARRATION: EVE AS THE BEARER OF THE PROPHETIC LIGHT[22]

In contrast to the previous *ḥadīth*, which sets up a creational hierarchy between man and woman, this next *ḥadīth* portrays Eve and Adam on a much more equal level. Like the previous one, this *ḥadīth* also comes across as characteristically Shiʿi, for it is flooded with Shiʿi spiritual cosmology, such as descriptions of pre-creation (*ʿālam al-dharr*),[23] the Prophetic light (*nūr Muḥammad*),[24] and the spiritual position of the family of the Prophet. However, it reflects more of an esoteric rather than an earthly view; if the previous *ḥadīth* was "left-brained," this is more "right-brained," in the sense of focusing on the intangible and intuitive or direct knowledge of spiritual realities. It can also be described as Sufi-esque.

This *ḥadīth* is recorded in al-Majlisī's gargantuan *Biḥār al-anwār* and was sourced from an earlier book called *Kitāb al-anwār*, which, in *Popular Culture in Medieval Cairo*, Boaz Shoshan identifies with the *Kitāb al-anwār*, which was circulated in Egypt and attributed to a (possibly fictional) compiler named al-Bakrī; this adds another interesting regional dimension. Shoshan argues that al-Majlisī endorsed *Kitāb al-anwār* because of his emphasis on the concept of the Prophetic light, and notes that some have considered *Kitāb al-anwār* to be the product of a Shiʿi.[25] While al-Majlisī is less forthright about the authorship of *Kitāb al-anwār*, in the first volume of *Biḥār* he indicates that it was approved of by the circle surrounding famous Shiʿi scholar al-Shahīd al-Thānī (Zayn al-Dīn al-ʿAmilī al-Jubaʿī, d. 966/1558), a founding father of later Shiʿi jurisprudence and *ḥadīth* studies.[26] When introducing this *ḥadīth*, al-Majlisī reiterates the link to al-Shahīd al-Thānī and also attributes it to "our shaykhs and forebears." The respect he shows here suggests that, regardless of its authenticity, (a) it was a live tradition, and perhaps one that was circulated as an esoteric tradition among the elite, and (b) it reflected views associated with the jurisprudential elite. This is quite a contrast to the previous *ḥadīth*, which was narrated by someone who did not enjoy the same social privilege. Since al-Shahīd al-Thānī lived in the Levant, and ʿAllāma al-Majlisī lived in Iran, while the *ḥadīth* itself may have originated in Egypt, this *ḥadīth* likely reflects a different set of regional views than the above one, which circulated in Iraq. This possibility does not necessitate fabrication; even the mere decision to transcribe one *ḥadīth* to the exclusion of another implies a tacit judgment that the transcribed text presents the "correct" views.

Since the *ḥadīth* is almost eighty pages long, I will not reproduce it in full here. However, I will include the introductory material to convey the flavour of the text, especially insofar as it differs from the previous *ḥadīth*:

> When Allah willed to create Muḥammad, peace be upon him and his family, He told the angels, "I intend to create a creation which is more excellent and more honourable than all other created things. [I intend] to make him the master of the first

and the last, and to grant him the ability to intercede for them on the Day of Judgment. Were it not for him, the gardens of Heaven would not have been bedecked, nor would the fires of Hell have been lit. So know his position. Honour him for the sake of My honour, and venerate him due to My greatness."

The angels said, "Our God and master! Slaves would never remonstrate to their master. We have heard, and we will obey."

Then, Allah, the Exalted, ordered Jibrā'īl, the angels of the loftiest level, and the bearers of the throne (*'arsh*) to take a handful of the dust from the tomb of the Messenger of Allah, peace be upon him and his family. Allah decreed to create him from that dust, and to lay him to rest in that dust, and to resurrect him from that dust. So they took a handful of that pure dust, which no sinner had yet stepped upon, and the trustworthy Jibrā'īl carried it up [to the heavens] and dipped it in the fountain of Salsabīl, until it shone like a white pearl. Every day, he dipped it into one of the rivers of Paradise and showed it to the angels, its lights shining. The angels would greet it, send salutations upon it, and honour it. Jibrā'īl [also] circled around the rows of angels with it, and whenever they gazed upon it, they said, "Our God and master! If you order us to prostrate [to it], we will prostrate [to it]." The angels had confessed to his [the Prophet's] excellence and honour even before [the time of] Adam, peace be upon him.

When Allah created Adam, peace be upon him, he heard a twittering in his loins, like the twittering of birds, and [heard] glorification [*tasbīḥ*] and sanctification [*taqdīs*] [of the divine]. Adam said, "O Lord! What is this?"

He said, "O Adam! This is the glorification [recited by] Muḥammad – the Arab, the master of the first and last. Happy be he who follows him, and wretched be he who crosses him! Adam, take a covenant with me, and only entrust him [i.e., his unborn self] to the loins of pure men, and the wombs of pure, good, chaste women."

Then Adam, peace be upon him, said, "O Lord! With this descendant, you have amplified my honour, light, resplendence, and dignity."

The light of the Messenger of Allah, peace be upon him and his family, [shone] upon Adam's face like the sun in the heavenly dome of the sky, or the moon on a dark night. It lit up the heavens and the earth, the heavenly pavilions, the throne [*ʿarsh*], and the divine seat [*kursī*].

When Adam, peace be upon him, wanted to lay with Eve, he told her to perfume and purify herself; and he told her, "May Allah grant you this light, and favour you with it, for it is Allah's trust and covenant." [This was] while the light of the Messenger of Allah, peace and blessings be upon him and his family, was still upon his face.

At this point, the *ḥadīth* breaks off and shifts to a lengthy discussion ascribed to ʿAlī ibn Abī Ṭālib about spiritual cosmology (such as the creation of the Tablet, the Pen, the angels, and the throne) and, of course, the creation of the Prophetic light. Here, God creates the otherworldly "infrastructure," such as Paradise and the Tablet – as well as intangible virtues, such as knowledge and forbearance – from the Prophetic light. It situates the Prophet's family above the angels, in that the angels pray for, bless, and acknowledge them. It also demonstrates that the relationship between God and the Prophet is one of love and closeness rather than authority and fear, for God speaks to the Prophet intimately, using expressions such as *ḥabībī* (my beloved). In essence, this section elaborates on the Prophet's authority over and permeation of all creation, as well as the nature of the Prophetic light that is being transmitted through Adam and Eve and ultimately to the Prophet, Fāṭima al-Zahrā, and the Imams. About five pages later, the *ḥadīth* returns to Imām al-Ṣādiq, and backtracks to retell the same story about Eve, with some twists, and then continues.

Nonetheless, the above still conveys subtexts regarding gender – in particular, sexuality and the sacred. For instance, it presents purity as an ideal for both men and women. According to many Shiʿi texts, the prophets and Imāms must be born to forefathers and foremothers who are free from blemishes such as idolatry or adultery; purity is both theological and sexual.[27] The purity assigned to the dust from which the Prophet is created is also ethical, in that the dust had hitherto not been touched by a sinner. This is in contrast to popular perceptions today, in that purity tends to be seen as a feminine virtue, usually a sexual rather than theological virtue. (To put it another way, Muslim women are judged far more often for how they dress than for what they believe.)

Along the same lines, the latter snippet of this excerpt portrays the conjugal relationship in a different light from the previous *ḥadīth*.

In the previous *ḥadīth*, it is treated as an earthly and physical matter; Eve's job, as a wife, is to satisfy Adam's physical desires. Here, however, rather than being treated as a "money for sex" arrangement – which is often how legalistic discussions of it come across – marriage is elevated to the level of a sacrament; in the next section of the *ḥadīth*, even the angels hover about while Adam is consummating their marriage. Additionally, while in the previous *ḥadīth* the narrative impetus was on explaining why woman was created to obey man, here the narrative impetus is on portraying Adam and Eve's humility before Allah and the Prophet; as a result, no gender hierarchy is set up between them. Eve's job here is not simply to service Adam, but rather to participate with him in a sacred act of creation. By elevating the sexual to the sacred, the *ḥadīth* presents man and woman as equals.

Lastly, there is an interesting sub-message in the portion of the *ḥadīth* attributed to ʿAlī ibn Abī Ṭālib (not quoted here). When the Prophetic light is created, Allah veils it with about a page worth of *ḥijābs*. It is not unusual for the word *ḥijāb* to refer to an otherworldly veil – after all, the Qurʾan uses it as such (Q. 7:46) – rather than to a curtain or an item of women's clothing. Also, spiritual veils recur in Shiʿi texts, and Shiʿi shrines tend to include a series of veiled inner sanctums. It is my belief that in the historical Shiʿi consciousness, the conceptualization of the *ḥijāb* as a veil to the sacred blended with the conceptualization of the *ḥijāb* as a garment to protect earthly modesty – even though, today, this usually gets lost in popular discussions about women's clothing. While this has the unfortunate effect of elevating women's seclusion to the point of sanctity, it also offers an alternative route to discussing the *ḥijāb* beyond notions of physical attraction and identity politics.

After the interlude by ʿAlī ibn Abī Ṭālib, the *ḥadīth* reintroduces Imām al-Ṣādiq as the speaker, and continues:

> The *rūḥ* [soul, spirit, divine breath] was in Adam's head for a hundred years, and his chest for a hundred years, and his back for a hundred years, and his thighs for a hundred years, and his shins and feet for a hundred years. When he, peace be upon him, stood upright, Allah ordered the angels to prostrate to him; that was after noon on a Friday. They continued prostrating until the afternoon.
>
> Adam, peace be upon him, heard a twittering in his loins, like the twittering of birds, and [heard] glorification [*tasbīḥ*] and

sanctification [*taqdīs*] [of the divine]. Adam said, "O Lord! What is this?"

Allah said: "O Adam! This is the glorification [recited by] Muḥammad – the Arab, the master of the first and last."

Then Allah, the Blessed and Exalted, created Eve from his curved rib, after He – the Exalted – had put him to sleep. When he awoke, he saw her by his head. He said, "Who are you?"

She said, "I am Eve. Allah created me for you."

He said, "How handsome your form is!"

At this particular juncture, the parallel between this and the previous *ḥadīth* becomes apparent. As in the previous *ḥadīth*, Allah puts Adam to sleep before creating Eve; however, it makes more sense here because Allah is going to create Eve from Adam's rib. The creation of Eve from Adam's rib is more in line with Genesis, and also the prominent Sunni *ḥadīth* that compares women to a bent rib.[28] However, unlike the previous *ḥadīth*, this account does not proceed to draw conclusions about the nature of woman. While Eve does say that she was created for Adam, she at least is aware of her own name, unlike in the above.

It continues with the wedding:

Allah revealed to him, "This is My slave [*ammatī*] Eve, and you are My slave [*ʿabdī*] Adam. I created you two for a realm known as My garden. Hence, both of you, glorify Me and praise Me. O Adam, seek Eve in marriage from me, and give me her *mahr* [bride-price]."

Adam said, "What is her *mahr*, O Lord?"

He said, "That you send blessings upon My beloved Muḥammad, peace and blessings be upon him and his family, ten times."

He said, "O Lord, for this, may praise and gratitude be to you, as long as I live!"

So he married her on that [condition]. The judge [*qāḍī*] was the Truth [*al-ḥaqq*, a name of Allah], Jibrāʾīl was the one who tied the knot [*al-ʿāqid*], the bride was Eve, and the witnesses were the angels.

Like the previous *ḥadīth*, this *ḥadīth* uses the terminology of slavery. However, unlike the previous *ḥadīth*, this one portrays slavery in the classical Islamic sense of being slaves of Allah. Both Eve and Adam are referred to as slaves, and here Eve is not treated as a commodity. While this marriage also involves a *mahr* to be ceded to Allah, the *mahr* here does not present Adam as the gatekeeper of knowledge or set him up as a "demigod" over Eve. Rather than setting up an authority dynamic of the man being in charge of the woman, it sets up an authority dynamic of the man and woman being under the authority of Allah and the Prophet. It is true that, as in the above *ḥadīth*, Eve is also not asked for her consent; however, she at least expresses some inclination toward Adam, and her presence is acknowledged.

Then it continues where the first section ended:

> He went unto her, while the angels were hovering behind Adam, peace be upon him. So Adam, peace be upon him, said, "O Lord, why are the angels standing behind me?"
>
> He said, "So they can gaze upon the light of your descendant Muḥammad, peace and blessings be upon him."
>
> He said, "O Lord, put it [the light] in front of me so that the angels can face me."
>
> So He put it on Adam's forehead [instead of in his loins], and the angels arrayed themselves in rows in front of him. Then Adam, peace be upon him, asked his Lord to put it somewhere where he could see it, so He put the light of Muḥammad (peace and blessings be upon him and his family) on his index finger, the light of ʿAlī (peace be upon him) on his middle finger, the light of Fāṭima (peace be upon her) on the finger next to that, the light of al-Ḥasan (peace be upon him) on his little finger, and the light of al-Ḥusayn (peace be upon him) on his thumb. Their lights were shining like the sun in the dome of the sky, or like the full moon.
>
> When Adam, peace be upon him, wanted to lay with Eve, he told her to perfume and purify herself; and he told her, "O Eve, may Allah grant you this light, and favour you with it, for it is Allah's trust and covenant." [This was] while the light of the Messenger of Allah, peace be upon him and his family, was still on Adam's face. [This continued] until she conceived Shayth (Seth). Then, the angels came to Eve and congratulated her. When she gave birth, she saw the light of the Messenger of Allah, peace be upon him and his family, shining brilliantly on his forehead, and was delighted.

It is here that the transferral of the Prophetic light reaches fruition. Since Eve now bears the Prophetic light, the angels move from honouring Adam to honouring Eve, thus showing that their honour is due to their spiritual link with the Prophet, and not their gender. Like Adam, Eve is also spoken to by the angels. Conception and childbirth are also treated with sanctity. Additionally, beauty is linked to the sacred and treated as something positive, rather than as an un-Islamic ideal or a temptation.

Just as the previous *ḥadīth* came across as an implicit exoteric exegesis of Q. 4:34, this *ḥadīth* comes across as an implicit esoteric exegesis of Q. 7:172 ("And when your Lord will have brought forth their descendants, from the loins of the children of Adam, and made them bear witness against themselves. 'Am I not your Lord?'"). Whether or not the spiritual cosmology presented in this *ḥadīth* is seen as being in accordance with the Qurʾan is largely a matter of one's theological orientation, since Shiʿis – like Muslims in general – hold differing viewpoints about what beliefs about pre-creation are "correct" and which *aḥādīth* about spiritual realities should be accepted or rejected. However, what can be said is that this *ḥadīth* is less anthropomorphic. While Allah still takes the role of Eve's guardian, the *ḥadīth* has a much stronger emphasis on the loftiness of the divine. Additionally, unlike the previous *ḥadīth*, this one does not present Eve and Adam as archetypes for male and female; this is closer to the approach of the Qurʾan.

In sum, this *ḥadīth* also sends messages about the nature and role of women – but the messages are different than in the previous *ḥadīth*. (a) This *ḥadīth* focuses on the equal position of women and men as servants of Allah. (b) There is an essentially equitable relationship between Eve and Adam, with no creational gender hierarchy. (c) The woman participates with man in the unfolding of sacred history. (d) This *ḥadīth* does not conflate marriage with slavery and instead treats slavery as a spiritual condition reflecting the relationship of the human with the divine. (e) It lacks the institutionalized patriarchy of the previous *ḥadīth*, and (f) it does not assign any gender roles. Although it respects the formalities of jurisprudence, it hints that the true focus of Islam should be spiritual or otherworldly. This is despite the fact that – all other material aside – the frame story of Eve's creation and wedding here is essentially the same as in the previous *ḥadīth*. It is similar in content but quite different in ramifications.

CONCLUSION

Both *aḥādīth* tell of how Eve was created and married to Adam. However, they convey completely different world views. The first, which can be attributed with reasonable confidence to ʿAbbāsid Iraq, codifies a strong patriarchy in which woman has no voice, no agency, and no role in sacred history. The second, which is attributed to the Levant and migrated to Iran, does not codify patriarchy. Instead, it involves both man and woman in sacred history and elevates sexuality to the level of the sacred. While the first *ḥadīth* emphasizes a legalistic perspective – and, in practice, reflects the paradigms and world views that became codified as "orthodox" – the second *ḥadīth* emphasizes a spiritual perspective. Between the two texts, the first can be considered more "acceptable" in the formal scholarly tradition, since it is in one of the most prominent Shiʿi source books and models the "correct" form of jurisprudential and theological reasoning, as well as "correct" views about the hierarchy between men and women. Nevertheless, the second text conveys fundamental beliefs about pre-creation, post-creation, and the nature and role of the Prophet, which is the basis for Shiʿi beliefs in the spiritual authority, infallibility, and knowledge of the Imams. That is, without this cosmological underpinning, the Imam would not be able to act as an omniscient narrator to tell us what happened in the beforetime. Thus, both approaches – the legalistic and the spiritual – are authentic to the Shiʿi tradition; yet they yield completely different world views. Placing the *aḥādīth* side by side and examining their subtexts brings these differences to the forefront.

Throughout the Islamic tradition – not just the Shiʿi tradition – there has been a tug of war between the legalistic and the esoteric. Here, the competition between these two approaches suggests that Shiʿis may have disagreed over whether post-Prophetic religious authority should be legalistic or charismatic. It also suggests that early Shiʿis may have disagreed over whose cultural values should be codified as "orthodox." In this case, rather than being the real issue, the question of gender roles would have been a pawn in part of a larger debate, just as, today, the *ḥijāb* is treated as a pawn in the "clash of civilizations."

Today, within the Twelver Shiʿi consciousness, there is an uneasy synthesis between (a) a patriarchal world view, which idealizes male authority and inherent differences between women and men, and (b) the belief that some women, such as Fāṭima al-Zahrāʾ, enjoy a spiritual position and spiritual authority beyond that of most men. Many Twelver Shiʿis resolve this apparent conflict by separating the worldly and the otherworldly. On earth, men are in charge; in other realms (such as pre-creation, dreams, and the afterlife), patriarchy disappears. However, this dichotomy leads to unanswered questions, not only about sacred history but also about how religiously committed women should live today. Must a pious woman situate herself under male authority? Muslim men have never required "permission" from women to exert authority over their faith and decree what God wills from them. So does a woman need "permission" from a man to exert authority over her faith, or is it a God-given right? Reading *ḥadīth* in this manner – that is, with an intent to unravel their subtexts – and critically comparing them not only to the Qur'an but to one another as well, may not answer all the questions, but doing so can at least help us define the questions and carry out more nuanced discussions.

NOTES

1 Al-Fadli, *Introduction to Hadith*, 68–71; Gleave, "Between *Ḥadīth* and *Fiqh*."

2 Jafarian, "The Encyclopaedic Aspect."

3 Matthee, "From the Battlefield," 97–8; Babayan, "Safavid Iran."

4 Al-Ṣadūq, *Man lā yaḥḍuruh al-faqīh*, vol. 3, 380, no. 4336.

5 Modarressi, *Tradition and Survival*, 404–5.

6 Al-Tustarī, *Qāmūs al-rijāl*, vol. 4, 415–16.

7 Al-Fadli, *Introduction to Hadith*, 198.

8 See, for instance, Leila Ahmed, Amina Wadud, and Kecia Ali argue this in *Women and Gender in Islam, Inside the Gender Jihad,* and *Sexual Ethics and Islam*, respectively. See also El Cheikh, *Women, Islam.*

9 Translations from the Arabic are mine.

10 See the discussion of Q. 4:1 in al-Tabatābā'ī, *al-Mizān*; Osman, *Female Personalities*, 17, 27; al-Majlisī, *Biḥār al-anwār*, vol. 11, 100, 116, 218; al-Ṣādūq, *Man lā yaḥḍuruh al-faqīh*, vol. 3, 381.

11 Elsewhere, al-Ṣādūq reiterates this argument to emphasize that Eve could not have been created from Adam's rib; he uses a similar argument to reject the (apparently popular) notion that the date palm was created from Adam, or else Adam would be eating a piece of himself every time he ate a date. Ibid., vol. 4, 327.

12 Biblical translation from the New International Version.

13 Osman, *Female Personalities*, 30–2.

14 Ali discusses the development of this paradigm in *Sexual Ethics and Islam*, 35-53.

15 Ali, *Marriage and Slavery*, 8.

16 Sa'diyya Shaikh shows how the exegesis of this verse developed over time in "Exegetical Violence," 49–73.

17 Ibid., 49–73. Gender hierarchy is a central theme of Wadud's *Inside the Gender Jihad*. El Fadl, *Speaking in God's Name*, 210–14, 218–22.

18 Al-Ḥākim al-Naysābūrī, *Al-Mustadrak 'alā al-ṣaḥīḥayn*, vol. 2, 396; al-Kulaynī, *al-Kāfī*, vol. 5, 516, no. 2; al-Ṣādūq, *Man lā yaḥḍuruh al-faqīh*, vol. 1, 374, no. 1089. This *ḥadīth* obviously communicates the unspoken assumption that men control knowledge for women. It is also in contrast to what is reported about attitudes towards female literacy in the Prophetic era, in that the Prophet is said to have encouraged his wives, and women in general, to learn to read and write.

19 For more on *Muṣḥaf Fāṭima*, see Mahdavirad, *History of Hadith Compilation*, 347–83. For more on the tradition of female scholars in classical Islam, see Nadwī, *al-Muḥaddithāt*.

20 Osman, *Female Personalities*, 22–5.

21 For more on the topic of gender hierarchy, one could see Bauer, *Gender Hierarchy in the Qur'ān*.

22 Al-Majlisī, *Biḥār al-Anwār*, vol. 15, 26–104, no. 48.

23 Amir-Moezzi discusses Shi'i narrations on pre-creation in depth in *The Divine Guide*, 29, 33, 37, 76, 79, 107, 128.

24 On questions of prophetic light and its use in the Islamic sources as passed down to Muḥammad from the earlier Israelite prophets, see Rubin, "Pre-Existence and Light." While the concept of the prophetic light is not limited to Shi'a, and Catherine Bronson says that this narration appears in a non-canonical Sunni text, it has been argued that this idea originated in Shi'ism. In any case, it is a frequently recurring concept in Shi'i texts. Bronson, *Imagining the Primal Woman*, 219–20, citing 'Umāra ibn Wathīma ibn Mūsā in Khoury, *Légendes Prophétiques*, 346–7.

25 Shoshan, *Popular Culture in Medieval Cairo*, 36–8.

26 Al-Majlisī, *Biḥār al-Anwār*, vol. 1, p. 41.

27 See Rubin, "Pre-Existence and Light," 62–119.

28 "A woman is like a rib – if you try to straighten her, you will break her; and if you would benefit from her, benefit from her while she still has crookedness." See al-Bukhārī, *Ṣaḥīḥ al-Bukhārī*, vol. 6, 145; vol. 4, 103.

REFERENCES

Ali, Kecia. *Marriage and Slavery in Early Islam*. Cambridge, MA: Harvard University Press, 2010.

Amir-Moezzi, Mohammad Ali. *The Divine Guide in Early Shi'ism: The Sources of Esotericism in Islam*, Trans. D. Streight. Albany: SUNY Press, 1994.

Babayan, Kathryn. "Safavid Iran: 16th to Mid-18th Century." In *Encyclopedia of Women and Islamic Cultures*, ed. Suad Joseph. http://dx.doi.org/10.1163/1872-5309_ewic_EWICCOM_0012

Bauer, Karen. *Gender Hierarchy in the Qurʾān: Medieval Interpretations, Modern Responses*. New York: Cambridge University Press, 2015.

Bronson, Catherine. "Imagining the Primal Woman: Islamic Selves of Eve." PhD diss., University of Chicago, 2010.

Bukhārī, Muḥammad ibn Ismāʿīl al-. *Ṣaḥīḥ al-Bukhārī*, 9 vols. N.p.: Dār al-Fikr li'l-Tibāʿa wa'l-Nashr wa'l-Tawzīʿ, 1981.

Cheikh, Nadia Maria El. *Women, Islam, and ʿAbbasid Identity*. Cambridge, MA: Harvard University Press, 2015.

Fadl, Khaled Abou El. *Speaking in God's Name*. Oxford: Oneworld, 2003.

Fadli, ʿAbd al-Hadi al-. *Introduction to Hadith*. Trans. Nazmina Virjee. 2nd ed. London, ICAS Press, 2012.

Gleave, Robert. "Between *Ḥadīth* and *Fiqh*: The 'Canonical' Imāmī Collections of *Akhbār*." *Islamic Law and Society* 8, no. 3 (2001): 350–82.

Jafarian, Rasul. "The Encyclopaedic Aspect of *Bihar al-Anwar*." Pts. 1 and 2. *Journal of Shiʿa Islamic Studies* 1, no. 3 (2008): 1–17; no. 4 (2008): 55–69.

Kulaynī, Muḥammad ibn Yaʿqūb al-. *al-Kāfī*. 8 vols. Tehran: Dār al-Kutub al-Islāmiyya, 1367 AH.

Mahdavirad, Muhammad Ali. *History of Hadith Compilation*. Trans. A. Khaleeli. London: ICAS Press, 2017.

Majlisī, Muḥammad Bāqir al-. *Biḥār al-anwār al-jāmiʿa li-durar akhbār al-aʾimma al-aṭhār*. 110 vols. Beirut: Muʾassasat al-Wafāʾ, 1983.

Matthee, Rudi. "From the Battlefield to the Harem: Did Women's Seclusion Increase from Early to Late Safavid Times?" In *New Perspectives of Safavid Iran: Empire and Society*, ed. Colin P. Mitchell, 97–120. New York: Routledge, 2011. Nadwī, Muḥammad Akram. *Al-Muḥaddithāt: The Women Scholars in Islam*. Oxford: Interface, 2007.

Naysābūrī, al-Ḥākim al-. *Al-Mustadrak ʿalā al-ṣaḥīḥayn*. 5 vols. Beirut: Dār al-Maʿrifa, n.d.

Osman, Rawand. *Female Personalities in the Qur'an and Sunna: Examining the Major Sources of Imami Shi'i Islam*. London and New York: Routledge, 2015.

Rubin, Uri. "Pre-Existence and Light – Aspects of the Concept of Nur Muhammad." *Israel Oriental Studies* 5 (1975): 62–119.

Ṣādūq, Muḥammad ibn ʿAlī ibn al-Ḥusayn ibn Bābāwayh al-Qummī al-. *Man lā yaḥḍuruh al-faqīh*. 4 vols. Qum: Jamāʿat al-Mudarrisīn fi al-Ḥawza al-ʿIlmīyya, n.d.

Shaykh, Sa'diyyah. "Exegetical Violence: *Nushūz* in Qur'ānic Gender Ideology." *Journal for Islamic Studies* 17 (1997): 49–73.

Shoshan, Boaz. *Popular Culture in Medieval Cairo*. Cambridge: Cambridge University Press, 1993.

Ṭabāṭabāʾī, al-Sayyid Muḥammad al-Ḥusayn al-. *Al-Mīzān fi tafsīr al-Qurʾān*. 21 vols. Beirut: Muʾassasat al-Āʿlamī li'l-Maṭbūʿāt, 1997.

Tustarī, Muḥammad Taqī al-, *Qāmūs al-rijāl*. 12 vols. Qum: Jamāʿat al-Mudarrisīn, 1419 AH.

Wadud, Amina. *Inside the Gender Jihad: Women's Reform in Islam*. Oxford: Oneworld, 2006.

5

Female Figures, Marginality, and Qur'anic Exegesis in Ibn al-Jawzī's *Ṣifat al-ṣafwa*

Aisha Geissinger

Muḥammad ibn al-Ḥasan ibn ʿAlī ibn Khalaf said: I heard Ibn Malūl – he was an aged man who had seen Dhū al-Nūn al-Miṣrī – say: I asked [Dhū al-Nūn], "Who is the most illustrious person you have ever seen?" He answered, "I have never seen anyone more illustrious than a woman that I saw in Mecca, who is called Fāṭima of Nishapur. She would discourse about the meaning of the Qur'an and I was amazed by it." So, I asked Dhū al-Nūn about her. He responded, "She is one of the friends of God the Mighty the Glorious, and she is my teacher."

Ibn al-Jawzī, *Ṣifat al-ṣafwa*[1]

In classical Muslim sources, those who are memorialized as having interpreted the Qur'an are nearly always (free) males. Yet this striking passage from Abū al-Faraj Ibn al-Jawzī's (510/1126–597/1200) biographical dictionary of pious figures, the *Ṣifat al-ṣafwa* (Characteristics of the Elite),[2] memorializes a woman, Fāṭima of Nishapur (d. 223/838),[3] as someone who expounded on the Qur'an's meaning. This raises the question of how one should understand its portrayal of her, as well as of a few other female figures who interpreted a Qur'anic verse or who quoted one in a way that implied an interpretive stance on their part.

Depictions of such women in the *Ṣifat al-ṣafwa* are few, quite laconic, and presented as historically marginal to the community's understandings of the Qur'an. There are a number of possible ways to approach textual dynamics of this kind, from reading them as reasonably accurate reflections of historical realities, to treating them as obstacles one must try to read behind or through in order to extract every hint that a woman might have engaged in exegetical activity. This chapter adopts the approach that the marginality of these female figures is an important aspect of their portrayal in the *Ṣifat al-ṣafwa* that should not be glossed over. Instead, it ought to be a focus of analysis. This marginality does not reflect an unmediated record of "what really happened," nor is it an incidental or accidental literary feature. Rather, it is textually produced and sustained. Analyzing its literary functions provides insight into a hitherto under-researched aspect of the *Ṣifat al-ṣafwa*,[4] while also further illuminating the ways in which constructions of exegetical authority are gendered in medieval Muslim texts[5] and contributing to ongoing debates about the boundaries of pre-modern Qur'anic exegesis (*tafsīr*).

This chapter carries out a close reading of four of these portrayals, while examining them in relation to the centuries-long literary process of their memorialization and analyzing them with reference to the broader textual structures of remembrance within which they are embedded in the *Ṣifat al-ṣafwa*. As will become apparent, these structures of remembrance have important consequences for how these depictions of female figures interpreting a Qur'anic verse or quoting it in a way that could be perceived as interpretive are shaped as well as framed. The work as a whole constructs particular "looking relations" – that is, ideas regarding who may look at whom, limitations on looking, and how looking relates to social hierarchies and relations of power. Such looking relations are made possible by specific historical, economic, social, and political conditions.[6] As we will see, the looking relations constructed here typically present the gazes of pious Muslim (and usually free) males as textually central, religiously significant, and authoritative unless otherwise indicated. By contrast, while female figures' looking is sometimes depicted in analogous ways, such cases are framed as exceptional. The *Ṣifat al-ṣafwa* also fashions gendered modes of piety, which it differentially associates with the exercise of interpretive authority. These factors, as well as editorial decisions regarding the framing of particular anecdotes, affect the memorialization of these female figures in various ways, and there are significant differences in the textual roles these portrayals perform. Yet the overall result is that even while they are idealized as pious women, the marginality of the words attributed to them as they relate to the community's understandings of the Qur'an is further reinforced.

INTRODUCING IBN AL-JAWZĪ AND THE *ṢIFAT AL-ṢAFWA*

Abū al-Faraj ʿAbd al-Raḥmān ibn ʿAlī ibn Muḥammad ibn al-Jawzī was a prominent and influential Ḥanbalī scholar and preacher in Baghdad, where he was born and also died. A very prolific author, his output includes books on various aspects of the *Ḥadīth*, and historical and biographical works, as well as writings that address an array of legal, pietistic, and admonitory matters and polemical questions. He also wrote several Qur'an commentaries (more on these presently). Ibn al-Jawzī was authorized to give sermons at the palace mosque by the caliph al-Mustanjid (r. 555–566/1160–1170), and by his successor, al-Mustaḍī' (r. 566–574/1171–1179). Through his teaching, preaching, writing, and supervision of several *madrasa*s in Baghdad, Ibn al-Jawzī energetically promoted Ḥanbalī ideas, and condemned the doctrines and practices of Shiʿi groups, as well as those of various Sunni jurists, mystics, and others that he deemed erroneous.[7]

Ibn al-Jawzī's *Ṣifat al-ṣafwa* constitutes but one node in the memorialization of the female figures under discussion here. In his portrayals of them, he quotes Abū ʿAbd al-Raḥmān al-Sulamī (d. 412/1021),[8] seemingly from the latter's biographical dictionary of Sufi women, *Dhikr al-niswa al-mutaʿabbidāt al-ṣūfiyyāt* (Memorial of Female Sufi Devotees).[9] As Rkia Cornell observes, Ibn al-Jawzī incorporated several of al-Sulamī's entries into the *Ṣifat al-ṣafwa* almost verbatim, as well as significant portions of others.[10] Comparing such passages sometimes allows us to make inferences about Ibn al-Jawzī's editorial concerns.[11] Moreover, this process of memorialization continues to some degree on the pages of Majd al-Dīn Ibn al-Athīr's (d. 606/1210)[12] *Al-Mukhtār min manāqib al-akhyār*, a compilation of the biographies of some of the Companions and some pious figures from subsequent generations. This work makes extensive use of the *Ṣifat al-ṣafwa*, copying a number of its biographical entries, while also variously rearranging, shortening, or omitting parts of the text.

As a number of studies have demonstrated, medieval biographical dictionaries and the information they contain need to be read with attention to historical context and to how literary, theological, and other considerations have shaped the presentation of the material.[13] Piety has historically been constructed in varying ways by different Muslim sects and movements. Through his selection and presentation of the materials he opted to include about the prophet

Muḥammad and the early generations in particular, Ibn al-Jawzī sought to (re)affirm and promote a sober, Sunni, *sharīʿa*-compliant approach to piety, over against what he regarded as wrong practices and misinterpretations.[14]

The *Ṣifat al-ṣafwa* contains 1,029 entries dedicated to a slightly larger number of pious figures, including several *jinn* (a type of supernatural being).[15] Some 157 entries are for Companions; 872 memorialize various figures from the generations of the Successors and for several centuries after them. Of the total number of post-Companion entries, 199 are for female figures (one of whom is a *jinn*) with widely varying positions in the social hierarchy, ranging from wealthy noblewomen to insane female slaves engaged in menial labour. While most of the entries for male figures are presented in fairly concrete terms, entries for females by contrast often give few if any biographical details, rarely even providing death dates.[16] One reason for such brevity is Ibn al-Jawzī's expressly stated wish to avoid repeating the same information in more than one entry,[17] and since the entries for male figures precede those of female figures from the same region, the latter often appear ethereal by comparison.[18] But a more salient factor is the inspirational/admonitory function that entries for female figures in particular are intended to play in this text. Much as Sufyān al-Thawrī (d. 161/778)[19] reportedly benefited from the instruction he received from Rābiʿa al-ʿAdawiyya (d. 185/801),[20] so the stories of devout women with their female deficiencies should spur religiously negligent men on to greater efforts, in Ibn al-Jawzī's view.[21] The implication is that such men should be embarrassed to be bested (literally or implicitly) by their inferiors.

ON *TAFSĪR*'S MARGINS

Historical evidence available at present does not appear to suggest that prior to the nineteenth century CE, very many women would have had the opportunity to study Qurʾan commentaries in depth, much less engage in exegesis of their own.[22] But in her pioneering work on ascetic and mystic female figures memorialized by al-Sulamī and Ibn al-Jawzī, Rkia Cornell has drawn attention to several portrayals of female figures interpreting a Qurʾanic verse or quoting it in a way that could be regarded as interpretive.[23] Apparently referring to an anecdote recounted in the *Ṣifat al-ṣafwa* in which the Basran Successor

Ḥafṣa bint Sīrīn (d. after 100/718) quotes a Qur'anic verse, Cornell states that Ibn al-Jawzī "notes her unique ability to interpret the Qur'an."[24] In another example, she describes a saying attributed to Maryam of Basra by al-Sulamī (and following him, Ibn al-Jawzī) as an instance of an "anecdotal form of Qur'an commentary."[25]

Whether or not sayings and anecdotes of this type can be said to constitute *tafsīr* depends in part on how *tafsīr* is defined: as a writing that belongs to the literary genre of Qur'an commentary, as a work that utilizes sources unique to exegetes, as written or oral materials designated by their author(s) as Qur'anic exegesis, or as Qur'anic interpretation in the broadest sense.[26] But for reasons that will become apparent, it is more relevant to ask when, where, why, and by whom such sayings and anecdotes are deemed to be "*tafsīr*" (or not), and to what effect. Categorizing these as examples of *tafsīr* even in the most general sense implies two things: (1) an intention to interpret the Qur'an on the part of their authors, and (2) that they are directly interpretive.[27] However, in the absence of any historical-critical research on these sayings and anecdotes, the "original" authorial intent behind them is unknown, and cannot be presumed without evidence to belong to the female figures portrayed. Moreover, judgments as to whether these sayings and anecdotes are directly interpretive can shift; as will become evident, much depends on how they are edited and framed.

Nonetheless, these sayings and anecdotes can be described as portrayals that have varying relations to *tafsīr*'s margins, and they should be studied as such. Exegetical discourses found in Qur'an commentaries constitute an important part of the backdrop against which an educated medieval reader/audience would have understood these depictions. Also, Ibn al-Jawzī's written output included several Qur'an commentaries. Shams al-Dīn Muḥammad ibn ʿAlī al-Dāwūdī (d. 945/1538) lists these as: *Zād al-masīr* (according to him, it was four volumes in length), *Al-Mughnī* (which he describes as very large in size), and *Tadhkirat al-arīb*.[28] Ibn al-Jawzī states that *Tadhkirat al-arīb fi tafsīr al-gharīb* is a summarized version of another of his Qur'an commentaries, the *Taysīr al-bayān fī ʿilm al-Qurʾān*, and that he penned the *Tadhkirat al-arīb* so that it could be memorized.[29] His familiarity with and active participation in such exegetical discourses informed his own views of the significance of these sayings and anecdotes. Therefore, the analysis that follows relates these portrayals to the relevant passages of Ibn al-Jawzī's *Zād al-masīr fī 'ilm al-tafsīr*, a Qur'an commentary that was intended to present (Sunni) exegesis as it existed in his time so concisely that students could memorize it.[30] In general, it provides an outline of what he regarded as the main interpretive issues associated with each Qur'anic verse.

To some extent, Ibn al-Jawzī seems to have defined his own exegetical activity over against Abū Isḥāq al-Tha'labī's (d. 427/1035) influential Qur'an commentary, *Al-Kashf wa'l-bayān*, which he singled out as an example of the books compiled by non-Arabs containing "far-fetched tales and corrupt ideas."[31] This charge is apparently a reference to certain stories of the prophets recounted in the *Kashf* that Ibn al-Jawzī regarded as theologically problematic. Nonetheless, al-Tha'labī's *Kashf* is among the sources that Ibn al-Jawzī used for his *Zād al-masīr*.[32] While he backhandedly acknowledges this with his assertion that his own Qur'ān commentaries have been cleansed of such erroneous materials,[33] he also seems to hope that his exegetical output will render the *Kashf* superfluous.[34]

Abū al-Ḥasan al-Māwardī (d. 450/1058) is another authority whom Ibn al-Jawzī cites. Therefore, al-Māwardī's *tafsīr*, *Al-Nukat wa'l-'uyūn*,[35] will be utilized below along with al-Tha'labī's *Kashf* in order to obtain a preliminary picture of the "mainstream" Sunni exegesis that Ibn al-Jawzī's *Zād al-masīr* aims to summarize.

INTERPRETIVE AUTHORITY AND GENDER

The closest that the *Ṣifat al-ṣafwa* comes to stating that a woman interpreted the Qur'an is the statement credited to the Egyptian renunciant Dhū al-Nūn (d. 245/860) quoted above, that a teacher of his, Fāṭima of Nishapur, "would discourse about the meaning of the Qur'an, and I was amazed by it."[36] Ibn al-Jawzī does not give any further details about this discoursing of hers. However, al-Sulamī provides an example of it in his rendition of the following exchange:

> When they were together in Jerusalem, Dhū al-Nūn said to her, "Advise me (*'iẓīnī*)."
>
> She said to him, "Hold fast to honesty [*ṣidq*], and strive against yourself in your actions and your words – because God Most High has said, '... when the decision [to fight] has been made, then if they were true to God [*fa-law ṣadaqū 'llāha*] it would be better for them.' (Q. 47:21)"[37]

Here, Fāṭima is commenting on the following two Qur'anic verses:

> Those who believe ask why no sūra has been sent down. Yet when a decisive sūra is sent down, and fighting is mentioned in it, you can see the sick at heart looking at you [Prophet] and visibly fainting at the prospect of death. Better for them would be obedience and fitting words, for when the decision [to fight] has been made, then if they were true to God it would be better for them." (Q. 47:20–1)

These Medinan verses refer to the unwillingness of some believers to fight against the pagans at the dawn of Islam. However, Fāṭima applies them to a significantly different situation. She takes the word *ṣadaqū* from verse 21 and derives from its root another word [*ṣidq*] that is related in meaning. Then she rereads the mention of fighting in battle in verse 20 as a reference to an individual's internal struggle against their desires. In this way, these rather prosaic verses are reframed, so that their import is extended from past events that involved particular people in a specific time and place to the present request for guidance from a student living more than a century and a half later. Sufi authors would later term this interpretive approach *ṭarīq al-fahm* (the way of understanding).[38] That al-Sulamī regarded interpretations ascribed to Fāṭima as insightful enough to merit at least occasional citation in a Qur'an commentary is indicated by his quotation of several of these in his *Ziyādāt ḥaqā'iq al-tafsīr*.[39]

Interestingly, Ibn al-Jawzī also relates this exchange between Fāṭima and Dhū al-Nūn, but without the Qur'anic verse at the end, so that when he requests that she advise him, she only responds, "Hold fast to honesty, and strive against yourself in your actions and your words."[40] Here, al-Sulamī's portrayal of her interpreting a couple of Qur'anic verses is transmuted into simple advice.

A number of female figures with very different positions in the social hierarchy are variously portrayed in the *Ṣifat al-ṣafwa* giving counsel or admonition to relatives[41] or others, as well as convening gatherings for the remembrance of God,[42] speaking to audiences, preaching, or teaching.[43] Such representations play varying textual roles, depending on the context. Some emphasize the depth and sincerity of a female figure's pious transformation.[44] In other cases, such anecdotes temporarily upend the reader's/audience's expectations, ultimately reinforcing certain ideas about the "correct" socio-religious order. Ibn al-Jawzī favourably depicts several early Muslim women telling inspiring tales, exhorting others, or teaching.[45] Yet he also utilizes female figures as symbols of *fitna* (disorder, temptation) in his criticisms of certain features of gatherings presided over by (male) preachers of his own time.[46]

A pious and knowledgeable female preacher thus inverts expectations, and her example can serve admonitory purposes, as illustrated by the entry for an elderly Basran woman who is referred to only as al-Māwardiyya (d. 466/1074). It describes her ascetic worship practices and highly restrained eating habits and then states that "she used to write, and recite [i.e., from the Qur'an] and preach to the women."[47] Her abstemious lifestyle along with her acquisition of at least some text-based religious learning is contrasted with (and thereby reproaches) the male preachers Ibn al-Jawzī exhorts elsewhere to live simply, and to seek knowledge so that they do not mislead audiences.[48] In a similar vein, the knowledge of the Qur'an's meanings imputed to Fāṭima of Nishapur enables her to play an inspirational/admonitory role in the *Ṣifat al-ṣafwa* as a teacher and source of advice. By calling attention to this aspect of her persona, Ibn al-Jawzī presents her in a way that is congruent with the broader themes of the work and amplifies them.

But his discussion of Q. 47:20–1 in his *Zād al-masīr* does not mention the interpretation of it that al-Sulamī's *Dhikr al-niswa* credits to Fāṭima of Nishapur. This is likely because Ibn al-Jawzī did not regard this interpretation as belonging to the Sunni exegetical mainstream, for the following hermeneutical as well as historical reasons: His attitude to Sufi exegesis appears to have been rather complex. While initially, Sunni Qur'an commentators typically rejected mystical approaches to Qur'anic interpretation as lacking authority, al-Thaʿlabī's incorporation of these in his *Kashf* promoted their acceptance within such exegetical circles. Al-Thaʿlabī quotes sayings ascribed to early ascetics, and interpretations of Sufis such as al-Sulamī, while also utilizing much the same interpretive approach in order to generate his own exegeses for many verses.[49] Although Ibn al-Jawzī harshly criticized some Sufi interpretive approaches, such as that of al-Sulamī's *Ḥaqā'iq al-tafsīr*,[50] he was willing to include a quotation attributed to al-Junayd (d. 298/910) from the *Kashf* in his *Zād al-masīr*, as we will see. It seems that al-Thaʿlabī's *Kashf* was too influential to be ignored in a Qur'an commentary intended to summarize Sunni *tafsīr*; furthermore, some such quotations had come to be regarded as part of the core of interpretations that an exegete might elect to cite or allude to.[51]

The interpretation of Q. 47:20–1 that al-Sulamī credits to Fāṭima in his *Dhikr al-niswa*, however, had never been incorporated into this core.[52] It did not deal with any of these verses' linguistic features, nor was it a *ḥadīth* or a view attributed to a well-known exegete. Rather, its authority rested on one woman's reputation for mystical insight. For these reasons, neither its form nor its content accorded with what Ibn al-Jawzī perceived as legitimately interpretive, so there would be little reason for him to quote it, either in his *Zād al-masīr* or in the *Ṣifat al-ṣafwa*.

It is interesting to note that a similar lack of interest in memorializing pious women's involvement in this type of exegesis seems to be evident in his entry for Maymūna, the half-sister of Ibrāhīm al-Khawwāṣ (d. 291/904). Al-Sulamī's entry for Maymūna presents an example of *ṭarīq al-fahm* in an anecdote in which she interprets Q. 9:118 in this manner when advising her brother; the same is true in al-Khaṭīb al-Baghdādī's (d. 463/1071) *Tārīkh Baghdād*. However, Ibn al-Jawzī's entry for her omits this entire exchange.[53] Nor is there any reference to it in his discussion of Q. 9:118 in his *Zād al-maṣīr*.

PIOUS MALE GAZES, AUTHORITY, AND GENDER

> ʿĀṣim al-Aḥwal said: We used to visit Ḥafṣa bint Sīrīn. She had put on her over-garment [*jilbāb*] like this, and veiled her face with it.
>
> So we said to her: "May God have mercy on you! God has said, 'No blame will be attached to older women who are not hoping for marriage, if they take off their garments, without flaunting their charms …' [Q. 24:60] – meaning, the *jilbāb*."
>
> He [ʿĀṣim] said: Then she replied, "Is there anything after that?"
>
> We answered, "'… but it is preferable for them not to do this.'"
>
> And she responded, "This is the evidence for [wearing] the *jilbāb*."[54]

This anecdote (hereafter "the Ḥafṣa's veil anecdote") attributed to ʿĀṣim al-Aḥwal (d. ca. 141/758), a freedman and *ḥadīth* transmitter,[55] presents a group of pious men in Basra who were in the habit of coming to see Ḥafṣa bint Sīrīn, perhaps in order to hear *aḥādīth* or inspiring words.[56] This anecdote places their perceptions at the forefront rather than hers. Through ʿĀṣim's voice and accompanying gesture ("She had put on her over-garment like this"), the reader/audience is shown Ḥafṣa as these men see her – an older woman wearing a *jilbāb* that she has wrapped in such a way that her face is covered. The men disapprove, and confidently correct her by quoting part of Q. 24:60. By so doing, they imply that there is no reason for her to wear a *jilbāb* at her age, much less veil her face. Given her family's slave past,[57] the suggestion is not only that she is being unnecessarily stringent, but as well that she is giving herself airs as she even exceeds what is required of elite freeborn older women.[58]

Thus far, the reader/audience has been primed to perceive Ḥafṣa solely through the men's eyes, to unreflectively adopt the men's gaze and its presumed religious authority as their own. But when she responds by posing a question that indirectly points to their failure to quote the entire verse, the reader/audience begins to suspect that Ḥafṣa knows more than they had assumed. The men reply by reciting its concluding portion, in this way indirectly conceding that their understanding of this verse is partial at best. Finally, Ḥafṣa is granted the last word, and with it she turns the tables on them (as well as on the reader/audience), asserting that its concluding words vindicate her sartorial choice.

In some ways, the Ḥafṣa's veil anecdote evokes *aḥādīth* (often quoted in Sunni *tafsīr* works) that portray the Prophet's wives secluded in their apartments exemplifying or expounding upon "correct" standards of attire and conduct for free and enslaved females alike.[59] But in the process, it vividly portrays the power relations underlying such exegetical discourses. For its part, the *Ṣifat al-ṣafwa* constructs particular looking relations that typically reaffirm the centrality of the gazes of pious Muslim males.

On one hand, religio-legal strictures on men's glances shape their gaze's construction in this work as one that must be disciplined. A pious man should exercise self-restraint so that he does not seek sensual pleasure by staring at any girl or woman to whom he does not have lawful sexual access.[60] Such self-discipline is presented as both a noteworthy aspect of male piety and as a potent symbol of it. At the same time, this pious male gaze is expressed in the exercise of authority over dependents[61] and in giving unsolicited advice or admonition to strangers.[62] In addition, the presumption is that such men are entitled to directly or indirectly view any scenes they might find edifying or inspiring (typically, with little attention paid to what those being observed in this way thought about it).[63] Such viewing could take place by actually looking at the situation in question, or an indirect and mediated view could be obtained through hearing or reading vivid anecdotes. The great majority of these are related on the authority of pious free male witnesses and transmitters. The underlying assumption is usually that such observers possess sufficient knowledge and insight to pass judgment on the religious worth of what they saw, as well as to determine what details and aspects of it should be passed on to others.[64]

These looking relations construct and naturalize the religio-interpretive authority of pious free males in particular. At the same time, they tend to position female figures in relation to males as sources of temptation,[65] or foils, or possibly as providers of inspiration, however unwittingly. As we have seen, some of the anecdotes in the *Ṣifat al-ṣafwa* portray female figures who initially appear to invert existing religious or social hierarchies. The Ḥafṣa's veil anecdote is a vivid example of this dynamic. But as the rhetorical force of such anecdotes turns on their seeming reversal of norms, and their focus is ultimately on the enlightenment of the female figure's male interlocutor(s), in the final analysis they reinforce such hierarchies rather than challenge them. One of the functions of this literary trope is to remind the reader/audience that things might not be quite as they seem, and that one should be humble enough to accept good advice or instruction even from those of lower status.[66]

Women's exercise of what could be termed generative religious authority – having the communally recognized power to generate new interpretations – tends to run against the grain of these broad textual dynamics. The *Ṣifat al-ṣafwa* presents a few such female figures, such as Fāṭima of Nishapur, who possess this; however, these women are also positioned as marginal to its overall construction of female piety.[67] But these textual dynamics are much more amenable to reproductive modes of female religious authority, in which women reproduce already-existing teachings, interpretations, and texts through admonition, teaching, or preaching.

Al-Sulamī has very little to say about Ḥafṣa bint Sīrīn. The entry for her in his *Dhikr al-niswa*, which simply recounts that her dwelling would become miraculously illuminated when she performed her nightly devotions, gives the vague impression of an ethereal, almost otherworldly figure.[68] While Ibn al-Jawzī relates this same anecdote in his (significantly longer and more detailed) entry for her in the *Ṣifat al-ṣafwa*, his placement of the Ḥafṣa's veil anecdote at the beginning of this entry grants her a far more concrete and memorable persona, while also portraying her life as thoroughly imbued with the Qur'an.[69] That she is a Successor was likely a factor in Ibn al-Jawzī's choice to significantly expand her entry in this way. The link between these two aspects of Ḥafṣa's image – her piety, and her deep familiarity with the Qur'an – is clear from the remainder of her entry in the *Ṣifat al-ṣafwa*. She is said to have recited half of the Qur'anic text every night, and in an anecdote related on her authority, she describes how her recitation of some verses eased her grief after her son's death.

It is also asserted that she learned to recite or read the Qur'an by age twelve,[70] and that when her brother Muḥammad did not know how to correctly recite a verse, he would send others to ask her about it. While this implies that Ḥafṣa knew more about their recitation than he did, it is unclear what level of knowledge these statements are intended to imply, as Ibn Sīrīn himself does not appear to have been remembered as an expert Qur'an reciter.[71] Also, such laconic remarks about her are modest indeed when compared to significantly more fulsome representations of some male Qur'an reciters' authority.[72] In any case, as Ibn al-Jawzī does not elect to provide details about it, Ḥafṣa's Qur'an recitation is represented here primarily as an expression of her piety.

Available evidence points to an early dispute about how to interpret Q. 24:60 and 24:31 – "Tell believing women that they should lower their eyes, guard their private parts, and not display their adornments beyond what is apparent" – in relation to each other. Treating the restrictions on free women's dress and conduct in Q. 24:31 as the rule, and 24:60 as specifying an exception, debate focused on which (free) women the latter verse refers to, what types of garments they may put aside, and under what circumstances. Interpretations of this exception's scope ranged from the relatively broad (such as allowing post-menopausal free women to dispense with over-garments and head-coverings in the presence of free men),[73] to the narrowly restrictive, which sought to reduce its practical implications as much as possible.[74] Social hierarchies were among the issues at stake; more permissive interpretations risked attenuating the visual distinction between older free women and female slaves.[75]

The Ḥafṣa's veil anecdote should be understood in light of such debates. It is quoted in the *ḥadīth*-based legal discussion of Q. 24:60 in al-Bayhaqī's (d. 458/1066) *Sunan* as evidence in support of a conservative stance (albeit not the most restrictive one): that while they are not obligated to do so, free post-menopausal women should preferably wear over-garments and face-coverings.[76] With her family's slave past and her all-encompassing *jilbāb*, Ḥafṣa textually embodies the porousness of the socio-legal boundaries differentiating enslaved and free women and, simultaneously, the highly consequential distinctions between them. That this anecdote does not seem to have typically been part of Sunni exegetical discourses on Q. 24:60[77] is likely one reason why it does not appear under this verse in Ibn al-Jawzī's *Zād al-masīr*. However, another factor is its lack of congruence with the interpretation of a leading Ḥanbalī jurist that Ibn al-Jawzī wishes to highlight – that a post-menopausal (free) woman may uncover her face and hands in front of unrelated males.[78]

FRAMING AND EXEGETICAL AUTHORITY

> Aḥmad ibn Abī al-Ḥawārī said: My wife Rābiʿa told me: I visited a sister of mine, a noble woman in Mosul. She said to me, "Do you know the meaning of His saying, 'except the one who comes before God with a heart (that is) *salīm*' (Q. 26:89)?"
>
> [Rābiʿa] said: I answered, "No."
>
> She replied, "The heart that is *salīm* is one that meets God, the Mighty and Glorious, while there is nothing in it except God, the Mighty and Glorious."
>
> Aḥmad said: I recounted this to Abū Sulaymān and he said, "This is not the speech of the female ascetic; this is the speech of the prophets."[79]

Significantly, this exchange (hereafter "the *rāhiba* anecdote") between two pious women, Rābiʿa bint Ismāʿīl[80] and an unnamed female ascetic (*rāhiba*) about the meaning of a word in Q. 26:89 is positioned between speech credited to two male renunciants. First, Aḥmad ibn Abī al-Ḥawārī (d. 230/844–45)[81] recounts this brief discussion in what we are told are his wife's words. That Aḥmad chooses to relate it could be taken to imply his approval of the female ascetic's interpretation; any doubt that he agrees with it is removed when he further states that when he told his teacher Abū Sulaymān al-Dārānī (d. 215/830)[82] about it, the latter endorsed it as akin to words that had been uttered by the prophets.

Here, this female ascetic is portrayed as interpreting a Qur'anic verse, and as doing so in a way that deeply impresses two prominent male renunciants. Yet, as this anecdote is the sum total of the information provided about this anonymous female figure in the *Ṣifat al-ṣafwa*, it is unclear whether the reader/audience is to infer that she has extensive knowledge of either the Qurʾan or its interpretation. In the absence of such details, the only basis provided for the reader/audience to evaluate her interpretation is its reception by Ibn Abī al-Ḥawārī and al-Dārānī. As a result, she seems much less concrete in comparison to the two men, who are named, and indeed are well-known. Such framing has the effect of highlighting the men's interpretive authority, while marginalizing that of the female ascetic by default.

A comparison between this entry and the entry in al-Sulamī's *Dhikr al-niswa* for "Ḥukayma/Ḥakīma [meaning "wise woman"][83] of Damascus, one of the noble women of Syria,"[84] provides a particularly pointed illustration of the difference that framing and editorial decisions about what to include can make. Al-Sulamī's entry foregrounds this wise woman's religious authority as well as the bond between her and Rābiʿa with its opening statement that the former was the latter's teacher and her companion. The setting he provides for the interchange about Q. 26:89 – that the wise woman is reciting the Qurʾan from a codex when Rābiʿa comes to see her – portrays the former as literate, while also implying that she is knowledgeable about the written Qurʾanic text (and likely also wealthy, if one infers that this is her personal copy).

Moreover, al-Sulamī presents the wise woman's interpretation of this Qurʾanic verse as part of her cuttingly ironic criticism of Ibn Abī al-Ḥawārī's decision to marry an additional wife, in which she rhetorically asks how the heart of someone known for his intellect (*ʿaql*) could be distracted from God by two wives. As a well-known *ḥadīth* presents women as deficient in *ʿaql* (intellect) as compared to men,[85] this question of hers inverts the expected for medieval readers/audiences. In this context, Abū Sulaymān al-Dārānī's endorsement of her interpretation of Q. 26:89 (which al-Sulamī renders as "in thirty years I have not heard speech better than this") appears to connote that he too agrees that Aḥmad is not acting wisely. The entry concludes with Rābiʿa moved to ecstasy by the wise woman's interpretation of the verse.

Al-Sulamī's version of this story features two teacher/student pairings, a female one (the wise woman and Rābiʿa) and a male one (Ibn Abī 'l-Ḥawārī and al-Dārānī). However, as the interpretation of Q. 26:89 is depicted as taking place as the wise woman instructs Rābiʿa, it is the female teacher/student pair that is the focus, while the male pair plays a satellite role. Al-Sulamī portrays both women in a significantly more authoritative light than Ibn al-Jawzī. Ibn Abī al-Ḥawārī's authority is depicted here through his humility, as he recounts an anecdote that criticizes him. However, the version recounted by Ibn al-Jawzī removes the implied criticism of Rābiʿa's husband's polygamy in favour of a more general and more directly exegetical focus.

In his discussion of Q. 26:89 in his *Zād al-masīr*, Ibn al-Jawzī lists six possible interpretations of a heart that is *salīm*: free from polytheism (*shirk*); free from doubt; sound; stung from the fear of God (this is credited to al-Junayd); free of distraction from wealth and offspring; or, finally, free from blameworthy innovation (*bidʿa*) and reliant on the *sunna*. While he states that the latter view is recounted by al-Thaʿlabī,[86] the entire list is taken from the *Kashf*, though with some alteration in the order.[87] While he seems to regard the interpretive possibilities here as fairly capacious, and the *rāhiba* anecdote is thematically congruent with several of the views listed by al-Māwardī (purity, sincerity),[88] Ibn al-Jawzī nonetheless does not elect to quote it.

GENDERED CONSTRUCTIONS OF PIETY AND THE QURʾAN

> ʿAbd al-ʿAzīz ibn ʿUmayr said: The devout worshipper, Maryam of Basra, stood [in prayer] at the beginning of the night and she said, "'God is subtle towards his servants' (Q. 42:19)." Then, she repeated it until dawn.
>
> And Maryam said, "I have not been worried about [my] livelihood, nor have I worn myself out seeking it since I heard that God the Glorious and Mighty says, 'In the heaven is your sustenance, and all that you are promised' (Q. 51:22)."[89]

The very brief entry for Maryam of Basra in the *Ṣifat al-ṣafwa* begins by tersely stating that she used to serve Rābiʿa al-ʿAdawiyya. Then it says that she would enter a state of ecstasy whenever she listened to a discourse about love and that she died when attending a gathering at which the speaker was discussing this topic. It concludes with this quotation. (This entry is almost identical to the one for her in al-Sulamī's *Dhikr al-niswa*; however, the latter also states that Maryam used to discourse on the subject of love.)[90]

While the first and second parts of this quotation from Ibn al-Jawzī might at first seem to have little to do with each other, his readers/audiences would generally know that Q. 42:19 continues: "He provides for whoever He will; He is the Powerful, the Almighty," and that the verse following it warns that one should wish for prosperity in the next life rather than in this world.[91] Both parts of the quotation thus deal with the theme of divine provision – and, depending on how the phrase "in the heaven" in Q. 51:22 is interpreted, possibly also with the notion that the next life has greater importance than life in this world. Not only are the two halves of this quotation thematically linked, but its first half refers to ritual actions (night prayers, prayer at dawn), which are described in verses preceding Q. 51:22:

> The righteous will be in gardens with [flowing] springs
> They will receive their Lord's gifts because of the good they did before
> Sleeping only little at night
> Praying at dawn for God's forgiveness (Q. 51:15–18)

Furthermore, the association of the theme of divine provision with a woman named Maryam who is a devoted worshipper evokes Qur'anic verses that describe Mary the mother of Jesus receiving divinely given sustenance, much to the amazement of her earthly guardian, Zachariah (Q. 3:37), and being instructed by angels to be assiduous in prayer (Q. 3:42–3). Thus, the entry for Maryam of Basra in the *Ṣifat al-ṣafwa* presents the reader/audience with a construction of piety that is thoroughly imbued with the Qur'an at the levels of myth as well as ritual. It addresses a doctrinal issue and also presents a gendered model of ritual practice that is textually oriented – yet one that does not necessarily presuppose much familiarity with the Qur'an, much less the ability to access it in written form.

The words attributed to Maryam regarding Q. 51:22 (hereafter "the livelihood saying"), when recounted by al-Sulamī in his *Dhikr al-niswa*, are intended to justify the Sufi practice of reliance on God (*tawakkul*) by providing Qur'anic support for it, as Rkia Cornell points out.[92] For his part, Ibn al-Jawzī objects to what he regards as misinterpretations of *tawakkul*, which he undertakes to correct in his *Ṣifat al-ṣafwa*.[93] The theme of the person whose piety is expressed through reliance on God is a literary *topos* in this work of his. Many anecdotes depict renunciants who elect to live in poverty and who when questioned about this maintain that they depend on God alone. A number of these feature pious women. In some of these tales, when men attempt to arrange financial help for impoverished women, or to give them charity, these female figures sharply reject this as unjustified interference in their affairs.[94] These dramatic depictions of women who shun the worldly comforts that benevolent men wish to bestow upon them invert the trope in which female figures personify worldly desires and temptations.

In the *Ṣifat al-ṣafwa*, the Qur'an functions as a vehicle for developing or demonstrating a person's piety in a number of ways. The livelihood saying is but one example of an anecdote in which a pious person is so deeply moved when they hear a particular Qur'anic verse or verses recited that they swiftly proceed to put its words into action.[95] In some tales, the devout faint or even die as they listen to the Qur'an being recited.[96] Also, numerous entries describe people performing long prayers during the day or standing in prayer throughout the night.[97] While *ṣalāt* requires the recitation of the opening chapter of the Qur'an and some other Qur'anic verses, and could involve much longer portions, [98] the number of suras or verses recited might be quite minimal.

The most common way by far that female piety is linked to the Qur'an in the *Ṣifat al-ṣafwa* is through *ṣalāt*. This ritual is presented as common to pious figures from a wide range of social locations – from the elite urban free male scholar who has expert knowledge of the technical minutiae of the Qur'an's various recitations, to the socially marginal and illiterate female slave who may have memorized a few very short suras. In these depictions, such hierarchies are paradoxically both relativized and upheld. While there is little doubt as to whose ritual performance would likely be deemed superior from a ritual-legal perspective, this is not necessarily the case when the worshipper's sincerity is considered. Much the same can be said about fluent and lengthy Qur'anic recitation by a named male authority (as opposed to an unnamed woman's short, slow, and – the reader might presume – less skilled recitation).[99] But the message for the reader/audience is admonitory. It is not intended to fundamentally call into question gendered hierarchies of access to textual authority – and in the end, it cements such hierarchies by constructing female piety as most typically linked to ritual practices that do not presuppose much if any formal learning or access to written texts.

In his *Zād al-masīr*, Ibn al-Jawzī notes that the sustenance in the heavens mentioned in Q. 51:22 has been variously held to mean precipitation (which he states is the majority view) or Paradise, while "and all that you are promised" could mean good and evil, or (again) Paradise.[100] In so doing, he summarizes the mainstream exegetical discourse on this verse, which neither includes the livelihood saying nor has much space for it,[101] which is probably one reason why he too does not quote it in this context.

CONCLUSION

The *Ṣifat al-ṣafwa* contains several portrayals of female figures interpreting a Qurʾanic verse or quoting it in a manner that could be thought to imply an interpretive stance. Ibn al-Jawzī apparently did not regard these anecdotes and sayings as belonging to the Sunni exegetical mainstream. In the examples examined above, it seems that this reflects the historical situation, as they do not appear to have been incorporated into the core of interpretations that Qurʾan commentators in his day would typically quote or allude to. That he did not opt to include any of them in his *Zād al-masīr* suggests that he did not think they ought to become part of this core either. While typical educated medieval readers/audiences of the *Ṣifat al-ṣafwa* often would have understood these anecdotes and sayings in relation to the exegetical discourses associated with the Qurʾanic verses that they comment upon or quote (and Ibn al-Jawzī certainly did), they are intended to serve admonitory and inspirational rather than interpretive purposes in that work.

Within the *Ṣifat al-ṣafwa*, these sayings and anecdotes are embedded in a broader discourse of memorialization that constructs them as marginal on multiple levels. The looking relations of the text most usually affirm the centrality of the gaze of the pious free elite Sunni Muslim male, with the examples of pious figures from the past chiefly presented so as to edify, admonish, and inspire this imagined typical reader/audience. This focus was in some ways hospitable to depictions of female figures exercising certain types of religious authority, in part because these could serve admonitory purposes through their momentary reversals of readers'/audiences' expectations. However, these textual dynamics are more congruent with portrayals of reproductive rather than generative modes of female authority. The *Ṣifat al-ṣafwa* depicts many female figures who set good examples in their own devotional practice, a number who exhort others to act righteously, and some who preach or teach. But perhaps not surprisingly, representations of female figures who have any degree of interpretive authority are very few in number, and details are rarely provided about their knowledge of the Qur'an or its interpretations.

Ibn al-Jawzī represents these latter portrayals of female figures in varying ways. He enhances the image of Ḥafṣa bint Sīrīn by incorporating the Ḥafṣa's veil anecdote into her entry, as well as by imputing knowledge of Qur'anic recitation to her. Yet he downplays Fāṭima of Nishapur's discoursing on the meaning of the Qur'an, as well as the anonymous female ascetic's interpretive authority. Such editorial choices seem to have been informed in part by certain theological factors, such as a wish to amplify a Successor's image while presenting her piety as more textually oriented, as well as by his opposition to some mystical exegetical approaches. But his construction of female piety and the admonitory and inspirational focus of this work also apparently played an important role in the shaping and framing of these portrayals as highly exceptional and in the end marginal, both to models of female piety as well as to the community's understandings of the Qur'an.

NOTES

A version of this chapter was presented in November 2014 at the American Academy of Religion Annual Conference in San Diego, CA; I would like to thank those present for their helpful feedback. Thanks also go to Laury Silvers for reading and commenting on an earlier draft of it, and Walid Saleh for assistance with interpreting several passages. Any errors of fact or interpretation are my own.

1 Ibn al-Jawzī, *Ṣifat al-ṣafwa*, entry #688. As this work circulates in a number of editions that have differing pagination, references to the *Ṣifat al-ṣafwa* will only provide the entry number. While most of my translations closely follow Rkia Cornell's in her *Early Sufi Women*, I have adjusted them at certain points, some of which involve minor divergences between the Arabic text provided in her book and this particular edition of the *Ṣifat al-ṣafwa*, which is a critical one.

2 Some classical sources render the title as *Ṣafwat al-ṣafwa* (The Elite of the Elite); see Melchert, "Before Ṣūfiyyāt," 117n4. However, as it is most commonly known today as the *Ṣifat al-ṣafwa* (Characteristics of the Elite), it is this latter version of the title that will be used in this study.

3 A female renunciant originally from Khorasan; Bāyazīd al-Bastāmī (d. 234/848 or 261/875) also reportedly attested to the scope of her

mystical knowledge: Cornell, *Early Sufi Women*, 20, 142–5. For more on her, see below.

4 Several studies have examined aspects of the female figures in the *Ṣifat al-ṣafwa*; see Roded, *Women*, 81, 91–113; Silvers, "Early Pious," 24–52; Melchert, "Before Ṣūfiyyāt." Cornell also translates some of the entries for female figures, and in her discussion of a number of their aspects calls attention to several anecdotes that she reads as examples of women interpreting the Qurʾān; for more on this, see below.

5 For gender and exegetical authority, see Geissinger, *Gender*.

6 For this term, which is from film studies, see Kaplan, *Looking for the Other*, 6–7. While there are obviously significant differences between films and medieval writings such as the *Ṣifat al-ṣafwa*, some of the issues dealt with in film studies suggest possible productive avenues of inquiry into texts. For more on the textual functions of male gazes in several different genres of classical Muslim writing, see, for example, Malti-Douglas, *Woman's Body*, 35, 43–4; Geissinger, *Gender*, 207–47.

7 See al-Dhahabī, *Tārīkh al-Islām*, 287–304, years 591–600 AH; Laoust, "Ibn al-Djawzī," *EI*².

8 He was a Sufi Shāfiʿī scholar from Nishapur whose prolific writings included a Qurʾān commentary, *Ḥaqāʾiq al-tafsīr*; see al-Dhahabī, *Tārīkh*, 304–7, years 411–420 AH; al-Dāwūdi, *Ṭabaqāt*, 394–5. For more on the *Ḥaqāʾiq*, see below. Al-Sulamī also wrote an appendix to it, the *Ziyādat ḥaqāʾiq al-tafsīr*.

9 For the question of whether it was "originally" a separate work, or part of al-Sulamī's *Tārīkh al-ṣūfiyya*, see Melchert, "Before Ṣūfiyyāt," 118. My references below to "al-Sulamī's *Dhikr al-niswa*" should not be understood as taking a stance on this issue, but as an expression of convenience.

10 Cornell, *Early Sufi Women*, 43. Some examples will be discussed below.

11 The manuscript of al-Sulamī's *Dhikr al-niswa* that Rkia Cornell used for her edition and translation of it is dated 474/1081, only sixty years after al-Sulamī's death: Cornell, *Early Sufi Women*, 44. However, as we do not know what recension(s) of this work Ibn al-Jawzī used or how it/they compare to this manuscript, it is not always clear if he is excluding material or if he might simply be quoting from the text as he had it. Other relevant primary sources have been used whenever possible to clarify which is more likely. Another possibility is that such divergences could result from scribal or printing errors in the *Ṣifat al-ṣafwa*. In order to reduce the likelihood of this affecting the results, I used a critical edition, and also checked the wording of key passages against a critical edition of Ibn al-Athīr al-Jazarī's *Al-Mukhtār*.

12 A Shāfiʿī scholar and author who spent much of his life in Mosul; his writings include a Qur'ān commentary; see al-Dhahabī, *Tārīkh*, 225–8, years 601–10 AH; al-Dāwūdī, *Ṭabaqāt*, 503–4. This commentary seems to be lost; see Saleh, *Formation*, 206.

13 For a discussion of these issues, see, for example, Cooperson, "Classical Arabic Biography," 177–87.

14 While this dynamic raises historical questions about the origins of certain details in the entries, as well as how such theological considerations may have affected their shaping, these are beyond the scope of this study. In what follows, the entries will be read as literary texts.

15 The Qur'an presents the *jinn* as beings created of smokeless fire who have certain kinds of supernatural powers, but whose existence is parallel to those of humans in some ways, such as in their ability to choose to be good or evil. At times, the faith of believing *jinn* serves as a reproach to disbelievers; see, for example, Q. 72 ("The Jinn").

16 Roded notes that only five entries for females give a death date: *Women*, 94.

17 Ibn al-Jawzī, *Ṣifat*, 1:21.

18 Roded, *Women*, 91, 93.

19 He was a jurist, *ḥadīth* scholar, and exegete; see Ibn al-Jawzī, *Ṣifat*, #443; al-Dāwūdī, *Ṭabaqāt* 135–7.

20 Ibn al-Jawzī provides a lengthy entry for Rābiʿa al-ʿAdawiyya (d. 185/801), this most famous female renunciant: *Ṣifat*, #588. The scholarship on her is voluminous; for the evolution of her image in Sufi sources, see Karamustafa, *Sufism*, 3–4; Cornell, *Early Sufi Women*, esp. 59–63, 74–81.

21 "*wa-maʿlūm anna dhikr al-ʿābidāt maʿa quṣūr al-unūthiyya yūthib al-muqassir min al-dhukūr, fa-qad kāna Sufyān al-Thawrī yantafiʿ bi-Rābiʿa wa-yataʾaddab bi-kalāmihā*" (It is well known that the mention of female worshippers despite their female deficiencies will spur on the deficient from among the males, for Sufyān al-Thawrī used to benefit from Rābiʿa, and allowed himself to be guided by her words.) Ibn al-Jawzī, *Ṣifat*, 1:31.

22 For several medieval Muslim women who are reported to have studied and/or transmitted particular exegetical works, see Geissinger, *Gender*, 248–50, 267–73.

23 Due to space constraints, only a couple of these instances will be discussed here.

24 Cornell, *Early Sufi Women*, 62. For more on this anecdote, see below.

25 Ibid., 84n24. If Maryam of Basra is a historical person, she would have lived in the second/eighth century. This anecdote is discussed below.

26 For a recent overview of debates about the boundaries of *tafsīr*, see Pink and Görke, "Introduction," 3–10.

27 For direct ("x means y") as opposed to secondary or adjacent interpretation, see Saleh, *The Formation*, 195.
28 Al-Dāwūdī, *Ṭabaqāt*, 192.
29 See Ibn al-Jawzī, *Nawāsikh al-Qurʾān*, 81.
30 For a translation of his introduction to *Zād al-masīr*, see McAuliffe, "Ibn al-Jawzī's Exegetical Propaedeutic." For some aspects of his hermeneutics, see McAuliffe, "The Tasks and Traditions," 181–8.
31 Ibn al-Jawzī, *Kitāb al-Quṣṣāṣ*, 103. For al-Thaʿlabī's hermeneutics and the reception of the *Kashf*, see Saleh, *Formation*.
32 Geissinger, *Gender*, 20 n. 84.
33 Ibn al-Jawzī, *Kitāb al-Quṣṣāṣ*, 145–6. The implication seems to be that while using al-Thaʿlabī as a source he was careful not to incorporate any questionable materials.
34 Ibid., 146.
35 He was a Shāfiʿī scholar, whose writings include books on *fiqh* and politics, as well as a Qurʾān commentary (al-Dāwūdī, *Ṭabaqāt*, 292–3). His commentary is based on al-Ṭabarī's *tafsīr*.
36 "*wa-kānat tatakallam fī fahm al-Qurʾān wa-taʿajjabtu minhā*": Ibn al-Jawzī, *Ṣifat* #688. Ibn al-Athīr has almost identical wording: *Al-Mukhtār* 3:228.
37 Cornell, *Early Sufi Women*, 144–5. I have slightly adjusted her translation. All translations of Qurʾanic verses in this article follow M.A.S. Abdel Haleem's translation, with a few minor modifications.
38 For this type of interpretation, see Sands, *Ṣūfī Commentaries*, 35–6.
39 Al-Sulamī, *Ziyādāt ḥaqāʾiq al-tafsīr*, 155, 184, 188. I would like to thank Laury Silvers for drawing my attention to these passages.
40 Ibn al-Jawzī, *Ṣifat* #688; Ibn al-Athīr, *Al-Mukhtār* 3:228.
41 E.g., Ibn al-Jawzī, *Ṣifat* ## 368, 597, 468.
42 E.g., ibid., ## 601, 630.
43 E.g., ibid., ## 235, 239, 619, 687. For portrayals of women's attendance at such gatherings, see Silvers, "Early Pious," 45–51; for women preaching, see Roded, *Women*, 104–6.
44 As in the conversion story of Abū Umama's freedwoman: Ibn al-Jawzī, *Ṣifat* #829.
45 E.g., ibid., ## 147, 157, 233, 585.
46 E.g., al-Jawzī, *Kitāb al-Quṣṣāṣ*, 108, 117, 124. For similar rhetoric by other medieval authors, see Berkey, *Popular Preaching*, 31–2; Armstrong, *Quṣṣāṣ of Early Islam*, 185–7.
47 "*wa-kānat taktub wa-taqraʾ wa-taʿiẓ al-niswān*": Ibn al-Jawzī, *Ṣifat* #619; Ibn al-Athīr, *Al-Mukhtār* 3:426. Her entry in Ibn al-Jawzī's chronicle has her preaching to "the people" (*al-nās*); see Ibn al-Jawzī, *Al-Muntaẓam*, 16:160.

48 Ibn al-Jawzī, *Kitāb al-Quṣṣāṣ*, 24–7.

49 Saleh, *Formation*, 152–61.

50 Sands, *Sūfī Commentaries*, 55. Ibn al-Jawzī was not alone in condemning it; see, for example, al-Dāwūdī, *Ṭabaqāt*, 395; Saleh, *Formation*, 152–3. For instances of its positive reception, see Cornell, *Early Sufi Women*, 41.

51 For historically evolving notions of "core" authorities and sources in Qur'anic exegesis, see Saleh, "Preliminary Remarks," 18–19.

52 See, for example, al-Thaʿlabī, *Al-Kashf*, 5:480; al-Māwardī, *Al-Nukat*, 5:301.

53 See Cornell, *Early Sufi Women*, 216–17; al-Khaṭīb al-Baghdādī, *Tārīkh* 14:438; cf. Ibn al-Jawzī, *Ṣifat* #364.

54 Ibn al-Jawzī, *Ṣifat* #585; Ibn al-Athīr, *Al-Mukhtār* 3:318.

55 He variously served as a judge in al-Madā'in and a market inspector in Kufa: Ibn Saʿd, *Al-Ṭabaqāt al-kubrā*, 7:290.

56 Earlier in the text, Ibn al-Jawzī names her as a transmitter of a *ḥadīth*: *Ṣifat* #151. Immediately following this anecdote, he depicts her exhorting young men.

57 Both her parents were captured and enslaved during the conquests: Ibn al-Jawzī, *Ṣifat* #504. While her brother Muḥammad is explicitly described as a freed slave (*mawlā*) of the Companion Anas ibn Mālik, neither his entry nor Ḥafṣa's says the same of her. However, Ḥafṣa is elsewhere said to have been the eldest child: Ibn Saʿd, *Ṭabaqāt* 7:225; if this is the case then she would have been born a slave.

58 For a study that examines the use of veiling by former slaves and their daughters as a signal of their changed status in a modern society, see Fair, "Veiling, Fashion," 18–28.

59 Geissinger, *Gender*, 207–11.

60 For devout men physically punishing themselves for illicit looking, see, for example, Ibn al-Jawzī, *Ṣifat* #421, 507.

61 For example, men should instruct their sons to avoid illicit looking: Ibn al-Jawzī, *Ṣifat* #522.

62 E.g., Ibn al-Jawzī, *Ṣifat* #471, 474. The idea that admonishing wrongdoers is a pious act (and in some circumstances a religious obligation) has a long history; see, for example, Cook, *Commanding Right*.

63 Some anecdotes depict the male watcher acting in such a way that a woman being observed in those circumstances might well fear for her safety; yet the focus of the text remains on *his* needs and perspectives. For portrayals that hint at renunciant women's vulnerability to sexual assault, see Silvers, "Early Pious," 45.

64 Some entries in the *Ṣifat al-ṣafwa* do contain anecdotes or sayings that are related by male transmitters from a female witness. However, as material

of this type comprises only a very small proportion of the total, and does not affect the overall prominence of pious male gazes in this work as a whole, it will not be examined here.

65 In some anecdotes, female figures personify a man's desire for food, rest, or other physical comforts that he is striving to master: e.g., Ibn al-Jawzī, *Ṣifat* ## 380, 403, 442, 521. For this theme in some later classical Sufi texts, see Schimmel, *My Soul Is a Woman*, 69–74.

66 Roded, *Women*, 104.

67 See, for example, the very short entries for two fourth/tenth century female scholars from Baghdad who gave *fatwa*s: Ibn al-Jawzī, *Ṣifat* ## 366, 367. Al-Khaṭīb al-Baghdādī provides slightly more detail: *Tārīkh* 14: 332–3.

68 Cornell, *Early Sufi Women*, 122–3.

69 Several entries feature female renunciants deflecting male criticism by quoting from the Qur'ān; e.g., Ibn al-Jawzī, *Ṣifat* ## 604, 617, 1016.

70 "*qara'at al-Qur'ān wa-hiya ibnat ithnatay 'ashra sana*" (she read/recited the Qur'ān when she was twelve years old). The entry in his *Muntaẓam* has "*khatamat al-Qur'ān*" (she completed the recitation of the Qur'ān) instead: Ibn al-Jawzī, *al-Muntaẓam*, 7:171.

71 In his well-known biographical dictionary for Qur'ān reciters, Ibn al-Jazarī (d. 833/1429) says little about Ibn Sīrīn except that some traditions regarding Qur'anic readings are related on his authority. Ibn al-Jazarī, *Ghāyat al-nihāya*, 2:134–5.

72 See, for example, the tale of a male reciters' vision: Ibn al-Jawzī, *Ṣifat*, #447.

73 Al-Māwardī, *Al-Nukat*, 4:121; al-Suyūṭī, *Al-Durr al-manthūr*, 6:222. Ibn al-Jawzī, however, holds that young or old, a (free) woman's hair must be covered: *Zād*, 6:63.

74 Al-Māwardī, *Al-Nukat*, 4: 121–2; al-Tha'labī, *Al-Kashf*, 4:398.

75 For veiling and free/slave distinctions in exegesis, see Geissinger, *Gender*, 207–10.

76 Al-Bayhaqī, *Al-Sunan al-kubrā*, 7:149–51.

77 Neither al-Māwardī nor al-Tha'labī quotes it, and of the (few) sources that al-Suyūṭī names for it, only one – Ibn al-Mundhir (*Durr*, 6:222-3) – might refer to a Qur'ān commentary, or perhaps the latter's legal writings. For Ibn al-Mundhir (d.ca. 318/930), a Nishapuri jurist who also authored a *tafsīr*, see al-Dāwūdī, *Ṭabaqāt*, 337–8; Geissinger, *Gender*, 21.

78 Ibn al-Jawzī, *Zād*, 6:63. He credits this view to al-Qāḍī Abū Ya'lā ibn al-Farrā' (d. 458/1065).

79 Ibn al-Jawzī, *Ṣifat* #731.

80 For her, see ibid., *Ṣifat* #823.

81 For him, see ibid., *Ṣifat* #764.

82 For him, see ibid., *Ṣifat* #757.

83 It is unclear whether this should be understood as her name or as a sobriquet; see Cornell, *Early Sufi Women*, 63. As I suspect that it is meant to be a sobriquet, I treat it as such here.

84 Cornell, *Early Sufi Women*, 126–7.

85 Classical *tafsīr* works also tie this notion to certain Qur'anic verses; see Geissinger, *Gender*, 39, 43–5.

86 Ibn al-Jawzī, *Zād*, 6:130–1.

87 Cf. al-Thaʿlabī, *Al-Kashf*, 4:454.

88 Al-Māwardī lists six possible interpretations; the other four are: doubt, shirk, free from sins, and safe from fear on Judgment Day: *Al-Nukat*, 4:177.

89 Ibn al-Jawzī, *Ṣifat* #592.

90 Cornell, *Early Sufi Women*, 84–5. The reader/audience may have been intended to understand that she did so at such gatherings.

91 "If anyone desires a harvest in the life to come, we shall increase it for him; if anyone desires a harvest in this world, we shall give him a share of it, but in the hereafter he will have no share": Q. 42:20.

92 Cornell, *Early Sufi Women*, 84n24.

93 See Ibn al-Jawzī's objections to Sufi tales that he says misrepresent *tawakkul*: *Ṣifat*, 1:26–30). But what constitutes *tawakkul* and how it should be put into practice were matters of debate: e.g., Karamustafa, *Sufism*, 43.

94 E.g., Ibn al-Jawzī, *Ṣifat*, ## 200, 232, 465, 1016.

95 For examples featuring female figures, see Ibn al-Jawzī, *Ṣifat* ## 941, 1013.

96 For women fainting, see Ibn al-Jawzī, *Ṣifat* ## 588, 819, 643. In the latter example, she also dies as a result. For more on stories of this type, see Saleh, *The Formation*, 59–65.

97 For examples with female figures doing this, see Ibn al-Jawzī, *Ṣifat* ## 654, 934, 612, 823, 929.

98 E.g., ibid., *Ṣifat* ## 445 and 446, 605, 606.

99 E.g., ibid., *Ṣifat* ## 473, 1019.

100 Ibn al-Jawzī, *Zād*, 8:34.

101 See al-Māwardī, *Al-Nukat*, 5:367–8; al-Thaʿlabī, *Al-Kashf*, 5:563–4.

REFERENCES

Abdel Haleem, M.A.S. *The Qur'an: A New Translation*. New York: Oxford University Press, 2005.

Armstrong, Lyall R. *The Quṣṣāṣ of Early Islam*. Leiden and Boston: Brill, 2017.

Bayhaqī, Abū Bakr Aḥmad ibn al-Ḥusayn ibn ʿAlī al-. *Al-Sunan al-kubrā*. Ed. Muḥammad ʿAbd al-Qādir ʿAṭā. 11 vols. Beirut: Dār al-Kutub al-ʿIlmiyya, 2010.

Berkey, Jonathan P. *Popular Preaching and Religious Authority in the Medieval Islamic Near East*. Seattle: University of Washington Press, 2001.

Cook, Michael. *Commanding Right and Forbidding Wrong in Islamic Thought*. Cambridge and New York: Cambridge University Press, 2000.

Cooperson, Michael. "Classical Arabic Biography: A Literary-Historical Approach." In *Understanding Near Eastern Literatures*, ed. Verena Klemm and Beatrice Gruendler, 177–87. Wiesbaden: Reichert Verlag, 2000.

Cornell, Rkia E. *Early Sufi Women: Dhikr an-niswa al-mutaʿabbidāt aṣ Ṣūfiyyāt*. Louisville: Fons Vitae, 1999.

Dāwūdī, Shams al-Dīn Muḥammad ibn ʿAlī ibn Aḥmad al-. *Ṭabaqāt al-mufassirīn*. Ed. ʿAbd al-Salām ʿAbd al-Maʿīn. Beirut: Dār al-Kutub al-ʿIlmiyya, 2002.

Dhahabī, Shams al-Dīn Muḥammad ibn Aḥmad ibn ʿUthmān al-. *Tārīkh al-Islām wa-wafayāt al-mashāhīr wa'l-aʿlām*. Ed. ʿUmar ʿAbd al-Salām Tadmurī. 52 vols. Beirut: Dār al-Kitāb al-ʿArabī, 1997.

Fair, Laura. "Veiling, Fashion, and Social Mobility: A Century of Change in Zanzibar." In *Veiling in Africa*, ed. Elisha P. Renne, 15–33. Bloomington: Indiana University Press, 2013.

Geissinger, Aisha. *Gender and Muslim Constructions of Exegetical Authority: A Rereading of the Classical Genre of Qur'ān Commentary*. Leiden and Boston: Brill, 2015.

Ibn al-Athīr al-Jazarī, Majd al-Dīn Abī al-Saʿādāt al-Mubārak ibn Muḥammad ibn Muḥammad ibn ʿAbd al-Karīm. *Al-Mukhtār min manāqib al-akhyār*. Ed. Muṣṭafā ʿAbd al-Qādir ʿAṭā'. 3 vols. Beirut: Dār al-Kutub al-ʿIlmiyya, 2009.

Ibn al-Jawzī, Abū al-Faraj ʿAbd al-Raḥmān ibn ʿAlī. *Al-Muntaẓam fī tārīkh al-mulūk wa'l-umam*. Ed. Muḥammad ʿAbd al-Qādir ʿAṭā and Muṣṭafā ʿAbd al-Qādir ʿAṭā. 19 vols. Beirut: Dār al-Kutub al-ʿIlmiyya, 1995.

– *Kitāb al-Quṣṣāṣ wa'l-mudhakkirīn*. Ed. and trans. Merlin L. Swartz. Beirut: Dar el-Machreq, 1971.

– *Nawāsikh al-Qur'ān*. Ed. Sāmī ʿAṭā Ḥasan. Amman: Amwāj, 2013.

– *Ṣifat al-ṣafwa*. Ed. Maḥmūd Fākhūrī and Muḥammad Rawwās Qalʿajī. 4 vols. Beirut: Dār al-Maʿrifa, 1979.

– *Zād al-masīr fī ʿilm al-tafsīr*. 9 vols. Damascus: al-Maktab al-Islāmī, 1964.

Ibn al-Jazarī, Shams al-Dīn Abū al-Khayr Muḥammad ibn Muḥammad ibn Muḥammad ibn ʿAlī. *Ghāyat al-nihāya fī ṭabaqāt al-qurrāʾ*. Ed. G. Bergstraesser. 2 vols. Beirut: Dār al-Kutub al-ʿIlmiyya, 2006.

Ibn Saʿd, Muḥammad. *Al-Ṭabaqāt al-kubrā*. Ed. Hamza al-Nashratī et al. 8 vols. Cairo: al-Maktaba al-Qayyima, n.d.

Kaplan, E. Ann. *Looking for the Other: Feminism, Film, and the Imperial Gaze*. New York: Routledge, 1997.

Karamustafa, Ahmet. *Sufism: The Formative Period*. Edinburgh: Edinburgh University Press, 2007.

Khaṭīb al-Baghdādī, Abū Bakr Aḥmad ibn ʿAlī al-. *Tārīkh Baghdād aw Madīnat al-Salām mundhu taʾsīsihā ḥattā sanat 463 H*. 14 vols. Cairo: Maktabat al-Khānjī, n.d.

Laoust, H. "Ibn al-Djawzī" *Encyclopaedia of Islam, Second Edition*, ed. P. Bearman, Th. Bianquis, C.E. Bosworth, E. van Donzel, and W.P. Heinrichs. Leiden: Brill, 1960. http://dx.doi.org/10.1163/1573-3912_islam_SIM_3139.

Malti-Douglas, Fedwa. *Woman's Body, Woman's Word: Gender and Discourse in Arabo-Islamic Writing*. Princeton: Princeton University Press, 1991.

Māwardī, Abū al-Ḥasan ʿAlī ibn Muḥammad ibn Ḥabīb al-Māwardī al-. *Al-Nukat wa'l-ʿuyūn Tafsīr al-Māwardī*. Ed. Sayyid ibn ʿAbd al-Maqṣūd ibn ʿAbd al-Raḥīm. 6 vols. Beirut: Dār al-Kutub al-ʿIlmiyya, n.d.

McAuliffe, Jane Dammen. "Ibn al-Jawzī's Exegetical Propaedeutic: Introduction and Translation." *Alif* 8 (1988): 101–13.

– "The Tasks and Traditions of Interpretation." In *The Cambridge Companion to the Qurʾān*, ed. Jane Dammen McAuliffe, 181–209. Cambridge: Cambridge University Press, 2006.

Melchert, Christopher. "Before Ṣūfiyyāt: Female Muslim Renunciants in the 8th and 9th Centuries CE," *Journal of Sufi Studies* 5 (2016): 115–39.

Pink, Johanna, and Andreas Görke. "Introduction." In *Tafsīr and Islamic Intellectual History: Exploring the Boundaries of a Genre*, ed. Andreas Görke and Johanna Pink, 1–23. New York: Oxford University Press, 2014.

Roded, Ruth. *Women in Islamic Biographical Collections: From Ibn Saʿd to* Who's Who. Boulder: Lynne Rienner, 1994.

Saleh, Walid. *The Formation of the Classical Tafsīr Tradition: The Qurʾān Commentary of al-Thaʿlabī–d. 427/1035*. Leiden and Boston: Brill, 2004.

– "Preliminary Remarks on the Historiography of *Tafsīr* in Arabic: A History of the Book Approach," *Journal of Qur'anic Studies* 12 (2010): 6–40.

Sands, Kristin Zahra. *Ṣūfī Commentaries on the Qur'ān in Classical Islam.* London and New York: Routledge, 2006.

Schimmel, Annemarie. *My Soul Is a Woman: The Feminine in Islam.* Trans. Susan H. Ray. New York: Continuum, 1999.

Silvers, Laury. "Early Pious, Mystic Sufi Women." In *The Cambridge Companion to Sufism*, ed. Lloyd Ridgeon, 24–52. New York: Cambridge University Press, 2014.

Sulamī, ʿAbd al-Raḥmān Muḥammad ibn al-Ḥusayn al-. *Ziyādāt ḥaqāʾiq al-tafsīr*. Ed. Gerhard Böwering. Beirut: Dar el-Machreq, 1995.

Suyūṭī, Jalāl al-Dīn al-. *Al-Durr al-manthūr fī tafsīr al-maʾthūr.* Beirut: Dār al-Fikr, 2002. 8 vols.

Thaʿlabī, Abū Isḥāq Aḥmad ibn Muḥammad ibn Ibrāhīm al-. *Al-Kashf wa'l-bayān fī tafsīr al-Qurʾān al-maʿrūf bi-tafsīr al-Thaʿlabī*. Ed. Sayyid Kasrawī Ḥasan. 6 vols. Beirut: Dār al-Kutub al-ʿIlmiyya, 2004.

6

Constructing the Image of the Model Muslim Woman

Gender Discourse in Ibn Saʿd's *Kitāb al-ṭabaqāt al-kubrā*

Amira Abou-Taleb

Role models are individuals who provide an example of the kind of success that one may achieve, and often also provide a template of the behaviors that are needed to achieve such success.

Penelope Lockwood, "Someone Like Me Can Be Successful"

The above is a quote from a contemporary psychology study about the impact of female role-modelling. For believing Muslim women, what better aspiration can there be than to emulate women whom God specifically addressed in the Qurʾan, as in the case of the wives of the Prophet Muḥammad?[1] They are often referred to as *ummahāt al-muʾminīn* (Mothers of Believers), and their mention in the sacred scripture has contributed to their significance and promoted their function as potential role models. The oldest extant text to provide detailed biographies of these women – and indeed, early Muslim women in general – is *Kitāb al-nisāʾ* (the Women's Volume) of the famous *Kitāb al-ṭabaqāt al-kubrā* (The Great Generations; hereafter KTK) by Abū ʿAbd Allāh Muḥammad ibn Saʿd (d. 230/845).[2] As Ahmad Nazir Atassi has demonstrated, this book had achieved canonical status by the sixth/ninth century and has since become an "expert witness" on the lives of early Muslims.[3] The type of information Ibn Saʿd emphasized in his portrayal of these women has served to construct their characters for centuries to follow, providing a template of expected behaviours and thereby impacting the development of the religious discourse toward women. One must note that Ibn Saʿd lived in Baghdad and authored the text at the time of the ʿAbbāsid imperial project, during the reigns of Harūn al-Rashīd (d. 193/809) and al-Maʾmūn (d. 218/833), a time that witnessed the production of many Sunni intellectual narratives, including *ḥadīth* collections, schools of jurisprudence (*fiqh*), and major historical annals. The two-hundred-year gap between the writing of the KTK and the events it narrates may well have had a significant impact on the text and the way in which Ibn Saʿd constructed the biographies. This begs for serious academic investigation, and to that end, this chapter critically examines the author's presentation of the biographies of the Prophet's wives in *Kitāb al-nisāʾ* to highlight Ibn Saʿd's influence and the context in which he constructed the image of the ideal Muslim woman.

Islam contends that its lack of an official clergy goes far to facilitate a direct relationship between the believer and God; yet the development of a "canonical" interpretive tradition has undermined this claim, by empowering certain perspectives over others. The resulting biases have played a role in moving Muslim societies away from the universal Qurʾanic call for justice.[4] Therefore, as Mir-Hosseini states, there is a need for "a critical reassessment of the entire Islamic intellectual tradition."[5] One approach is to interrogate the relationship between power and knowledge production as per Michel Foucault (d. 1984), who argued that one is not able to remove oneself from society and history so as to make the claim to generate objective and truthful knowledge of these disciplines.[6] His ideas reinforce the notion that there are strong links between historical narratives and the socio-political contexts in which they were created. Indeed, history can be written from different points of view to represent alternative realities. Catherine Belsey thus argued that the best approach a modern critical historian or "historicist"[7] can take is "to use the text as a basis for the reconstruction of an ideology."[8] That is precisely the direction this chapter takes: it examines Ibn Saʿd's biographies of the Prophet's wives and compares them to those written by other authors who lived at different times and in other places. The study then compares Ibn Saʿd's presentation of these prominent women to how he himself presents other Muslim women of the community in the KTK.

The analysis is divided into three parts. The first introduces *Kitāb al-nisāʾ* and identifies its main themes: the women's pledge, physical segregation, and bodily concealment. The second part is comparative and consists of two sections. The first compares presentations of the Prophet's wives in the KTK to those of other biographical works, specifically those of Abū'Umar Yūsuf ibn ʿAbd al-Barr (d. 463/1070) and Ibn Ḥajar al-ʿAsqalānī (d. 852/1449). The second section demonstrates the variance between how Ibn Saʿd chose to present the most prominent women such as the wives of the Prophet, versus how he presented other Muslim women in the early Muslim community. The third and final part of this chapter sheds light on Ibn Saʿd's historical context and suggests possible influences that may have contributed to the specific portrayals he offers in the KTK. The findings reveal how the lives of the Prophet's wives are presented differently across the various biographical dictionaries. Ibn Saʿd's portrayal seems to have been influenced by his own cultural milieu, which celebrated patriarchal ideals as part of the ʿAbbāsid imperial project – ideals that bolstered the perception that women were physical temptations to be avoided if one was to be a pious Muslim (man). Ibn Saʿd overlooked the strong character some of the Prophet's wives had claimed in other sources, in effect reducing them to models reflecting the ideal of gender segregation and body concealment but offering little else. The result is a canon of biographical representations that strip women of their individual agency while rendering them as a collective role model serving the cause of a patriarchal power discourse.

KITĀB AL-NISĀʾ

The KTK contains the largest number of women's biographies presented in any Islamic biographical dictionary.[9] The Leiden edition consists of eight volumes, with the first seven dedicated to the lives of the Prophet and Muslim men. The last volume, *Kitāb al-nisāʾ*, is dedicated to women of the Meccan and early Medinan periods, including some third-generation Muslim women. That volume is divided into two parts. The first part covers the biographies of women of the Prophetic household, while the second part is devoted to the biographies of other women living at the time. Volume Eight's overall structure thus establishes a clear distinction between women of the Prophetic household (the Prophet's daughters and wives) and other Muslim women of the community. This distinction is enforced through the tactics of order (earlier placement), entry size, and interjection of a middle narrative separator section about the Prophet as a husband.[10] Ibn Saʿd seems to be deliberately setting the Prophet's wives and daughters in a league of their own, as an exemplary model for all other Muslim women to aspire to. The separator section places these women in seclusion, setting them apart from the other women of the community. Volume Eight offers around 630 biographies in total. The women in the Prophet's family represent approximately 2 percent of the total number of women covered in the entire volume. Yet their section, along with the narrative section on the Prophet's marital customs and traditions, comprises 47 percent of Volume Eight. The listing of the entries of the KTK is based on the notion of *ṭabaqāt*, which denotes the concept of stages or a hierarchy in generations. This sentiment is also present within the work itself, where the layers form what appears to be a ripple effect in which the Prophet is the nucleus. Volume Eight's entries on women of the Prophetic household, particularly the wives of the Prophet, include themes that relate to them as individuals, such as seclusion, physical beauty, jealousy, and asceticism (*zuhd*). Marriage details, such as bridal payment (*mahr*), guardianship (*walī)*, and waiting period (*ʿidda*), constitute a significant portion of the entries and vary from one entry to another. All of the above areas are emphasized through exaggerated repetitions and use of dramatic literary tools, such as switching to active voice and the use of *topoi* and Qur'anic verses. Due to size limitations, this chapter focuses on the themes of gender segregation and body concealment. It also describes the women's pledge, which sets the tone for the themes of gender segregation and body concealment that run throughout the section.

The Pledge (bayʿa)

Kitāb al-nisāʾ starts with the rendition of the *bayʿa* (pledge of allegiance to Islam and the Prophet). Although these first few pages covering the *bayʿa* mention the names of the women who participated, other important information is lacking, such as the time and place of the *bayʿa(s)*. Even though there is no pertinent information about the actual *bayʿa* setting, there is remarkable detail that describes the various ways in which the Prophet avoided touching the bare hands of the women while accepting their pledge. In fact, the opening sentence of *Kitāb al-nisāʾ* reads, "we were told by ʿAbd Allah ibn Idrīs al-ʿAwdī, on the authority of Ḥusayn ibn ʿAbd al-Raḥmān, on the authority of ʿĀmīr al-Shuʿabī, who said: 'the Prophet accepted the women's pledge with a cover on his hand.'"[11] In a clear reflection of the author's own concerns, the *bay'a* section then goes on to reiterate that same fact by explicitly stating – twenty-one times in the seven-page section – that the Prophet did not touch the women's hands. This tremendous emphasis on the physical segregation of man and woman can by no means be purely coincidental. The entry continues giving different reports relating to the same topic. Some simply state that the Prophet refused to shake hands with women; others show him covering his hand while shaking theirs; still others show him dipping his hand in a bucket of water and then having them dip their hands into the same bucket to signal a *bay'a*. Regardless of the method used, across all cases the message is the same: men and women should not touch hands, more so that the man in question here is the Prophet himself. In her analysis of the interpretations rendered about the *bay'a*, Stowasser notes a huge discrepancy between what is presented in the tradition and how the women's *bay'a* is referenced in the Qur'an, which indicates that the Prophet accepted their *bay'a* without denying that he touched their hand when doing so (Q. 60:12). She concludes that "the interpretations are clearly later distortions of the text." She goes on to share something that other scholars concur with – that the persistence of the image of the Prophet not touching the hands of the women reflects the spirit, not of the first/seventh century, but of the third/ninth century of Islam.[12]

It appears reasonable to begin a biographical dictionary of Muslim women with a general section on accepting Islam. But here it also serves as an archetype for consigning the entire female Muslim community. Starting with the opening line and repeatedly emphasizing one key message within this section – which is, that a man should not touch a woman's hand – not only diminishes the grandeur of the historical moment but also appears to establish a meta-narrative for the philosophy of the entire text. Let us then look at the biographies of the Prophet's wives to identify the main themes and examine how the need for segregation and physical concealment reflects the overriding preoccupation of the author.

Physical Segregation

The author appears to convey the ideal of staying within the home through his portrayal of the way the Prophet's wives of elevated status, such as 'Ā'isha (d. 56/678), Sawda bint Zam'a (d. 52/674), and Zaynab bint Jaḥsh (d. 19/641), behaved. Ibn Saʿd states that the Prophet married ʿĀʾisha when she was six years old and consummated the marriage three years later, when she was nine.[13] The entry goes on to state that before her marriage, ʿĀʾisha spent most of her time playing with other girls outdoors, but when she got married, she remained inside the house. On one of the rare occasions in which the author gives ʿĀʾisha an active voice, she says, "I was playing outside with my friends when my mother came and took me in and locked me inside the house; it was only then that I realized that I got married."[14] This story is repeated several times in ʿĀʾisha's entry, which is the longest in *Kitāb al-Nisāʾ*, covering seventeen pages. This emphasis goes hand in hand with the entry stating that she was also the Prophet's favourite wife. Such statements set ʿĀʾisha on a high pedestal, as if to make her behaviour the ideal model to emulate. In those seventeen pages, Ibn Saʿd mentions neither the Battle of the Camel nor ʿĀʾisha's leadership role in it. The Battle of the Camel was the first civil strife (*fitna*) in Islam in which ʿĀʾisha participated against ʿAlī ibn Abī Ṭālib (d. 39/661) in retaliation for his alleged failure to avenge the murder of ʿUthmān ibn ʿAffān (d. 34/656).[15] Ibn Saʿd refers several times to ʿĀʾisha's general state of regret in her later years without alluding to the reason for her regret. Yet that regret is so deep that she herself refers several times to how she wished she had never been born. Once again, the author gives ʿĀʾisha an active voice as we hear her lamenting, "I wish I were a tree or a piece of earth or a rock and had never existed."[16] The fact that the battle itself is not mentioned, but her remorse is, may be due to the author's own disapproval of women's involvement in political affairs. In another example, it is stated that ʿĀʾisha would cry profusely when she heard the Qur'anic verse referring to the Prophet's' wives staying home (Q. 33:33).[17] This dramatic scene helps drive the premise home that she should have never left her house in the first place.

The biographical entry on the Prophet's wife Sawda states that she went on pilgrimage with the Prophet on his final *ḥajj*. The following year, after the Prophet's death, some women wanted to go to perform the lesser pilgrimage (*ʿumra*) and asked Sawda to go with them; however, she replied, "Nothing can move me after the Messenger of God, not even a camel."[18] There are two further references to similar stories in Sawda's entry: one shows Zaynab bint Jaḥsh staying behind with Sawda, while others go on *ḥajj*; the other shows Sawda answering the same *ḥajj* request by stating, "I have performed *ḥajj* and *ʿumra* and now I shall stay in my home and follow the word of God." She then recites part of Q. 33:33 about staying at home.[19] It is interesting to note that none of the above examples are included in these women's entries in the other biographical dictionaries examined later in this chapter, namely those of Ibn ʿAbd al-Barr (d. 463/1070) and al-ʿAsqalānī (d. 852/1449).

Another reference to *ḥajj* takes us back to ʿĀʾisha's entry, where she states that "a woman's *jihād* [effort, struggle, activism] is the *ḥajj.*"[20] This example assures the reader that women should not take to the battlefield, especially in light of Ibn Saʿd's omission of any mention of the Prophet's wives' participation in battle, whether during the Prophet's life or after his death, even though it is mentioned in the other biographical works, as will be noted later, in the case of Umm Salama and others.[21] By limiting woman's public participation to *ḥajj,* which is the only Islamic obligation that dictates women's presence outside the home, the author sends an important message that promotes the isolation and seclusion of pious Muslim women. It is quite interesting that in the section of the book dedicated to other Muslim women of the community, Ibn Saʿd does include presence on the battlefield in some of their entries, such as in the case of Umm ʿUmāra and Umm Salīm (see below).[22]

Bodily Concealment

Another aspect of female seclusion is concealment, a concept we encounter in the author's mention of the types of clothing worn and in his emphasis on women covering up when men are present. Ibn Saʿd mentions several types of clothing in his entries, including *khimār*, *niqāb*, *izār*, and *dirʿ*. The definitions of these terms are somewhat fluid and rely significantly on what was commonly referred to at the time, as opposed to how we may comprehend them today. For example, the term *ḥijāb* is more commonly used as a verb (*ḥajab-*, to conceal), in reference to a woman being concealed from others behind something (usually a curtain).[23] As the entries of ʿĀʾisha, Zaynab bint Jaḥsh, and Ṣafiyya are among the longest in the *KTK,* it is no surprise that Ibn Saʿd's methodology utilizes the biographies of these particular women to reflect his own emphasis on the fact that they observed the highest degrees of concealment.

An example from the entry for Ṣafiyya bint Ḥuyayy drives home the point.[24] Ibn Saʿd reports that the Prophet used his own clothes to conceal Ṣafiyya while riding on his camel as they departed Khaybar after their marriage in 6/628.[25] The entry states that throughout the ride, Ṣafiyya was very concerned about being physically exposed in case the camel tripped. This statement resembles a prophecy by an omnipotent narrator who is somehow privy to her thoughts. Oddly enough, the author then states that the camel did indeed trip and both the Prophet and Ṣafiyya fell off; however, the Prophet immediately covered her up. In another reference about that predicted fall, the entry states that a man named Abū Ṭalḥa ran to assist them, and that as he approached Ṣafiyya, he used his own clothes to cover his face (so as not to see her) before proceeding to cover her up. Covering her up while his own face was covered would have presented some difficulty; however, Ibn Saʿd's clear focus was on emphasizing women's concealment without regard to such practical logistics.

Another instance in the same biography states that Ṣafiyya was riding a mule on her way to help the leader of the Muslim community at the time, the caliph ʿUthmān (d. 34/656), when a man struck the face of her mule, causing the mule to sway. Ṣafiyya then said, "Take me back lest I get exposed."[26] It is important to note here that Ibn Saʿd does not give any details about the situation ʿUthmān was in or how Ṣafiyya was trying to help. Instead, the statement merely focuses on conveying Ṣafiyya's fear of exposure. When we refer to other biographical dictionaries, we note that the later al-ʿAsqalānī, for example, shares the incident of Ṣafiyya going to help ʿUthmān without any mention of her concern for concealment. As a matter of fact, al-ʿAsqalānī's version emphasizes Ṣafiyya's wisdom, strength, and courage, as well as her defiance: he focuses on how she tried to help the caliph ʿUthmān by delivering food to his besieged household.[27] Regardless of which historian portrayed the "real history," the differences seem to show that history was not being written in an objective fashion; rather, each historian's agenda played a role in his portrayal of past events.

Ibn Saʿd's account is loaded with explicit and implicit messages about a woman's obligation to conceal her body. The details of the Prophet's efforts on two occasions to cover Ṣafiyya and of the foreign[28] man (Abū Ṭalḥa) hiding his own face show a deliberate effort to highlight seemingly trivial information when presenting someone's life in a biographical dictionary. Ṣafiyya's worry about a possible fall stemmed from her fear of being exposed, not her concern about suffering physical harm by falling off a camel. Ibn Saʿd's statement sets a hierarchal priority, placing greater concern on the social shame of female exposure than on the woman's physical well-being. The fact that Ṣafiyya's entry focuses so intently on such an issue, but fails to share information about her own character, sheds light on how the author perceived the objective of the biographical entry. In other words, the notion that Ṣafiyya was taking a stand by trying to help ʿUthmān, a caliph in distress, seems insignificant when compared to what appears to be the narrator's main purpose, which is to reinforce her need to remain concealed. Yet the Ṣafiyya we encounter when reading al-ʿAsqalānī's account of the same incident shows a woman of courage, committed to standing by a caliph – a Muslim man – in distress, a woman who participates actively in the public life of her community. Indeed, she is presented as a woman who shows no signs of being intimidated as a "woman" and who does not appear to be obsessed with fear of exposure and the shame associated with it.

Fear of exposure resonates equally in ʿĀʾisha's entry through the author's many references to her use of a *niqāb* or a *khimār*.[29] In one instance, ʿĀʾisha is reported as circumambulating around the Kaʿba in a *niqāb;* in another she is mending her *niqāb*. Later on, in her old age, it is reported that she cries with regret and her tears soak her *khimār*. Overall, Ibn Saʿd shares more than twenty-six reports about ʿĀʾisha's clothing. One reference even shows her swiftly covering up when a blind man enters the room. When asked why she concealed herself if he could not see her, she replied that even if he could not see her, she could see him.[30] ʿĀʾisha adhered to the highest standards of concealment and advised the other wives to do the same. Ibn Saʿd reports that she once saw Ḥafṣa bint ʿUmar wearing a light, translucent *khimār,* and pulled it off and handed her a heavier one. Another narration shows ʿĀʾisha scolding Ḥafṣa and asking her if she [Ḥafṣa] was unaware of what God had ordained in Surat al-Nūr (Q. 24).[31] Since the author reports that ʿĀʾisha was the Prophet's favourite wife and gives her the longest entry in the volume, the fact that she takes such extreme care to remain concealed, and urges other prominent women to do the same, shows how the author constructed a correlation between being a model woman in Islam and concealment. This emphasis may be a reflection of the narrator's own intellectual context and milieu, as will be shown below.[32]

Ibn Saʿd reports that the concept of concealment was ordained by God. It was the occasion of Zaynab bint Jaḥsh's wedding to the Prophet that triggered the revelation of the famous *ḥijāb* verse (Q. 33:53) instructing the Prophet to place a barrier between his wives and the men.[33] The term used for the Prophet placing a curtain to conceal his wives from the visitors inside his house is "concealed her" (*ḥajabahā*) or "imposed concealment upon her" (*ḍaraba ʿalayhā al-ḥijāb*). Ibn Saʿd states that following Zayd ibn Ḥāritha and Zaynab bint Jaḥsh's divorce, the Prophet sent Zayd to deliver a message to Zaynab. The entry then states that Zayd spoke to Zaynab while giving her his back. This same encounter is mentioned by other biographers as a normal conversation between two adults with no reference to such strained concealment efforts.[34] Ibn Saʿd's methodology reveals how he may have taken it upon himself to elaborate and emphasize the notion of concealment by making it a central message when presenting the role models of Muslim women: the wives of the Prophet.

What could be the reasons behind Ibn Saʿd's emphasis on promoting such concepts as the Prophet's wives staying at home, women covering up, and women not shaking hands with men? Was the cultural context of Baghdad conducive to such calls? Many scholars agree that women seem to have enjoyed much more freedom in early Islamic Arabia than what is presented through the *fiqh* literature of medieval times.[35] Amira Sonbol argues that the rise of the *ʿulamāʾ* allowed them to produce *fiqh* material that reflected their own patriarchal tendencies more than it narrated the actual lives of women of the early days and their lived realities. She adds that the upper-class elite of Mesopotamia practised veiling long before the onset of Islam and found a way to do so afterwards. Sonbol thus believes that medieval discourse "must be seen as the efforts of the *fuqahāʾ* to establish a moral code, rather than as a representation of the actual life that women of that period lived."[36] The expansion of Muslims into the greater territories beyond Mecca and Medina witnessed a sweeping change in social structure. Captive women of varying races and classes ended up in a variety of situations: some were consigned to the Caliph's harem, some trained to be singers, and still others found themselves auctioned in slave markets. Abbott writes that this situation resulted in a "definite class distinction between free Arab woman of noble race and lineage, haughty but generally virtuous, and foreign slave women, singers or concubines, with pride of beauty and talent but unconcerned and of comparatively loose morals."[37] As Ibn Saʿd was a scholar close to the court of al-Maʾmūn, who claimed to be the Imām and guardian of the faith, his religious zeal could have prompted him to counter the eroding morals of the time in such an explicit manner.[38] The fact that Ibn Saʿd does not allude to poetry, or to female poets or singers, in his *Kitāb al-Nisāʾ*, despite the prominence of poetry and music in Arab society, including during pre-Islamic times, is another strong indicator of his role as the guardian of ultra-conservative religious mores. Referring to the changing social order between Medina and Baghdad, Abbott concludes: "It was they [the new social conditions] rather than any really religious or political factors that gradually but steadily forced the veil and seclusion on more and more of the aristocratic and the free Arab women."[39]

Ibn Saʿd emphasizes the great attention these women paid to ensuring their seclusion and concealment; in doing so he in effect undermines their individual agency as women with active public roles in society. The fact that other biographical dictionaries display these women's individuality and endow them with unique positive traits, while Ibn Saʿd does not, suggests that the KTK set a generic prototype of pious women that undermined their own individual characters. That is not to say that later biographical dictionaries offer less biased representations of their subjects, as every author left his own imprint on the text.

COMPARISON WITH OTHER BIOGRAPHICAL DICTIONARIES

To assess the extent of uniqueness or universality in the KTK's portrayals of the above women, in the following sections their entries in the KTK are juxtaposed against their biographies in two other biographical dictionaries: *Al-Istīʿāb fī maʿrifat al-asḥāb* by the Cordovan scholar Muhammad Ibn ʿAbd al-Barr (d. 463/1070) and *Al-Iṣāba fī tamyīz al-ṣaḥāba* by the Cairene scholar Ibn Ḥajar al-ʿAsqalānī (d. 852/1449). The two authors lived two and six centuries after Ibn Saʿd respectively. This section examines the details recorded in these two works as well as the discrepancies between them in presentation. The biographies of Umm Salama and ʿĀʾisha are used as examples of how the same person can be presented differently across various texts. The objective is not to assess which renditions more accurately depict their lives, but rather to comprehend how one person's life can be rendered so differently depending on how a given author constructs the character and what information is highlighted or suppressed.

Umm Salama

Umm Salama's individual entry in the KTK shows a pious wife. Ibn Saʿd portrays her labouring for hours to prepare a meal to feed the

Prophet's household on the occasion of their marriage. The entry goes on to give the information that Ibn Saʿd typically provides for all wives' entries, such as details on lineage, occasion of marriage, dowry, just division of time between all wives, jealousy among the wives, and death and burial details.[40] The reader finishes her biography sensing that Umm Salama was an older, beautiful, and pious wife who displayed the same typical signs of seclusion as the others. There is no reference to individual characteristics in her entry, nor is there to her status as an important *muḥaddītha* (traditionist, narrator of *ḥadīth*) who narrated hundreds of the Prophet's *aḥādīth*.[41]

Yet when works by other biographers are consulted, Umm Salama emerges as a strong, powerful woman – qualities that are absent in Ibn Saʿd's biography. Al-ʿAsqalānī, for example, refers to an incident in which Umm Salama intervened publicly to advise the Prophet regarding the Treaty of Ḥudaybiyya – advice the Prophet took due to the wisdom it reflected.[42] Also, Ibn ʿAbd al-Barr reports that Umm Salama witnessed the Battle of Khaybar, noting that she was so close to the battlefield that she could hear the sound of a sword striking a combatant's teeth.[43] Umm Salama's history as presented by al-ʿAsqalānī states that in her earlier years she had escaped her captors and attempted to ride a camel alone through the desert to find her first husband; during that journey, she encountered a stranger who escorted her to her final destination. The man was not a Muslim, yet al-ʿAsqalānī reports that Umm Salama lauded him as the best man she ever encountered.[44] In conclusion, readers who restricted their learning about Umm Salama to her biographical entry as composed by Ibn Saʿd would be left with a hazy and generic impression, if not a severely distorted one.

ʿĀʾisha

When we compare Ibn Saʿd's biography of ʿĀʾisha to those in the other two works mentioned, again she seems barely recognizable. Ibn Saʿd utilized ʿĀʾisha's entry to promote notions of segregation, whereas the other two authors share anecdotes about her role as a scholar and *ḥadīth* narrator. Even more telling is that al-ʿAsqalānī and Ibn ʿAbd al-Barr make no references to her relentless efforts to conceal herself.

Ibn Saʿd portrays ʿĀʾisha as the Prophet's favourite wife, one who repeatedly and vehemently condemned the mixing of the sexes, yet he fails to highlight her prominent role in the community. Conversely, the other authors mainly emphasize her public role and make no reference to her thoughts about gender segregation or female seclusion. For example, Ibn ʿAbd al-Barr shares no information about ʿĀʾisha's clothes, or her isolation, or her regrets in her old age, as does the KTK; but he does reference the *ifk* incident (Affair of the Lie) and shares information about the Qur'an acquitting her of the accusations levelled against her.[45] Ibn ʿAbd al-Barr reveres ʿĀʾisha as a pious and very special wife of the Prophet, and he does so without shying away from sharing well-known information about aspects of her life that are part of Islamic history as attested to in numerous other sources. Indeed, Ibn ʿAbd al-Barr focuses largely on ʿĀʾisha's public role, stating that the council of the most revered *ṣaḥāba* (companions) used to seek her advice on religious issues following the Prophet's death. He goes on to share a narration by ʿAṭāʾ ibn Abī Rabāḥ, who said: "ʿĀʾisha was the most revered person in issues of *fiqh*. She was the most knowledgeable of all people and was known to have the best opinion in public."[46] In another narration, Hishām ibn ʿUrwa is quoted saying that he had never seen anyone as knowledgeable on issues of *fiqh*, medicine, or poetry as ʿĀʾisha. This type of information is mostly absent in the KTK. Also, while Ibn Saʿd makes no mention of ʿĀʾisha's role in the Battle of the Camel, Ibn ʿAbd al-Barr shares a report narrated on behalf of the Prophet in which he foretold ʿĀʾisha's participation in a battle involving a camel; the report goes on to state that in that battle many around her would be killed, but she would be rescued. Ibn ʿAbd al-Barr comments on this particular *ḥadīth*, stating that it was later perceived to be one of the prophetic signs of Muhammad (*aʿlām nubuwattih*).

When we examine ʿĀʾisha's representation in al-ʿAsqalānī's work, we find that she is much closer to the ʿĀʾisha portrayed by Ibn ʿAbd al-Barr and quite different from the woman we encounter through Ibn Saʿd.[47] Al-ʿAsqalānī does not mention the Battle of the Camel, but he does share accounts of ʿĀʾisha's great knowledge. He also reports that when the men faced a problem they could not solve, they would seek ʿĀʾisha's help, because she always had the answer. He also includes a narration that reveres ʿĀʾisha as the best poet, stating that she was so talented she could instantly improvise poetry in any situation.[48] Al-ʿAsqalānī ends ʿĀʾisha's biography by listing the names of more than thirty people who narrated *ḥadīth* on her authority.

When comparing Ibn Saʿd, Ibn ʿAbd al-Barr, and al-ʿAsqalānī, we find that all three present ʿĀʾisha as a beloved wife and (probably) the most revered of all *ummahāt al-muʾminīn*. They share similar information about her early marriage to the Prophet, her being the Prophet's wife in heaven, her being privileged by having Qur'anic verses revealed in her presence, and the Prophet dying and being buried in her home. All three authors establish ʿĀ'isha as the highest female authority in Islam; but they choose to construct this model in extremely different ways. Ibn Saʿd utilizes ʿĀ'isha's authority to craft a patriarchal imperial ʿAbbāsid portrait of the "ideal" woman as one who does not mix with men. Most importantly, she is one who finds comfort in the private setting of her home and stays far from the public domain. In his telling, her knowledge, talents, and character traits appear insignificant. Yet both Ibn ʿAbd al-Barr and al-ʿAsqalānī use ʿĀ'isha's heightened authority to portray a highly talented woman whose mental rigour, poetic talent, and advanced medicinal skills set her high above many men in the community. She is a public figure living in a community in which men do not shy away from seeking knowledge wherever it lay, even if it is in the hands of a woman. Clearly, both authors had access to Ibn Saʿd's information, for they often referenced the *KTK* in their own entries, an indication that they could choose to write down what they believed was relevant to their entries.

KTK'S ENTRIES ON OTHER MUSLIM WOMEN IN THE COMMUNITY

For lack of a better term, the entries reviewed in this section are labelled as "other women's entries." That is not to say that these individual women did not play a significant role in early Muslim history, for many of them were heroines in their own right. This definition is simply for differentiation purposes. The objective here is to highlight the major areas of difference in the portrayals of the two groups of women. Inconsistencies in representation are examined in order to identify discrepancies in Ibn Saʿd's methodology when presenting the Prophet's wives versus his methodology in presenting other Muslim women in the same community.

The "other" Muslim women appear to have enjoyed more liberties than their counterparts examined above. Ibn Saʿd portrays them participating in battle, speaking up against unwanted suitors, demanding divorce, and, in fact, working and earning money. Such independent character is not presented in the biographies of the Prophet's wives, which portray them as more of a monolith, despite what other biographers share about their strength of character and their public engagement. To further illustrate this point, the following analysis examines "other" Muslim women's presence on the battlefield and their integration (as opposed to segregation) in the community.

Presence on the Battlefield

While the biographies of the Prophet's' wives in the KTK do not reflect the characteristics of courage or independence, some of the other entries in the book's latter section show a significantly different side of the women of early Islam. In the latter part of the KTK, Ibn Saʿd shares stories of a few women who participated in battles in various ways. He states that Umm ʿUmāra (Nusayba bint Kaʿb) fought in battles using a sword and arrows.[49] She was one of the women at the ʿAqaba pledge (*bayʿa*), the earliest instance of men and women pledging themselves to the Prophet, prior to his arrival in Medina. She also participated in the battles of Uḥud, Khaybar, Ḥunayn, and Yamāma, as well as the Treaty of al-Ḥudaybiyya. Her entry states that she had initially gone to Yamāma to serve water to the soldiers, but when she saw the Prophet under attack, she took it upon herself to defend him. Umm ʿUmāra suffered twelve wounds and eventually lost her hand. The fact that the entry does not denounce her participation may indicate that such action was not condemned. Ibn Saʿd also states that Umm Salīm participated in the Battle of Uḥud while pregnant and had a dagger (*khanjar*) tied around her stomach.[50] Additionally, Umm ʿAtiyya's entry states that she was present at seven battles, where she helped feed and nurse the troops.[51]

In Umm Sinān's entry, the author reports the Prophet's own perspective on women's participation in battle. The entry shows her asking the Prophet's permission to join the battle, and him replying that many women had already asked him and that he had already granted his consent. The Prophet even gave Umm Sinān the option of joining his troop or remaining with that of her own tribe.[52] This approval by the Prophet reflected his lenient attitude toward women's presence on the battlefield, a dangerous public space involving foreign men. Examples like this are only to be found outside the biographies of the Prophet's wives, although other sources state that *ummahāt al-muʾminīn,* such as Umm Salama and ʿĀʾisha, played important roles in the history of Muslim warfare. Indeed, Ibn Saʿd himself reports that Sumayya bint Khayyāt was the first martyr in Islam.[53]

The above discrepancies between Ibn Saʿd's biographies of Muslim women living in the same community, but endorsing different values, reflects how the author may have manipulated the text in order to construct a particular image relating to how "model" Muslim women were to behave. The liberties the author showed in sharing how the Prophet approved of women engaging in battle in the latter part of the text are difficult to reconcile with the way of life presented for the women of the Prophetic household in the first part of the work. Additionally, as addressed in the previous section, works by other biographers show the Prophet's wives living in a manner that resembles more closely that of the women in the latter part of the *KTK*. For example, the fact that Umm Salama is shown in other biographical dictionaries as being repeatedly at the heart of the battle, while Ibn Saʿd is completely silent on the matter, may reveal his own bias in representation. By stripping the Prophet's wives' biographies of mentions of public engagement and battle participation, the author is sending a message to pious Muslim women that they should aspire to be like them: at home. Securing the notion that a woman should be confined to her home is key to the patriarchal ideology encouraging male control over women's mobility – something that Ibn Saʿd vehemently stresses in his rendition of the wives of the Prophet himself.

Integration versus Segregation

Gender segregation is a core concept propagated in the entries on the Prophet's wives. However, an examination of other entries in the same volume reflect casual gender interaction and indicate that male and female intermingling may have been common, even when it involved the Prophet. The *KTK's* entry for Asmāʾ bint Abū Bakr states that one day she was working in the field and carrying a heavy load of dates on top of her head. When the Prophet approached and saw her, he halted his mule and asked her to ride with him. She rejected the offer, fearing her husband's (al-Zubayr ibn al-ʿAwwām) known jealousy.[54] What is interesting in this anecdote, other than that a woman was working outside the home, is that the Prophet himself encouraged the interaction, while the refusal was rooted in the husband's jealousy. In other words, Islam as a religion (symbolized by the Prophet) had no issue with gender interaction, but social pressure and fear of the husband did. The entry also states that Asmāʾ suffered from a huge lump in her neck and that the Prophet himself sat by her side stroking her neck and praying for God to cure her. We note that the Prophet seemed to show no hesitation in mingling with the women of the community, a fact that is clearly suppressed in the entries discussed in the previous section. Another entry shares a story in which Umayya bint Qays boasted that she had a necklace that the Prophet had personally placed around her neck.[55] In the case of Umm Khālid (Ama bint Khālid ibn Saʿīd), the entry states that the Prophet had a new garment and wanted to put it on someone special, so he asked the people to fetch Umm Khālid, whom he then adorned with the new garment.[56]

These anecdotes reflect what may have been common practice. In some cases, it was precisely such male–female interaction that saved the Prophet's life. The entry for Raqīqa bint Abū Sayfī states that it was she who warned the Prophet that Quraysh were plotting to murder him one night. Accordingly, the Prophet asked ʿAlī ibn Abī Ṭālib to sleep in his place, and thus his life was spared.[57] Ibn Saʿd reports that when the Prophet migrated to Medina, the very first place the Prophet and Abū Bakr stayed was that of a woman named Umm Miʿbid (ʿAtika bint Khālid).[58] The entry goes on to share the conversation that took place between her and the Prophet and how the Prophet miraculously milked her goat, causing it to produce an abundant supply. Encounters like these show that the Prophet interacted with "foreign" women and even stayed at their homes. In another example, Ibn Saʿd states that the Prophet used to frequently visit Umm Salīm at her home. He adds that the Prophet would often nap in her house and that she would collect his sweat drops in a vial to use later as a fragrance.[59] This suggests how common it may have been for the Prophet to visit community members in their homes regardless of their gender; it also shows close contact between Umm Salīm and the Prophet, given that she attempted to gather his sweat drops. Also, the entry for the Prophet's relative Umm al-Faḍl, Lubāba bint al-Ḥārith, states that the Prophet used to nap in her house and that she used to put *kuḥl* (kohl) in his eyes while he was lying on her lap. She also used to inspect his head for lice.[60]

Public intermingling was present in the mosque as well. According to the KTK, Umm Sabiyya bint Qays claimed that in the Prophet's time, it was common practice for her and her female friends to linger in the mosque, where they would chat, weave, and sew. She states that such practices continued during Abū Bakr's caliphate, until ʿUmar prohibited them shortly after his accession to power.[61] It is difficult to reconcile the above anecdotes with the myriad mentions in the *bayʿa*'s opening section emphasizing that the Prophet refused to shake hands with women.[62] According to the latter part of the text, men and women intermingled during the time of the Prophet, notwithstanding Ibn Saʿd's later vociferous efforts to segregate them in the earlier pages of his work. All of these examples suggest that Ibn Saʿd's repeated attempts to advance gender segregation in the earlier section of the volume are much too constructed. These discrepancies endorse the notion that the biographies of the women of the Prophetic household may have been tailored to reflect "desired" and idealized values, rather than values that were practised as lived realities during the Prophet's time. This conclusion is affirmed by Afsaruddin's study of later biographical dictionaries, in which she states: "The male and female *salaf* were regarded as the moral and spiritual predecessors of later generations of Muslims, whose example the pious claimed to follow meticulously. Divergences in behavior from the reported lifestyles of the Companions of the Prophet thus potentially had grave moral repercussions for the scrupulous Muslim."[63]

The examples of women's active involvement in the well-being of society as contributors to *ḥadīth* and *fiqh,* and as working in the fields of medicine and trade, is limited to the sections on "other" Muslim women. Although the Prophet's wives' entries were much longer than those of the others, Ibn Saʿd shared more information about the other women's professional contributions to society than he did in the earlier section. The long entries about the wives of the Prophet focused on driving home the concepts of segregation and seclusion as well as sharing rituals related to funeral and marital practices, but they did not address the women's individual characteristics, talents, or professional inclinations. This variance in representation supports the theory that Ibn Saʿd may have utilized the biographies of the wives of the Prophet to establish an idealized "persona" of how elite women behaved, without any real emphasis on who these women really were as individuals. So to comprehend Ibn Saʿd's discourse, a better understanding of patriarchy and early Islam is thus necessary.

CONTEXT OF THE TIME

Ibn Saʿd lived during the rule of the ʿAbbāsid caliphs Harūn al-Rashīd (d. 193/809) and his son al-Maʾmūn (d. 217/833), both of whom injected their rule with a socio-religious dimension. On the social front, they were patrons of the arts, sponsored poets and musicians, and encouraged intellectual work by commissioning scholars and establishing libraries. They also attempted to dominate the religious platform by acting as the guardians of the faith, as well as through their sponsorship of scholarly activities.

Religious scholarship was dominated by *mawālī* (clients, plural of *mawlā*) whose allegiance was to the court. A *mawla* was a non-Arab convert to Islam, often of Persian origin, and the *mawālī* played a crucial role in the formation of the Islamic faith and Islamic law. Ibn Saʿd was one of these scholars, a *mawla* of the Arabian tribe of the Banū Hāshim, and also worked as a scribe for al-Wāqidī (d. 207/822), author of the famous *Kitāb al-maghāzi*.[64] In this context, *ʿulamāʾ* (religious scholars) came to be regarded as the guardians, transmitters, and interpreters of religious knowledge. With the expansion of Islam into new territories and the gaining of new converts, the role of religious scholars became very important, for they offered guidelines on how to reconcile local traditions with Islamic values. Gradually, the *ʿulamāʾ* as a group gained strength, as well as a more concrete structure, particularly as *ḥadīth* became the best way for people to learn about the Sunna of the Prophet. Offering biographies of the various *ḥadīth* narrators in an attempt to establish their credibility in the chain of narration (*isnād*) became a major step, particularly with the formation of jurisprudence. Most scholars believe that the *Ṭabaqāt* works were created mainly to serve this purpose.[65]

Other scholars, however, argue that biographical dictionaries were constructed for the purpose of conveying behavioural patterns.[66] In his study of the genre, Gibb argued that entries do not reflect personality traits as much as they convey clichéd models of what the authors wished to reveal.[67] Some scholars argue that simply compiling information in "book" format makes it easier to propagate agendas.[68] It follows that biographical dictionaries allow us to understand the mental images the authors had in mind at the time of writing. Cooperson argues that a major dilemma facing scholars of biographical dictionaries is that the same figures' lives are portrayed differently in various works and concludes that "the biographer's own preoccupations had a decisive influence upon their representations of the human subject."[69] Such mental images are not unique to the author; rather, they represent a conglomeration of the social, political, and religious ideologies prevalent at the time. So it is important to investigate the cultural setting in which Ibn Saʿd authored the KTK if we are to better understand the possible factors influencing them.

POSSIBLE INFLUENCES

Foreign/Persian Influence

Upon the Muslim conquest of the Iraq–Iran region, the mores of the incoming Muslims were fused with those of the incumbent Sasanian society, whose official religion was Zoroastrianism. The *mawālī* cultures infiltrated the Muslim world and altered the Arabs' lifestyle in many ways, including by changing how they dressed and what they ate as well as the songs they sang and the entertainments in which they partook.[70] As the ʿAbbāsids established Baghdad, it acquired a cosmopolitan character, and the influence of its Persian majority grew as more of them converted to Islam. Along with these new territories came an abundance of wealth, which translated into luxuries and the creation of a new class hierarchy that the tribal societies of early Islam had never before known. Keddie argues that the resulting social and gender stratification led to the development of domestic slavery and elite harems as well as the veiling and seclusion of women.[71]

The new lifestyle affected the society's mores and reconfigured the values of the ʿAbbāsid families, an impact that might have had a reversing effect on the status of free women compared to early Islam.[72] In reviewing the available literature, Nadia Maria El Cheikh writes: "The narrative presents a reading to the effect that while the early Muslims had allowed women to participate in public life and had empowered them in their personal lives, the late Umayyad and the ʿAbbāsid periods ushered in conditions that debased the position and the conception of women."[73] Leila Ahmed's study of the Code of Hammurabi and Assyrian law (1752 and 1200 BCE, respectively) in ancient Mesopotamia demonstrates that the subordination of women was institutionalized as a result of the growth of urban societies.[74] So it is possible that these pre-Islamic customs were the backdrop against which the imperial narrative was constructed, and (most pertinently here) that most of the authors of the seminal texts, including the *KTK*, were *mawālī* men of Persian origins.

As al-Maʾmūn claimed to be the guardian of the faith, his patronage of scholars was likely an attempt to protect that faith from historical oblivion by documenting the early venerated Muslim models. However, as a consequence of the subjectivities of the authors and the deeply embedded cultural setting of the time, the "history" documented by these patrons likely reflected political objectives and personal biases, along with a recounting of the past, all at once. So revisiting gender representation in medieval texts becomes a necessary endeavour for any scholar interested in furthering our understanding of the influences of social norms and political conditions on the output of authors of the time. Hugh Kennedy argues that it was in the middle of the second/eighth century – around Ibn Saʿd's time – that the "harem" developed into a separate and secluded structure for women of the Caliphal court.[75] In patriarchal societies where women as a group are viewed as the "other," their oppression is often regarded as not only natural, but indeed necessary, in order to maintain what is perceived to be society's proper balance. In such societies, powerful women are perceived as a threat and as a danger to the overall balance. Examples of strong female agency during Ibn Saʿd's own time contributed to fears of upsetting the patriarchal power structure the ʿAbbāsids wanted to maintain.

Fear of Female Power

Fear of women meddling in state affairs may have been very widespread in Ibn Saʿd's time. One great example is Hārūn al-Rashīd's own mother, who was known to have controlled government affairs until her death.[76] Historical reports state that Harūn's early years in the court were heavily influenced by his mother, al-Khayzurān (d. 172/789), and by his Barmakid tutor Yaḥya b. Khālid (d. 190/806).[77] Some stories even blame al-Khayzurān for plotting the death of her own son Mūsa in order to clear the way for his brother Hārūn to ascend the throne. Records show that local customs did not accept such powerful female roles, which is why these women usually had to exert their power through conspiracies with top viziers.[78]

There are various other examples of caliphs having overpowering mothers. Indeed, this led the administration – following the death of al-Muqtadir (d. 295/908) – to establish the death of the mother as a criterion for selecting the next caliph.[79] When Ibn Saʿd establishes the "ideal" that good Muslim women stay at home, he is in fact sending a message to the women of his own time to follow the model of their forebears and stop meddling in public affairs. In other words, the discrepancy between how Ibn Saʿd portrays the Prophet's wives and how he portrays other women may reflect the author's own lived reality along with his society's fears and concerns.

Combating Moral Decay of the Time

The KTK's conservative attitude is further reflected in the author's failure to feature music and poetry in the biographies examined, despite the many records documenting the significant role of male and female musicians, both in the early days of Islam and at the courts of al-Rashīd and al-Maʾmūn.[80] Despite Hārūn al-Rashīd's strict religious stance, he was known to be very generous toward musicians and poets, who in turn memorialized his name in famous works such as *Kitāb al-Aghānī* (Book of Songs) and the *Arabian Nights*.[81] These works show scores of examples of situations where music, gender intermingling, love stories, and anecdotes of power, lust, and deceit were at play together during the vibrant times of al-Rashīd and al-Maʾmūn. The works often associate female slave singers and musicians with an abundance of wealth and power.[82]

In her study of Ibn al-Ḥajj's treatise *Al-Madkhal*, Huda Lutfi demonstrates how the ultraconservative writings of religious scholars may not have reflected their lived realities, but rather served as a strategy for combating the moral decline of their times.[83] The writings of Ibn Saʿd can thus be viewed as the author's attempt to combat the decadence he perceived in his own society, by showing how the prominent women in Islam did *not* engage in public life. Examples of strong female agency during Ibn Saʿd's own time likely contributed to fears of upsetting the patriarchal power structure that the ʿAbbāsids aspired to maintain. This may in turn have triggered a need to establish the ideal Muslim woman as one who is silent, segregated, secluded, and submissive. Such a portrayal not only supported the call of the conservative *ʿulamāʾ* but also triumphantly propagated the patriarchal discourse adopted by the ʿAbbāsid imperial project and legitimized the norms of the existing heritage. Afsaruddin argues that Muslim women lost more freedom over time and describes the eleventh- to fifteenth-century biographical dictionaries she examined as works that "should not be taken as reflective of actual social practices and realities but rather as a masculine 'wish-list' of desirable qualities in the proper and decorous Muslim lady of the late Middle Ages."[84] It is highly conceivable that what applies to the authors of these late biographies also applies to Ibn Sa'd and that his work reflected his "wish list" of desirable qualities in the pious Muslim woman of early Islam.

It may also be that Ibn Saʿd simply portrayed the women of the Prophetic household in the light he deemed appropriate based on his own cultural values. Jerry Bentley's study on what is referred to as "myth-history" offers a theoretical framework for this phenomenon. Proponents of this theory argue that historians often produce knowledge that is based on professional historical scholarship but that also "draws inspiration from perspectives that offer idealized visions of a community and endow its historical accounts with meaning."[85] He adds that historians generally reflect an urge for attachment and identity. In this regard, Ibn Saʿd's efforts to ground the early Muslim tradition in terms familiar to his own value system constitute one likely reason for his unique portrayal of the prominent Muslim women.

CONCLUSION

This chapter has demonstrated how a "canonical" text that is valued within the Islamic tradition as a key source of information about early Muslim figures seems to reflect biased representations. First, it has revealed how the biographical portrayal of the Prophet's wives in the *KTK* does not follow the same methodology Ibn Saʿd used when presenting the biographies of other Muslim women of the time. Second, Ibn Saʿd's presentation of the Prophet's wives differs greatly from how other authors depict them in other biographical dictionaries. All of this suggests that the *KTK* emphasizes different qualities when presenting the Prophet's wives, who are treated as role models for Muslim women, in that it focuses on the concepts of seclusion and concealment. In contrast, "other" Muslim women are presented as more actively engaged in the public sphere, even to the point of participating on the battlefield. In this way, the text effectively subdues the significant role the Prophet's wives played in early Muslim history by not presenting information that reflects strong individual characteristics or active participation in public life. Such information is present in other biographical dictionaries, as demonstrated above. The *KTK* focuses mainly on how the wives of the Prophet in early Islam adhered to the highest levels of gender segregation and made great efforts to remain concealed from the public eye. The text leaves the reader with the notion that an ideal Muslim woman is one who is not seen or heard beyond the confines of her home; it sends a message that propagates the essence of patriarchal values.

As the text was authored about two centuries after the Prophet's time by a non-Arab *mawlā* of Persian descent and was created in Iraq during the construction of the imperial ʿAbbāsid project, the possible influencing factors are infinite. This examination suggests that the promotion of such patriarchal ideals was influenced by the author's Persian heritage, the fear of women meddling in state affairs (as in the case of al-Khayzurān), and the religious zeal of scholars aiming to combat the eroding morals of the time. Although there may be many reasons behind the skewed representations, the fact remains that the portrayal of the wives of the Prophet in the KTK seems alarmingly subjective. One can conclude that there is an imminent need for academic scholars to re-examine the "canonical" texts to ferret out any biases, identifying and highlighting them as they are encountered. This examination is a step forward in the ongoing efforts made by scholars of Islamic studies to bridge the vast rift between the egalitarian message of the Qurʿan and the centuries-old patriarchal interpretations that have burdened the Islamic tradition and adversely affected the lived realities of Muslim women, men, and families to this day.

NOTES

This chapter is based on my MA thesis titled "Gender Discourse in *Kitāb al-Ṭabaqāt al-kubrā*: Deconstructing Ibn Saʿd's Portrayal of The Model Muslim Woman," American University in Cairo, 2013, under the supervision of Dr Amina ElBendary and the readership of Dr Mohamed Serag and Dr Huda Lutfi.

1 Q. 33:30–2 directly addresses the wives of the Prophet, instructing them to adhere to certain rules of conduct.

2 This study utilizes the Leiden edition, Ibn Saʿd, *Kitāb al-ṭabaqāt al-kubrā*.

3 Atassi, "History," 1.

4 See, for example, Q. 4:135; 5:8.

5 Mir-Hosseini, "Muslim Legal Tradition," 37–8.

6 Munslow, *Deconstructing History*, 12.

7 The concept of "historicism" holds that all knowledge and cognition are historically conditioned. For more, see Hamilton, *Historicism*.

8 Belsey, *Critical Practice*, 144.

9 Roded, *Women*, 59.

10 The intermittent narrative section that separates the Prophet's family from the rest of the Muslim women is sixty-one pages long, comprising 18 percent of the volume.

11 Ibn Saʿd, *Kitāb*, 1. All translations from the Arabic are mine, unless otherwise stated.

12 Stowasser, "Women's Bay'a," 95.
13 Ibn Sa'd, *Kitāb,* 40.
14 Ibid.
15 For details on the Battle of the Camel see Haider, "Camel, Battle of the."
16 Ibn Sa'd, *Kitāb,* 51.
17 "And stay quietly in your houses, and make not a dazzling display, like that of the former Times of Ignorance; and establish regular Prayer, and give regular Charity; and obey Allah and His Messenger. And Allah only wishes to remove all abomination from you, ye Members of the Family, and to make you pure and spotless." Yusuf 'Ali's interpretation.
18 The word used in Arabic is not camel but *dāba,* which is defined in *Lisān al-'Arab* as any animal that produces a sound while walking. See Ibn Sa'd, *Kitāb,* 37.
19 Ibid., 38. See Q. 33:33 in above note.
20 *Jihād* is often rendered "holy war" in English, although it more accurately means "effort." For more on *jihād* see Afsaruddin, *Striving.*
21 Ibn 'Abd al-Barr, *Al-Istī'āb.* For more examples of Muslim women in the battlefield, see Sonbol, "Rise of Islam," 3–9.
22 Ibn Sa'd, *Kitāb,* 291, 302, 312.
23 *Lisan al-'Arab* defines the terms as follows: *khimār* stems from the *kh-m-r* root, meaning cover. *Niqāb* stems from the root meaning of creating a hole; "*nuqb*" and refers to either a cover around the face, or a face cover with holes for the eyes; *izār* stems from the root word "to engulf" and refers to any type of dress that engulfs the body; *dir'* refers to a woman's shirt or a shield of iron or a loose outer garment. *Ḥijab* stems from the root word "to conceal" and refers to anything that serves such purpose. See, Ibn Manzūr, *Lisan al-'Arab*, vol. 1, 298–89, 761–70; vol. 4, 16–19, 254–9; vol. 8, 81–4.
24 Ibn Sa'd, *Kitāb,* 85.
25 Ibid., 91.
26 Ibid.
27 Al-'Asqalānī, *Al-Iṣāba,* 14.
28 In this instance, "foreign" is the equivalent of the Arabic *gharīb* and refers to Abū Ṭalḥa not being a close relative of Ṣafiyya. He was not a "foreigner" in the outsider or non-native sense.
29 Ibn Sa'd, *Kitāb,* 39.
30 Ibid., 47.
31 Although Ibn Sa'd does not specify which verse in *Surat al-Nūr* 'A'isha is referring to, it is likely that the verse in question is verse 31.
32 Ibn Sa'd, *Kitāb,* 39.

33 Ibid., 72.
34 Al-ʿAsqalānī, *Al-Iṣāba,* 275.
35 For studies promoting similar theories, see, for example, Ahmed, *Women and Gender*; Deniz Kandiyoti, "Islam and Patriarchy"; Fatima Mernissi, *Veil and the Male Elite*; Sonbol, *Beyond the Exotic*; and Spellberg, "History Then, History Now."
36 Sonbol, "Rise of Islam," 8.
37 Abbott, "Women and the State," 351.
38 Atassi argues that only those who agreed with the Caliph's opinion were considered to be true believers who could be trusted in aiding the court's mission of protecting the religion. See Atassi, "A History," 60.
39 Abbott, "Women and the State," 368.
40 Ibn Saʿd, *Kitāb,* 67.
41 For details on Umm Salama's integral role in the history of early Islam, see Amin, "Umm Salama and Her Ḥadīth."
42 The Ḥudaybiyya treaty took place in year (6/628). For more details on the treaty see Montgomery Watt, "al-Ḥudaybiyya." As referenced earlier, for in depth information about Umm Salama and her pivotal role in early Islamic history see Amin, "Umm Salama and Her Ḥadīth."
43 Ibn ʿAbd-al-Barr, *Al-Istīʿāb*, 1939. In the year 6/628, Muhammad marched with over 1,500 men and more than 100 horses to surprise the Jews of Khaybar. See for example L. Veccia Vaglieri, "Khaybar," in *Encyclopaedia of Islam*, 2nd ed., ed. P. Bearman, Th. Bianquis, C.E. Bosworth, E. van Donzel, and W.P. Heinrichs.
44 Al-ʿAsqalānī, *Al-Iṣāba,* vol. 13, 221.
45 Ibn ʿAbd al-Barr, *Al-Istīʿāb,* 1883.
46 Ibid.
47 Al-ʿAsqalānī, *Al-Iṣāba*, 40.
48 Ibid.
49 Ibn Saʿd, *Kitāb,* 283.
50 Ibid., 291.
51 Ibid., 312, 175. There are many other examples of women who participated in battle according to Ibn Saʿd. For details, see the biographies of Kuʿayba bint Saʿd, Umm Mūṭāʿ, Umm Sinān, Ummayya bint Qays, Umm Mānīʿ bint ʿAmr, and Umm ʿAṭiyya al-Anṣāriyya. Ibid., 213–14, 280, 311.
52 Ibid., 214.
53 Ibid., 193.
54 Ibid., 183.
55 Ibid., 214.

56 Ibid., 168.
57 Ibid., 162.
58 Ibid., 211.
59 Ibid., 290.
60 Ibid., 203.
61 Ibid., 217.
62 Ibid., 1.
63 Afsaruddin, "Islamic Biographical Dictionaries," 33.
64 Fück, J.W. "Ibn Sa'd."
65 Some scholars attribute the primary cause for the rise of the *ṭabaqāt* genre to the establishment of genealogy as a means of asserting kinship to the Prophet. Gilliot, "*Tabaḳāt*."
66 Hurvitz, "Biographies," 43.
67 Gibb, "Islamic Biographical Literature," 55.
68 Atassi, "History," 18.
69 Cooperson, "Ibn Hanbal," 72.
70 Keddie, *Women in Middle Eastern*, ,15. For song and entertainment see Ḍayf, *al-Shi'r wa'l-ghinā'*, 29.
71 Keddie, *Women in Middle Eastern,* 15.
72 El Cheikh, *Women, Islam*, 7.
73 Ibid.
74 Ahmed, *Women and Gender*, 12.
75 Kennedy, *When Baghdad Ruled*, 161.
76 Omar, "Hārūn al-Rashid."
77 Ibid.
78 Kennedy, *Early 'Abbāsid Caliphate*, 112.
79 El Cheikh, "Gender and Politics," 161.
80 For details see Ḍayf, "*Al-Shi'r*"; al-Hamawi, *Tajrid al-aghāni*; Sawa, "Status and Roles," 69–82.
81 Kennedy, *Early 'Abbāsid Caliphate*, 115.
82 Farag, "Arabian Nights," 204.
83 Lutfi, "Manners and Customs."
84 Afsaruddin, "Islamic Biographical Dictionaries," 34.
85 Bentley, "Myths," 51.

REFERENCES

Abbott, Nabia. "Women and the State in Early Islam." *Journal of Near Eastern Studies* 1, no. 3 (1942): 341–68.

Afsaruddin, Asma. "Islamic Biographical Dictionaries: 11th to 15th Century." In *Encyclopedia of Women and Islamic Cultures*, ed. Suad Joseph, vol. 1, 32–6. Leiden: Brill, 2003.

– *Striving in the Path of God: Jihad and Martyrdom in Islamic Thought*. Oxford: Oxford University Press, 2013.

Ahmed, Leila. *Women and Gender in Islam: Historical Roots of a Modern Debate*. New Haven: Yale University Press, 1992.

Amin, Yasmin. "Umm Salama and Her Ḥadīth." MA thesis, American University in Cairo, 2011.

ʿAsqalānī, Shihāb al-Dīn Abī al-Faḍl Aḥmad ibn ʿAlī "Ibn Ḥajar" al-. *Al-Iṣāba fī ṭamyyīz al- ṣaḥāba*. Cairo: Maktabat al-Kulliyyāt al-Azhariyya, 1968.

Atassi, Ahmad Nazir. "A History of Ibn Saʿd's Biographical Dictionary *Kitāb al-ṭabaqāt al-kabīr*." PhD diss., University of California–Santa Barbara, 2009.

Belsey, Catherine. *Critical Practice*. London: Methuen, 1980.

Bentley, Jerry H. "Myths, Wagers, and Some Moral Implications of World History." *Journal of World History* 16, no. 1 (2005): 51–82.

Cooperson, Michael. "Ibn Ḥanbal and Bishr al-Ḥāfi: A Case Study in Biographical Traditions." *Studia Islamica* 86 (1997): 71–101.

El Cheikh, Nadia Maria. "Gender and Politics in the Harem of al-Muqtadir." In *Gender in the Early Medieval World: East and West, 300–900*, ed. Leslie Brubaker and Julia M.H. Smith, 147–64. Cambridge: Cambridge University Press, 2004.

– *Women, Islam, and ʿAbbasid Identity*. Cambridge, MA: Harvard University Press, 2015.

Fück, J.W. "Ibn Saʿd." In *Encyclopaedia of Islam, Second Edition*, ed. P. Bearman, Th. Bianquis, C.E. Bosworth, E. van Donzel, and W.P. Heinrichs. http://dx.doi.org/10.1163/1573-3912_islam_SIM_3343.

Gibb, H.A.R., "Islamic Biographical Literature." In *Historians of the Middle East*, ed. B. Lewis, 54–9. New York: Oxford University Press, 1962.

Gilliot, Cl. "*Tabaḳāt*." In *Encyclopaedia of Islam, Second Edition*, ed. P. Bearman, Th. Bianquis, C.E. Bosworth, E. van Donzel, and W.P. Heinrichs. http://dx.doi.org/10.1163/1573-3912_islam_COM_1132.

Haider, Najam I. "Camel, Battle of the." In *Encyclopaedia of Islam, THREE*, ed. Kate Fleet, Gudrun Krämer, Denis Matringe, John Nawas, and Everett Rowson. Leiden: Brill, 2013. http://dx.doi.org/10.1163/1573-3912_ei3_COM_25465.

Ḥamawī, Muḥammad ibn Wāṣil al-. *Tajrīd al-Aghānī*. Beirut: Dār Iḥyā' al-Turāth al-'Arabī, 1955.
Hamilton, Paul. *Historicism*. 2nd ed. London: Routledge, 2003.
Hurvitz, Nimrod. "Biographies and Mild Asceticism: A Study of Islamic Moral Imagination." *Studia Islamica* 85 (1997): 41–65.
Ibn 'Abd al-Barr, Abū 'Umar Yūsuf ibn 'Abd Allāh ibn Muḥammad. *Al-Istī'āb fī ma'rifat al-asḥāb*. Ed. A.M. Bijawi. Cairo: Nahḍat Miṣr, 1959.
Ibn Manẓūr al-Ifrīqī al-Miṣrī, Abū al-Faḍl Jamāl al-Dīn Muḥammad ibn Mukarram. *Lisan al-'Arab*, 3rd ed. 15 vols. Beirut: Dār Ṣādir, 1994.
Ibn Sa'd, Muḥammad. *Kitāb al-ṭabaqāt al-kubrā*. Ed. Carl Brockelmann. Leiden: Brill, 1904.
Kandiyoti, Deniz. "Islam and Patriarchy: A Comparative Perspective." In *Women in Middle Eastern History: Shifting Boundaries in Sex and Gender*, ed. N. Keddie and B. Baron. New Haven: Yale University Press, 1991.
Keddie, Nikki R. *Women in the Middle East: Past and Present*. Princeton: Princeton University Press, 2007.
Kennedy, Hugh. *The Early 'Abbāsid Caliphate: A Political History*. London: Croom Helm, 1981.
– *When Baghdād Ruled the Muslim World*. Cambridge, MA: Da Capo Press, 2005.
Lockwood, Penelope. "'Someone Like Me Can Be Successful': Do College Students Need Same-Gender Role Models?" *Psychology of Women Quarterly* 30, no. 1 (2006): 36–46.
Lutfi, Huda. "Manners and Customs of Fourteenth-Century Cairene Women: Female Anarchy versus Male Shar'ī Order in Muslim Prescriptive Treatises." In *Women in Middle Eastern History*, ed. N. Keddie and B. Baron, 99–121. New Haven: Yale University Press,1991.
Mernissi, Fatima. *The Veil and the Male Elite: A Feminist Interpretation of Women's Rights in Islam*. Lakeland: Perseus Books, 1991.
Mir-Hosseini, Ziba. "Muslim Legal Tradition and the Challenge of Gender Equality." In *Men in Charge? Rethinking Authority in Muslim Legal Tradition*, ed. Ziba Mir-Hosseini, Mulki Al-Sharmani, and Jana Rumminger, 13–42. London: Oneworld, 2015.
Munslow, Alun. *Deconstructing History*. London: Routledge, 1997.
Omar, F. "Hārūn al-Rashid." In *Encyclopaedia of Islam, Second Edition*, ed. P. Bearman, Th. Bianquis, C.E. Bosworth, E. van Donzel, and W.P. Heinrichs. http://dx.doi.org/10.1163/1573-3912_islam_COM_0002.

Roded, Ruth. *Women in Islamic Biographical Collections: From Ibn Sa'd to Who's Who*. Boulder: Lynne Rienner, 1994.
Sawa, George Dimitri. "The Status and Roles of the Secular Musicians in the Kitāb al-Aghānī (Book of Songs) of Abu al-Faraj al-Iṣbahānī (356 AH /967 AD)." *Asian Music* 17, no. 1 (1985): 69–82.
Sonbol, Amira El-Azhary. *Beyond the Exotic: Women's Histories in Islamic Societies*. Syracuse: Syracuse University Press, 2005.
– "Rise of Islam: 6th to 9th Century." In *Encyclopedia of Women and Islamic Cultures* 1, ed. Suad Joseph, 3-9. 2003.
Spellberg, Denise. "History Then, History Now: The Role of Medieval Islamic Religio-Political Sources in Shaping the Modern Debate on Gender." In *Beyond the Exotic: Women's Histories in Islamic Societies*, ed. Amira Sonbol, 3–14. Syracuse: Syracuse University Press, 2005.
Stern, Gertrude H. *Marriage in Early Islam*. London: Royal Asiatic Society, 1939.
Stowasser, Barbara Freyer. *Women in the Qur'ān, Traditions, and Interpretation*. New York: Oxford University Press, 1994.
– "The Women's Bay'ā in Qur'an and Sīra." *Muslim World* 99, no. 1 (2009): 86–101.
Wāqidī, Muḥammad ibn 'Umar ibn al-. *Kitāb al-Maghāzi*. Ed. M. Jones. Oxford: Oxford University Press, 1966.

7

The Love of Prophet Muḥammad for the Jewish Woman Rayḥāna bint Zayd

Transformation and Continuity in Gender Conceptions in Classical Islamic Historiography and *Aḥādīth* Literature

Doris Decker

This chapter focuses on the relationship between the Prophet Muḥammad and the Jewish woman Rayḥāna bint Zayd, whom the Muslims captured in 5/627 after they defeated Banū Qurayẓa. The relationship that unfolded between the two is noteworthy, allowing that early Islamic historiography and the *aḥādīth* literature from the second/eighth to the seventh/thirteenth centuries provide numerous contradictory narratives. Even a brief comparison reveals, first, a transformation in the gendered conceptions of Rayḥāna and Muḥammad, and, second, the continuity of such narratives. Against this background, this chapter examines the transformation and continuity of the individual traditions, in terms of the following questions:

1. Which literary images of Muḥammad and Rayḥāna and their relationship are conveyed in the texts, and which themes dominate?
2. How do changes and continuities in the conceptions of and the relationship between genders develop over five centuries?

Two basic problems are considered: (1) canonization, and (2) interreligious marriage.

In contradiction to a distinguishing feature of Islam, that is, its lack of central authority or an institutional body through which something can be formally defined as "canonical," scholars have recently taken up the terms "canon" and "canonization"[1] and begun to apply concepts such as "canonical texts" and "canonical laws" to describe historical and literary developments in *ḥadīth* and *fiqh* in the Islamic context.[2] Drawing on transformations in depictions of Muḥammad and Rayḥāna's relationship, this chapter examines whether such "canonization" is actually evident in early Islamic historiography and the *aḥādīth* literature. It focuses on canonization as the ascription of authority, reconstructing the methods early compilers used to construct their texts as authorities on the history of early Islam. In this example, canonization refers to both figurative representations – conceptions of and relationships between genders – and the literary narrative of the particular version of the tradition. Texts and symbols and so on can be considered canonized when they are determined to be authoritative and normative and thus retain continuity over several centuries.

Since the love between Muḥammad and Rayḥāna centres on an interreligious relationship, this chapter also focuses on the theme of interreligious marriage, a subject that continues to be controversial, for its legal repercussions vary. For example, Sunnis forbid a Muslim woman to marry a non-Muslim man – a stance that is said to derive from the Qurʾan (Q. 2:221 and 60:10). Yet a Muslim man can marry a non-Muslim woman provided she belongs to a religion of the book (*ahl al-kitāb*), which Sunnis base on Q. 5:5. Some Sunni scholars deem such marriages "undesirable."[3] Nowadays, in order to circumvent the prohibition of interreligious marriage, some couples marry abroad.[4] In light of such considerations, it is necessary to ask which positions vis-à-vis interreligious marriage are represented in the individual traditions; due to the differing content in the traditions, this chapter limits itself to the relationship between a Muslim man and a non-Muslim woman.

METHODOLOGICAL APPROACH

The analyzed material comprises thirty traditions from eleven compilations of early Islamic historiography and *aḥādīth* literature by ten scholars from the second/eighth to the seventh/thirteenth centuries. It includes al-Wāqidī's *Kitāb al-maghāzī*; Ibn Hishām's *Sīrat rasūl Allāh*; Ibn Saʿd's *al-Ṭabaqāt al-kabīr fī al-nisāʾ*; al-Balādhurī's

Ansāb al-ashrāf; al-Ṭabarī's historical work, *Taʾrīkh al-rusul wa'l-mulūk wa'l-khulafāʾ*; al-Ṭabarānī's *Al-Muʿjam al-kabīr*; al-Ḥākim al-Naysābūrī's *Al-Mustadrak ʿalā al-ṣaḥīḥayn*; Abū Nuʿaym al-Iṣfahānī's *Maʿrifat al-ṣaḥāba*; Abū Bakr al-Bayhaqī's *Dalāʾil al-nubuwwa* and *Al-Sunan al-kubrā*; and ʿIzz al-Dīn ʿAlī ibn al-Athīr's *Usd al-ghāba fī maʿrifat al-ṣaḥāba*.[5]

Research shows that the compilers who attempted to document the events of the early first/seventh century often back-projected later experiences or idealized distortions of previous eras and their personalities in their accounts. Indeed, depictions were manipulated, for example, through attempts at legitimization by ruling dynasties, through the establishment of the Islamic legal system, or by rival theological groups.[6] So it is questionable whether such compilations represent an "authentic" image of past events. A historical reconstruction of the period is further complicated by the approximately 150 to 200 years between the Prophet's death and the oldest records, during which a specific Islamic identity was pursued through the canonization of particular narratives.[7] Accordingly, consideration must be given to the different norms and values that are back-projected onto the time of the Prophet from different temporal and regional contexts. At the same time, it is important to note the particular norms that have been canonized and that have suppressed other narratives through their continual reiteration in the records. This is particularly important for the descriptions of men and women in such texts, which may have sought to legitimize contemporary or desired gender and social orders and thus cannot be accepted as historical fact.[8]

Despite this generally complex state of the sources (in that several often contradictory narratives were recorded about the same event), researchers often continue to reconstruct linear historical events from the records, and this has resulted in the establishment of weak theses. For example, Fatima Mernissi's thesis is, in my opinion, not convincing, as she often analyzes the traditions inadequately but nevertheless treats them as historical accounts. For instance, her interpretation of the figure of Rayḥāna is rather one-sided, drawing historical inferences from only one version of the narrative.[9] Neglecting the diversity of the records gives the false impression that a uniform picture of the history of early Islam can be reconstructed based on the existing sources; this inevitably leads to a kind of "canonization," favoured by her preferred version of tradition, and, at the same time, to a normalization of particular gender conceptions from which social or legal conventions could be derived.[10]

Accordingly, while this chapter reconstructs and analyzes the transformation as well as the continuities of the gender conceptions of both Muḥammad and Rayḥāna and their relationship in historical retrospective, it is ultimately about the messages of the texts themselves.[11] This allows for insight into how scholars depicted and evaluated gender relations in early Islam in and around Mecca and Medina. The diversity of the narratives also facilitates inferences about which representations they accepted (canonized) and which they rejected. In this respect, this chapter traces the cultural *Zeitgeist* of the later centuries (as manifested in the texts) in which the narratives were compiled rather than some potentially false linear history of the early Islamic period.

TRADITIONS FROM THE SECOND/EIGHTH TO THE THIRD/NINTH CENTURIES

AL-WĀQIDĪ (130–207/747–823)

Tradition 1.1

They said: Rayḥāna bint Zayd of the al-Naḍīr tribe was married [to someone] in the Qurayẓa tribe. The Messenger of God had already chosen her as part of the war booty. She was beautiful. The Messenger of God offered her to become a Muslim, but she refused everything expect Judaism. Thereupon, the Messenger of God kept her at a distance from himself, but suffered therefore from lovesickness. He sent for Ibn Saʿiyya and told him about it. Ibn Saʿiyya said: "By my father and mother, she will become a Muslim!" He looked for her and began to say to her (many times): "Do not follow your people; you have already seen what has befallen Ḥuyayy ibn Akhṭab.[12] Become a Muslim instead, so that the Messenger of God may choose you for himself." When the Messenger of God was with his companions one day, he heard the sound of sandals and said: "These are the sandals of Ibn Saʿiyya, who brings me glad tidings of Rayḥāna's Islam." Then he came and said: "O Messenger of God, Rayḥāna has already become a Muslim!" That pleased him.[13]

Tradition 1.2

ʿAbd al-Malik ibn Sulaymān told me from Ayyūb ibn ʿAbd al-Raḥmān ibn Abī Ṣaʿṣaʿa from Ayyūb ibn Bashīr al-Muʿāwiyy, who said: The Messenger of God sent her to the house of Salmā bint Qays Umm al-Mundhir. She was with her until she menstruated and then this ended. Then Umm al-Mundhir went and reported to the Prophet (about what had occurred). Then the Messenger of God came to her in the house of Umm al-Mundhir. The Messenger of God said to her: "If you would prefer it, I will free you and marry you. I could do that. But if you would prefer to be in my possession [*fī milk*], I will sleep with you according to the right of possession [*aṭaʾuki biʾl-milk*]. I could make it so." She said: "O messenger of God, it is easier for you and for me when I am in your possession." So she remained in his possession and he slept with her until she died with him [in his lifetime].[14]

Tradition 1.3

Ibn Abī Dhiʾb told me, he said: I asked al-Zuhrī about Rayḥāna. He answered: She was a slave woman [*ama*] of the Messenger. He manumitted and married her. She used to live a reclusive life with her family [*iḥtajabat*] and would say: "No one sees me but the Messenger of God." And this is for us the more reliable version of the two stories. Rayḥāna's husband before the Prophet was al-Ḥakam.[15]

The three traditions about Muḥammad and Rayḥāna included in the *Kitāb al-maghāzī* focus primarily on Rayḥāna's social status as Muḥammad's possession or the Prophet's wife, and on her conversion. These topics are not always discussed together: conversion is only included in 1.1, while marriage is mentioned in 1.2 and 1.3, and 1.1 covers marriage only implicitly.

In 1.1, in comparison to the subsequent twenty-nine versions, Ibn Saʿiyya's conviction that Rayḥāna had converted is unique, in that it is mentioned only in this version. Indirectly, it appears as though the text might also introduce the idea of marriage, as Ibn Saʿiyya recounts that Rayḥāna was promised "that the Messenger of God may choose you for himself." Here, it is important that Muḥammad had stayed away from Rayḥāna, because she had not converted, which means that because of her Jewish faith, he had forbidden himself any involvement with her. It is also clear in this version that a woman captured as war booty had the right not to convert to Islam and to retain her religion and that Muḥammad accepted her decision. He was, however, unhappy about it as it meant he would have to keep his distance from her. He later rejoiced, following her conversion, for the same reason, since nothing then stood in the way of them being together. Moreover, Muḥammad's lovesickness[16] is clearly depicted (*wajada fī nafsihi*), and this emotional characteristic is repeated again in other versions. The depiction of the Prophet in 1.1 suggests that he chose Rayḥāna as war booty because he wanted to take her as his wife – likely because of her beauty – and that her Jewish faith initially kept him from being with her. Whether this depicted behaviour imparts the opinion that a Muslim man is not allowed to have a relationship with a Jewish woman, is discerned from the Prophet's words and deeds only if they are considered normative. Nevertheless, Rayḥāna is portrayed as a woman who wanted to remain faithful to her faith and to her people, and who, therefore, rejected Islam. Based on this account, it must have taken several rather persuasive attempts to convince her to convert to Islam.

1.2 and 1.3 do not focus on faith or conversion but rather on marriage in terms of social status. 1.2 depicts the type of relationship Muḥammad and Rayḥāna had: he, willing to marry her, first waited for her menstruation to ensure that she was not pregnant (although a prior husband was not mentioned). For this, he placed Rayḥāna in the care of Salmā bint Qays, a woman from the Khazraj tribe of Medina and his maternal aunt. After any chance of pregnancy was excluded, he proposed to manumit and marry her, giving her the option to become his wife or to remain a slave in his possession [*fī milk*], so that he, according to the rights of ownership, could sleep with her. On the subject of marriage and slavery in early Islam, Ali remarks: "The existence of slavery during Islam's early centuries resulted in a complex set of linkages between marriage and slavery in Islamic law, both seen as forms of ownership, *milk*, that legitimized sex (in the case of slavery, only when the owner was male and the owned, female)."[17] Rayḥāna chose the latter: she declined Muḥammad's marriage proposal, preferring to remain his slave. What she meant by "easier" (*akhaff*) can only be assumed. Perhaps she was not prepared to accept specific obligations or to tolerate the particular restrictions that marriage to the Prophet imposed. One reason could be the segregation imposed by the Qurʾan on the Prophet's wives; another could be the obligation not to marry after his death (Q. 33:32–4 and Q. 33:53).

It is rather conspicuous that both Muḥammad and Rayḥāna are cited in direct speech in 1.2; this brings the tradition alive and places the reader in close proximity to the events of the past – a kind of "past lived reality."[18] Also, this version depicts Rayḥāna as a self-determined woman. While it may sound paradoxical as she rejects freedom, it was indeed her own choice to make: she is allowed to speak; she decides for herself whether to accept or reject the proposal; and she chooses to reject it, justifying her rejection. To compare, in 1.1 only Muḥammad and Ibn Saʿiyya are cited in direct speech, and this banishes Rayḥāna to the background of the tradition. Finally, 1.2 reports that Muḥammad regularly slept with her and that she died before him. Her religion, Judaism, is not mentioned and plays no role in her relationship with Muḥammad.

1.3 is ascribed to al-Zuhrī and includes a new aspect: on the one hand, there is the concept *ama*, describing her as "slave," and *iḥtajabat*[19] (see also version 2.1), which implies that she returned to live a reclusive life with her family. On the other hand, this also implies that he manumitted and married her and that no one saw her after him, as she herself explains (in 1.3, this is cited only in direct speech). The statement that no one else saw her after the Prophet conforms with Q. 33:53 and with the commandment that the Prophet's wives speak to men only from behind a curtain.[20] We cannot know how willingly Rayḥāna married Muḥammad or whether he even gave her the option to decide as 1.2 describes, but she is depicted in her own explanations as an exemplary and modest wife who followed the Qurʾan's commandments. The fact that her Jewish faith was irrelevant in 1.3 – and in 1.2 – indicates that her faith was not an obstacle to her relationship with Muḥammad, regardless of whether it entailed marriage or ownership. That she remained Jewish without converting thus indicates that even as an enslaved woman, she maintained her right to freely choose her faith. It is also interesting that this tradition discusses her manumission for the first time. In 1.1 and 1.2, Muḥammad was not concerned with manumitting Rayḥāna from slavery, whether she converted to Islam or not, as 1.1 proposes.

The introduction to 1.3, "I asked al-Zuhrī about Rayḥāna," suggests that people were uncertain about her and her position. The accuracy of al-Zuhrī's assessment is bolstered by the addition that this tradition is the more reliable of the two accounts that were likely circulating in the community. Perhaps, in claiming greater reliability, 1.3 is comparing itself to 1.2. It thus seems to imply that Rayḥāna married Muḥammad, whereas 1.2 suggests that she remained a concubine. In 1.3, the name of Rayḥāna's former husband is given for the first time.

It is striking that in comparison to 1.1 and 1.2, the narrative in 1.3 does not indicate there were any problems with Rayḥāna, particularly in terms of her relationship with Muḥammad. This version lacks any references to difficulties or inconveniences, and Rayḥāna is described as a pious and exemplary wife. She is also not portrayed as being unruly regarding her faith or being against the marriage proposal. Thus, this version, in comparison to 1.1 and 1.2, idealizes Rayḥāna's gender conception. The Prophet is hardly mentioned; his thoughts and actions are rarely described. This positions him in some way as both sovereign and rational. The brevity of the version and the information it is missing that was contained in 1.1 and 1.2 give the impression that al-Zuhrī wanted to address the question whether the two had been married or not in an uncomplicated and concise manner.

IBN HISHĀM (D.~215/830)

Tradition 2.1

> He said [Ibn Isḥāq]: The Messenger of God had chosen for himself from their women Rayḥāna bint ʿAmr ibn Junāfa, a woman from the ʿAmr ibn Qurayẓa tribe. She was with the Messenger of God until he died with her, as she was in his possession [as a slave]. The Messenger of God had asked her to marry him and to uphold the *ḥijāb*, but she answered: "O Messenger of God, let me remain in your possession so that it will be easier for me and you." So he left her. It was already during her capture that she had opposed Islam and refused everything except Judaism. So the Messenger of God kept his distance from her and suffered from lovesickness for her. When he was with his companions one day, he heard the sound of sandals behind him and said: "That is Thaʿlaba ibn Saʿiyya, who brings me glad tidings of Rayḥāna's Islam." He came and said: "O Messenger of God, Rayḥāna has already become a Muslim." That pleased him.[21]

Ibn Hishām's *Sīra* includes only one tradition about Rayḥāna and Muḥammad. It is nearly identical to traditions in other compilations.

Accordingly, some of the following versions are not cited explicitly (for example, the tradition of al-Ṭabarī), but are instead compared to 2.1.

2.1 picks up both themes, marriage and conversion, and as the phrase "already during her capture" indicates, offers a reversed chronology that seems to imply that her conversion occurred before Muḥammad's proposal. In the first section, we learn that Muḥammad had chosen her as war booty and that she was in his possession until he died. 2.1 then reports that he asked her to marry him and uphold the *ḥijāb* – the first time this information appears in the narrative. The expression *wa-yaḍriba ʿalayhā al-ḥijāb* is understood in this context as "and she was to adopt the *ḥijāb*, i.e., to make it obligatory." The noun *ḥijāb* could be understood – particularly in the context of Muḥammad's wives – to imply some kind of "curtain"[22] used as a form of segregation for his wives, as formulated in Q. 33:53. In this context, the reference to *ḥijāb* is similar to Rayḥāna's reclusive life, described in 1.3 and expressed as *iḥtajaba* (1.3 has *taḥtajib*).

In 2.1, Rayḥāna also decides to remain in the Prophet's possession, based on the same reasoning provided in 1.2: it would be "easier" for them both. This is followed by a section that focuses on her time in captivity, which may have preceded the marriage proposal. This version mentions that she had refused Islam and remained loyal to Judaism. Accordingly, Muḥammad kept his distance from her, but at the same time also suffered from "lovesickness" for her. In the final section, Muḥammad learns, as he did in 1.1, of her conversion, which may have taken place at another time. This likely gave him the opportunity to make advances toward her again and to marry her. In comparison to al-Wāqidī, it is noticeable that 2.1 could be a combination of 1.1 and 1.2 (except for the reference to waiting for her menstruation, Ibn Saʿiyya's attempt to convince her to convert to Islam, and the statement that Rayḥāna died before Muḥammad). Such an assumed development could indicate that in the mind of the transmitters of these traditions, the question was primarily one of whether a Muslim man could enter into a relationship with a Jewish woman, which 2.1 and 1.1 deny based on Muḥammad's behaviour, inasmuch as his behaviour is understood as being exemplary for all Muslims to derive legal stipulations. Without the two paragraphs beginning at "It was already during her capture [...]," 2.1 would convey a relationship between a Muslim man and a Jewish woman for which nothing stands in the way.

Gender conceptions in 2.1 are those of an emotional Prophet suffering from lovesickness and a longing for Rayḥāna, whose Jewish faith keeps him from being with her. Rayḥāna, on the other hand, is described as self-determined in that she adheres to Judaism and refuses to marry him. The conversion narrative, which plays out the same in 1.1, appears to be a retroactive addition, indicating that it was no longer acceptable among scholars of later times for Rayḥāna to reject Islam. This assumption is supported by the Prophet's words when Ibn Saʿiyya brings him the glad tidings of Rayḥāna's conversion in 2.1. When Ibn Saʿiyya approached Muḥammad from behind, he recognized him and knew the content of his tidings even before they were delivered.

IBN SAʿD (168–230/784–845)

Tradition 3.1

Muḥammad ibn ʿUmar [al-Wāqidī] told us that ʿAbd Allāh ibn Jaʿfar had recalled from Yazīd ibn al-Hād from Thaʿlaba ibn Abī Mālik, who said: Rayḥāna bint Zayd ibn ʿAmr ibn Khunāfa of the al-Naḍīr tribe was married to a man who some said was al-Ḥakam. As the Qurayẓa tribe was captured, the Messenger of God took her for himself, then manumitted and married her. She died with him [in his lifetime].[23]

Tradition 3.2

Muḥammad ibn ʿUmar told us that ʿĀṣim ibn ʿAbd Allāh ibn al-Ḥakam told from ʿUmar ibn al-Ḥakam, who said: The Messenger of God manumitted Rayḥāna bint Zayd ibn ʿAmr ibn Khunāfa. She was with her husband, who had loved and adored her. She said: "I will not accept anyone after him [as her husband]." And she was a beauty. [Rayḥāna said]: "And when the Qurayẓa tribe was captured, the women were brought before the Messenger of God. I was one of those brought in front of him. I was ordered [to come], then I was separated from the others. And I was to become a part of the war booty for him from all the spoils. When I was separated from the others, God chose me. Then they sent me to the house of Umm al-Mundhir bint Qays for a few days, until the captives were executed and the women were distributed. Then the messenger of God came to me. I was filled with shame in front of him, and he took me and sat before me and said: "If you chose God and his Messenger, then the Messenger of God shall choose you for himself." I answered: "Truly, I choose God and His Messenger." When I became a Muslim, the Messenger of God manumitted and married me. He gave me twelve *ūqiyya*[24] and one *nashshan*,[25] as he also gave his other wives as dowry. He took me as his bride in the house of Umm al-Mundhir and sent for me, what he also sent for his other wives, and I adopted the *ḥijāb*." The Messenger of God was delighted with her and she received everything for which she asked from him. That is why they said to her, "If you had asked the Messenger of God about the Qurayẓa, he would have released them." And she used to say: "He was never alone with me before the captured women were distributed as slaves." Indeed, he was often alone with her and he had a great longing for her [he often slept with her]. She stayed with him until she died when he returned from his [last] pilgrimage. He buried her in al-Baqīʿ[26]. He had married her in the month of Muḥarram, six years after the Hijra.[27]

Tradition 3.3

Muḥammad ibn ʿUmar told us: Ṣāliḥ ibn Jaʿfar told me about Muḥammad ibn Kaʿb, who said: Rayḥāna was part of the war booty, that God had given to him. She was a beautiful, attractive woman. When her husband was killed, she was captured [as a slave]. She was part of the Messenger of God's war booty from the day of the [battle against the] Qurayẓa. The Messenger of God asked her to choose between Islam and her religion, and she chose Islam. Then the Messenger of God manumitted and married her, and he placed the *ḥijāb* upon her. She was extremely jealous over him, so he left her. She stayed in her place and did not leave it. This was unbearable for her and she cried more and more about it. Once the Messenger of God came to her when she was in this state. Then he took her back. She stayed with him until she died with him [in his lifetime] before he died.[28]

Tradition 3.4

Muḥammad ibn ʿUmar reported to us: Bakr ibn ʿAbd Allāh al-Naṣrā told us from Ḥusayn ibn ʿAbd ar-Raḥmān from Abū

Saʿīd ibn Wahb from his father, who said: Rayḥāna was of the al-Naḍīr tribe and she was married to a man from the Qurayẓa tribe, said to be Ḥakīm. The Messenger of God manumitted and married her. As she was one of his wives, he had given to her what he had given to all his wives, and he placed the *ḥijāb* upon her.[29]

Tradition 3.5

Muḥammad ibn ʿUmar told us: Ibn Abī Dhiʾb told me from al-Zuhrī, who said: Rayḥāna bint Zayd ibn ʿAmr ibn Khunāfa was a Quraẓiyya. She was in the possession of the Messenger of God, under his right hand [*kānat min milk rasūl Allāh bi-yamīnih*]. He manumitted and married her. Then he parted from her. With her family, she used to say, "No one sees me after the Messenger of God."[30]

Tradition 3.6

Muḥammad ibn ʿUmar said: In this *ḥadīth*, two perspectives are presumed, she was a Naḍariya and died with the Messenger of God [in his lifetime] and that is what we were told of her manumission and marriage, and those are the most confirmed statements for us. And so it is for the scholars. And I have already heard that it was transmitted that she was with the Messenger of God and that he had not manumitted her. He used to sleep with her according to his right of possession by his right hand, until she died.[31]

Tradition 3.8

Muḥammad ibn ʿUmar reported to us: ʿUmar ibn Salma told me from Abū Bakr ibn ʿAbd Allāh ibn Abī Juhm, who said: When the Messenger of God captured Rayḥāna, he offered her [conversion to] Islam. She declined and said, "I belong to the religion of my people." Then the Messenger of God said: "When you become a Muslim, the Messenger of God would choose you for himself." But she refused. This was unbearable for the Messenger of God. When the Messenger of God once sat amongst his companions, he heard the sound of sandals. He said: "That is Ibn Saʿiyya,

> he brings me the glad tidings of Rayḥāna's Islam." He came to him and reported: "Truly, she has already become a Muslim." The Messenger of God used to sleep with her according to the principles of the rights of possession, until he died with her [in her lifetime].[32]

Ibn Saʿd lists eight traditions that provide a particularly comprehensive and wide-ranging spectrum of content about Muḥammad and Rayḥāna's relationship. Al-Wāqidī and Ibn Saʿd's teacher/student relationship is evident in the *isnād* of the analyzed traditions, which identifies al-Wāqidī as transmitter.

Ibn Saʿd begins with a rather brief tradition (3.1). It does not cite direct speech or conversations between the Prophet and Rayḥāna. The tradition reports that the Prophet captured, manumitted, and then married Rayḥāna, and therefore, similar to version 1.3, also lacks any sort of reference to complications between the two. Her Jewish faith does not emerge as a topic or an obstacle to their relationship. Although Ibn Saʿd draws his version from al-Wāqidī, it does not appear – with the same *isnād* as mentioned by Ibn Saʿd – in the *Kitāb al-maghāzī*; this also applies to 3.2, 3.3, 3.4, 3.6, and 3.8.

3.2 is much longer than 3.1. Of the thirty versions discussed in this chapter, it is the longest and most comprehensive tradition of them all. New aspects of the account are added, some of which are found only in 3.2. Moreover, Rayḥāna is interestingly positioned as the narrator. She recounts that it was not Muḥammad who had chosen her, but that she had been chosen for the Prophet by God (*khāra Allāhu lī*). This suggests that her relationship with Muḥammad was divinely ordained, which raises her status and clearly identifies her as one of the Prophet's wives. Thus, the question whether she was his wife or his slave becomes obsolete. Rayḥāna also explains here for the first time that she did not want to accept another man after her first husband, who loved her very much. She is brought to Umm al-Mundhir's house for a different reason (the captives' execution) than in 1.2.

The description of the emotions between the two is striking. This begins as early as when Rayḥāna is ashamed of being visited by the Prophet. His proposal is predicated on the requirement that she convert to Islam. According to his statement ("if ... then ..."), conversion has to come before they are married – that is, *if* she chooses God and His messenger, *then* he will choose her for himself. Here, Rayḥāna refuses neither to convert nor to marry him, responding: "Truly, I choose God and His messenger," which is rather astonishing and unrealistic in the context of her capture and the execution of members of her tribe, as well as the prior loving relationship she had with her husband. In addition to the reference to *ḥijāb* (similar to 2.2), here a bridal dowry is mentioned for the first time, specifically that it was the same amount that Muḥammad had given to all his wives. Again, this underscores Rayḥāna's equal status with his other wives and her legal marriage to him.[33] That he was deeply attached to her comes through in the remark that he had given her everything for which she had asked. In addition, Rayḥāna assures the reader that her sexual relationship began after the captive women had all been distributed, which shows both of them as virtuous. After her sexual relationship with Muḥammad is legitimized, it is described as extremely active – he was often alone with her and had great longing for her. In 3.2, she dies before him and we learn where he buried her and when the marriage took place. Such detailed information (the amount of the dowry, the year of marriage) had never been provided in earlier versions.

There are other peculiarities in 3.3, which reports for the first time that the two had separated for a time, seemingly the result of Rayḥāna's jealousy. It is also explicitly mentioned here that it was God's plan for Rayḥāna to become Muḥammad's war booty. In contrast, variants 1.1, 2.1, and 3.1 report that the Prophet had chosen her for himself. Similarly, we learn that Rayḥāna decided to convert to Islam after the Prophet allowed her to choose between Islam and her religion, and – similar to 3.2 and 1.1 – not only that she was beautiful, but also that he was attracted to her. The tradition reports – albeit not in direct speech or in any conversation about the matter – that after she became a Muslim, she had been manumitted by the Prophet, married him, and adopted the *ḥijāb* (obligatory, see 2.1). In this version as well, the relationship between the two corresponds with her conversion. This is followed by a section not included in the other versions: because of her jealousy, likely directed at the Prophet's other wives, he may have left her, which affected her greatly. In comparison to 1.1 and 2.1, the gender conceptions between Rayḥāna and Muḥammad are particularly prominent in 3.3 because they are inverted. While Rayḥāna is emotional and jealous, and suffers from her separation from Muḥammad in 3.3, the Prophet is not described as suffering from lovesickness. In almost all versions (except in 3.8) Ibn Saʿd abandoned the depiction of the Prophet as being emotional in that way. So this marks the canonization of a certain figurative representation of the Prophet.

3.4 is as short as 3.1 and adds nothing new to the narrative; however, it rearranges the individual sections in a different order from prior versions.

3.5 is similarly short, but also has a special feature in terms of formulation. In this version, the two separate, as in 3.3, but it also informs us that no one else saw Rayḥāna after the Prophet, similar to 1.3. The *isnād* of 3.5 is the same as that of 1.3; even so, this version of the tradition differs in terms of content (the separation, the formulation of *bi-yamīnih*,[34] the mention of her tribe). The phrase "she was in the *possession* of the Messenger of God, under his right hand," in comparison to earlier formulations, such as *fī milkih* and the addition *bi-yamīnih*, echo Q. 4:3, 4:24, and 23:6. In the Qur'an, the expression "what their/your right hands possess" indicates control or ownership of someone (slaves).[35] In the context of the tradition, the phrase implies that Rayḥāna was Muḥammad's slave and that he could sleep with her whenever he wanted.

The formulation *min milk rasūli Allāh bi-yamīnih* appears similar to 3.6 as *bi-milk al-yamīn*, in that 3.5 and 3.6 are the only versions that add "*yamīn*." 3.6 refers to two versions, which are contradictory in terms of context and are prototypical answers to the question whether Muḥammad and Rayḥāna had married, and whether she remained his possession or he manumitted her. This underscores the degree to which the scholarly compilers of these texts were unclear about the actual relationship between Muḥammad and Rayḥāna.

Since 3.7 has the same *isnād* and content as 1.2,[36] the citation has been omitted. It should be emphasized, however, that this version is the last one to refer to Muḥammad waiting for Rayḥāna's menstruation before he entered into a relationship with her. This is mentioned only twice in the thirty transmitted versions (1.2 and 3.7).

The last of Ibn Saʿd's versions offers a new and unique description. The second part of the tradition is already known from 1.1 and 2.1. Here as well, it seems as though it is a later addition, which also addresses why this version always appears the same but is preceded by different narratives. The first part, however, is unique. Here, Rayḥāna first rejects Muḥammad's offer to accept Islam and then also refuses to enter into a relationship with him. The degree to which her rejection must have offended Muḥammad is expressed by the term "unbearable" (*shaqqa ʿalā*). The form of the relationship offered to her ("the Messenger of God would choose you for himself") only indirectly implies a marriage proposal, similar to Ibn Saʿiyya's statement in 1.1. However, since a marriage eventually takes place as described with the same formulation as 3.2, this can also be taken as a marriage proposal. The connection between conversion and relationship is also striking; the latter can only happen if the former takes place. This means that in order for her to enter into a relationship with Muḥammad, she was required to become a Muslim.

Ibn Saʿd's traditions offer a wide range of possibilities as to how Rayḥāna reacted to Muḥammad's desires and wishes, as well as different representations of both protagonists. However, some tendencies manifest themselves clearly. For example, Rayḥāna is more often depicted as emotionally insecure (3.2, 3.3), Muḥammad less often (3.8). By comparison, al-Wāqidī and Ibn Hishām report Muḥammad's lovesickness but not Rayḥāna's insecurity or jealousy. In terms of her conversion, it is striking that when her faith is addressed, she always converts, even if it had been previously reported that she had rejected Islam. This condition is included only in 3.8, as she immediately accepts Islam in 3.2 and 3.3, and this is rather new in comparison to al-Wāqidī and Ibn Hishām. Accordingly, there seems to be a tendency for Ibn Saʿd to portray Rayḥāna as determined to convert. Furthermore, in certain summaries, Rayḥāna is idealized as an exemplary and pious wife of the Prophet, which, in the context of Ibn Saʿd's traditions, can be considered a canonization of such characteristics. This is true not only for the particularly short traditions, but also and especially for the embellished traditions. It is noteworthy that in each of the traditions Muḥammad desires to have a relationship with Rayḥāna and that he marries her in six of the eight versions. In 3.2 and 3.8, it seems that her conversion is required before a relationship between the two is possible. Taken as a whole, all traditions are about their relationship; however, the topic of faith is addressed in only three out of the eight, each time requiring her conversion.

TRADITIONS FROM THE THIRD/NINTH CENTURY

AL-BALĀDHURĪ (D. 279/892)

Tradition 4.1

They said: The Messenger of God had chosen Rayḥāna bint Shamʿūn ibn Zayd ibn Khunāfa ibn ʿAmr from the Qurayẓa when he conquered the Qurayẓa. He offered Islam to her, but she rejected everything but Judaism. He kept his distance from her. Then she became a Muslim. He offered that she marry him and adopt the *ḥijāb*. She said: "Leave me rather in your possession." He used to sleep with her, as she was in his possession. She was under a man [had a husband], and about that man, he is said to be ʿAbd al-Ḥakam or al-Ḥakam and he was the son of her uncle and he adored her. She hated to marry after him. Some said: The name of the Quraẓiya is Rubayḥa. The Prophet made sure that she was lodged in the date farm [Nakhl] that belonged to him. It was called Nakhl al-Ṣadaqa. It is said that he perhaps fell ill with her or that he was ill at that time. Then he went to Maymūna's house, and then he moved to ʿĀ'isha's house. They said: Rayḥāna was from the al-Naḍīr by a Qurayẓa man, called Abū al-Ḥakam. And God knows best.[37]

Tradition 4.2

Muḥammad ibn Saʿd told me from al-Wāqidī from Ibn Abī Dhi'b from al-Zuhrī, who said: Rayḥāna bint Shamʿūn ibn Zayd ibn ʿAmr ibn Khunāfa was a Quraẓiyya. She was in the possession of the Messenger of God. He manumitted and married her and her dowry was her freedom. Then he parted from her. With her family, she used to say: "No one sees me after the Messenger of God."[38]

Tradition 4.3

Al-Wāqidī transmits in his *isnād* of Muḥammad ibn Kaʿb al-Quraẓī, he said: At that time Rayḥāna of the Qurayẓa was part of the war booty of the Messenger of God. The Messenger of God manumitted and married her. She was extremely jealous over him, so he parted from her. Then he took her back. She was with him until she died, before he passed away. Rayḥāna used to say: "The Messenger of God married me and my dowry was like that of his wives. He gave it to me. He placed the *ḥijāb* upon me. His marriage to me took place in the month of Muḥarram in the sixth year after the Hijra."[39]

Tradition 4.4

ʿAlī ibn al-Madīnī and Ibrāhīm ibn Muḥammad ibn ʿArʿara told me, they said: It was told to us by ʿAbd al-Razzāq from

> Maʿmar from al-Zuhrī, that the Messenger had two concubines [*surriyya*]: al-Qubṭiyya[40] and Rayḥāna bint Shamʿūn.[41]

Four traditions[42] in al-Balādhurī's *Ansāb al-ashrāf* focus on the relationship between Muḥammad and Rayḥāna. At the very beginning, 4.1 introduces new aspects. We learn that Muḥammad himself chose Rayḥāna as war booty and proposed that she convert to Islam. Since she rejected his offer and held tightly to her Jewish faith, he kept her at a distance. This version does not reference any lovesickness on his behalf. It then, without any embellishment or mention of any other persons, reports that Rayḥāna became a Muslim. After that, Muḥammad proposed marriage to her and required that she adopt the *ḥijāb*. In contrast to 1.2 and 3.7, Muḥammad is not cited here in direct speech. With this sequence, the tradition suggests that (as in 1.1 and 2.1) a Muslim man – to the degree that the Prophet's behaviour can be considered normative – should not enter into a relationship with a Jewish woman.

Rayḥāna's answer to Muḥammad's marriage proposal is similar to the narratives in 1.2, 2.1, and 3.7 but is written in direct speech: she chooses to remain his property, and this is followed by the information that he slept with her (as in 1.2, 3.2, 3.6, 3.7, 3.8). Additionally, the tradition mentions her prior marriage, the name of her husband, and, for the first time, how the two were related (her uncle's son), that he had adored her (as in 3.2), and that she hated to remarry after him. This may have served as an explanation for her negative attitude toward Muḥammad, indicating that it had nothing to do with him per se but was rooted in her prior love marriage. The tradition is also the first to include reference to uncertainty about her name and to where Rayḥāna lived during her relationship with the Prophet (a date farm belonging to the Prophet called al-Ṣadaqa). Another new element is that the tradition indicates that the Prophet may have fallen ill while he was with her, referring to the illness that led to his death in 10/632. It is, however, unclear whether he fell ill "with her" or "at that time" without actually being with her. After he fell ill, he went to the chamber of his wife Maymūna and then to that of his wife ʿĀʾisha. This version then mentions Rayḥāna's tribe, which nearly all traditions include, and concludes with another new addition in the sentence: "And God knows best." This indicates that not everything can be known or confirmed about Rayḥāna and Muḥammad's relationship.

In this version, the gender conceptions appear more objective. This version includes direct speech only from Rayḥāna; the Prophet does not speak. The development of the tradition's content is striking, particularly the new aspects such as the naming of the date farm where she lived and references to Muḥammad's illness. This is also the first time that the *isnād* appears in this manner, which could explain this version's development in terms of content. Furthermore, al-Balādhurī is the only one of all ten compilers to cite Anas ibn Mālik, the last of the Prophet's companions, believed to have died in Baṣra in 93/712.

The uniqueness of 4.2 can be found in the clear connection between al-Balādhurī's teacher, Ibn Saʿd, and his teacher, al-Wāqidī. This is also apparent in the *isnād*, as 4.2 has the same *isnād* as 3.5 and 1.3, supplemented by the respective teachers. In particular, similarities can be seen between 4.2 and 3.5, as al-Balādhurī also reports in 4.2 their separation and Rayḥāna's tribe. Here, the formulation *min milk* appears as in 3.5, but without the addition, *bi-yamīnih*. A new element in 4.2 is the description of the bridal dowry, not as a material present but as Rayḥāna's liberation from slavery. There are no references to her faith, and accordingly, these traditions are linked to those that indicate that a Muslim man can marry a Jewish woman.

4.3 has nearly the same *isnād* as 3.3, but the content differs in some places. Rayḥāna is described as being part of the war booty that God had given the Prophet in 3.3, but she is described only as being his war booty in 4.3. Al-Balādhurī simply reports that the Prophet manumitted and married her, that she became jealous, that he therefore left her and then took her back, and that she stayed with him until she died. This part is not embellished with details as in 3.3, with a description of her beauty, her husband, her conversion, or her despair as a result of their separation. Here, it appears that only the relationship between the two is of interest. Nevertheless, one statement is added about her dowry, which underscores that she was afforded the same status as Muḥammad's other wives after he married her. Rayḥāna then reports that Muḥammad had imposed the *ḥijāb*, also adding when the marriage took place. Such phrases should – as Stern emphasizes – make it clear that Rayḥāna was a legitimate wife of the Prophet.[43]

How important this assurance must have been for the process of memory for Muslims is demonstrated in one of the traditions recorded in the *Ansāb al-ashrāf*, which states: "Muḥammad ibn al-Aʿrābī said, I heard … , a man came to Rayḥāna during the harvest(44) and he said to her, 'Truly God did not want you to become the Mother of the

Faithful'." In this version of the tradition, Rayḥāna responds quickly: "And God did not want for you to become my son." [45] This suggests not only that there were different memories as to whether Rayḥāna had been married to Muḥammad, but also that she was not accepted in certain circles as the Prophet's wife. A further difference from 3.3 is that in 4.3 the exact dates of the marriage are provided. Here as well, it is noteworthy that the gender conceptions are less detailed (the description of Rayḥāna's appearance is missing) and less emotional (Rayḥāna was jealous but did not suffer from the separation). The most striking detail is that, in contrast to 3.3, the question is not one of faith and conversion; thus, conversion does not become a prerequisite for a marriage or a relationship between Muḥammad und Rayḥāna.

4.4 is very short, barely comprising the elements of the previous versions. It is remarkable that while the tradition draws on al-Zuhrī, it follows a different chain of transmitters than 4.2 (and therefore also 3.5 and 1.3). The only information provided about Rayḥāna and her relationship with Muḥammad is that she was one of Muḥammad's two concubines. For the first time in the thirty versions the Arabic name used to denote Rayḥāna's social status is *surriyya*,[46] translated in this context as "concubine." *Surriyya* primarily refers to a female slave who was also a concubine, meaning those slaves who had sexual relationships with their owners. This means that Rayḥāna maintained her status as Muḥammad's slave and that he slept with her whenever he wanted. Lane defines the term *surriyya* as "a concubine-slave; a female slave whom one takes as a possession and for *concubitus* (lat. for sexual intercourse); a female slave to whom one assigns a house, or chamber, in which he lodges her, and whom he takes as a possession and for *concubitus*." Similarly, in the *Lisān al-ʿArab*, *surriyya* means *ama* (see 1.3), a woman who is also provided a house.[47] The information that a female slave was provided a house or a room is interesting, as it is in 4.1 rather than 4.4 that we learn about the place where Muḥammad had brought Rayḥāna in order to visit and sleep with her.

Ninth-century Islamic legal sources such as the *Kitāb al-umm* by the legal scholar al-Shāfiʿī (150–204/767–820) indicate that the number of wives and concubines a man was entitled to have was controversial. [48] Al-Shāfiʿī permitted concubinage, arguing based on the Qurʾan: a man could have as many concubines as he wished, as God had not defined a limit in the Qurʾan.[49] Ali described the status of a concubine:

> Concubines often received additional privileges – better quality food and clothing, and usually exemption from duties of household service – and were subject to additional restrictions, usually related to keeping them exclusively available to their masters. The status of concubine was informal; however, law and custom allowed a master to have sex with any of his (unmarried) female slaves. It was also insecure: a concubine could be freed and married by her owner, or she could be sold off, so long as he had not impregnated her.[50]

With al-Balādhurī, the gender conceptions are less emotional and appear more factual compared to those presented by prior scholars: neither lovesickness nor jealousy is mentioned except in 4.3, and only then in reference to Rayḫāna. Two new aspects are brought into the narrative: the date farm where Rayḥāna lived and the assumption that the Prophet was with her when he fell ill. This new information notwithstanding, the traditions follow the narratives of the prior compilations and reveal, together with Ibn Saʿd's versions, some peculiarities for the third/ninth century, which can be taken as canonical for this period: the separation, the conversion (in 4.1 only), the marriage, the bridal dowry, and non-marriage as well as the *ḥijāb*. Conversely, some themes no longer play a role, such as the waiting period before they entered into a relationship, the description of Rayḥāna's appearance, and Muḥammad's desire for her.

TRADITIONS FROM THE THIRD/NINTH TO THE FOURTH/TENTH CENTURIES

AL-ṬABARĪ (225–310/839–923)

Al-Ṭabarī reports a tradition about Rayḥāna and Muḥammad that draws upon Ibn Isḥāq (5.1).[51] Since 5.1 is almost identical to 2.1, it is not cited here. It is surprising that al-Ṭabarī includes only one version of the narrative, given that his collection of traditions is quite substantial.[52] In contrast, as demonstrated, prior scholars had included multiple versions of the tradition: al-Wāqidī lists three, Ibn Hishām one (the same as al-Ṭabarī), Ibn Saʿd eight, and al-Balādhurī four versions. In addition, the probability that al-Ṭabarī knew of other versions is high. Perhaps he trusted that one version more than the others and therefore included it exclusively? On the other hand, this argument seems weak, as al-Ṭabarī often presents different narrative versions of the same events, side by side, without commenting on the historicity of the narratives.[53]

AL-ṬABARĀNĪ (260–360/873–971)

Tradition 6.1

> Al-Qāsim ibn ʿAbd Allāh ibn Mahdī al-Akhmīmī al-Miṣrī told us: This was told to me by my uncle, Muḥammad ibn Mahdī: It was told to us by ʿAnbasa: It was told to us by Yūnus from al-Zuhrī from Abū Umāma ibn Sahl from his father: [...] And he took Rayḥāna from the Qurayẓa as concubine [*istasarra*]. Then he manumitted her. She followed her tribe. She lived a reclusive life with her tribe.[54]

Although al-Ṭabarānī was one of the most popular *ḥadīth* scholars and compilers of his time, *Al-Muʿjam al-kabīr* contains very little information about Muḥammad and Rayḥāna. In 6.1, we learn that Muḥammad chose Rayḥāna to be his concubine. This is expressed here for the first with the verb *istasarra*[55], derived from the noun *surriyya*, which appears in al-Balādhurī's 4.4. This version also depicts that Muḥammad manumitted her and that she remained secluded with her tribe (*iḥtajabat*). It is unclear whether the latter means that Muḥammad married her and that she therefore lived reclusively according to the Qurʾanic rules (perhaps after his death), which is already depicted in 1.3. There is no information explicitly related to marriage, but it can be assumed that they married, as all prior versions refer both to their relationship and to eventual marriage. Similarly, nothing is reported about Rayḥāna's conversion, which suggests that although she was Jewish, Muḥammad could take her as his concubine.

While it is unnecessary to list the information omitted in 6.1, it is important to note that al-Ṭabarānī breaks with the typical narrative. The turn of the third/ninth century to the fourth/tenth century can therefore be understood as a turning point in the narrative, linked to the geographical shift in the centre of Islamic life and scholarship from the Iraqi to the Iranian area,[56] as evidenced, for example, in Persian influences such as the term *istasarra*. As Ali explains, the Arabs' emulation of the Sasanians' concubinage is expressed in the traditions with the inclusion of such verbs, which indicated the keeping of slaves for sexual pleasure.[57]

The additional emphasis on the sexual relationship placed further importance on understanding the relationship as concubinage, and this is reflected in 6.1 in the omission of other themes.

It is interesting that the *isnād* maintains al-Zuhrī as the tradent despite its differences from the previous tradition chains that include al-Zuhrī, who is said to have passed on Yūnus's tradition. Moreover, the transmission chain extends beyond al-Zuhrī as tradent here for the first time, with this version naming Abū Umāma ibn Sahl and his father.

6.2 is not cited for it is identical to 6.1.[58]

The student/teacher relationship between al-Ṭabarānī and al-Ṭabarī does not appear to have any influence on the tradition, so that al-Ṭabarānī also presents different versions.

TRADITIONS FROM THE FOURTH/TENTH TO THE FIFTH/ELEVENTH CENTURIES

AL-ḤĀKIM AL-NAYSĀBŪRĪ (321–404/933–1014)

Tradition 7.1

> Abū al-ʿAbbās told us: Abū Usāma al-Ḥalabī told us: Ḥajjāj ibn Abī Manīʿ told us from his grandfather from al-Zuhrī, he said: The Messenger of God took Rayḥāna from the Qurayẓa as his concubine. Then he manumitted her. She followed her tribe.[59]

Tradition 7.2

> Abū ʿUbayda Maʿmar ibn al-Muthannā said: She was one of the concubines of the Messenger of God, Rayḥāna ibn Zayd bin Shamʿūn. At that time, the Messenger of God used to say: "Her capture was in the month of Shawwāl in year four."[60]

7.1 and 7.2 by al-Ḥākim al-Naysābūrī are similar to al-Ṭabarānī's 6.1 and 6.2. Differences are found in the *isnād*, as al-Zuhrī once again reports that the tradition was passed on from another person (to this point there have been four different narrators). Additionally, there is no reference that Rayḥāna lived a reclusive life with her tribe, which also reduces the likelihood of marriage even if it is reported that Muḥammad manumitted her. 7.2 differs from all prior versions in its *isnād*, and only one person is named as the transmitter, Abū ʿUbayda Maʿmar ibn al-Muthannā. The latter may be identical to Maʿmar from 4.4, which justifies a comparison between 4.4 and 7.2. The two provide equally limited information: Rayḥāna was the Prophet's concubine, and 7.2 replaces the singular *surriyya* with the plural *sarārī*. The plural expresses that the Prophet had several concubines. This could be indicative of the Persian influence and of a legitimization – if not an Islamization – of concubinage. It is interesting to note that there is no question about Rayḥāna's liberation in 7.2. Muḥammad's statement about the month and year of her captivity is a new element in this version.

In terms of al-Ṭabarānī and al-Ḥākim al-Naysābūrī, some aspects of the narrative that were important for the other transmitters of the tradition do not play a role, and accordingly, their versions differ greatly from the previous ones. Most striking is that a marriage is not mentioned and it remains unclear whether Rayḥāna's manumission and her reclusive life imply that she had been married to Muḥammad. Rayḥāna's faith is also not addressed. The narratives are short and rather uniform; the versions are not contradictory, and unlike prior versions, they do not describe the relationship or the character of the protagonists. There is no portrayal of emotions, and direct speech is rare. In terms of the description of the gender relations, the terms *istasarra* and *surriyya* draw the focus to concubinage. Hence, the legitimization of concubinage seems to be the priority for the compilers and transmitters here.

ABŪ NUʿAYM AL-IṢFAHĀNĪ (336–430/948–1038)

Tradition 8.1

It is reported to us by Sulaymān ibn Aḥmad [al-Ṭabarānī]: Al-Qāsim ibn ʿAbd Allāh ibn Mahdī al-Akhmīmī told us: My uncle Muḥammad ibn Wahb told us: ʿAnbasa ibn Khālid ibn Yazīd told us: My uncle Yūnus ibn Yazīd told me from Ibn Shihāb [al-Zuhri] from Abū Umāma ibn Sahl from his father, he said: [...] And he took Rayḥāna from the Qurayẓa as his concubine. Then he manumitted her. She followed her tribe. With her tribe she lived a reclusive life.[61]

Tradition 8.3

Muḥammad ibn ʿAlī told us: Abū ʿArūba al-Ḥusayn ibn Abī Maʿsharin told us: Abū al-Ashʿath al-ʿIjlī Aḥmad ibn al-Miqdām told us: Zuhayr ibn al-ʿAlāʾ told us: Saʿīd ibn Abī ʿArūba told us from Qatāda, he said: The Prophet had two walīda. [...] And Rayḥāna belonged to him. And some of them said: Rumayḥa al-Quraẓiyya, one of the women of the Khufāfa. Then he was with us in the date farm [Nakhl] near al-ʿĀliya [a place west of Mecca]. And he lived with her [Rayḥāna] sometimes when the date farm was harvested. They claimed that the first time he had the pain, from which he died, it happened when he was with her.[62]

Tradition 8.4

Muḥammad ibn Aḥmad ibn al-Ḥasan told us: Abū Shuʿayb al-Ḥarrānī told us: Abū Jaʿfar al-Nufaylī told us: Muḥammad ibn Salama told us from Muḥammad ibn Isḥāq, who said: As the Messenger of God conquered the Qurayẓa tribe, he chose Rayḥāna bint ʿAmr ibn Junāfa for himself from these women, one of the women from the ʿAmr ibn Qurayẓa tribe. She was with the Messenger of God until he died with her [in her lifetime], as she was in his possession [as a slave]. The Messenger of God had offered Islam to her and that she would leave her religion; he had offered to marry her and make her uphold the *ḥijāb*, but she answered: "O Messenger of God, leave me rather in your possession, so that it is easier for me and for you." It was during her capture that she had hated Islam and rejected everything except Judaism. So the Messenger of God kept his distance from her and suffered from lovesickness for her. Once when he was with his companions, he heard the sound of sandals behind him and said: "That is Thaʿlaba ibn Saʿiyya, who is bringing me the glad tidings of Rayḥāna's Islam." He came and said: "O Messenger of God, Rayḥāna has already become a Muslim." That pleased him. Muḥammad ibn ʿUmar al-Wāqidī said: She died in the year 16 AH. ʿUmar prayed for her. He buried her in al-Baqīʿ.[63]

With Abū Nuʿaym al-Iṣfahānī, the number of versions returns to four. His connection to his teacher al-Ṭabarānī is apparent in 8.1, as he is the last person named in the *isnād*. With the exception of the *isnād*, 8.1 is nearly a word-for-word replication of 6.1, as 6.1 refers to "my uncle Muḥammad ibn Mahdī," while 8.1 provides details such as "my uncle Muḥammad ibn Wahb." The editor of the *Maʿrifat al-ṣaḥāba*, al-ʿAzāzī, notes that concerning "ibn Wahb," one of his manuscripts added "ibn Mahdī" (as in 6.1).

As 8.2 is similar to 8.1, it is not cited separately.[64] Its *isnād* differs: after the mention of Yūnus ibn Yazīd, 8.2 lists other people, and accordingly, the tradition draws, as in 8.1, on al-Zuhrī (but does not go beyond him).

A new *isnād*, only recorded once in all thirty versions, appears in 8.3. In terms of content, we learn that Rayḥāna belonged to the Prophet and that there was likely some confusion about her name. This version is the first to use the term *walīda*,[65] meaning "female slave" or "slave girl," to define her social status. Other terms such as *fī milk*, *istasarra*, and *surriyya* do not appear. This tradition reports for the second time that the Prophet was at the date farm (first time was in 4.1) but includes the farm's exact location in al-ʿĀliya. Furthermore, the tradition reports that Muḥammad lived with her there occasionally during the harvest. Finally, this version mentions, similar to 4.1, that Muḥammad had been with "them," that is, the people who had lived at the date farm including Rayḥāna, when he first felt the pain that would eventually lead to his death, which, in contrast to 4.1, 8.2 explains in detail.

8.4 draws on Ibn Isḥāq, but in contrast to 2.1 and 5.1, it includes the names of other transmitters. The *isnād* builds upon Ibn Isḥāq and leads to Abū Nuʿaym al-Iṣfahānī himself. Ultimately, 8.4 reproduces the contents of 2.1 and 5.1, adding two additional narrative elements. First, it states that Muḥammad requested that Rayḥāna convert to Islam before he proposed marriage to her. Second, as per the customary end of the Ibn Isḥāq tradition similar to 2.1 and 5.1, this version includes information from al-Wāqidī, such as the year of her death and, furthermore, that she was buried by ʿUmar in al-Baqīʿ. 3.2 also names this place, which Ibn Saʿd ascribes to al-Wāqidī (however, it was not included in the *Kitāb al-maghāzī*). Otherwise, gender conceptions and the relationship constellation remain the same as in 2.1 and 5.1.

Abū Nuʿaym al-Iṣfahānī connects his versions to the traditions of his predecessors and teachers, al-Ṭabarānī and al-Ḥākim al-Naysābūrī, particularly in 8.1 and 8.2. Yet he also breaks from those traditions in

8.3 and 8.4 and thereby broadens particular themes. Nonetheless, an explicit reference to a marriage between the two is not mentioned in the text. Rayḥāna is identified once as Muḥammad's concubine, what al-Ṭabarānī, al-Ḥākim al-Naysābūrī, and Abū Nuʿaym al-Iṣfahānī indicate with *istasarra* and *sarārī*, but she is also described as *walīda*, a new term that is distanced from the meaning of concubine, for it places less attention on the sexual relationship. All versions of the traditions by the last three compilers draw on al-Balādhurī's version in 4.4, which uses the noun of the same root, *surriyya*, for the first time. While the three compilers mention that Rayḥāna had been manumitted from slavery, they interestingly do not mention marriage. Nevertheless, al-Ṭabarānī and Abū Nuʿaym al-Iṣfahānī (but not al-Ḥākim al-Naysābūrī) retained material that may indicate a marriage with the hint that Rayḥāna had lived a reclusive life with her tribe. However, they have not preserved any explicit mentions of a marriage.

TRADITIONS FROM THE FIFTH/ELEVENTH CENTURY

ABŪ BAKR AL-BAYHAQĪ (384–458/994–1066)

Tradition 9.2

Abū ʿAbd Allāh al-Ḥāfiẓ told us, he said: Aḥmad ibn Kāmil told us, he said: al-Ḥasan ibn ʿAlī al-Bazzāz told us, he said: Muḥammad ibn ʿAbd al-Aʿlā told us, he said: Al-Muʿtamir ibn Sulaymān told us from his father, that the Messenger of God in the night of the 22nd of the month of Ṣafar became ill. His pain began when he was with a *walīda*, who belonged to him. They said about her, Rayḥāna. She was one of the women captured from the Jews. The first day he fell ill was a Saturday and he died on the tenth day. Two nights had passed since Rabīʿ al-Awwal. It had been ten years since he had arrived in the city (Medina).[66]

Tradition 9.3

Yaʿqūb said: Ḥajjāj said: My grandfather told me, he said: Muḥammad ibn Muslim, which means al-Zuhrī, that ʿUrwa ibn al-Zubayr had told him(67), that Āʾisha, the wife of the Prophet, said: [...] and he had a *walīda*, which was said to be Rayḥāna bint Shamʿūn from the People of the Book from the Khunāqa

> tribe. She was part of the Qurayẓa tribe. The Messenger of God manumitted her and they claimed that she had lived a reclusive life.[68]

As with Abū Nuʿaym al-Iṣfahānī, four versions appear in Abū Bakr al-Bayhaqī's works. In 9.1, Abū Bakr al-Bayhaqī draws on Ibn Isḥāq. As it is identical to the versions in 2.1 and 5.1, it is not cited.[69]

9.2 comprises known details but also adds new aspects to the narrative. First, we learn exactly when the Prophet fell ill and with whom he was at the time, namely that he was with a *walīda* who belonged to him. Here, the term *walīda* appears again as in 8.3. The *walīda* is specified with her name as well as with the information that she was one of the captive Jewish women. No information is provided about her tribe, in contrast to most other versions. Furthermore, the exact day of the week that Muḥammad fell ill and when he died is provided. About Rayḥāna, we learn only that she was his *walīda*, that she was one of the captive Jewish women, and that he fell ill when he was with her. Doubts as to whether he was with her at the beginning of his illness – as indicated in 4.1 or 8.3 – are not found.

9.3 distinguishes itself from all prior versions. The *isnād* draws on the Prophet's wife, ʿĀʾisha, who also identifies Rayḥāna as *walīda*. In the context of her tribal affiliation, which is very precisely identified here, ʿĀʾisha states that Rayḥāna was one of the "People of the Book," which is a term the Qurʾan uses for Christians and Jews (see, for example, Q. 4:64; 5:5; 29:46).[70] This is also the first time that this expression appears, and its addition confirms that she did not convert to Islam and remained Jewish. ʿĀʾisha describes that the Prophet had manumitted Rayḥāna but raises doubt as to whether she lived her life in seclusion with the expression "alleged" (*yazʿamūn*). This is in contrast to 6.1, 6.2, 8.1, and 8.2, and calls the marriage into question.

As 9.4 is identical to 9.3, it is not cited here.[71]

Abū Bakr al-Bayhaqī also rejects, like his predecessor, Abū Nuʿaym al-Iṣfahānī, the narrative uniformity that prevails with al-Ṭabarānī and al-Ḥākim al-Naysābūrī. The teacher/student relationship between al-Ḥākim al-Naysābūrī and Abū Bakr al-Bayhaqī is not visible in the versions, except for sharing some of the few scholars in the *isnād*. It is striking that Rayḥāna's social status is no longer defined with terms such as *istasarra* or *surriyya*; instead the term first used by Abū Nuʿaym al-Iṣfahānī, *walīda*, becomes prevalent. This term distances the relationship between Muḥammad and Rayḥāna noticeably from concubinage, and thereby places less emphasis on the sexual relationship between the two. Finally, the tradition does not explicitly state that Muḥammad slept with her, as it does in 1.2, 3.2, 3.6, 3.7, 3.8 and 4.1. However, for all the narrative variety in the versions of Abū Bakr al-Bayhaqī and Abū Nuʿaym al-Iṣfahānī, they do not include the themes addressed by scholars from the second/eighth to the third/ninth centuries. Furthermore, the richness of detail and the emotional descriptions are also missing. In comparison to earlier traditions, these reports are rather short and have little to no direct speech, concentrating on fewer topics. Furthermore, the reports are mainly *about* the protagonists rather than depicting them actively thinking and acting.

TRADITIONS FROM THE SIXTH/TWELFTH TO THE SEVENTH/THIRTEENTH CENTURIES

ʿALĪ IBN AL-ATHĪR (555–630/1160–1233)

Tradition 10.1

> Abū Jaʿfar told us with his isnād *from* Yūnus from Ibn Isḥāq, that the Prophet passed away with her [in her lifetime] as she was in his possession. The Messenger of God had offered to marry her and to place the *ḥijāb* upon her, but she answered: "O Messenger of God, leave me rather in your possession, so it will be easier for me and for you." So he left her. It was during her capture that she had already opposed Islam and rejected everything except Judaism. Thus, the Messenger of God suffered from lovesickness. One time when he was with his companions, he heard the sound of sandals and said: "That is Thaʿlaba ibn Saʿiyya, who is bringing me the glad tidings of Rayḥāna's Islam." Then he brought him the glad tidings of her Islam. This is also recorded by Abū ʿUmar and Abū Mūsā [in their works]. Abū Mūsā said: Rayḥāna bint ʿAmr is a concubine of the Messenger of God. Al-Ḥafiẓ Abū ʿAbd Allāh, which actually refers to Ibn Mundh,[72] mentioned her in the biography of Māriya. He had nothing about her [Rayḥāna's] life. She was called Rubayḥa.[73]

The last version considered here is by ʿAlī ibn al-Athīr. The *isnād* of 10.1 maintains, in comparison to 2.1, 5.1, and 9.1, which also draws on Ibn Isḥāq, the peculiarity that Yūnus and Abū Jaʿfar are mentioned.

These names refer to Ibn Isḥāq's student Yūnus ibn Bukayr (d. 199/815) and to al-Ṭabarī; however, how the two are connected is not explicitly identified here. In terms of content, 10.1 differs from 2.1, 5.1, and 9.1, which also draw on Ibn Isḥāq, in some respects, not only with the addition of new information, but also with the removal of certain narratives from previous versions. 10.1 does not mention that Muḥammad chose Rayḥāna for himself or that he distanced himself from her when she refused Islam. The content also differs in terms of narrative sequence in that the account begins with the information that the Prophet died before Rayḥāna, while she was still his property. Furthermore, although he had proposed to her, marriage does not take place in this version. Her initial negative attitude toward Islam and marrying the Prophet is mentioned, as are Muḥammad's lovesickness and her subsequent conversion. However, as this version does not refer to the Prophet maintaining his distance from her, we can only assume from the mention of lovesickness that he had forbidden himself to have any contact with her because of her Jewish faith.

The final paragraph contains new information, explaining that this tradition is included in other compilations as well. This version also describes Rayḥāna as the Prophet's concubine (*surriyya*), marking the first time the terms *fī milkih* and *surriyya* appear together in one version; this seems to combine the Iraqi versions of the traditions (al-Wāqidī and Ibn Saʿd) with the Persian ones (al-Ḥākim al-Naysābūrī and Abū Nuʿaym al-Iṣfahānī). Moreover, this paragraph highlights that different versions of the tradition were in circulation and indeed competed against one another. Accordingly, individual versions needed assurances and confirmations to attest to their historicity, such as additional mentions of other scholars and their compilations to indicate the version's veracity.

RESULTS OF THE ANALYSIS

This chapter's analysis of thirty versions of the relationship between Muḥammad and Rayḥāna depicts the wide-ranging themes explored within them; it also reveals the importance of particular questions and subjects for the scholars and compilers discussed. The frequency of appearance and the continuity in the narratives over the course of five centuries together point to what was of greater/lesser importance for the scholars – that is, to the canon of a particular period.

Two questions are of particular importance: first, whether Rayḥāna remained Muḥammad's slave or whether he manumitted and married her, and, inherently, whether a Muslim man could marry or have a sexual relationship with a Jewish woman; and second, whether she converted to Islam. Certain tendencies are evident:

1. Muḥammad's marriage proposal only appears in 1.2, 2.1, 3.7, 4.2, 5.1, 8.4, 9.1, and 10.1, and in combination with her conversion in 3.2 and 3.8; following al-Ṭabarī's version, the records no longer explicitly mention marriage. Thus, the reference to marriage is period-specific and likely related to the question of whether a Muslim man can marry a Jewish woman. Only al-Wāqidī, Ibn Saʿd, and al-Balādhurī directly report the marriage. When it is recorded – with one exception – it is not preceded by a marriage proposal, and all versions except one indicate that Rayḥāna rejected it. Only one-third of all versions mention the interreligious relationship between them. These versions indicate that a Muslim man should not enter into a sexual relationship with a Jewish woman (including marriage), insofar as the Prophet's behaviour is considered normative. In 1.2, 1.3, 3.1, 3.4, 3.5, 3.6, 3.7, 4.2, and 4.3, her Jewish faith is not an obstacle to the Prophet's marriage proposal. As she is a slave, her faith does not prevent Muḥammad from engaging in a sexual relationship with her in 4.4, 6.1, 6.2, 7.1, 7.2, 8.1, 8.2, 8.3, 9.2, 9.3, and 9.4. Nonetheless, nearly every version prioritizes Rayḥāna's social status as Muḥammad's wife or slave more than her religion. The topic of concubinage dominates – in terms of terminology as well – after al-Ṭabarānī's compilation. Beginning with Ibn Saʿd, six of the eight versions reference marriage; after al-Balādhurī, this is no longer the case.
2. Interest in Rayḥāna's faith faded over the centuries, likely the result of the changing lived reality of Muslims over the course of the Islamic conquest and the normalized and deproblematized coexistence of Muslims, Jews, and Christians. Apart from the transmission of her conversion through Ibn Saʿiyya (1.1, 2.1, 3.8, 5.1, 8.4, 9.1, 10.1), she is reported to have converted only in the three traditions included by Ibn Saʿd and al-Balādhurī (3.2, 3.3, 4.1).

Both continuities and transformations in gender conceptions are evident, and some are completely inversed over time. Rayḥāna's dismissive attitude toward Muḥammad, her refusal to marry him, and his subsequent lovesickness are replaced temporarily by a more idealized image of the two. Rayḥāna becomes a pious wife and a self-determined convert, who conversely suffered from jealousy and lovesickness because of him (for instance, in Ibn Saʿd). Accordingly, a specific characteristic emerges, particularly in al-Zuhrī's versions, in which Rayḥāna is completely unremarkable. While the other versions, such as those by Ibn Isḥāq and others (1.1, 1.2, 4.1, 3.8), often depict Rayḥāna as determined, unruly, and dominant, and Muḥammad as troubled by her unruliness, no such difficulties are referenced in al-Zuhrī's versions. Her representation appears to be smoothed over by al-Zuhrī so that the Prophet can abandon her easily and at will. This indifference is also evident in versions where she is not quoted in direct speech or not depicted as an active subject and in which emotional descriptions such as lovesickness or jealousy are omitted. These figurative representations thus serve to canonize particular narratives about gender conceptions. The analysis also reveals apparent competition between Ibn Isḥāq and al-Zuhrī for authority. The two scholars only agree that the two were not married (with the exception of 1.3, 3.5, 4.2). They disagree on the matter of her conversion. In Ibn Isḥāq's versions, Rayḥāna always converts, while Rayḥāna's status as a Jewish woman does not play a role in the relationship between her and the Prophet in al-Zuhrī's versions.

It is only Ibn Saʿd's and al-Balādhurī's versions from the third/ninth century that depict the Prophet's temporary separation from Rayḥāna and that she develops emotions, such as shame or jealousy, albeit less so than the Prophet. In contrast, al-Wāqidī's and Ibn Hishām's prior reports merely portrayed Muḥammad's lovesickness, not Rayḥāna's emotions. Later compilations that draw on Ibn Isḥāq's versions up to ʿAlī ibn al-Athīr present similar narratives. Indeed, the idealization of the protagonists reaches its pinnacle in the third/ninth century, as accentuated by emotional details. Ibn Saʿd's and al-Balādhurī's versions differ insofar as al-Balādhurī's depictions are more objective, adding new information such as where they lived and Muḥammad's illness.

With the fourth/tenth century, the gender conceptions take on a new direction, particularly in al-Ṭabarānī's versions and for subsequent scholars such as al-Ḥākim al-Naysābūrī and Abū Nuʿaym al-Iṣfahānī. This indicates that the repositioning of the centre of Islamic life and scholars from Iraq to Iran transformed or shifted the narrative. Some of the more dominant aspects of the earlier versions such as prior descriptions of the protagonists' relations or characteristics are omitted; also, the versions are shorter, and details are scarce and lack any direct speech. There is a fleeting tendency toward narrative uniformity, and scholars such as al-Ṭabarānī no longer include contradictory versions. It is also during this period that concubinage comes to the fore. This seemingly temporal narrative uniformity is broken, beginning with Abū Nuʿaym al-Iṣfahānī and continuing with Abū Bakr al-Bayhaqī, and the term *walīda* further distances Rayḥāna from her depiction as one of the available concubines used to satisfy sexual desire. Although the final three compilations draw on al-Balādhurī's tradition, they do not reach the diversity of the compilations from the second/eighth and the third/ninth centuries.

CONCLUSION: TEMPORAL CANONIZATION

From the earliest times, narratives about Rayḥāna and Muḥammad were unclear and/or controversial, and there appears to have been competition among the various versions. Scholars attempted to position their respective versions as authoritative, underscored in phrases such "and this is for us the more reliable version of the two stories" (1.3), "those are the most confirmed statements for us" (3.6), and "This is also recorded by [...]" (10.1). References to additional scholars in certain narratives serve to confirm a version's authority and thereby canonize its narrative. The diversity in the records thus indicates that there was no consensus in terms of which version was of greater historical accuracy and canonical; at the same time, most scholars seemed to have had no real problem including different versions of the narratives next to one another. Accordingly, scholars' isolated endeavours cannot be considered some sort of fixed canon. While Ibn Isḥāq's version is the most stable version and appears to have been subjected to some form of canonization by at least half the compilations, not one of the traditions appears uniformly over the course of the five centuries. Furthermore, even Ibn Isḥāq's version is not homogenous – it is transmitted with deviations and inconsistencies over the centuries. The version could thus be regarded at most as canonical with certain limitations. It cannot, however, claim exclusivity, for it does not replace the other available versions.

The obvious transformations inevitably raise questions about the historical value of the traditions and thus their authority, revealing the complex tensions between the transmission process and the living practices of Islamic interpretation. In terms of content, the texts cannot be perceived as historical accounts of the events of the early first/seventh century. Instead, the narratives highlight temporarily and regionally contested canons. The example of Muhammad and Rayḥāna underscores the degree to which issues such as gender conceptions were continuously reconstructed through lived realities and then back-projected onto historical events. The focus on concubinage can, for example, be explained through the understanding that Islamic legal discourse of the first century[74] was relatively elitist and androcentric, as Ali contends,[75] and was exposed to Persian influence. It can also be inferred that the change in gender conceptions resulted from the contestation of, for example, legal power. Even the focus on Rayḥāna and the *ḥijāb* diminished over time. Variations in the traditions from each of the centuries indicate that specific aspects (social, religious) served various interests at different times and are therefore given more or less weight depending on the scholars, the period, and even the dominant centre of Islam. The diverse aspects of Muḥammad and Rayḥāna's relationship are depicted, preserved, transmitted, or even neglected and omitted to the degree that only "temporal" canons can be spoken of. Revealing the narrative variety in terms of the references to Muḥammad and Rayḥāna's relationship in the transmitted traditions, this chapter has emphasized that we cannot reconstruct a linear history of early Islam based solely on the compilers' varied retrospectives

APPENDIX: BIOGRAPHICAL INFORMATION

Al-Wāqidī[76]

Muḥammad ibn ʿUmar ibn Wāqid al-Wāqidī was born in Medina in 130/747, where he operated a grain shop. He first acquired extensive knowledge of Islamic traditions in his hometown. In 171/787, he became acquainted with the caliph Hārūn al-Rashīd (~146/763–193/809) and vizier Yaḥyā ibn Khālid al-Barmakī (d. 190/806) while they were on their pilgrimage to Mecca and Medina and served as their guide. This possibly placed him in the favour of the ʿAbbāsid Court. He left his hometown in 180/796 – likely because of debt – and travelled to Baghdad, where he was probably appointed to a judicial office by Hārūn. From there he went to al-Raqqa, the Caliph's residence at the time. Yaḥyā ibn Khālid al-Barmakī became al-Wāqidī's patron. In later years, after a stay in Khurāsān and a few years before his death, he was (once again) appointed to the position of judge by the caliph al-Maʾmūn (~170–218/786–833). Although al-Wāqidī spent the last thirty years of his life in Baghdad, where he died in 207/823, he was one of the historians of Medina. As an expert on early Islamic history, he provided extensive information on *ḥadīth* and *fiqh*. He described the *futūḥ* book of his predecessor Ibn Isḥāq (see section on Ibn Hishām) as his primary source for his conquest books, but did not mention it in his *Kitāb al-maghāzī*.[77] In this work, he reports on the campaigns that Muḥammad undertook after his migration to Medina. It is believed that he wrote more than thirty books, but only the *Kitāb al-maghāzī* (which contains the traditions considered here) is extant. Along with Ibn Hishām's *Sīrat rasūl Allāh*, it is the oldest of the eleven compilations discussed here. For this reason, the versions he includes about Muḥammad and Rayḥāna can be considered the earliest versions of the narrative.

Ibn Hishām[78]

The historian, grammarian, and genealogist Abū Muḥammad ʿAbd al-Malik ibn Hishām from Baṣra is primarily known for his contribution to the *Sīrat rasūl Allāh*, the biography of Muḥammad by Ibn Isḥāq[79] (~85–150/704–767). He lived approximately two generations after Ibn Isḥāq and was a student of Ibn Isḥāq's disciple, Ziyād ibn ʿAbd Allāh al-Bakkāʾī (d. 183/799).[80] Ibn Hishām spent most of his life in Fusṭāṭ (Egypt), where he died around 215/830.[81] In his record of the *Sīra*, he neglected the histories of other Prophets and events that had nothing to do with the life of Prophet Muḥammad or that were not mentioned in the Qurʾan as well as material that was not relevant for the Prophet's career.[82] He also provided abridged passages with remarks about what was meant.[83] His work is thus a conscious editorial intervention (for example, it eliminates Muḥammad's suicidal thoughts,[84] which according to Ibn Hishām did not correspond to the image of a prophet). Some of the *Sīra* passages Ibn Hishām removed are included in al-Ṭabarī's and other authors' records.[85] The deliberate shortening or elimination of certain narratives marks a first step towards a canonization process.

Ibn Saʿd[86]

The historian Abū ʿAbd Allāh Muḥammad ibn Saʿd was born in Baṣra around 168/784 and died in Baghdad in 230/845. He belonged to the *ahl al-ḥadīth* (Traditionists). In search of traditions, he travelled to the

Ḥijāz, lived for some time in Medina, and studied under different scholars. In Baghdad, he joined al-Wāqidī as both his student and his secretary. Among other books, he composed the *Kitāb al-ṭabaqāt al-kabīr*,[87] which contains the traditions discussed here and depicts the life of Muḥammad and his companions. It is his only surviving work and is conducive to the study of traditions, as it provides information on approximately 4,250 people (including around 600 women) who played a role as narrators or tradents of the Prophet's traditions. The main source of Ibn Saʿd's work was his teacher al-Wāqidī, but he also drew his knowledge from many other sources, such as, for example, Ibn Isḥāq's records of the traditions.

Al-Balādhurī[88]

Abū al-ʿAbbās Aḥmad ibn Yaḥyā ibn Jābir al-Balādhurī is one of the most important Arab historians of his time. Very little is known about him. The date of his death can be vaguely estimated as some time in 279/892. He was likely of Persian descent and was born in the first decades of the third/ninth century in Baghdad, where he spent most of his life. His studies brought him to Damascus, Emesa (Homs), Antioch, and then Iraq. He studied under Ibn Saʿd, among other scholars. Two of his great works have survived: *Futūḥ al-buldān* and *Ansāb al-ashrāf*.[89] Like the *Ṭabaqāt* of Ibn Saʿd, the *Ansāb* is written genealogically and begins with the life of the Prophet and a biography of his relatives. It contains the traditions that are of interest in this contribution. In the *Ansāb,* al-Balādhurī attempted to connect material from Ibn Saʿd's *Ṭabaqāt* books and other works, such as the chronicles of Ibn Isḥāq.

Al-Ṭabarī[90]

The widely read Islamic scholar of Persian origin, Abū Jaʿfar Muḥammad ibn Jarīr al-Ṭabarī, marks the transition from the third/ninth century to the fourth/tenth century. Al-Ṭabarī was born in Āmul (northern Iran, Ṭabaristān) in 225/839 and died in Baghdad in 310/923. He is said to have been able to recite the Qurʾan by the age of seven and qualified as an Imām at the age of eight. By nine, he had already studied the Prophet's traditions. It is said that by the time he was twelve years old, he had embarked on a journey to enrich his knowledge in various fields of scholarship. He studied with countless scholars in Rayy, Baghdad, Wāsiṭ, Kūfa, and Baṣra and travelled to Syria, Lebanon, Palestine, and Egypt. After his return from Egypt, he followed the Shāfiʿī School until he founded his own *fiqh* school, the Jarīriyya. Around 256/870, he settled in Baghdad, where he lived and taught until his death. Among his most important works are *Taʾrīkh al-rusul wa'l-mulūk wa'l-khulafāʾ* (*History of the Messengers, Kings, and Caliphs*) and a commentary on the Qurʾan. In both works, he edited older writings, which have now been partly lost.[91] In the *Taʾrīkh*, he places Muḥammad in the complete history of the Prophets and writes from an all-encompassing perspective. The work appears to take the entire world into account, and accordingly, only a few volumes explicitly address the Prophet's life story.

Al-Ṭabarānī[92]

Abū al-Qāsim Sulaymān ibn Aḥmad ibn Ayyūb ibn Muṭawayyir al-Lakhmī al-Ṭabarānī was one of the most important and most sought after Arabic *ḥadīth* scholars of his time. With him, we progress not only in terms of time moving into the fourth/tenth century, but also geographically. This is a result of the relocation of the life and teaching centres of the scholars considered here from Iraqi to Persian regions, which influenced the recorded traditions. In the tenth century, in the region of modern-day Iraq and Iran, the Buyid, a Shiʿi dynasty in Persia, came to power. With the conquest of Baghdad in 334/945, they took over control from the ʿAbbāsid caliphate, which they held until 454/1062. The ʿAbbāsid caliph was divested of political power and thereafter acted only as the Muslim spiritual head. The Buyid dynasty promoted Persian culture during its reign and favoured the spread of Shiʿi Islam in Iran.[93] In this way, they continued the tradition of the Samanids, who had already fostered east Iran's (Samarkand, Bukhara) "fusion of Arab-Islamic culture with Iranian culture and thus contributed decisively to the emergence of Persian-language Islam, which quickly gained a completely independent face."[94]

Al-Ṭabarānī was born in ʿAkkā in 260/873. His parents came from Tiberias (Galilee). At the young age of thirteen, he began to study *ḥadīth*. For more than thirty years, he travelled throughout Syria, Iraq, Ḥijāz, Yemen, and Egypt, studying under countless scholars, including, among others, al-Ṭabarī. Around 290/902, he settled in Iṣfahān, where he died in 360/971. He belonged to a group of *ahl al-ḥadīth* in Iran who continued to compile Musnad works that contained weak or forgotten *aḥādīth*, in contradistinction to the *Ṣaḥīḥ* collections of al-Bukhārī and Muslim.[95] Above all, he is known for three works on *ḥadīth*: *Al-Muʿjam al-kabīr*, *Al-Muʿjam al-awsaṭ*, and *Al-Muʿjam al-ṣaghīr*.[96] The former contains *aḥādīth* that deal with the Prophet and Rayḥāna's relationship.

Al-Ḥākim al-Naysābūrī[97]

The Persian Muḥammad ibn ʿAbd Allāh ibn Muḥammad Abū ʿAbd Allāh al-Ḥākim al-Naysābūrī was born in 321/933 in Naysābūr, which became the capital of the Tahirid dynasty, the first Islamic family to rule on Iranian soil in the third/ninth century. He died there in 404/1014. He is alleged to have begun his *ḥadīth* studies as early as the age of nine and to have studied with more than two thousand teachers in Kufa, Rayy, Baghdad, Ābādān, Hamadhān, Merv, and his native city Naysābūr. He also travelled to Khurāsān and Transoxania. He is said to have visited Baghdad twice, once during his youth, and once during 368/978–79. Al-Ḥākim al-Naysābūrī belongs to the *ahl al-ḥadīth* and is considered a moderate Shāfiʿī jurist, following the Ashʿarī school of theology. Upon the instruction of one of his teachers, he led a small *ḥadīth* school, *Dār al-sunna*, and acted as a guardian of their *waqf* (endowment). He was a leading member of the *ḥadīth* scholarly community in Naysābūr, and most of his works were already known from Egypt to Andalusia during his lifetime. One of his last works, *Al-Mustadrak ʿalā al-ṣaḥīḥayn*, is of interest here as it includes traditions about the Prophet and Rayḥāna. This work is an *ilzāmāt* (obligations) work; it was widely read even in his lifetime and provoked reactions from many scholars. It comprises approximately 8,800 *aḥādīth* and supplements the *aḥādīth* of al-Bukhārī and Muslim, containing a multitude of *aḥādīth* that were in his opinion authentic but had not been included in the *Ṣaḥīḥayn*.[98]

Abū Nuʿaym al-Iṣfahānī[99]

Aḥmad ibn ʿAbd Allāh ibn Isḥāq ibn Mūsā ibn Mihrān al-Shāfiʿī Abū Nuʿaym al-Iṣfahānī was born in 336/948 in Iṣfahān, where he also died in 430/1038. He was of Persian origin. His grandfather was a famous ascetic, the first of his family to accept Islam. His father, also a scholar, sent Abū Nuʿaym to learn from important scholars beginning with the age of six. He travelled to Iraq, Ḥijāz, and Khurāsān and studied with great scholars such as al-Ṭabarānī and al-Ḥākim al-Naysābūrī. He had copies of some of al-Ḥākim al-Naysābūrī's books, for example, the *Tārīkh naysābūr* and the *Madkhal ilā al-ṣaḥīḥ*. Traditions about Rayḥāna and Muḥammad are included in his work, *Maʿrifat al-ṣaḥāba*, one of the hundreds of works he wrote. According to Brown, the Shāfiʿī jurist and Sunni Abū Nu'aym al-Iṣfahānī is part of the Sufi tradition,[100] in which he was even considered a "major figure."[101]

Abū Bakr al-Bayhaqī[102]

The Sunni Abū Bakr Aḥmad ibn al-Ḥusayn ibn ʿAlī ibn Mūsā al-Khusrawjirdī al-Bayhaqī was a Shāfiʿī legal expert and an Ashʿarī theologian who worked mainly in the *aḥādīth* field. He was born in 384/994 in Khusrawjird, a village in the Bayhaq district (present-day Sabzevār) in Khurāsān in northeastern Iran. He studied with distinguished teachers across Iran, Iraq, and the Arabian Peninsula. Chronicles depict him as the most prominent student of al-Ḥākim al-Naysābūrī. Shortly before his death, he travelled to Naysābūr, where he taught numerous students the content of his works, thereby spreading them across the Islamic world and gaining great prestige. "Both later Shāfiʿī/Ashʿarīs and Ḥanbalī/über-Sunnis respected and relied on his work."[103] He likely died in Naysābūr in 458/1066.[104] The traditions he compiled that are discussed here are found in his work *Dalāʾil al-nubuwwa* and *Kitāb al-sunan al-kubrā*. The latter is a large *ḥadīth* collection, consisting of ten volumes, which attests to Abū Bakr al-Bayhaqī's mastery of the compilation of *ḥadīth*. According to Brown, this is "a landmark in the Shāfiʿī legal school, supporting every detail of its law code with a myriad of reports from the Prophet and his companions."[105]

'Ali ibn al-Athīr[106]

The Sunni historian and Ashʿari theologian Abū al-Ḥasan ʿIzz al-Dīn ʿAlī ibn Muḥammad ibn ʿAbd al-Karīm ibn ʿAbd al-Wāḥid al-Jazarī al-Shaybānī was born in Cizre (Turkey) in 555/1160 and was of Arab descent. He spent most of his life as a private tutor in Mosul, where he died in 630/1233. In his work *Usd al-ghāba fī maʿrifat al-ṣaḥāba*, a prosopography of the Prophet's contemporaries, he includes a tradition about Rayḥāna and Muḥammad. With him, we once again encounter a compiler from the Iraq region – with whom we incidentally finish.

His travels took him to Aleppo; he spent a year in Damascus and taking several trips to Baghdad. At the age of twenty-eight, he served in the army under the command of Ṣalāḥ al-Dīn and fought against the Crusaders.

NOTES

1 See Brown, *Canonization*; El-Shamsy, *Canonization*.

2 The term "canon" comes from Hebrew (hebr. *qānæh* "rod, measuring tape") and was adopted into Greek (Greek *κανών*) to mean "benchmark, guiding principle." Canonization "describes the process in which a set of symbols, texts, actions or artefacts are defined as being authoritative and normative. The collection, ordering and writing of self-evident everyday forms of behaviour, cultural practices, piety, and moral conceptions into a canon serves to secure tradition": Bahr, "Kanon/Kanonisierung," 159. Canons have diverse characteristics: They secure a community's identity. They are formed, especially in the face of a threatened loss of tradition, as a means to protect a tradition. Accordingly, canonizations are often reactions to crises: They are connected to power, as a canon often substantiates traditions tied to a specific normative authority that possesses a monopoly on interpretation. Canonization processes are ambivalent, in that they do not preserve certain traditions but, through a process of chosen selection, exclude others: Bahr, "Kanon/Kanonisierung," 159–61. In terms of Islam, apart from the Qur'an, the *aḥādīth* compilations, legal schools' interpretation are often understood to be canonical.

3 Rohe, *Das islamische Recht*, 82–3. Translation mine.

4 In Lebanon, for example, couples travel to Cyprus "because they know that according to the Lebanese Law of Conflict, their future family legal relationships are governed by the laws of the place where the marriage was ratified." Rohe, *Das islamische Recht*, 358; translation mine.

5 Biographical information for each is provided in the Appendix.

6 See Noth, "Der Charakter der ersten großen Sammlungen von Nachrichten zur frühen Kalifenzeit"; idem, *Quellenkritische Studien*; Nagel, "Ḥadīth"; El Cheikh, *Women, Islam*.

7 See Decker, "Frauen zwischen Selbst- und Fremdbestimmung."

8 See Decker, *Frauen als Trägerinnen religiösen Wissens*; Stowasser, *Women in the Qur'an*; Ahmed, *Women and Gender*.

9 Mernissi, *Geschlecht*, 67. Other scholars offer rather one-sided interpretations of the relationship between Rayḥāna und Muḥammad; see Yitzhak, "Muhammad's Jewish Wives"; Gilli-Elewy, "Soziale Aspekte."

10 For example, Mernissi purports the thesis that in terms of "family structure" in pre-Islamic times "the family was built upon the wife's self-determination" and Islam brought about a new structure where "the family is defined based upon the principal of the superiority of the man." The introduction of Islam therefore meant that the "interests of the patriarchy were protected": Mernissi, *Geschlecht*, 59. Taking into account her methodological approach, such theses are doubtful (whether they are advocated or not).

11 The underlying theoretical-methodological concept is that of the *intentio operis* by Eco, *Die Grenzen der Interpretation.*

12 Ḥuyayy ibn Akhṭab was the leader of the Jewish tribe Banū Naḍīr, who were expelled by the Muslims from Medina. He was also the father of one of Muḥammad's wives, Ṣafiyya bint Ḥuyayy, also originally Jewish.

13 Al-Wāqidī, *Kitāb al-maghāzī*, 520.

14 Ibid., 521.

15 Ibid.

16 In this contribution, the translation *lovesickness* is used rather than *yearning* or *longing*, which does not appropriately reflect the degree to which the original German versions of the tradition emphasized love, pain, and heartache. For further reasons for this translation see *wajada* and *wajd* in Wehr, *Arabisches Wörterbuch*; Wahrmund, *Handwörterbuch*; Brünnow and Fischer, *Arabische Chrestomathie*.

17 Ali, *Sexual Ethics and Islam*, 43.

18 In terms of the linguistic structure of direct speech and conversation, Nagel concludes that the *ḥadīth* serves the "annihilation of history": *Vernichtung der Geschichte*; meaning an abolishing of the historical and alienating distance between the Muslims and the Prophet: Nagel, "Ḥadīth," 126.

19 Arab. *iḥtajabat* (3. Pers. Sg. f., *ḥajaba* VIII): "Disappear from sight, to conceal oneself; to be hidden; to retreat" (Wehr); "To hide oneself; to sit behind a curtain (like a king)." Stern argues that the verb "implied a general idea of seclusion and did not in any single case refer to the custom of veiling": Stern, *Marriage in Early Islam*, 120.

20 Ibid., 113.

21 Ibn Hishām, *Sīra*, vol. 1, 693.

22 In terms of the translation of *ḥijāb* as "curtain," see the translation of the Qurʾan by Khoury, for example, Q. 33:53. See also, Stern, *Marriage in Early Islam*, 113, 118, 120. Additionally, the term *ḥijāb* is actually a metaphor (as it appears in Q. 42:51). See Ibid., 117.

23 Ibn Saʿd, *Ṭabaqāt*, 92.

24 Arab. *ūqiyya*, "a weight, originally 7 *mithqāl* or 40 *dirham*" (Wahrmund).

25 Arab. *nashsh*, "Weight of 20 Dachmen" (Wahrmund).

26 Al-Baqīʿ is the name of the first and oldest Islamic cemetery, which today is next to the Prophet's mosque in Medina.
27 Ibn Saʿd, *Ṭabaqāt*, 92–3.
28 Ibid., 93.
29 Ibid.
30 Ibid.
31 Ibid.
32 Ibid., 94.
33 See also Stern, *Marriage in Early Islam*, 51–3.
34 Arab. *yamīn*, "a covenant confirmed by an oath; *yamīnu llāh* the oath by attestation of God" (Lane); "Right, on the right side, right side, right hand"; "Oath" (Wehr).
35 Ali, *Sexual Ethics and Islam*, 44.
36 Ibn Saʿd, *Ṭabaqāt*, 93–4.
37 Al-Balādhurī, *Ansāb al-ashrāf*, vol. 2, 91.
38 Ibid.
39 Ibid., 91–2.
40 Here, Māriya the Copt is referenced.
41 Al-Balādhurī, *Ansāb al-ashrāf*, vol. 2, 92.
42 The traditions that place Rayḥāna only in the context of military campaigns are not discussed: al-Balādhurī, *Ansāb al-ashrāf*, vol. 2, 78, 92.
43 Stern, *Marriage in Early Islam*, 121.
44 Arab. *mawsim*, "Season, festival, annual market, harvest, harvest time" (Wehr). Based on this information, we can assume that the man encountered Rayḥāna at the date farm belonging to the Prophet (4.1).
45 Al-Balādhurī, *Ansāb al-ashrāf*, vol. 2, 91.
46 Arab. *surriyya*, pl. *sarārī*, "concubine; lover" (Wehr); "Person with whom you sleep; concubine; married slave woman" (Wahrmund).
47 Ibn Manẓūr, *Lisān al-ʿArab*.
48 Ali, *Sexual Ethics and Islam*, 14–15.
49 Ibid., 42.
50 Ibid., 40.
51 Al-Ṭabarī, *Taʾrīkh*, series I, 1497–78.
52 The English translation of the *Taʾrīkh ar-Rusul wal-Mulūk wal-Khulafāʾ* comprises forty volumes. See al-Ṭabarī, *The History of al-Tabari.*
53 See, for example, the multitude of versions contained in al-Ṭabarī's compilations about the first revelatory experiences of Muḥammad: *Taʾrīkh*, series I, 1146–56.
54 Al-Ṭabarānī, *Al-Muʿjam al-kabīr*, vol. 6, no. 5588, 85.
55 Arab. *istasarra* (*sarra* X.), "to hide oneself; to hide; to take one as a concubine (a woman)" (Wehr); "to hide, to hide from a" (Wahrmund); "he, or it,

became concealed; or he or it, concealed himself or itself: it (a thing, or an affair) became hidden or concealed or secret: it (the moon) became concealed by the light of the sun for one night, or for two nights" (Lane).

56 See Appendix, "Al-Ṭabarānī." Differences between the Iraqi and Persian versions result from the scholars' varied life and work contexts; for further information see general Appendix.

57 Ali, *Sexual Ethics and Islam*, 40.

58 Al-Ṭabarānī, *Al-Muʿjam al-kabīr*, vol. 22, no. 1087, 445–6.

59 Al-Hākim al-Naysābūrī, *Al-Mustadrak*, vol. 4, 41–2.

60 Ibid.

61 al-Iṣfahānī, *Maʿrifa al-ṣaḥāba*, no. 7366.

62 Ibid., no. 7486.

63 Ibid., no. 7492.

64 al-Iṣfahānī, *Maʿrifa al-ṣaḥāba*, no. 7484.

65 Arab. *walīda*, "Daughter, girl, wench, slave woman" (Wehr); Arab. *walīd*, "a new-born child: a young infant; a youth: a boy who has arrived at the age when he is fit for service, before he attains to puberty: a youthful servant; one is so called from the time of his birth until he attains to manhood: the servant of a man in paradise is a *walīd* always, never changing in age: a slave; or, as some say, one born in servitude: fem. in these senses, a female slave is called *walīda* even if aged" (Lane).

66 Al-Bayhaqī, *Dalāʾil al-nubuwwa*, vol. 7, 234.

67 This is likely an error, and actually means that al-Zuhrī had told him from ʿUrwa ibn al-Zubayr.

68 Al-Bayhaqī, *Dalāʾil al-nubuwwa*, vol. 7, 286–7.

69 Ibid., vol. 7, 234.

70 The definition of "People of the Book" is oft-discussed by Islamic scholars, and the question about whether a marriage can take place between a Muslim man and a non-Muslim woman was not so uncomplicated that it could just be allowed. The discussion centres on, among others things, who counts as the "People of the Book." Ali, *Sexual Ethics and Islam*, 14–16.

71 Al-Bayhaqī, *Al-Sunan al-kubrā*, vol. 7, no. 13424, 115.

72 Ibn Mundh (~??–395/–1004–5) (Brown writes Ibn Manda) of Iṣfahān was a student of al-Ṭabarānī and colleague of al-Ḥākim al-Naysābūrī. Brown, *Canonization*, 172. See also Sezgin, *Geschichte*, 214–15.

73 Ibn al-Athīr, *Usd al-ghāba*.

74 Some of the subjects in the traditions are directly in the centre of legal discourses, and these cannot be more fully discussed here. See, for example, the questions about a person's social status and religious freedom; waiting for a woman's menstruation before engaging in a sexual relationship; and

whether a Muslim man is allowed to enter into a sexual relationship with a slave woman if she does not convert to Islam. Also, the liberation of slaves was an important topic of Islamic jurisprudence and has been the matter of rather controversial discussions.

75 Ali, *Marriage and Slavery in Early Islam*, 3.

76 See Sezgin, *Geschichte*, 294–7; Leder, "Al-Wāḳidī,“ 101–2; Bobzin, *Mohammed*, 46–8; Brockelmann, *Geschichte*, 141. A list of his work can be found in Sezgin, *Geschichte*, 296–97. For further information on his research, see Leder, "Al-Wāḳidī," 102.

77 According to Schoeler, al-Wāqidī secretly used Ibn Isḥāq's *Kitāb al-maghāzī* as the main source for his own work. Schoeler, *Charakter und Authentie*, 25.

78 See Watt, "Ibn Hišām," 800; Sezgin, *Geschichte*, 297–9.

79 Muḥammad ibn Isḥāq was one of the most important *Sīra* authors, born around 85/704 in Medina and, according to most sources, died in Baghdad in 150/767. Ibn Isḥāq's family belonged to those of the early transmitters, and he began to collect *aḥādīth* early in his life. He stayed in Alexandria after 119/737 to study; then, after returning to Medina, he went to Baghdad. He also travelled to al-Jazira, al-Ḥīra, Kūfa, Rayy, and Baṣra. In addition to the *Sīra* he composed in the final years of the Umayyad era, Ibn Isḥāq has been attributed as the author of other books, of which not one copy – not even from his students – remains. Sezgin, *Geschichte*, 288; Schoeler, *Charakter*, 49; Bobzin, *Mohammed*, 36. Other dates for his death lie between 761 and 762; Jones, "Ibn Isḥāq," 810–11. About his further works, see Sezgin, *Geschichte*, 290.

80 Schoeler, *Charakter*, 50.

81 Watt specifies the years 828 and 833, Sezgin 834. The exact date of birth is unknown. Watt, "Ibn Hišām," 800; Sezgin, *Geschichte*, 297-9.

82 Watt, "Ibn Hišām," 800.

83 Sezgin, *Geschichte*, 289.

84 Schoeler, *Charakter*, 92–3.

85 Al-Ṭabarī, *Ta'rīkh*, series I, 1147, 1150, 1155. Al-Ṭabarī kept the *Sīra* almost in their original form. Schoeler, *Charakter*, 94.

86 See Bobzin, *Mohammed*, 47–9; Sezgin, *Geschichte*, 300–1; Loth, "Ursprung," 602; Al-Samuk, *Die Historischen Überlieferungen nach Ibn Isḥāq*, 88; Fück, "Ibn Saʿd," 922–3. A list of his works can be found in Sezgin, *Geschichte*, 300–1.

87 It is also believed that al-Wāqidī also composed a *Ṭabaqāt* (Generations) book that Ibn Saʿd likely used as source material. Loth, "Ursprung," 604. About *Kitāb al-ṭabaqāt*, see also Loth, *Das Classenbuch*.

88 See Becker and Rosenthal, "al-Balādhurī"; Sezgin, *Geschichte*, 320–1.
89 About *Ansāb al-ashrāf* see Khalidi, *Arabic Historical Thought*, 58–61.
90 See Bosworth, "Al-Ṭabarī," 11–15; Sezgin, *Geschichte*, 323–8. About his works, see Bosworth, "Al-Ṭabarī," 13–15.
91 For example, he edited some of the traditions from Ibn Isḥāq, which Ibn Hishām left out. Raven, "Sīra," 661; Bobzin, *Mohammed*, 43; Watt, "Ibn Hišām," 800; Schoeler, *Charakter*, 50.
92 See Sezgin, *Geschichte*, 195–7; Fierro, "al-Ṭabarānī."
93 Nagel, *Die islamische Welt*, 96–101; Busse, *Chalif und Großkönig*.
94 Nagel, *Die islamische Welt*, 96. Translation mine.
95 Brown, *Hadith*, 41, 48.
96 As a rule, authors chose a particular topic from *muʿjam* works and then compiled as many *aḥādīth* as possible on the same topic to demonstrate the breadth of their knowledge of the *ḥadīth* corpus on the topic. According to Brown, such works functioned as some sort of CV of a *ḥadīth* scholar, as it, among other things, indicated the range of teachers with whom the author had studied. Brown, *Hadith*, 50.
97 See Sezgin, *Geschichte*, 221–2; Brown, *The Canonization*, 155–60; Robson, "al-Ḥākim al-Naysābūrī."
98 Brown, *Hadith*, 42.
99 See Pedersen, "Abū Nuʿaym al-Iṣfahānī"; Brown, *Hadith*, 37; idem, *Canonization*, 158; Melchert, "Abū Nuʿaym's Sources," 145–59.
100 Brown, *Hadith*, 46.
101 Brown, *Canonization*, 62.
102 See Dickinson, "al-Bayhaqī, Abī Bakr"; Brown, *Canonization*, 219–20; Brown, *Hadith*, 34, 37, 39.
103 Brown, *Canonization*, 219.
104 According to other sources, he died in Bayhaq in 454/1062. See Dickinson, "al-Bayhaqī, Abī Bakr."
105 Brown, *Hadith*, 41.
106 See Rosenthal, "Ibn al-Athīr."

REFERENCES

Primary Sources

Balādhurī, Abū al-ʿAbbās Aḥmad ibn Yaḥyā ibn Jābir al-. *Ansāb al-ashrāf: Kitāb jumal min ansāb al-ashrāf ṣannafahu al-imām Aḥmad ibn Yaḥyā ibn Jābir al-Balādhurī*. Ed. Suhayl Zakkār and Riyāḍ Zarkalī. 13 vols. Beirut: Dār al-Fikr, 1996.

Bayhaqī, Abū Bakr Aḥmad ibn al-Ḥussayn ibn ʿAlī ibn Mūsā al-Khusrawjirdī al-. *Dalāʾil al-nubuwwa: Dalāʾil al-nubuwwa wa-maʿrifat aḥwāl ṣāḥib al-sharīʿa li-Abī Bakr Aḥmad ibn al-Ḥusayn al-Bayhaqī*. Ed. ʿAbd al-Muʿṭī Qalʿajī. 7 vols. Beirut: Dār al-Kutub al-ʿIlmiyya, 1988.

– *Al-Sunan al-kubrā: al-Sunan al-kubrā li'l-imām Abī Bakr Aḥmad ibn al-Ḥusayn ibn ʿAlī al-Bayhaqī*. Ed. Muḥammad ʿAbd al-Qādir ʿAṭā. 11 vols. Beirut: Dār al-Kutub al-ʿIlmiyya, 2003.

– Hākim al-Naysābūrī, Abū ʿAbd Allāh Muḥammad ibn ʿAbd Allāh ibn Muḥammad al-. *Al-Mustadrak: Al-Mustadrak ʿalā al-ṣaḥīḥayn li-Muḥammad ibn ʿAbd Allāh al-Hākim al-Naysābūrī*. 4 vols. Hyderabad, 1915–23.

Ibn al-Athīr, ʿIzz al-Dīn ʿAlī. *Usd al-ghāba: Usd al-ghāba fī maʿrifat al-ṣaḥāba*. Ed. Muḥammad Ibrāhīm al-Bannā and Muḥammad Aḥmad ʿĀshūr. 7 vols. Kairo. (Cited in *Jawāmiʿ al-kalim* V 4.5. Ed. Muḥammad Ībrāhīm al-Bannā and Muḥammad Aḥmad ʿĀshūr. Cairo: Dār al-Shaʿb.)

Ibn Hishām, Abū Muḥammad ʿAbd al-Malik. *Sīra: Kitāb Sīrat rasūl Allāh: Das Leben Muhammad's nach Muhammad Ibn Ishāk bearbeitet von Abd el-Malik Ibn Hischām*. Ed. Ferdinand Wüstenfeld. 2 vols. Göttingen: Dieterichsche Universalitäts-Buchhandlung, 1858–60.

Ibn Manẓūr, Abū al-Faḍl Jamāl al-Dīn Muḥammad ibn Makram. *Lisān al-ʿArab*. 15 Vols. Beirut: Dār Bayrūt, 1955.

Ibn Saʿd, Abū ʿAbd Allāh Muḥammad. *Ṭabaqāt: Ibn Saʿd, Biographien Muhammeds, seiner Gefährten und der späteren Träger des Islams bis zum Jahre 230 der Flucht*, vol. 8: *Biographien der Frauen*. Ed. Carl Brockelmann. Leiden: E.J. Brill, 1904.

Iṣfahānī, Abū Nuʿaym Aḥmad ibn ʿAbd Allāh ibn Isḥāq ibn Mūsā ibn Mihrān al-Shāfiʿī al-. *Maʿrifat al-ṣaḥāba: Maʿrifat al-ṣaḥāba li-Abī Nuʿaym al-Aṣbahānī*. Ed. ʿĀdil ibn Yūsuf al-ʿAzāzī. Riyad: Dār al-Waṭan, 1998.

Ṭabarī, Abū Jaʿfar Muḥammad ibn Jarīr al-. *Taʾrīkh: Annales quos scripsit Abu Djafar Mohammed ibn Djarir at-Tabari*, cum aliis edidit M.J. de Goeje. Leiden: E.J. Brill, 1964.

– *The History of al-Tabari: An Annotated Translation*. Ed. Ihsan Abbas et al. 40 vols. New York, Albany: SUNY Press, 1985–98.

Ṭabarānī, Abū al-Qāsim Sulaymān ibn Aḥmad ibn Ayyūb ibn Muṭawayyir al-Lakhmī al-. *Al-Muʿjam al-kabīr: Al-Muʿjam al-kabīr li'l-ḥāfiẓ Abī al-Qāsim Sulaymān ibn Aḥmad al-Ṭabarānī*. Ed. Ḥamdī ʿAbd al-Majīd al-Salafī. 25 vols. Cairo: Maktabat Ibn Taymiyya, 1983.

Wāqidī, Muḥammad ibn ʿUmar ibn Wāqid al-. *Kitāb al-maghāzī: The Kitāb al-maghāzī of al-Wāqidī*. Ed. Marsden Jones. 3 vols. London: Oxford University Press, 1966.

Secondary Sources

Ahmed, Leila. *Women and Gender in Islam. Historical Roots of a Modern Debate*. New Haven: Yale University Press, 1992.
Ali, Kecia. *Marriage and Slavery in Early Islam*. Cambridge, MA: Harvard University Press, 2010.
– *Sexual Ethics and Islam*. Oxford: Oneworld, 2006.
Bahr, Petra. "Kanon/Kanonisierung." In *Metzer Lexikon Religion. Gegenwart – Alltag – Medien*, ed. Christoph Auffarth, Jutta Bernard, and Hubert Mohr, vol. 2, 159–61. Stuttgart: J.B. Metzler, 2005.
Becker, C.H., and F. Rosenthal. "al-Balādhurī." In *Encyclopaedia of Islam, Second Edition*, ed. P. Bearman, Th. Bianquis, C.E. Bosworth, E. van Donzel, and W.P. Heinrichs. http://dx.doi.org.proxy.ub.uni-frankfurt.de/10.1163/1573-3912_islam_COM_0094.
Bobzin, Hartmut. *Mohammed*. München: C.H. Beck, 2000.
Bosworth, Clifford E.: "Al-Ṭabarī, Abū Djaʿfar Muḥammad B. Djarīr b. Yazīd." In *Encyclopaedia of Islam, Second Edition*, ed. P. Bearman, Th. Bianquis, C.E. Bosworth, E. van Donzel, and W.P. Heinrichs, vol. 10, 11–15. Leiden: E.J. Brill, 2000.
Brockelmann, Carl. *Geschichte der Arabischen Literatur*, vol. 1. Leiden: E.J. Brill, 1943.
Brown, Jonathan. *The Canonization of al-Bukhārī and Muslim: The Formation and Function of the Sunnī Ḥadīth Canon*. Leiden: E.J. Brill, 2007.
– *Hadith: Muhammad's Legacy in the Medieval and Modern World*. Oxford: Oneworld, 2009.
Brünnow, Rudolf-Ernst, and August Fischer. *Arabische Chrestomathie aus Prosaschriftstellern*. 7th ed. Wiesbaden: Harrassowitz, 1988.
Busse, Heribert. *Chalif und Großkönig. Die Buyiden im Iraq (945–1055)*. Wiesbaden: Steiner, 1969.
Decker, Doris. *Frauen als Trägerinnen religiösen Wissens. Konzeptionen von Frauenbildern in frühislamischen Überlieferungen bis zum 9. Jahrhundert*. Stuttgart: Kohlhammer, 2013.
– "Frauen zwischen Selbst- und Fremdbestimmung. Wandel weiblicher Geschlechterkonstruktionen in religiösen Veränderungsprozessen am Beispiel frühislamischer Überlieferungen." In *Doing Gender – Doing Religion. Fallstudien zur Intersektionalität im frühen Judentum, Christentum und Islam*, ed. Ute E. Eisen, Christine Gerber, and Angela Standhartinger, 193–223. Tübingen: Mohr, 2013.
Dickinson, Eerik. "al-Bayhaqī, Abī Bakr." In *Encyclopaedia of Islam, THREE*, ed. Kate Fleet, Gudrun Krämer, Denis Matringe, John Nawas,

and Everett Rowson. http://dx.doi.org.proxy.ub.uni-frankfurt.de/10.1163/1573-3912_islam_COM_23711.
Eco, Umberto. *Die Grenzen der Interpretation*, 3rd ed. München: dtv, 2004.
El Cheikh, Nadia Maria. *Women, Islam, and Abbasid Identity*. Cambridge, MA: Harvard University Press, 2015.
El-Shamsy, Ahmed. *The Canonization of Islamic Law: A Social and Intellectual History*. New York: Cambridge University Press, 2013.
Fierro, Maribel. "al-Ṭabarānī." In *Encyclopaedia of Islam, Second Edition*, ed. P. Bearman, Th. Bianquis, C.E. Bosworth, E. van Donzel, and W.P. Heinrichs. http://dx.doi.org.proxy.ub.uni-frankfurt.de/10.1163/1573-3912_islam_SIM_7246
Fück, Johann W. "Ibn Saʿd." In *Encyclopaedia of Islam, Second Edition*, ed. P. Bearman, Th. Bianquis, C.E. Bosworth, E. van Donzel, and W.P. Heinrichs, vol. 3, 922–3. Leiden: E.J. Brill, 1971.
Gilli-Elewy, Hend. "Soziale Aspekte frühislamischer Sklaverei." *Der Islam* 77 (2000): 116–68.
Jones, J.M.B. "Ibn Isḥāq." In *Encyclopaedia of Islam, Second Edition*, ed. P. Bearman, Th. Bianquis, C.E. Bosworth, E. van Donzel, and W.P. Heinrichs, vol. 3, 810–11. Leiden. E.J. Brill, 1971.
Khalidi, Tarif. *Arabic Historical Thought in the Classical Period*. Cambridge: Cambridge University Press, 1996.
Lane, Edward William. *An Arabic–English Lexicon*. 8 vols. Beirut: Librairie du Liban, 1968.
Leder, S. "Al-Wāḳidī." In *Encyclopaedia of Islam, Second Edition*, ed. P. Bearman, Th. Bianquis, C.E. Bosworth, E. van Donzel, and W.P. Heinrichs, vol. 11, 101–13. Leiden: E.J. Brill, 2002.
Loth, Otto. *Das Classenbuch des Ibn Saʿd. Einleitende Untersuchung über Authentie und Inhalt nach den handschriftlichen Überresten*. Habilitationsschrift. Leipzig: Druck von G. Kreysing, 1869.
– "Ursprung und Bedeutung der Ṭabaḳât, vornehmlich der des Ibn Saʿd." *Zeitschrift der Deutschen Morgenländischen Gesellschaft* 23 (1869): 593–614.
Melchert, Christopher. "Abū Nuʿaymʿs Sources for *Ḥilyat al-awliyāʾ*, Sufi and Traditionist." In *Les Maîtres Soufis et Leurs Disciples Des IIIe–Ve Siècles de l'Hégire (IXe–XIe)*, ed. Gobillot, Geneviève, and Thibon, Jean-Jacques, 145–59. Damaskus and Beirut: Presses de l'Ifpo, 2012.
Mernissi, Fatima. *Geschlecht – Ideologie – Islam*, 3rd ed. München: Kunstmann Antje, 1989.
Nagel, Tilman. "Ḥadīth – oder: Die Vernichtung der Geschichte." In *XXV. Deutscher Orientalistentag*, Vorträge, ZDMG Supplementa 10 (1994): 118–28.

– *Die islamische Welt bis 1500*. München: Oldenbourg, 1998.
Noth, Albrecht. "Der Charakter der ersten großen Sammlungen von Nachrichten zur frühen Kalifenzeit." *Der Islam* 47 (1971): 168–99.
– *Quellenkritische Studien zu Themen, Formen und Tendenzen frühislamischer Geschichtsüberlieferungen*. Teil I: *Themen und Formen*. Bonn: Selbstverlag des Orientalischen Seminars der Universität Bonn, 1973.
Pedersen, J. "Abū Nuʿaym al-Iṣfahānī." In *Encyclopaedia of Islam, Second Edition*, ed. P. Bearman, Th. Bianquis, C.E. Bosworth, E. van Donzel, and W.P. Heinrichs. http://dx.doi.org.proxy.ub.uni-frankfurt.de/10.1163/1573-3912_islam_SIM_0239.
Raven, Wim. "Sīra." In *Encyclopaedia of Islam, Second Edition*, ed. P. Bearman, Th. Bianquis, C.E. Bosworth, E. van Donzel, and W.P. Heinrichs, vol. 9, 660–3. Leiden: E.J. Brill, 1997.
Robson, J. "al-Ḥākim al-Naysābūrī." In *Encyclopaedia of Islam, Second Edition*, ed. P. Bearman, Th. Bianquis, C.E. Bosworth, E. van Donzel, and W.P. Heinrichs. http://dx.doi.org.proxy.ub.uni-frankfurt.de/10.1163/1573-3912_islam_SIM_2638.
Rohe, Mathias. *Das islamische Recht. Geschichte und Gegenwart*. München: C.H. Beck, 2009.
Rosenthal, F. "Ibn al-Athīr." In *Encyclopaedia of Islam, Second Edition*, ed. P. Bearman, Th. Bianquis, C.E. Bosworth, E. van Donzel, and W.P. Heinrichs. Accessed 06 March 2017. http://dx.doi.org.proxy.ub.uni-frankfurt.de/10.1163/1573-3912_islam_SIM_3094.
Schoeler, Gregor. *Charakter und Authentie der muslimischen Überlieferung über das Leben Mohammeds*. Berlin and New York: De Gruyter, 1996.
Sezgin, Fuat. *Geschichte des Arabischen Schrifttums*, vol. 1: *Qurʾānwissenschaften, Ḥadīth, Geschichte, Fiqh, Dogmatik, Mystik bis ca. 430 H*. Leiden: E.J. Brill, 1967.
Stern, Gertrude H. *Marriage in Early Islam*. London: Royal Asiatic Society, 1939.
Stowasser, Barbara Freyer. *Women in the Qur'an, Traditions, and Interpretations*. Oxford: Oxford University Press, 1994.
Wahrmund, Adolf. *Handwörterbuch der neu-arabischen und deutschen Sprache*, 3rd ed. 2 vols. Beirut: Librairie du Liban, 1985.
Watt, W. Montgomery. "Ibn Hišām." In *Encyclopaedia of Islam, Second Edition*, ed. P. Bearman, Th. Bianquis, C.E. Bosworth, E. van Donzel, and W.P. Heinrichs, vol. 3, 800–1. Leiden: E.J. Brill, 1971.
– "Ibn Hishām." In *Encyclopaedia of Islam, Second Edition*, ed. P. Bearman, Th. Bianquis, C.E. Bosworth, E. van Donzel, and W.P.

Heinrichs. http://dx.doi.org.proxy.ub.uni-frankfurt.de/10.1163/1573-3912_islam_SIM_3203.

Wehr, Hans. *Arabisches Wörterbuch für die Schriftsprache der Gegenwart.* Wiesbaden: Harrassowitz, 1952.

Yitzhak, Ronen. "Muhammad's Jewish Wives. Rayhana bint Zayd and Safiya bint Huyayy in the Classic Islamic Tradition." *Journal of Religion and Society* 9 (2007): 1–14.

PART THREE

Fiqh and Its Applications

8

Fiqh Rulings and Gendering the Public Space

The Discrepancy between Written Formality and Daily Reality

Hoda El-Saadi

This chapter examines rulings concerning the visibility of women and their presence in public spaces in Islamic law literature (*fiqh*) and in daily lived experience as recorded in historical chronicles and annals. It investigates a variety of legal and historical sources to determine whether or not the rulings reflect the lived realities of women, thereby furthering our understanding of the complexity of *fiqh* and how it intersects with social, political, and economic factors. In doing so, this chapter questions the claim that women's seclusion stems from the Qur'an and Sunna, and illustrates how discrimination against women was the product of patriarchal authority striving to impose its power over women, especially during times of decline and social instability. It also demonstrates how the lived realities, as recorded in historical chronicles, often diverged from the ideal models constructed by the scholars and how in many cases the medieval legal scholars' arguments were a reaction to the lived reality, not a reflection of it. More importantly, it shows how medieval Muslim women's activities serve to contest the *fiqh* interpretive narrative. Although the lived experience of the law has received scholarly attention in recent years, it has focused mainly on the Ottoman Empire, because of the wealth of court records that survive from this period.[1] Very few studies focus on the same topic in the pre-Ottoman period, because of the complete absence of court archives. This chapter is an attempt to fill that gap and contribute to our understanding of medieval Islamic socio-legal history with a specific focus on women and gender relations in the public space.

This chapter has three parts. The first part focuses on *fiqh* rules concerning women and gender relations in the public space. It illustrates how *fiqh* aimed to extract God's law from the Qur'an and Sunna; yet *fiqhī* rules were often more severe than those decreed by the Qur'an and by the Prophet. Therefore, it begins by contrasting Qur'an-based *sharīʿa* with *fiqh* and presents a brief historical overview of the seclusion of women in *fiqh*. It shows that *fiqh* was contextual and was in a constant state of negotiation with social, political, and economic factors. This part also provides the reader with a sample of *fiqh* manuals that reinforced the seclusion of women and limited their role in society. The second part focuses on *siyāsa sharʿiyya*, the sultan's decrees, another source of legal authority that exerted significant influence on women in the public sphere. Islamic law is composed of both *siyāsa sharʿiyya* and *fiqh*. This part illustrates how *fiqh* and *siyāsa* cooperated, competed, and in many cases clashed over issues regarding women as well as gender relations in the public space. The third part deals with the dynamics of law implementation and the role of law enforcers, particularly the role of the *muḥtasib* (supervisor of bazaars and trade and market inspector). It shows how everyday life and customs influenced the implementation and practice of Islamic law, including *fiqh* rules and sultanic decrees. All three parts together illustrate different factors at work in regulating the place of women in the public sphere, as well as the dynamics of subversion and change in the pre-Ottoman period, and highlight the discrepancy between theory and practice, between the ideal model and the lived reality.

WOMEN IN THE QUR'AN VERSUS WOMEN IN *FIQH*

I contend that women's seclusion and their confinement to the private sphere do not originate in Islam's sacred text, the Qur'an.[2] Indeed, the seclusion of women in Muslim societies does not reflect the spirit of the Qur'an, its teachings, or the image that emerges from early Islamic history. The *sharīʿa*, which is "the totality of God's will as revealed to the Prophet Muḥammad"[3] and thus an eternal set of guidelines, grants women the right to work, own property, and run businesses; it does not limit women to the private sphere, nor does it grant men exclusive rights to the public sphere, where commercial interactions are conducted and wealth is generated. On the contrary, Muslim men *and* women are expected to conduct professional transactions honestly, strive to earn their living, and pay *zakāt* (alms): "Hence do not covet the bounties which God has bestowed more abundantly on some of you than on others. Men shall have a benefit from what they earn and women shall have a benefit from what they earn. Ask, therefore God to give you out of his bounty: behold. God has indeed full knowledge of everything" (Q. 4:32).[4] Generally, no verses in the Qurʾan circumscribe women's activities, except those that address the wives of the Prophet – for example, Q. 33:32–3, 53, which state: "O wives of the Prophet! You are not like any other women" and commands them to "[s]tay quietly in your houses and do not make dazzling display like that of the earlier *jāhiliya* … for God only wishes to remove all scandal from you, members of the Prophet's family and to make you pure and pristine." These verses specifically address the wives of the Prophet and therefore should not be made to apply to all Muslim women and to marginalize or limit their role in society. For if these verses apply to all Muslim women, then all women will have to refrain from remarrying after the death of their husbands, as detailed in Q. 33.53: "[N]or that you should marry his wives after him ever," singling out the Prophet's wives. Moreover, there is no verse in the Qurʾan that clearly requires all Muslim women to follow the specific rules addressed to the prophet's wives, who indeed are distinguished and set apart by the words "you are not the same as other women" in Q. 33:32.

Fiqh is the human effort to understand, interpret, and extract legal rulings from the Qurʾan; however, it is precisely this human effort that constructs the basis for gendering the public sphere and isolating women. Unlike the divine and infallible *sharīʿa*, *fiqh* is man-made and thus liable to human error. Nevertheless, there is an observable trend in some of the Islamic literature of equating *fiqh* with *sharīʿa* and understanding the two to be interchangeable.[5] *Fiqh* is not to be construed as both divine and infallible, for it is purely a product of human efforts to find solutions to life issues and to regulate these at particular moments in history.[6] It follows that women's seclusion is not a Qurʾanic dictate, but a mere product of the Islamic law literature – *fiqh*, which is how jurists and scholars interpreted the Qurʾan. *Fiqh* is a comprehensive discourse that reflects what the *ʿulamāʾ* (religious scholars) deemed spiritual and moral, and it often reflected patriarchal, social, cultural, and political expediencies.[7] In defining the position of women and their relation to men in society, the *fiqh* texts neglect the objectives of the *sharīʿa* and the egalitarian spirit of the revelation; all they do is reflect the patriarchal beliefs of the world in which the jurists lived.[8] Jurists, in understanding the Quran, were guided by the norms, beliefs, and values of their times. These patriarchal beliefs formed the bases of many myths and legends that seeped into the literature, belittling women and portraying their sexuality as a grave danger to men and as a threat to social order.[9] Thus, segregating and secluding women from men's company was deemed necessary, and this ultimately rendered women invisible.

A Historical Overview: The Seclusion of Women in Fiqh Literature

During the third/ninth century, religious and legal canonical works established the tenets of orthodox Islam. Theologians composed elaborate manuals explicating the parameters of proper feminine conduct. Such manuals became essential indices, dictating societal attitudes toward women's presence in the public domain at the time and allowing us today to grasp the transformation in the role of women when compared to the earlier period of Islam.[10] During this particular period, many political, social, and cultural changes took place in the Islamic world, with a strong impact on society, leading to a shift in attitude toward women. By then the Islamic community had developed from a small state to a vast empire, one in which Muslims encountered new peoples of different religions, ethnicities, and cultures, and in which the Muslim faith interacted and clashed with the strong social customs of new converts, significantly shaping women's position and affecting their social mobility. Indeed, it has been argued that the marginalization of women, as well as the restrictions pertaining to their movement, visibility, and participation in the public sphere, emerged during the first three centuries of Muslim history.[11] This was a time when many ancient and medieval concepts infiltrated social norms and customs, which the community assimilated to reflect the patriarchal traditions of the new locales.[12] Some authors remark, instead, that Islam significantly restricted the presence and social participation of Middle Eastern Jewish and Christian women. However, due to the scarcity of relevant evidence, both arguments appear to reflect the leanings of the scholars involved.[13]

The Muslim community found itself in a dilemma, torn between the challenge of adopting new patriarchal perceptions concerning women, the fear of straying from the early ideals of the Islamic community, and the dread of impending social disorder (*fitna*). According to the jurists, sexual desire presented a real threat to societal order and stability. To put an end to its harm, women, who were perceived as the source of sexual temptation, had to be controlled. It was this fear of *fitna* (temptation, social disorder) that ignited and fuelled the legal discourse on male–female interaction.[14] Jurists issued rules to regulate the interaction between men and women in an attempt to control sexual activities. However, as mentioned earlier, the Qurʾanic discourse was not the impetus for the development of the *fitna* discourse; rather, the primary role was played by a large number of traditions and reports that violated the ethical principle of Islam and its egalitarian spirit.[15] The most widely circulated one was probably the *ḥadīth* (Prophetic report), "I have not left in my people a *fitna* more harmful to men than women."[16] Jurists placed women in the role of the treacherous and the dangerous; they wanted to control them in order to protect society from the temptations they posed. They limited their interactions with men in public spaces and set conditions for women's presence in the public sphere: women were to go out on the streets early in the morning, at dawn or late at night when darkness would conceal them. They also directed young women in particular to wear humble clothes and forbade them to wear perfume, display their jewellery, or walk on crowded streets.[17] Yet it is important to note that the *fitna* discourse did not describe a historical reality; it mainly reflected the aspirations, claims, and prescriptions of the jurists of this age.[18] The historical annals, chronicles, travel narratives, and biographical dictionaries give a different picture, showing a society in which men and women mixed liberally on the streets of Cairo and in the marketplace.[19]

By the early sixth/twelfth century, manuals of religious scholars reflected a shift in emphasis in the discourse of *fitna*. According to these, the real threat to society was no longer the sexual temptation women posed, but rather the delinquency and corruption of society as a whole. Consequently, jurists advocated the seclusion of women in order to protect them from possible harassment by unruly people and from the disruptive elements in society. In this sense, it was men's inability to control their sexual instincts and desires that led to the confinement of women. Terms like *fasād* (corruption) and *fussāq* (wrongdoers) found their way into jurists' manuals.[20] Women were now secluded not because they were the source of *fitna* but because the public sphere was infested with corrupt and sexually aggressive men, who endangered the well-being of women. Men now wanted to seclude women not because they feared them or saw them as a threat to society, but in order to protect them from unruly people on the streets. Jurists positioned themselves as the caretakers of women. Their manuals reflected a patriarchal tone that empowered men in society and gave them a legitimate reason to control and seclude women.

Between the sixth/twelfth century and the eighth/fourteenth, the Islamic world passed through a tumultuous period of wars, as well as political and social turmoil, and this caused another shift and a growing concern about delinquency and corruption. This unstable period witnessed the disintegration of the Muslim civilization into feudalism, the invasion of the Crusaders, and mounting conflict between Sunna and Shia, which created an atmosphere of fear and chaos. But the Mongol Invasion was by far the most alarming and devastating event, for it resulted in the sack of Baghdad in 656/1258 and put an end to the ʿAbbāsid Caliphate, the symbol of Sunni Islam. The Mongols occupied Central Asia and Persia, establishing their rule in these regions and spreading terror in the hearts of all Muslims until they were defeated by the Mamluks of Egypt in 658/1260. Unfortunately, the menace of the Mongols never ceased – they continued to raid against the Mamluks. The Mongols being originally pagan, Muslim scholars were unable to trust even those of them who had converted to Islam, fearing they would hold on to their pagan traditions and corrupt the faith. Further complicating the situation was that the Mongols favoured Shiʿi subjects and allowed Ismāʿīlī propaganda to increase, besides allowing the spread of Sufism, which included popular religious practices that venerated saints. All of this constituted a major threat to orthodox Islam and its scholars.[21]

During this turbulent age, many prescriptive manuals were composed by the *ʿulamāʾ* and theologians of the late Seljuk and Mamluk periods (twelfth to sixteenth centuries), elucidating the parameters of proper feminine behaviour. As Huda Lutfi's research on fourteenth-century Cairene women seems to suggest, during periods of social instability and political chaos, societies in fear of change tend to adopt conservative positions, turning their attention toward the private domestic domain and focusing on regulating women's behaviour. In line with this observation, the jurists and the *ʿulamāʾ* adopted an attitude of conservatism and rigidity, mainly directed toward women, as their manuals indicate. The *ʿulamāʾ* and rulers used women as scapegoats to explain political decline, chaos, and natural catastrophes. It seems that only by restricting women's access to the public sphere could men feel empowered and in control of the social order.[22] Next, I disucss three such manuals, composed by famous medieval Muslim theologians: Abū al-Faraj ibn al-Jawzī (d. 597/1201), Ibn Qayyim al-Jawziyya (d. 751/1350), and Abū ʿAbd Allāh ibn al-Ḥajj (d. 737/1336–37).

A Sample of the Manuals Composed during the late Seljuk and Mamluk Eras

A prominent example is the manual titled *Aḥkām al-nisāʾ* (Rulings Concerning Women), compiled by Ibn al-Jawzī, the Hanbalī theologian of the Seljuk period. Two chapters of this manual focus on the importance and desirability of secluding women. Chapter 26, "Cautioning Women from Going Outside the Home" (*taḥdhīr al-nisāʾ min al-khurūj*),[23] relates Ibn al-Jawzī's advice to women to stay at home, explaining that only after obtaining her husband's permission can a woman leave her house, in which case she, looking unattractive and simple, must avoid crowded streets. In a similar vein, chapter 27, "Mention of the Merit of Staying Home for Women" *(dhikr faḍl al-bayt li'l-marʾa)*, cites a non-prophetic report of the Companion ʿAbd Allāh ibn Masʿūd, stating that a woman who goes out of her house is always accompanied by the devil; therefore, she should always stay at home where she is close to God.[24]

Another manual, *Akhbār al-nisāʾ* (Information on Women), attributed to another Ḥanbalī theologian, Ibn Qayyim al-Jawziyya, also reflects a rigid attitude toward women and advocates their seclusion.[25] Having lived during eighth/fourteenth-century Mamluk Damascus in the midst of all the social and political instability, Ibn al-Qayyim believed that many evil forces threatened the Islamic community. He claimed that the *ʿulamāʾ*, being the inheritors of prophets, the commanders of the Islamic nations, and the leaders whom people should follow, were entrusted with authority to purify the community from evil and organize the public sphere.[26] Ibn al-Qayyim firmly believed, as becomes apparent from his writing, that male–female encounters in the public sphere threatened the purity of the community. His writings reflect his deep concerns about this matter, to the extent that his book calls for the complete barring of women from the public sphere and the imposition of strict rules to prevent any encounters between the two sexes.[27] Not only that, but Ibn al-Qayyim's misogynistic statements also claimed that women were created from a crooked rib that could never be straightened, and criticized them for being sly, ignorant, and deceptive.[28] His book includes a chapter titled "The Perfidy of Women" *(ghadr al-nisā')*[29] in which he cites a *ḥadīth* without an *isnād* (chain of narrators) or any proof of authenticity: "Consult with women and do the opposite of what they recommend; for indeed, in opposing them is blessing."[30] This report clearly contradicts the *ḥadīth* stating that "Never was a *ḥadīth* unclear to us – companions of the Messenger of Allah – and we asked 'Ā'isha, except that we found some knowledge concerning it with her,"[31] and represents a clear departure from the reports included in the early biographical dictionaries citing 'Ā'isha as the primary source of knowledge in the early Islamic period. She remained a trusted adviser to most of the prominent companions of the Prophet after his death and issued legal judgments during the reigns of 'Umar (r. 13/634–33/644) and 'Uthmān (r. 23/644–35/656) and continued to do so until her death in (58/678).[32] Furthermore, Umm Salama is credited for being the Prophet's political adviser, especially during the Ḥudaybiyya treaty.[33]

Another eighth/fourteenth-century scholar who was preoccupied with the issue of male–female interaction in the public sphere was the Mālikī jurist Ibn al-Ḥajj al-'Adbārī al-Fāsī. In his prescriptive manual *al-Madkhal ilā tanmiyat al-a'māl bi-taḥsīn al-niyyāt* (An Introduction to the Development of Deeds through the Improvement of Intentions)," he harshly criticized women, accusing them of having a weak, corrupt nature, leading to loose social behaviour.[34] He also chastised women for their improper behaviour in the marketplace, where they socialized with men and attended public festivals and weddings, and he publicly lamented and wailed over the dead. What seems to have frustrated him to a great extent was the activities of popular preachers and storytelling circles that were conducted in mosques or more commonly in cemeteries. He believed that such circles, where men and women mixed freely in an unregulated manner, threatened gender boundaries. He saw them as a threat not just to formal gender boundaries but to all standards of decency and propriety. Ibn al-Ḥajj was very harsh in his condemnation of those preaching circles that allowed the genders to mix. However, one must be careful not to embrace the scholar's treatise and his strict rules regarding such circles as reflecting the social life of his time. As mentioned earlier, the descriptive historical sources give us a different image of the medieval Islamic societies than the one communicated by the legal manuals. Gathering references to women's presence in the public space in medieval Cairo from historical chronicles, annals, and traveller's narratives gives a different impression than the one communicated by Ibn al-Ḥajj's legal manual. Ibn al-Ḥajj had "obsessive" fears of illicit and immoral behaviour, which he saw as threatening to spread throughout society as a result of the mixing of the sexes. This was reflected in the way he treated the issue. He firmly believed, as his writing shows, that there should be a sharp division between the public space of men and the private space of women. Any infringement on these spatial restrictions would present temptation to men and would lead to chaos and social anarchy.[35]

All of the above manuals reinforced the seclusion of virtuous women. Jurists interpreted Qur'anic verses and prophetic reports in ways that solidified specific patriarchal views regarding the proper role of women in the later medieval period, particularly views about their activities in the public sphere. Yet there is no indication that these restrictive rules had legal weight or that they significantly limited women's social and economic roles during this period. In fact, many scholarly studies record women's notable involvement and participation in economic, civic, and scholarly activities during the Seljuk and Mamluk eras. Mamluk chronicles and biographical dictionaries include hundreds of examples of women who were active in the fields of religion, medicine, and urban economy.[36] Women were engaged in various professions, and they offered their services or their wares to both men and women. Some female physicians worked in hospitals and treated both men and women. In *Histoire des bimaristans (hôpitaux) à l'époque islamique,* the historian Aḥmad ʿĪsā mentions a female physician known by the name Ibnat Shihāb al-Dīn al-Ṣāʾigh who succeeded her father in the *mashyakha* (the presidency of medicine) at al-Manṣūrī hospital in Cairo. She not only practised medicine in the hospital but also presided over the physicians of her time.[37] Moreover, biographical dictionaries are full of entries for female religious scholars, which indicates that women were active in the religious arena and came there into direct contact with men.[38] In fact, many male scholars of the time stated that they got their knowledge from female scholars. They respected them and expanded on the admirable qualities related to their strength of character, cleverness, and respected presence. Most of them are referred to by honorific titles such as *shaykha*, or *sitt al-wuzarāʾ* (Master/Mistress of Ministers/ Viziers), *sitt al-fuqahāʾ* (Master of Jurists), *sitt al-quḍāh* (Master of Judges), *sitt al-ʿulamāʾ* (Master of Scholars), titles that indicate clearly how society and male scholars viewed female *ḥadīth* and how they looked on female scholars with high esteem.[39] In addition, women, both elite and non-elite, contributed to and were active participants in the urban economy.

The references detailing women's lives and activities are vital to efforts to redress the false impression communicated by the legal manuals, which belittle and condemn women's presence in the public sphere. It is imperative to juxtapose legal and non-legal literature to better understand the dynamics of medieval Islamic societies. Still, one should not assume that the legal discourses were completely divorced from social realities; for scholars did not dictate behavioural norms that were unquestionably carried out by ordinary men and women. On the contrary, legal scholars engaged in a more complex dialogical relationship with reality. As mentioned above, it is obvious that the most fervent categorical laws prohibiting women's activities and presence in the public sphere were issued in cases where women were highly visible, a fact that was explicitly stated.[40] The repeated bans issued from the seventh/thirteenth century to the ninth/fifteenth barring Egyptian women from visiting graveyards and shrines are clear examples of how the scholars reacted to the high public visibility of women. Both religious and political authorities were frustrated by this phenomenon of the visiting of graveyards, for it was an extremely popular activity that entailed long absences of women from their homes and a high degree of public presence.[41] Jurists often had a reactive role, and scholars often lamented their inability to control various activities.

Generally, the legal *fiqh* literature was written by strongly patriarchal men, who took it upon themselves to define the position and proper behaviour of women in society. The home became the domain of women, while the marketplace, where wealth was generated, became the domain of men; at least this was the image the male establishment projected as real. Manuals also implied that women's seclusion was desirable among influential and elite circles. These manuals were fashioned as models to be emulated in order to counter the political chaos, threats, and fears that were spreading in society at that time and to discredit the participation of Mamluk women in the public domain. For jurists, the main aim behind their work was not to organize the public space but to secure firm control of the human sexual drive and the marital institution.

In addition, jurists did not always present a unified front; there were many significant divergences among them, especially concerning gender issues. While the great theologian Abū Ḥāmid Muḥammad ibn Muḥammad al-Ghazālī (d. 505/1111) wrote that a good wife "should remain in the inner sanctum of her house and tend to her spinning,"[42] the Andalusian philosopher Ibn Rushd (d. 595/1198) rejects the idea that a woman is only good for sewing and giving birth. In fact, he asserts that a woman can govern and run a state, in addition to conducting war. He believed that restricting women to procreating, spinning, and weaving resulted in female poverty and dependence on men.[43] Jurists failed to reach a consensus on contentious issues such as seclusion, segregation, and women's appropriate attire. Although many were anxious about male–female interactions, most jurists did not believe that the seclusion of women and their expulsion from the public space held the answer. Since jurists were not unanimous in their views, this conflict considerably affected the enforcement of the law. Jurists discussed the case of the *mukhaddara*, women of a specific class and age group, who never left their houses under any circumstances. Still, the way these women lived did not present the standard practice; in *fiqh* literature, there was no reference to support this lifestyle. In fact, legal literature is imbued with examples of women's testimony in courts being approved – indeed, being considered an ordinary occurrence.[44] Besides, the protection and seclusion of women was unattainable and unrealistic for most of the population, for many women had to work to support themselves and their families through their wages. Women who lacked male financial support had to go to out to earn their living. Women's work was integral to the economy. Their wages, no matter how modest, were part of the capital circulating in the economy. So any attempt to confine women at home and restrict their presence in the marketplace would surely have damaging effects on the economy.[45] Despite all that, religious patriarchal authorities continued to advocate the seclusion of women, especially during times of social disorder and political chaos. The strict legal manuals cited above of Ibn Qayyim al-Jawziyya, Ibn al-Jawzī, and Ibn al-Ḥajj were products of such times.

Unlike the previously cited patriarchal jurists, the Ḥanafī scholar al-Marghinānī (d. 593/1197) presented a more moderate position. In his famous book *al-Hidāya* (The Guide), he states that in business dealings and commercial transactions women do not need to cover their faces, hands, or forearms in the presence of men.[46] Al-Marghinānī discusses the role of women in the world of trade and business; his vision of the gendered space is one in which women come into daily contact with men who are not related to them. Unlike jurists who favoured the seclusion of women, he believed that women were part of the marketplace and that they had the right to engage in trade and various commercial activities, even though it would bring them into close contact with men who were not their *maḥram* (a *maḥram* of a woman is her husband, father, brother, son, or uncle). What he discusses is how women should dress in the company of such men during these business dealings.[47] Also, the Egyptian Shāfiʿī scholar and judge Ibn Ḥajar al ʿAsqalānī (d. 852/1449) referred to "the continuous practice based on the permissibility of women's going out to mosques, markets, and journeys when they are veiled so that men cannot see them" (*istimrār al-ʿamal ʿalā jawāz khurūj al-nisāʾ ilā al-masājid wa'l-aswāq wa'l-asfār mutanaqqibāt li-allā yarāhunna al-rijāl*).[48] Ibn Ḥajar here shares the same position as al-Marghinānī on the right of women to the public space and shares his concern regarding their attire in the company of men they meet in the public space and markets. Ibn Ḥajar's acceptance of women in the public space is evident in his historical recording of the famous scholars of his age. In his biographical dictionary, *al-Iṣāba fi tamyīz al-ṣaḥāba,* he included the lives of 1,543 female scholars, 53 of whom were his direct tutors. There is no mention of segregation or seclusion in such biographies of the women, nor does the question of anonymity arise. Ibn Ḥajar describes the female scholars in positive words, relating to them admirable qualities of strength, wisdom, and patience in teaching.[49] It is interesting to note that the veil and the issue of the covering of women does not appear in the biographical dictionaries. Unlike in Ibn Ḥajar's *fiqh* works, the uncovered faces of the female scholars are not made an issue or shown as an exception when recording the lived reality in the biographical dictionaries. The liberal mixing of sexes and the uncovered faces of women is also clear in the writings of Ibn Ḥajar's student Shams al-Dīn al-Sakhāwī (d. 902/1497), who dedicated one volume of his biographical dictionary *al-Ḍawʾ al-lāmiʿ* to the women scholars, most of whom specialized in *ḥadīth* science. Like his teacher, he praised their wisdom and substance and developed intellectual camaraderie and friendship with them.[50] Accordingly, Ibn Ḥajar and his student al-Sakhāwī do not display negative attitudes toward women scholars or even great surprise, amazement, or embarrassment at their accomplishments and participation in the public sphere. As mentioned earlier, they referred to most of them by highly honorific titles. These works further underscore that women's presence in the public sphere and their mixing with men was an accepted common practice. Finally, it is worth highlighting that a scholar like Ibn Ḥajar, when writing in his capacity as a *faqīh* (jurist), often focused on the issue of the veil and the covering of women, but when writing in his capacity as a historian, he did not pay the issue of women's attire any attention, and only spoke of women's accomplishments in the field. Scholars differed among themselves over the issue; indeed, a scholar would change his position on the same issue from one context to another, adding to the diversity and complexity of the situation.

The multifaceted nature of the *fiqh* literature made its implementation difficult, since it was subject to changes and inconsistencies. As can be discerned from the points discussed above, jurists were not unanimous, and their manuals did not reflect one reality; on the contrary, the interpretation of the source texts yielded multiple readings and understandings, due in part to juristic preferences of methodology and to other contextual factors. Not only did earlier scholars lack consensus concerning many issues, but in some cases their opinions were not binding. The incongruities of views developed into what we know as the *ikhtilāf* (differences, disagreements) genre, which has been one of the main features of *fiqh* ever since its conception during the early days of Islam.[51] *Fiqh* has never been seen as definitive; it is a scholarly endeavour to explain God's law, and therefore it has always been subject to change and alteration.

POLITICAL DIMENSION OF ISLAMIC LAW: *SIYĀSA SHARʿIYYA*

What exacerbated the situation and impaired the enforcement of the law was that jurists' manuals did not represent the sole legal authority. The ruler's legal authority, known as the authority of policy-based decisions, *siyāsa* or *siyāsa sharʿiyya,* also held significant weight. Rulers were involved in the development of Islamic law, acting in their capacity as the protectors of the believers and the defenders of the faith. Due to the legal indeterminacy created by the *ikhtilāf* (disagreement) among *fuqahāʾ*, rulers had room to issue decrees that were compatible with the *sharīʿa* and binding in the territories under their control.[52] The juristic doctrines and the rulers' policies coexisted; they interacted, forming a symbiotic relationship. Each recognized that its source of authority could not govern solely, and meanwhile, the two competed for jurisdiction over the regulation of society.[53] Both significantly influenced the formulation of Islamic law. In what follows, the dynamics between the rulers and the jurists are discussed, and examples are provided of how these two legal sources of Islamic law manifested themselves on a daily basis, and how their cooperative, competing, and symbiotic relationship affected the formulation of laws regulating the presence of women in public spaces. Jurists and rulers were not primarily occupied with the gendering of public space and the seclusion of women. Jurists, as discussed above, were more interested in controlling the human sexual drive and organizing the marital space; rulers concentrated on taxation and currency.[54]

Regarding women's presence in the public space, the historical chronicles mention only a few cases where rulers issued explicit orders declaring that women should stay at home and forbidding their presence in public spaces. The most famous example is probably that of the fifth/eleventh century Fatimid caliph al-Ḥākim (r. 375–411/985–1021), who issued strict orders to that end. He also forbade women from going to markets and public baths and even from visiting tombs.[55] Such extreme misogynistic declarations were usually issued at times of crisis, drought, famine, or plague. Religious scholars, for their part, presented women as scapegoats to explain the causes of political crises and natural disasters. Medieval societies interpreted these manifestations as consequences of the decline of faith and the degeneration of social norms. Women were usually singled out as the main threat to social norms. Al-Ḥākim's decrees were not implemented for long, because they encountered the resistance of both men and women. Gradually, this opposition triggered the first clear manifestation of women's agitation for their freedom. It was impossible for many women, who lacked men's financial support, to abide by these rules, because they had to leave their houses, earn a living, and obtain provisions. They enjoyed their freedom of movement on the streets and markets of Cairo, something they would not give up easily.[56] Men became adamant adversaries as well, because they were affected by the absence of women from the markets. Merchants complained to al-Ḥākim about the financial and economic difficulties they faced because of these policies of confining women, who were their main customers, to their homes.[57]

During the Mamluk era (648/1250–932/1517), issues of public morality, regulation of households, and gender boundaries took centre stage. Several decrees issued by the Mamluk sultans were short-lived, and many encountered resistance, because of their damaging economic effects. Yossef Rapoport observes that one ban, issued in 844/1440, lasted for a single day. He considers resistance to such decrees by society as clear evidence of the importance of women to the urban economy.[58] When a plague devastated Cairo and *Fusṭāṭ* in 841/1438, causing many deaths, the Mamluk sultan Ashraf Barsbay (d. 841/1438) issued a decree forbidding women from appearing on the streets or going to the marketplace during the month of Ramadan. The sultan asked the jurists and judges to identify the sins that God punished with plague; the jurists responded that that sin was *zinā* (fornication).[59] Most scholars gave a moral interpretation of the plague, perceiving it as divine punishment for corrupt behaviour and social malaise. When asked about the reasons for the plague, Jalāl al-Dīn al-Suyūṭī (d. 910/1505) explained in *al-Ḥāwī li'l-fatāwī* that "I believe people committed too many sins, so they were punished by this epidemic."[60] Yet not all Muslim scholars held the same views, for Ibn Ḥajar al-ʿAsqalānī (d. 852/1449) did not view plagues as punishment, as implied by the title of his epistle on plague *Badhl al-māʿūn fī faḍl al-ṭāʿūn* (An Offering of Kindness on the Virtue of the Plague).

Many medieval scholars pointed out that women walked on the streets in their finest attire day and night, which increased the chances of fornication.[61] The jurists' misogynist argument and outlook demonstrated how personal discretion can significantly influence legal decisions. For if these jurists had instead highlighted the unruly and disrespectful behaviour of men walking on the streets, and accused them of openly flirting with women in ways that could lead to fornication, the debate would have developed in a completely different manner and would probably have led to a different legal decision. Unfortunately, most of the jurists held the same opinion, believing that women's presence in public spaces led to immoral behaviour and sinful acts. This is what spurred the decision to forbid women from going out on the streets, excluding only old women and women of modest appearance. Even so, the sultan was still inclined to prohibit all women without exception, thinking that this would lift the plague.[62] Still, the sultan and the jurists agreed to issue a single decree. This case highlights the dynamics of medieval politics: where rulers' policies and juristic doctrines coexisted, the two sides cooperated to enforce the same law.[63]

One case of rulers and jurists not seeing eye to eye on interpreting the law, so that their disagreement escalated into a constitutional crisis, arose at the end of the Mamluk rule during the reign of sultan Qanṣūh al-Ghūrī (r. 906/1501–922/1516). A military chamberlain heard a case filed by a deputy *qāḍī* (judge) against his wife and her lover, where he accused them of adultery. After pleading guilty, both the wife and the lover were flogged and then fined one hundred dinars. The woman pled poverty and refused to pay. Since she was still technically financially dependent on her husband, the officers asked him to pay the fine. It was absurd to ask a husband to pay the fine for his adulterous wife. When he refused to do so, he was imprisoned. Upset to hear of such injustice, Sultan Qanṣūh ordered the stoning of the adulterers. This punishment was unusual, for no stoning had been carried out for many years.[64] His sentence was highly controversial and led to a serious debate and struggle over who had the right to interpret the law and pass sentences, as well as what the right punishment for such transgressions was. The sultan eventually ended this debate by having the lovers executed, then later hanged for two days to instill fear and order in society. In this case, we can see the juristic doctrine actively competing with the ruler's policy over the jurisdiction to regulate society. This time, it ended with the sultan manifesting himself as the sole ruler of the public space and as dominating the domestic front. This account of the two lovers and their tragic execution is fascinating, for it affirms clearly the role of the state and sultan in regulating the private sphere and disciplining women. The incident took place in the year (919/1513), toward the end of the Mamluk era, an age of decline, struggle, and political chaos. The impetus for this new role of the sultan at this moment in history is unclear; perhaps he was attempting to consolidate his position in the face of social changes and political decline by directly controlling his subjects and disciplining women.

THE DYNAMICS OF LAW IMPLEMENTATION AND THE ROLE OF LAW ENFORCERS

The formulation of laws in medieval Islam was a complex matter; the dynamics of devising and implementing them were also quite intricate. Who introduced these laws to societies? How was the work of the law enforcers affected by the societal backdrop? How did the people receive these laws and respond to their implementation? All of these questions arise when we examine the subtle interactions surrounding the practical application of the law. The *qāḍī* and the *muḥtasib* were both responsible for enforcing the law. The *qāḍī*, who was at the top of the official hierarchy, was responsible for settling disputes among people, while the *muḥtasib* was his direct subordinate. Any disputes between the people and the government, however, were referred to a judge presiding over a parallel court system that dealt with administrative matters related to the state, the *qāḍī mazālim* (injustices, grievances). The role of the *qāḍī* was confined to a type of court known as the *qāḍī* court; this was a single-judge court, where only the *qāḍī* could pass judgment.[65] He also had crimes investigated and personally interviewed both the accuser and the offender in his court before passing sentence. Crimes punishable by the criminal law and *ḥudūd* (penal code) were not part of a *muḥtasib*'s jurisdiction, because he usually punished wrongdoings without conferring with plaintiffs or defendants. The *muḥtasib* was responsible for settling any violation of the law affecting the community, that is, offences that took place in markets or public spaces. He constantly monitored public spaces to ensure there were no transgressions such as alcohol drinking, drug consumption, and prostitution. The *muḥtasib* was also responsible for policing the marketplaces, monitoring the condition of roads and buildings, and overseeing public morality. Thus, he represented the law and was tasked with implementing it in public spaces.[66]

Despite the jurists' strict manuals that barred women from public spaces, there is no record of the *muḥtasib* ever enforcing such rules. In fact, the *muḥtasib's* manuals contained instructions on how to deal with women in the marketplace and how to regulate gender relations in public spaces. Ibn al-Ukhuwwa's (d. 729/1329) *Ma'ālim al-qurba fī aḥkām al-ḥisba* (Milesones of Proximity in the Rules of Accountability), the best-known *muḥtasib* manual of the Egyptian Mamluk period, presents general instructions for governing gender relations in the marketplace.[67] Although there is a clear private/public dichotomy in this manual, the marketplace – the most public of spaces – is accessible to both genders. Indeed, Ibn al-Ukhuwwa instructs the *muḥtasib* never to bar women from public spaces. On the contrary, women are to be treated cautiously and with great sensitivity and protected from unwanted male attention. In the marketplace, cotton carders and flax spinners are instructed to discourage women from lingering in front of their shops and are forbidden to address them.[68] These regulations recognized that women's presence in the public space was a deeply rooted reality that *fiqh* rulings could not easily abolish. Still, the *ḥisba* manuals illustrate the dilemma that *muḥtasibs* faced at the time; they were torn between allowing customary daily practices and violating *fiqh* rulings. In *Ma'ālim al-qurba fī aḥkām al-ḥisba,* Ibn al-Ukhuwwa provides another example of how the *muḥtasibs* dealt with reality, kept the peace, and safeguarded women on the streets. This one refers to astrologers. In his manual, the practice of astrology is forbidden, yet the profession itself never is. Instead, rules are set to regulate it. Ibn al-Ukhuwwa instructs astrologers to practise their profession in public areas, where they can easily be supervised, instead of in alleyways, because astrologers are usually sought out by women, who might be bothered by men lingering in those areas. By imposing such regulations, the *muḥtasib* ensured peace on the streets and could regulate the behaviour of men and women.[69]

As seen in the above examples, the *muḥtasib* generally tried to enforce *fiqh* rulings without disturbing or clashing with local customs and practices. This meant allowing women access to public spaces. The *muḥtasib* enforced the rules barring them from the streets only in times of crisis when the sultan demanded it. Believing that plague was God's punishment for fornication and sinful behaviour, the *muḥtasibs* barred women from public spaces in accordance with the sultan's decree. These orders, however, were usually short-lived and were constantly defied and challenged by men and women alike. For example, in the year 825/1422, the *muḥtasib* Ṣadr al-Dīn al-ʿAjamī (d. 833/1430) prohibited women from sleeping in front of shops in the marketplace, where they were trying to catch sight of the *maḥmal* (pilgrimage caravan) that would pass through in the morning. He ordered women to return home, fearing that inappropriate behaviour would take place between men and women during these campouts. Women complied with these rules as long as the *muḥtasibs* were around to enforce them, but once they left, they went back to secure their spots.[70] Women did not fear the wrath of the *muḥtasibs* enough to be deterred from violating the prohibition.

At other times, the *muḥtasib* resorted to fear and violence in order to impose the rules. This was uncommon, especially since he usually enforced the laws using discretionary punishment (*taʿzīr*). During the reign of the Mamluk sultan Barsbay, Dawlat Khuja (d. 841/1438) was appointed *muḥtasib* during the aforementioned outbreak of plague. Dawlat Khuja was a military and administrative man as well as the governor of Cairo. The sultan needed an uncompromising man to carry out his orders to keep women from the markets as part of a broader plan to end the plague.[71] Dawlat Khuja succeeded in forcing women off the streets by threatening to execute any transgressor. This threat obliged women to stay home for a while. However, the law was short-lived: partial relief came after only three days, so that slave girls and old women could go out to purchase their necessities; then a week later the ban was completely lifted and women resumed their activities in the public space.[72] However strict a *muḥtasib* was, it was impossible to impose sultanic rules for extended periods of time, especially when they violated women's intrinsic need for freedom of movement. This case is valuable as it clearly shows the relations among all the actors on the legal scene in medieval Islamic Egypt: the sultan, the jurists, the *muḥtasib*, and the common people. It poins to the complexity of their relations and to how contextual and environmental factors accounted for their actions.

The implementation and enforcement of both *fiqhī* and sultanic rules depended greatly on the character of the *muḥtasib*, the social context, and life's daily realities. The public's reception and response also significantly affected implementation. Historical records are filled with examples of men and women defying and challenging rules. In an apparent subversion of authority, they contested the imposed rules by simply refusing to comply.[73] Other women, who were unable to defy the rules outright, found ways to weaken them, as in the case of the women who were determined to see the pilgrimage procession and stayed out on the streets once the *muḥtasibs* had left. Many laws faded away with time because they could not change the daily customs and practices of people.

The position of *muḥtasib* is an expression of the Qur'anic injunction to command public morality and prohibit evil (Q. 3:104, 110, 114; 7:157; 9:71, 112; 31:17). Although the concept is simple, the dynamics of its implementation are complex. *Fiqh* and *siyāsa* enjoyed a symbiotic relationship, constituting the two main sources of authority that dictated the rules the *muḥtasib* had to enforce. Not only that, but the education, life experiences, biases, beliefs, and personal characteristics of the *muḥtasib* drastically influenced how he ran things and handled misconduct in the public domain. In addition, the common people affected how the rules were implemented, for the ways they responded to various orders compelled the *muḥtasib* to change his tactics. All of these variants added to the complexities of law implementation.

CONCLUSION

This chapter has examined the complex relation between *fiqh* rulings and the visibility of women in the public space, showing how different factors affected the implementation of rulings barring women from public spaces in real life. First, *fiqh* rules were in a constant state of negotiation with social, political, and economic factors. Although the primary objective of *fiqh* is to extract God's law from the Qur'an and Sunna, in many cases the scholars' interpretations were more severe than what can be found in either source.

Second, *fiqh* rules were not the only source of authority; the *siyāsa shar'iyya* also exerted considerable influence. The symbiotic relationship between *fiqh* and *siyāsa* significantly affected the formulation of law; in fact, both powers cooperated, competed, and in many cases clashed over issues concerning women and gender relations in the public space. *Fiqh* rules were occasionally more lenient than rulers' decrees. On the few occasions that a sultan intervened to bar women from public spaces, his rules were enforced even though they were challenged on *fiqh* grounds.

Third, daily life and customs influenced how Islamic law, including both *fiqh* rules and sultanic decrees, was practised in society. The implementation of Islamic law proved to be very difficult due to its eclectic nature and the complex dynamics at work when it came to formulating and enforcing it. The multiple interpretations, the fact that there was more than one source of authority, and the lack of consensus regarding some of the *fiqh* rules complicated matters even more. The personal background, character, and beliefs of the law enforcers also played a major role in how the law was implemented. Finally, the people who lived during these times themselves contributed to the way law was imposed and enforced.

Indeed, the fact that rulers and jurists repeatedly attempted to restrict women's mobility hints at how common and prevalent their presence on the streets and in marketplaces was. The laws addressed actual events and common practices. In turn, social circumstances and norms gradually compelled a change in imposed laws. Accordingly, one can argue that Islamic law is responsive to social norms and customs; it is also eclectic, having more than one source of authority. These two features can be sources of empowerment for women demanding equality today.

NOTES

1 See, for example, Pierce, *Morality Tales*; Ergene, *Local Court*; Tucker, *In the House of the Law*.

2 See, for example, Sonbol, "How Sharīʿah Sees," 159–79; Tucker, *Women, Family, and Gender*, 175–217. Tucker in her chapter on "Woman and Man in Gendered Space" discusses how *fiqh* concerning the seclusion of women is a product of the intellectual, social, and political context in which it developed.

3 Mir-Hosseini, "Construction of Gender," 2.

4 All translations of Qur'anic verses in this chapter follow Muhammad Asad's translation with a few minor modifications: Asad, *Message of the Quran.* All non-Qur'anic translations are by the author unless otherwise stated.

5 See, for example, Amer, *What is Veiling*, 35.

6 Mir-Hosseini, "Construction of Gender," 2.

7 Ibid., 4.

8 Ibid., 1, 3.

9 Abou El Fadl, *Speaking in God's Name*, 474–6. Abou El Fadl argues that the jurists' determinations on women's seclusion are not based on the Qurʾanic verses but on a large number of reports and traditions. After carefully scrutinizing those traditions he discerned that there were too many patriarchal vested interests circulating and advocating them.

10 Keddie, *Women in the Middle East*, 24. Keddie discusses in detail how women were publicly active in the earliest Islamic period supporting men in warfare by nursing the wounded and taking on occasional combat roles. She argues that the religious establishment that developed in the mid-eighth century interpreted Quranic rules related to women's position in society in ways that reflected the practices and cultural assumptions of their own era, not early Islamic times. See also Roded, *Womenin Islam*, 32–47.

11 Keddie, *Women in the Middle East*, 30.

12 Ibid.

13 Katz, *Women in the Mosque*, 119.

14 Abou El Fadl, *Speaking in God's Name,* 472–3.

15 Ibid., 474.

16 ʿAmāra, *Jawāhir al-Bukhārī*, 240:553.

17 See Katz, *Women in the Mosque*, 28–30; Tucker, *Women, Family, and Gender*, 184.

18 Abou El Fadl, *Speaking in God's Name*, 480.

19 For how women and men mixed liberally in the streets of Cairo, see al-Maqrīzī, *Kitāb al-mawāʿiẓ*, vol. 1, 488; vol. 2, 108.

20 Katz, *Women in the Mosque*, 83.

21 Frenkel, "Islamic Utopia," 78–9.

22 Lutfi, "Manners and Customs," 101.

23 Ibn al-Jawzī, *Aḥkām al-nisāʾ*, 53–4.
24 Ibid., 54–6.
25 Ibn Qayyim al-Jawziyya, *Akhbār al-nisāʾ*, 1982.
26 Frenkel, "Islamic Utopia Under the Mamluks," 76.
27 Ibid., 79-81.
28 Ibn Qayyim al-Jawziyya, *Akhbār al-nisāʾ*, 144.
29 Ibid., 144–67.
30 Ibid., 145.
31 Al-Tirmidhī, *Al-Jāmiʿ al-ṣaḥīḥ*, no. 3884.
32 Roded, *Women*, 28–9; Katz, *Women in the Mosque,* 52. Katz discusses how many medieval scholars not only ignored and departed from the prophetic *aḥādīth* but also manipulated their historical context to meet their own ends. She cites the example of Ibn Daqīq al-ʿĪd (d. 700/1302), a famous Shāfiʿī scholar, who alleged that the Prophet's statement deterring men from barring women from going to mosques was not an indicator that women should be allowed to move freely, but presented an exception to the general rule that limited women's movement away from their homes.
33 Ibn Saʿd, *Kitāb al-ṭabaqāt al-kabīr*, vol. 2, 95.
34 Ibn al-Ḥajj, *Al-Madkhal*, vol. 4, 104.
35 Lutfi, "Manners and Customs," 100.
36 For more information on the economic role of women in Egypt, see al-Saʿdī, "Al-Nashāṭ al-iqtiṣādī al-ḥaḍārī"; idem, "Al-Nisāʾ wa-mihnat al-ṭibb"; idem, "Al-Marʾa wa'l-ḥayāh al-dīniyya"; and ʿAbd al-Razzāq, *Al-Marʾa fī Miṣr al-mamlūkiyya.*
37 ʿĪsā, *Histoire des bimaristans*, 165.
38 See, for example, Ibn Ḥajar, *Al-Durar al-kāmina*, vol. 3, 177, 395; al-Sakhāwī, *Al-Ḍawʾ al-lāmiʿ*, vol. 12, 27, 107–22; Ibn Khallikān, *Wafayāt alʿyān*, vol. 2, 172.
39 Ibid.
40 Lutfi, "Manner and Customs," 99-121.
41 Ibn al-Ḥajj, *Al-Madkhal*, vol. 1, 193–4.
42 Al-Ghazālī, *Iḥyāʾ ʿulūm al-dīn*, vol. 2, 54.
43 Ibn Rushd, *Averroes on Plato's* Republic, 59.
44 Tucker, *Women, Family, and Gender,* 183.
45 Al-Saʿdī, "al-Nashāṭ al-iqtiṣādī al-ḥaḍārī," 17.
46 Al-Marghinānī, *Hidāya*, 2000.
47 Tucker, *Women, Family, and Gender,* 181–2.
48 Ibn Ḥajar al-ʿAsqalānī, *Fatḥ al-bārī bi-sharḥ Ṣaḥīḥ al-Bukhārī*, vol. 9, 337 (commentary on al-Bukhārī, *Saḥīḥ, Kitāb al-nikāḥ, bāb naẓar al-marʾa ilā al-ḥabsh wa-naḥwihim min ghayr rība*, no. 5045 [5236]).

49 Ibn Ḥajar, *Al-Durar al-kāmina*, vol. 3, 177.

50 Al-Sakhāwī, *Al-Daw' al-lāmi'*, vol. 12, 46, 107–12.

51 See, for example, Masud, *Ikhtilaf al-Fuqaha*.

52 Masud, "Doctrine of *Siyāsa*," 1–29. Masud has a thorough study on *siyāsa shar'iyya* in which he discusses in great detail the different opinions raised by jurists on the topic. See also Rapoport. "Royal Justice," 71–102. Rapoport lays out how sultanic authority in integrated within the legal framework and explains how the Islamic state during the Mamluk era played an active role in adapting the sacred law to social practice.

53 Frenkel, "Islamic Utopia," 78; Stilt, *Islamic Law in Action*, 33. The jurists largely recognized the authority of rulers and devised and developed detailed theories to regulate the relationship between the two. Scholars like Ibn Taymiyya and Ibn Qayyim al-Jawziyya tried to solidify the role of the *'ulamā'* over that of the sultans in the *sharī'a* system, claiming that the *'ulamā'* had the final say in religious issues when disagreement arose. Ibn al-Qayyim went further, claiming that among the *'ulamā'*, the Ḥanbalis were the most perceptive, knowledgeable, and trustworthy.

54 Stilt, *Islamic Law in Action*, 189; Tucker, *Women, Family, and Gender*, 184

55 Al-Maqrīzī, *Itti'āẓ al-ḥunafā'*, vol. 2, 38, 53, 95–6, 8790–1. See this source for more on al-Ḥākim's restrictive measures.

56 Al-Maqrīzī, *Kitāb al-mawā'iẓ*, vol. 1, 488; vol. 2, 108. See this source to see how men and women mingled freely on the streets of Cairo.

57 Al-Dawādārī, *Kanz al-durar*, vol. 6, 298. See this source for more information on the effect of women's absence from the marketplace.

58 Rapoport, *Marriage, Money and Divorce*, 36.

59 Al-Maqrīzī, *Kitāb al-sulūk*, vol. 4, 1031–3. Rapoport discusses the damage that fell on the markets as a result of this decree banning women from the streets and markets. Rapoport, *Marriage, Money and Divorce*, 36.

60 Al-Suyūṭī, *Ḥāwī*, 381.

61 Ibn al-Ukhuwwa, *Kitāb ma'ālim al-qurba*, 157; Ibn al-Ḥajj, *Al-Madkhal*, 1:168.

62 Stilt, *Islamic Law in Action*, 104–5.

63 Ibid., 104.

64 Rapoport, "Women and Gender," 1–3.

65 Masud, Peters, and Powers, *Dispensing Judgement in Islam*, 21–2. See this reference for more information on the courts and court sessions. The judge court sessions were held in a location that was easily accessible to the public. Many jurists were against the holding of court sessions in mosques, for non-Muslims could not access them.

66 For more information on the Hisba and the Muhtasib, see Cahen et al., "Ḥisba."
67 Ibn al-Ukhuwwa, *Kitāb ma'ālim al-qurba.*
68 Ibid., 225–6.
69 Ibid., 275–26.
70 Stilt, *Islamic Law in Action*, 101.
71 Al-Maqrīzī, *Kitāb al-sulūk*, vol. 4, 1031–3, 1063. See this reference for more information on how appointing military men as *muḥtasibs* had become common practice by the end of the Mamluk era, especially during times of plague or economic crisis, when the sultans needed strong men to carry out their orders. This practice was strongly criticized, however, by religious scholars, who were offended by the encroachment of military men on their authority.
72 Rapoport, *Marriage, Money and Divorce*, 36.
73 Stilt, *Islamic Law in Action*, 204.

REFERENCES

Primary Sources

'Amāra, Muṣṭafā Muḥammad. *Jawāhir al-Bukhārī wa-sharḥ al-Qasṭalānī: Sub'umi'at ḥadīth mashrūḥa*. Ed. Khālid al-'Aṭṭār. Beirut: Dār al-Fikr, 2008.

Dawādārī, Abū Bakr 'Abd Allāh ibn Aybak al-. *Kanz al-durar wa- jāmi' al-ghurar:al-durra al-muḍī'a fī akhbār al-dawla al-Fāṭimiyya*. Ed. Ṣalāḥ al-Dīn al-Munajjid. Vol. 6. Cairo: Qism al-Dirāsāt al-Islāmiyya, al-Ma'had al-Almānī li'l-āthār bi'l-Qāhira, 1961.

Ghazālī, Abū Ḥāmid Muḥammad ibn Muḥammad al-. *Iḥyā' 'ulūm al-dīn*. Vol 2. Cairo: Dār al-Ṣābūnī, n.d.

Ibn al-Ḥajj, Abū 'Abd Allāh ibn Muḥammad al-'Abdarī. *Al-Madkhal ilā tanmiyat al-a'māl bi-taḥsīn al-niyyāt*. 4 vols. Cairo: al-Maṭba'a al-Miṣriyya, 1929.

Ibn al-Jawzī, Abū al-Faraj 'Abd al-Raḥmān ibn 'Alī ibn Muḥammad. *Aḥkām al-nisā*. Ed. 'Abd al-Qādir Aḥmad 'Abd al-Qādir. Al-Manṣūra, Egypt: Maktabat Dār Ibn Qutayba, 1989.

Ibn al-Ukhuwwa, Muḥammad ibn Muḥammad ibn Aḥmad al-Qurashī. *Kitab ma'ālim al-qurba fī aḥkām al-ḥisba*. Cairo: al-Hay'a al-Miṣriyya, 1976.

Ibn Ḥajar al-'Asqalānī, Aḥmad ibn 'Alī. *Badhl al-mā'ūn fī faḍl al-ṭā'ūn*. Ed. Aḥmad 'Iṣām 'Abd al-Qādir al-Kātib. Riyadh: Dār al-'Āṣima, 1990.

– *Al-Durar al-kāmina fī aʿyān al-miʾa al-thāmina*. Vol. 3. Beirut: Dār al-Jīl, 1977.

– *Fatḥ al-bārī bi-sharḥ ṣaḥīḥ al-Bukhārī*. Ed. Muḥammas Fuʾād ʿAbd al-Bāqī, Muḥibb al-Dīn al-Khaṭīb, and Quṣayy Muḥibb al-Dīn al-Khaṭīb. 14 vols. Cairo: Dār al-Rayyān li'l-Turāth, 1986.

Ibn Khallikān, Abū al-ʿAbbās Shams al-Dīn Aḥmad. *Wafayāt al-aʿyān wa-anbāʾ abnāʾ al-zamān*. Vol 2. Cairo: Maktabat al-Nahḍa al-Miṣriyya,1948.

Ibn Qayyim al-Jawziyya, Shams al-Dīn Abū ʿAbd Allāh Muḥammad ibn Abī Bakr ibn Ayyūb al-Zurʿī al-Dimashqī al-Ḥanbalī. *Akhbār al-nisāʾ*. Ed. Nizār Riḍā. Beirut: Dār Maktabat al-Ḥayāh, 1982.

Ibn Rushd, Abū al-Walīd Muḥammad. *Averroes on Plato's Republic*. Trans. Ralph Lerner. Ithaca: Cornell University Press, 1974.

Ibn Saʿd, Muḥammad. *Kitāb al-ṭabaqāt al-kubrā*. Ed. Carl Brockelmann. Leiden: Brill, 1904.

Maqrīzī, Taqī al-Dīn Aḥmad ibn ʿAlī al-. *Ittiʿāẓ al-ḥunafāʾ bi-akhbār al-aʾimma al-Fāṭimiyyīn al-khulafāʾ*. Ed. Jamāl al-Dīn al-Shayyāl and Muḥammad Ḥilmī. 3 vols. Cairo: Maṭbaʿat Lajnat Īḥiyāʾ al-Turāth al-Islāmī, 1967–73.

– *Kitāb al-mawāʿiẓ wa'l-iʿtibār fī dhikr al-khiṭaṭ wa'l-āthār al-maʿrūf bi'l-khiṭaṭ al- maqrīziyya*. 2 vols. Beirut: Dār Ṣādir, 1853.

– *Kitāb al-sulūk li-maʿrifat duwal al-muluk*. Ed. Saʿīd ʿAshūr and Musṭafā Ziyāda. 2nd ed. 4 vols. Cairo: Maṭbaʿat Lajnat al-Taʾlīf wa'l-Tarjama wa'l-Nashr, 1956–73.

Marghīnānī, Burhān al-Dīn ʿAli ibn Abī Bakr al-. *Al-Hidāya fī sharḥ bidāyat al-mubtadiʾ*. 4 vols. Cairo: Dār al-Salām, 2000.

Sakhāwī, Shams al-Dīn Muḥammad ibn ʿAbd al-Raḥmān al-. *Al-Ḍawʾ al-lāmiʿ li-ahl al-qarn al-tāsiʿ*. Vol 12. Cairo: Maktabat al-Qudsī, 1355 AH [1936 CE].

Suyūṭī, Jalāl al-Dīn ʿAbd al-Raḥmān al-. *Al-Ḥāwī li'l-fatāwī*. Ed. ʿAbd al-Laṭīf Ḥasan ʿAbd al-Raḥmān. 2 vols. Beirut: Dār al-Kutub al-ʿIlmiyya, 1983.

Tirmidhī, Abū ʿĪsā Muḥammad ibn ʿĪsā ibn Sūra al-. *Al-Jāmiʿ al-ṣaḥīḥ wa-huwa sunan al-Tirmidhī*. Ed. Aḥmad Muḥammad Shākir and Musṭafa Muḥammad Ḥusayn al-Dhahabī. Cairo: Dār al-Ḥadīth, 1999.

Secondary Sources

ʿAbd al-Razzāq, Aḥmad. *Al-Marʾa fī Miṣr al-mamlūkiyya*. Cairo: al-Hayʾa al-Miṣriyya al-ʿĀmma li'l-Kitāb, 1999.

Abou El Fadl, Khalid. *Speaking in God's name: Islamic Law, Authority, and Women*. Oxford: Oneworld, 2001.

Amer, Sahar. *What Is Veiling?* Chapel Hill: University of North Carolina Press, 2014.

Asad, Muhammad. *The Message of the Qur'an*. Gibraltar: Dar Al-Andalus, 1980.

Cahen, Cl., M. Talbi, R. Mantran, A.K.S. Lambton, and A.S. Bazmee Ansari. "Ḥisba." In *Encyclopaedia of Islam, Second Edition*, ed. P. Bearman, Th. Bianquis, C.E. Bosworth, E. van Donzel, and W.P. Heinrichs. http://dx.doi.org/10.1163/1573-3912_islam_COM_0293.

Ergene, Bogaç A. *Local Court, Provincial Society, and Justice in the Ottoman Empire: Legal Practice and Dispute Resolution in Çankiri and Kastamonu (1652–1744)*. Leiden: E.J. Brill, 2003.

Frenkel, Yehoshua. "Islamic Utopia Under the Mamluks: The Social and Legal Ideals of Ibn Qayyim Al-Ğawziyyah." In *A Scholar in the Shadow: Essays in The Legal and Theological Thought of Ibn Qayyim al-Ğawziyyah*, ed. Caterina Bori and Livnat Holtzman, 67–87. Rome: Istituto per l'Oriente C.A. Nallino, 2010.

ʿĪsā, Aḥmad. *Histoire des bimaristans (hôpitaux) à l'époque islamique. Discours prononcé au Congrès médical tenu au Cairè a l'occasion du centenaire de l'École de médecine et de l'Hôpital Kasr-el-Aïni en décembre 1928*. Cairo: Imprimerie Paul Barbey, 1928.

Katz, Marion Holmes. *Women in the Mosque: A History of Legal Thought and Social Practice*. New York: Columbia University Press, 2014.

Keddie, Nikki R. *Women in the Middle East: Past and Present*. Princeton: Princeton University Press, 2007.

Lutfi, Huda. "Manners and Customs of Fourteenth Century Cairene Women: Female Anarchy versus Male Ṣhar'i Order in Muslim Prescriptive Treatises." In *Women in the Middle Eastern History: Shifting Boundaries in Sex and Gender*, ed. Nikkie Keddie and Beth Baron, 99–121. New Haven: Yale University Press, 1991.

Masud, Muhammad Khalid. "The Doctrine of *Siyāsa* in Islamic Law." *Recht van de Islam* 18 (2001): 1–29.

– *Ikhtilaf al-Fuqaha: Diversity in Fiqh as a Social Construction*. http://www.musawah.org/sites/default/files/Wanted-MKM-EN.pdf.

Masud, Muhammad Khalid, Rudolph Peters, and David Powers. *Dispensing Judgement in Islam: Qadis and their Judgments*. Leiden: E.J. Brill, 2012.

Mir-Hosseini, Ziba. "The Construction of Gender in Islamic Legal Thought and Strategies for Reform." *Hawwa* 1, no. 1 (2003): 1–28.

Pierce, Leslie P. *Morality Tales: Law and Gender in the Ottoman Court of Aintab*. Berkeley: University of California Press, 2003.
Rapoport, Yossef. *Marriage, Money and Divorce in Medieval Islamic Society*. Cambridge, Cambridge University Press, 2005.
– "Royal Justice and Religious Law." *Mamluk Studies Review* 16 (2012): 71–102.
– "Women and Gender in Mamluk Society." *Mamluk Studies Review* 11, no. 2 (2007): 1–47.
Roded, Ruth. *Women in Islam and the Middle East: A Reader*. London: I.B. Tauris, 2008.
Saʿdī, Hudā al-. "Al-Nashāṭ al-iqtiṣādī al-ḥaḍārī li'l-nisāʾ fī Miṣr." *Awrāq al-dhākira*, no. 4. Cairo: Women and Memory Forum, 2007.
– "Al-Nisāʾ wa-mihnat al-ṭibb fi'l-mujtamaʿ al-islāmī" [Women and The Medical Profession in Islamic Societies]. *Al-Muʾarrikh al-Mīṣrī*. Cairo University, 23 July 1999.
– "Al-Marʾa wa'l-ḥayāh al-dīniyya fi'l-ʿuṣūr al-Islāmiyya" [Women and Religious life in Medieval Islamic History]. *Dawr al-marʾa al-siyāsī wa'l-ḥaḍārī ʿabr al-ʿuṣūr*. Cairo: Cairo University–Markaz al-Buḥūth wa'l-Dirāsāt al-Tārīkhiyya, 2002.
Sonbol, Amira al-Azhary. "How Shariʿa Sees Women's Work." *Society and Economy in Egypt and the Eastern Mediterranean, 1600–1900: Essays in Honor of André Raymond*, ed. Nelly Hanna and Raouf Abbass, 159–79. Cairo: American University Press, 2005.
Stilt, Kristen. *Islamic Law in Action: Authority, Discretion, and Everyday Experiences in Mamluk Egypt*. Oxford: Oxford University Press, 2011.
Tucker, Judith. *In the House of the Law: Gender and Islamic Law in Ottoman Syria and Palestine*. Berkeley: University of California Press, 1998.
– *Women, Family, and Gender in Islamic Law*. Cambridge: Cambridge University Press, 2008.

9

Mysterious Legislation

ʿUmar ibn al-Khaṭṭāb's Role in the Legalization of the Stoning Punishment in the Sunni Islamic Tradition

Sarah Eltantawi

Idhā ikhtalafa al-nās fī shay' fa-'nẓurū mā ṣanaʿa ʿUmar fa-khudhū bih.
(If there is a disagreement among the people on any matter, look to what ʿUmar did and emulate it.)

Mujāhid ibn Jabr (d. 100/718 or 104/722), early Qur'anic exegete[1]

In my recent book on *sharīʿa* (re)implementation in northern Nigeria, I tracked the process by which a peasant woman, Amina Lawal, was sentenced to death by stoning for committing *zinā* in 2002, two years after twelve northern states began (re)implementing full Islamic legal penal codes.[2] In this ethnographic work in Nigeria, during which I sought to understand why many northern Nigerians supported the stoning punishment, I came away with the understanding that people thought the stoning punishment was a demonstration of Islamic law's seriousness. The stoning punishment portrays Islamic law as so severe that it is the only moral system that can combat the poverty and corruption that is at the heart of this grassroots demand for *sharīʿa*. When I discussed with Nigerians the contentious intellectual history of the stoning punishment in Islam, I was routinely met with surprise: they wanted to quash this information, for it did not demonstrate the severity and stability of Islamic law. I also found that intellectuals at the heart of the *sharīʿa* movement themselves harboured doubts about the legality of the stoning punishment but did not want to pursue the matter publicly – casting doubt on the perceived appropriateness of stoning as a legal punishment in Islamic law would entail too high a political price.

This volume as a whole explores the tensions between canonization, methodological foundations, and lived reality in the Islamic interpretive tradition, with the focus on gender justice. The strange story of how the stoning punishment came to be legalized in the Islamic tradition falls squarely within this problematic. This chapter offers one perspective (there are several) that can help us understand how the stoning punishment, despite being a contingent, ambivalent, and unstable one in the Islamic tradition, nevertheless became law. I focus here on the labyrinthine intellectual history that resulted in the punishment being legalized in the four major schools of Islamic law.[3] In particular, I focus on the role ascribed to ʿUmar Ibn al-Khaṭṭāb (d. 644/1244) (hereafter ʿUmar), Islam's second caliph, in legalizing the stoning punishment for the crime of *zinā*, or illicit sexual activity. First, stoning occurs in an abrogated "verse" that does not appear in the Qurʾan in recited form yet has retained its legal implications (*naskh al-tilāwa dūna al-ḥukm*). The Qurʾan does prescribe a punishment – flogging – for the same crime of *zinā* (Q. 24:2), creating a contradiction that needed to be resolved. This peculiar form of abrogation is only applied – and hence, I would surmise, was only developed – to legalize stoning. Second, Islamic intellectuals applied the concept of *takhṣīṣ* (specification) to resolve this contradiction. *Takhṣīṣ* is applied in such a way that the punishment for *zinā* found in the Qurʾan – flogging – is applied to virgins (*bikr*), whereas stoning is applied to married adulterers. These hermeneutical tools, developed solely to legalize stoning, are noteworthy for their intellectual "acrobatics." That ʿUmar is the protagonist of this verse in important *aḥādīth* (that work to legalize the punishment) is notable for what it tells us about this historical figure and how (hegemonic) Sunni Muslim intellectuals have read and interpreted him. This, in turn, focuses the lens on the gender values, among other values, of ʿUmar's interpreters, if not the gender values of ʿUmar himself – at least insofar as we can accurately assess them.

ʿUMAR

The historical figure of ʿUmar is significant for his central role, as Sunni Islam's second caliph, in expanding the Islamic empire. He is also the only figure in the Islamic tradition who is represented as credibly rivalling the Prophet as a lawgiver and recipient of divine *waḥy* (revelation). ʿUmar is reported to have three times been vindicated by God in his pre-empting of revelation. Far from treating treat this extraordinary fact as a problem for the conceptualization and consolidation of Prophetic authority, traditional exegetical sources (*tafsīr*) do not appear to regard this issue as a theological problem. Instead, these sources invest ʿUmar with "quasi-divine authority." This apparent lack of concern regarding the issue of Prophetic authority during the period of the early *tafsīr* supports the theory that it was only after Muḥammad ibn Idrīs al-Shāfiʿī (d. 204/820) that Muslim practice became tied to the person of Muḥammad.[4] What *is* a theological problem for early exegetes and jurists is the epistemological instability of the *rajm* (stoning) verse that comes through the tradition through several *aḥādīth* attributed to ʿUmar. It is clear that the version of *naskh* (abrogation) theory that conceptualizes the abrogation of certain recitations without stripping them of their legal force (*naskh al-tilāwa dūna al-ḥukm*) was probably developed in direct response to ʿUmar's stoning verse – it was certainly the quintessential, if not the only, example of this type of abrogation. Jalāl al-Dīn ʿAbd al Rahmān al-Suyūṭī (d. 911/1505) a polymath whose thoughts on abrogation we will focus on below, links this particular form of abrogation directly to ʿUmar's authority.[5]

As I show below, the exegesis of Qurʾanic verses that reportedly vindicate ʿUmar (*muwāfaqāt* ʿUmar) rely heavily on *aḥādīth*, and when examined next to al-Suyūṭī's discussion of abrogation in general and the stoning verse in particular, we can identify trends in the early sources. First, we notice at the outset that discourses such as *tafsīr*, *fiqh* (jurisprudence), and *asbāb al-nuzūl* (occasions of revelation) are interdependent, each building on and reinforcing the assumptions of the others. This suggests that the "aggrandizing" of ʿUmar as a source of law in the *tafsīr* sources influenced the scholars who developed the *naskh* theory that resolved the theological contradictions presented by the stoning verse. Hence the *tafsīr* aggrandizes ʿUmar and testifies to his nearly prophetic power, even while producing a report of an abrogated verse mandating stoning, which is represented as being of the utmost importance to ʿUmar. ʿUmar's endorsement of the stoning verse may well inform *naskh* theorists' willingness to accept its legality (at least within traditionalist, Sunni Islam.) We should note, however, that this acceptance was questioned by the Khawārij and the Muʿtazila in the early centuries of Islam and then again by modern exegetes in the twentieth century.[6]

It is clear that the *rajm* verse is represented as of central importance to ʿUmar – important enough that he urged Muslims to remember it even on the occasion of the Prophet's death. To get at why, one avenue I explore is what we know of ʿUmar's broader attitudes toward women. First, it must be clarified that the stoning punishment is to be meted out equally to both men and women who are married adulterers – this is not a punishment that treats women differently from men. However, there is some evidence that ʿUmar's record of disdain for women influenced decisions that restricted their movement and access to the mosques and public spaces and, relatedly, their expressions of sexuality. Hence, though it is fallacious to establish a direct link between ʿUmar's advocacy of the stoning punishment and his occasional negative fixation on women, there is quite a bit of evidence to suggest that (1) upholding the patrilineal family structure was central to ʿUmar's agenda, both during the Prophet's life and during his own caliphate, and (2) he quite clearly disregarded women and considered them primarily objects of sexual temptation whose movements must be regulated. The stoning verse would aid in this goal, if only because of its *takhwīf* (deterrence) value. While the stoning verse applies equally to men and women in Islamic law (unlike in Judaic and Mesopotamian law, both of which influenced the punishment's entrance into Islam, which viewed adultery as a property crime against fathers and husbands),[7] the context of the verses' entrance into Islam implies a desire to contain female sexuality.

I show below that ʿUmar succeeded in implementing his vision of women's role in society, even though he was subservient to the Prophet, who is represented as possessing more gentle and accommodating attitudes and stances toward women and their "rights." It is noteworthy that Ṣaḥīḥ al-Bukhārī's *ḥadīth* collection describes instances in which the Prophet and ʿUmar got into disputes about various issues. Although the Prophet was quite capable of standing up to ʿUmar when he was so inclined, he is not represented as feeling that inclination with respect to issues concerning women. We can only speculate as to why the Prophet was rather passive toward ʿUmar when it came to questions of "women's rights," but one reasonable theory is that given that the Prophet valued ʿUmar so highly as a *ṣāḥib* (close companion), and given that the Prophet was used to managing ʿUmar's strong opinions, the Prophet did not wish to pick these particular battles, perhaps choosing the consolidation of political authority instead, even if it meant the sacrifice of some "women's rights."

ʿUMAR AND THE QURʾAN

The Islamic tradition considers the Qurʾan to be the narration of the unfettered word of God as transmitted through the Prophet Muḥammad. The second most authoritative source in the Islamic legal tradition is the *ḥadīth* collections, which comprise the Sunna of the Prophet Muḥammad. The Sunna is a general category that records a set of precedents and examples of the Prophet for Muslims to emulate. It is further held that the revelation of the Qurʾan from God through Muḥammad via the angel Jibrīl (Gabriel) is the sole means through which Muslims have received God's Qurʾanic revelations. Yet several traditions portray ʿUmar as having directly intervened in the revelatory process between Muḥammad and God. These instances of direct influence on the Qurʾan appear in the broader context of several *ḥadīth* reports, which describe ʿUmar contradicting and challenging the Prophet on certain issues regarding which he was eventually vindicated by God in the form of divine revelation. The most famous report of ʿUmar's influence on divine revelation is when he says "*wāfaqanī rabbī ʿalā thalāth*" (God agreed with me three times). This tradition is reported in al-Bukhārī's *ḥadīth* collection and is narrated by ʿUmar as follows:

> My Lord agreed with me three times: (1) I said, "O Allah's Apostle, I wish we took the station of Abraham as our praying place [for some of our prayers]." So came the Divine Inspiration: And take you (people) the station of Abraham as a place of prayer [for some of your prayers, e.g., two Rakʿāt of Ṭawāf of Kaʿba] (Q. 2:125). (2) And as regards the [verse of] the veiling of the women, I said, "O Allah's Apostle! I wish you ordered your wives to cover themselves from the men because good and bad ones talk to them." So the verse of the veiling of the women [namely 66:5] was revealed. Once the wives of the Prophet made a united front against the Prophet and I said to them, "It may be if he [the Prophet] divorced you, [all] that his Lord [Allah] will give him instead of you wives better than you." So this verse (the same as I had said) was revealed. (Q. 66:5)[8]

According to this report, God agreed with ʿUmar about rendering the place where Abraham stood (*maqām*, station) a place of prayer and also regarding two verses mandating the *ḥijāb* (veil). Accordingly, the tradition's most authoritative *ḥadīth* collection presents ʿUmar as having anticipated revelation. In another narration captured by Abū Bakr al-Bayhaqī (d. 458/1065), Umm Salama, one of the Prophet's wives, offers an objection: "'Oh ʿUmar, oh how the Prophet [*pbuh*] reveres his wives, and you are going to set them straight?' And then she went silent. And then, God, the Most High, revealed, 'It may be that if he divorces you, his God would give him wives in your stead who are better than you.'"[9]

In this narration, Umm Salama's compelling point – that the Prophet himself revered his wives, and thus ʿUmar was out of bounds in his criticism of these women – is represented as being silenced by the Qurʾan itself, which repudiates Umm Salama with a verse vindicating ʿUmar.

This narration also tells the extraordinary story of ʿUmar ordering the Prophet – using the grammatical command form of the verb *ḥ-j-b* (*uḥjub nisāʾak*) – to veil his wives.

Ibn Ḥajar al-ʿAsqalāni's (d. 852/1449) commentary on al-Bukhārī provides a further narration where Umar once again persists in his point that the Prophet's wives should take the *ḥijāb* so that they will set an example for other women and purify their own hearts. In this narration, ʿĀʾisha describes how she was reaching into the same bowl as ʿUmar during a meal, and their fingers touched, causing ʿUmar to cry out that he should be listened to regarding the *ḥijāb*. Subsequently, a verse was revealed, vindicating ʿUmar (*fa-nazala al-ḥijāb*):

> I was eating with the Prophet [*pbuh*] together from a large bowl when ʿUmar came by, so the Prophet invited him to join us, and he did. His finger touched my finger, and he said, "Ooh! Ooh! If the Prophet would agree with me, then I would not lay eyes on you in the first place. And then the *ḥijāb* verse was revealed. And the people agreed that this [incident with ʿĀʾisha] happened before the story of Zaynab.

The fact that these two incidents happened one after the other is one of the reasons for the revelation of the *ḥijāb* verse. And it is not a problem to have several reasons for the revelation. And Ibn Mardawayh narrated a *ḥadīth* from Ibn ʿAbbās which said:

> A man came to the house of the Prophet [*pbuh*] and sat down for a long time, so the Prophet [*pbuh*] got up and left three times and returned to give him a hint to leave, but he did not leave. Then ʿUmar came and saw annoyance on the face of the Prophet [*pbuh*], and said to the man, "It seems you have annoyed the Prophet [*pbuh*]" And the Prophet [*pbuh*] said, "I got up and left three times so [the man] would follow me, but he did not." So ʿUmar said to the Prophet [*pbuh*], "Oh Messenger of God, if you mandated the *ḥijāb* for your wives, the most exalted of all women, it would purify their hearts." So, the *ḥijāb* verse was revealed.[10]

Nūr al-Dīn al-Haythamī (d. 807/1404) reports the same story of revelation vindicating ʿUmar – this time in response to Zaynab, one of the Prophet's wives, who accused ʿUmar of *ghāyra* (jealousy, to display zeal or vie for) over the wives of the Prophet: "Zaynab said to ʿUmar, 'You are always [against us] Ibn al-Khaṭṭāb, even though the Qurʾan is revealed in our homes!' So, God the Most High revealed the verse, 'And when you ask anything of [the Prophet's – *pbuh* – wives], ask from behind a veil.'"[11]

ʿUmar also is reported to have anticipated the verse regarding *khalq* (creation):

> We created the man of an extraction of clay, then We set him, a drop, in a receptacle secure, then We created an extraction of clay, then We set him, a drip, in a receptacle secure, then We created of the drop a clot, then we created of the clot a tissue, then we created of the tissue bones, then We garmented the bones in flesh, then We produced him as another creature.[12]

Upon hearing this detailed description of God's creation, ʿUmar is supposed to have exclaimed: "So blessed be God, the fairest of creators!" And the Prophet said: "This is the way it was revealed, O ʿUmar!" The *ḥadīth* is quoted in al-Suyūṭī's *Tārīkh al-khulafāʾ* with this addition: "The Prophet [*pbuh*] invocated, 'Oh, God, strengthen Islam, with ʿUmar!' And ʿUmar was the first to pledge allegiance to Abū Bakr."[13] ʿUmar's authority as a predictor of divine will is buttressed by reminding the reader of how he was the first to underscore Sunni political authority in his support of Abū Bakr during the struggle for succession.[14]

Building on instances in which ʿUmar seems to have all but willed the *ḥijāb* verse, against the Prophet's wishes, Avraham Hakim points to patterns later in ʿUmar's career that suggest ʿUmar viewed his position as a successor of the Prophet politically and as a religious leader extending the Prophet's mandate as lawgiver. Hakim discusses ʿUmar's opposition to the practice of *mutʿa*, both of marriage (temporary conjugal relations) and of the *ḥajj* (the right to perform the rites of both pilgrimages, the *ʿumra* and the *ḥajj*, in one trip to Mecca, as opposed to having to go twice). Hakim cites Abū Qulāba al-Jarmī (d. between 104/722 and 107/726), who reports ʿUmar saying, "There were two kinds of *mutʿa* at the time of the Prophet. I hereby prohibit them and punish whomever practices them, *mutʿa* of *hajj* and *mutʿa* of marriage."[15]

Hakim points to further tensions in the Islamic tradition between the Sunna of the Prophet and the rulings of ʿUmar. He cites one example, that of ʿAlī ibn Abī Ṭālib (d. 40/661) saying he preferred the Prophet's Sunna to that of ʿUmar on the matter of how many times to lash ʿUqba ibn Abī Muʿayṭ, the governor of Kufa, for leading prayers while intoxicated. ʿAlī is reported to have said "*wa-hādhā aḥabbu ilayya*"[16] with regard to the Prophet's ruling.[17] That ʿAlī had to explicitly state that he preferred the Prophet's Sunna over ʿUmar's suggests a serious rival to the Prophet's authority. Despite this challenge, however, Hakim concludes, "Once this [the construction of Muhammad as the ultimate spiritual, moral and religious authority in Islam] was achieved, the *ummah*, rallied around the Prophet and the image of ʿUmar was diminished. The community preferred the image of a Prophet as its source of authority to that of a caliph."[18] Hakim does not detail the epistemological or historical process that brought about this outcome, nor does he trace the alternative history of ʿUmar's status of lawgiver. This is another example of how the process of "orthodoxization" is not total. "Total orthodoxy" implies there are no elements of a tradition to exclude. In a context in which ʿUmar has clearly made such a strong mark on Muslim intellectual, political, and military history, perhaps Hakim's conclusion that ʿUmar's influence is diminished is too firm.

THE *RAJM* VERSE AND ABROGATION

The examples I have provided from traditional sources make clear that ʿUmar's influence on divine revelation was not considered a theological problem at the time the scholars wrote about it. As Hakim argues, this could be because the construction of the Prophet as the sole lawgiver was the result of that very process of scholarly consolidation of norms and sources, and so could not have been at that time self-consciously argued. That ʿUmar's influence on revelation, and hence his potential rivalry with the Prophet, was not considered a problem suggests that in the early period of Islamic intellectual history, a more oligarchical conception of authority was acceptable, as opposed to in later periods when the tradition had more strongly congealed.

What was a problem, however, was that the divine injunction to stone adulterers to death for adultery was an "abrogated verse" not found in the Qurʾan and that ʿUmar is represented as instrumental in introducing it into Islamic law and tradition. The evident differences in scholarly concern about the two issues might lead us to postulate that questions of spiritual and political authority during this intellectual period were secondary to sorting out the theological difficulties presented by "verses," such as the stoning verse, that are considered divine even though they did not make it into the Qurʾan.

John Burton helps us understand how the idea of a stoning verse whose legal maxim has been retained while its recitation has been abrogated (*naskh al-tilāwā dūna al-ḥukm*) could have been squared with al-Shāfiʿī's *uṣūl*, which holds that the Qurʾan must always supersede *ḥadīth*.[19] "For Shāfiʿ ... Ḳurʾān and *muṣḥaf* are not coterminous. For *muṣḥaf* refers to the Ḳurʾān document. But Ḳurʾān refers to the Ḳurʾān source – to all that was revealed to Muḥammad, not all of which, as we see, has survived the *muṣḥaf*. The distinction implies that, to some, those reports on the Prophet's 'forgetting' revelations refer to some hypothetical proto-Ḳurʾān once revealed to the Prophet."[20] Al-Shāfiʿī is, of course, correct that the Qurʾan and the *muṣḥaf* are not coterminous, but for the purposes of streamlining the *uṣūl*, this distinction would open the door to more problems than it would generally be worth. Al-Shāfiʿī's willingness to do so here speaks once again to the extraordinary status of the stoning punishment as one that was deemed very important to legalize.

CLOSE READING OF AL-SUYŪṬĪ'S DISCUSSION OF *NASKH* AND THE *RAJM* VERSE

The beginning of al-Suyūṭī's (d. 911/1505) discussion concentrates on all the possible meanings of *naskh* (removal, substitution, and transfer), and grounds each of those readings in a Qur'anic verse that functions as a proof text for this concept. *Naskh* becomes an important tool theologically, for there are reports of verses that were recited but not written down during the ʿUthmānic collection of the codex. That the science of *naskh* was developed to logically accommodate these occurrences in the tradition tells us that the principle of coherence and non-contradiction in the Qur'anic text is of a higher epistemological order than what we might call the "lesser" contradiction of an unrecited *āya* (verse), which is, by definition, divine.[21]

Al-Suyūtī argues that whatever abrogated verses do not make it to the Qur'an appear in the "higher Qur'an," or the *lawḥ al-maḥfūẓ*.[22] Al-Suyūtī argues that some *ʿulamāʾ* held that the Qur'an can only be abrogated by Qur'an while others held that it was possible to abrogate Qur'an with Sunna; however, he does not specify which *ʿulamāʾ*. Al-Suyūṭī reports that it was also said that abrogation of Sunna is permissible if it is *bi-amr Allāh min tarīq al-waḥy* (with the permission of God through divine inspiration), but not if the abrogation is arrived at via *ijtihād* (independent reasoning). Some scholars, such as Ibn Jarīr al-Ṭabarī (d. 310/923) in his *Tafsīr*, objected to the notion of abrogation based on Q. 2:106: "We do not abrogate a verse or cause it to be forgotten without bringing a better one like it."[23] Al-Shāfiʿī argues that when the Qur'an is abrogated by Sunna, there will be a Qur'anic verse reinforcing that abrogation; and when Sunna is abrogated by Qur'an, then the Sunna will reinforce that abrogation. This process makes clear the mutually supportive relationship between the Qur'an and the Sunna.[24] Al-Suyūtī then discusses different types of *naskh*: some commands (*maʾmūr bih*) are abrogated before they become codified or solidified (*qabla imtithālih)*, and some verses are abrogated because they were revealed for prior communities. An example of the latter is the command to pray to Mecca rather than Jerusalem. There is also the case of suspension of a ruling at times when Muslims are few or weak (*ka'l-amr ḥīna al-ḍaʿf wa'l-qilla*). Regarding this category, al-Suyūtī argues: "and these in reality are not abrogated, but are in the category of the postponed or deferred" (*wa-hādhā fī al-ḥaqīqa laysa naskhan bal huwa min qism al munsaʾ*).[25]

Al-Suyūtī then describes the three basic categories of *naskh*: those whose recitation and law were abrogated together (*naskh tilāwatih wa-ḥukmih maʿan*), those whose law was abrogated, but not their recitation (*naskh hukmih dūna tilāwatih*), and the third kind, those whose recitation was abrogated, but not their law (*naskh tilāwatih dūna hukmih*).[26] The stoning verse falls under this third category.

Al-Suyuṭī narrates the following discussion in the voice of ʿUmar, which explains why the *rajm* verse's *tilāwa* was not transmitted:

> Ibn Idris transmitted in the *faḍā'il* al-Qur'an, on the authority of Ya'lā ibn Hakīm, on the authority of Zayd ibn Aslam: "ʿUmar addressed the people, and said: 'Do not dispute stoning, for it is legal, and I had intended to write it into the *muṣḥaf* [the ʿUthmānic codex],' so I asked Ubayy ibn Ka'b, and he said: 'Did you not come to me when I was trying to decode the verse from the Prophet of God [*pbuh*], and he pushed me in my chest and said: "I have decoded the stoning verse – they were having sex with each other like animals."' Ibn Ḥajar said: "And here is a sign that reveals the reason for its [the stoning verse's] recitation, and that is the difference of opinion about it."[27]

The fact that ʿUmar is represented as having shoved Ubayy ibn Ka'b when he questioned the revelation of the stoning verse indicates both ʿUmar's sense of urgency about stoning and, perhaps, his own sense that the legality of the punishment would seem questionable to his interlocutors. That "they were having sex with each other like animals" is noted by Ibn Ḥajar as an explanation for the unlikely verse. Public sexual displays are represented here as objectionable on their face, an offence to public morality. Despite what might seem like an obvious justification, however, al-Suyūṭī is still compelled to follow this *ḥadīth* with a justification of this peculiar form of *naskh* (*naskh al-tilāwa dūna al-ḥukm*):

> Ibn al-Ḥiṣār said on this subject: "It has been said, 'what happens to that which has been abrogated without a replacement?' When God the Most High said, 'We have not abrogated any verses or causes, but we substitute something better or similar' (Q. 2:106). Is there no debate on this *tilāwa*?" We say the answer is, everything that has been established in the Qur'an and which has not been abrogated is a replacement for that whose recitation has been abrogated [*tilāwatuh*]; and everything abrogated from the Qur'an that we have no way of knowing at this time has been replaced by that which we have learned, and its recitation and meaning have been passed down to us.[28]

Here, al-Suyūṭī presents us with a closed hermeneutic circle: nothing has been abrogated; verses have simply been replaced by something close or better. Immediately following this we are presented with a contradiction: "Everything which has been presented in the Qur'an which has not been abrogated is a replacement for that whose recitation has been abrogated," which clearly suggests that there are indeed verses, at least in theory, that have been abrogated, at least in their recitation. The final category is "everything which has been abrogated that we have no way of knowing at this time" – that is, verses, such as stoning, that we might assume exist in *al-lawḥ al-maḥfūẓ* in heaven, are replaced with "that which we have learned, and whose recitation and meaning have been passed down to us," that is, the stoning *ḥadīth* transmitted on the authority of 'Umar. So for al-Suyūṭī, abrogation theory is built around the empirical evidence we have – however contradictory and perhaps self-serving it may be. The evidence is not sifted out and discarded if it does not conform to a pre-existing theory. This logic, with its reverse causality, clearly indicates that *naskh* theory was developed to accommodate stoning; stoning was not outlawed because it contradicted a theory of abrogation that could have been more simple and straightforward.

Al-Suyūṭī's elaboration of abrogation theory reveals the tremendous amount of intellectual energy and rational contortions that went into legalizing stoning. In accommodating stoning, jurists and exegetes were unable to question the validity of abrogated verses, which muddied the waters considerably. Why were those verses abrogated in the first place?[29] Yet legalizing stoning was deemed important enough that jurists and exegetes were willing to inject contradictions and logical fallacies into the Islamic intellectual tradition. Given that most of the *tafāsīr* (exegetical works) al-Suyuṭī cited were produced after major collections of *aḥādīth* were compiled, one might ask why he and his contemporaries were willing to take this risk. Burton argues that since all the *fuqahā'* (jurists) abided by the stoning penalty, only differing about its source, "*naskh* theorizing is characteristic of a secondary science, *uṣūl al-fiqh*. Since *naskh* involves such delicate issues as the alleged 'suspension' of Qur'an rulings (their inoperability for *fiqh* purposes), it was obviously expedient to seek to base the entire theory of *naskh* on a secure Qur'anic foundation."[30] Burton is pointing to the interdependent nature of these discourses – *tafsīr*, *ḥadīth*, *uṣūl al-fiqh* – which suggests that aggrandizing 'Umar as a lawgiver has influenced the *fuqahā'*'s stance of total agreement on the validity of stoning. Since the facticity of the stoning verse was eventually accepted uncritically by the *fuqahā'*, their task was therefore to harmonize that verse with *usūl al-fiqh* epistemology. This acquiescence to a ruling that was considered controversial even by those standards can only be justified by the authority of ʿUmar, who is understood as a secondary lawgiver.

Kevin Reinhart analyzes another discourse affected by ***naskh: asbāb al-nuzūl***, "The supersession concept reflects or creates the genre of 'occasions of revelation' [*asbāb al-nuzūl*] which details the circumstances provoking revelation of a given Qurʾanic periscope."[31] Reinhart's's use of the phrase "reflects or creates" points again to the interdependence of all of these genres in the Islamic sciences.

THE TERMS OF ʿUMAR'S RIVALRY WITH THE PROPHET

Linda Lee Kern undertook a study of ʿUmar's relationship with the Prophet in a dissertation completed at Harvard University in 1996. In it, she details each time this relationship is referred to in al-Bukhārī's *Kitāb al-jāmiʿ al-ṣaḥīḥ*.[32] Here is one example of interpretive conflict regarding Q. 9:80: "Seek forgiveness for them, or seek not forgiveness for them. If thou seekest forgiveness for them seventy times, God will not forgive them. That is because they disbelieve in God and His Messenger. And God guides not iniquitous people."[33] According to al-Bukhārī, ʿUmar interpreted this verse narrowly to mean that a hypocrite should not be prayed over under any circumstances, while the Prophet interpreted the verse more liberally to suggest that redeeming the souls of the hypocrites might mean praying over them more than seventy times. ʿUmar's interpretation of this first verse seems to have been confirmed by God in Q. 9:48: "Indeed, even before this time have they tried to stir up discord and devised all manners of plots against thee, [O Prophet,] until the truth was revealed, and God's will be came manifest, however hateful this may have been to them."[34] ʿUmar may be unique among major Muslim figures with respect to the impact his often fiery comportment had on his actions and thus on Islamic history. In the section below on contemporary accounts of the Prophet and ʿUmar's relationship, I explore this psychological dimension further, but it should also be mentioned alongside the example above. It is worth noting that ʿUmar went so far as to physically assault the Prophet to prevent him from praying over ʿAbd Allāh ibn Ubayy's grave, and then repented, reportedly saying, "I was amazed at my strength in persisting against the Messenger of God on that day, and God and His messenger know best."[35] Al-Bukhāri's *aḥādīth* on the relationship between the Prophet and ʿUmar unearth how particular gender norms in the Islamic tradition were constructed. Below are examples of the dynamic between the Prophet and ʿUmar regarding issues that do not concern gender. The following *ḥadīth* expands on the previously mentioned one and opens with ʿUmar "pouncing" upon the Prophet:

> As [the Prophet] stood up [to pray over ʿAbd Allāh], I pounced on him and said, "Oh Messenger of God, are you [really going to] pray over ʿAbd Allāh ibn Ubayy, after he said such and such on the day of such and such?" And I enumerated for him the things he had said. The Messenger of God [*pbuh*] smiled and said, "Get out of my way ʿUmar." And when I continued all the more [to challenge] him about it, he said, "I was given the choice [whether or not to seek forgiveness for the hypocrites] and I've made my choice. And if I knew that [praying] more than seventy [prayers over him] would [cause God to] forgive him, I would certainly pray more than seventy [prayers]." Then the Messenger of God [*pbuh*] prayed over him and left.[36]

The Prophet and ʿUmar were of different opinions on this issue, and the Prophet gently, yet firmly, held his ground against ʿUmar, who had just physically assaulted him. I note this instance because it is clear from this example that in cases where the Prophet wanted to assert his will over that of ʿUmar, he was perfectly able to do so. ʿUmar here was defaulting back to a behaviour pattern of expressing impatience and impetuousness followed by profound guilt and subservience to the Prophet. Indeed, ʿUmar's reaction to the Prophet's mild reprimand in this instance was so severe that he spent a period fasting, giving alms, praying, and freeing slaves to absolve himself of what he must have regarded as the enormous sin of questioning the Prophet's judgment.

Another example of the Prophet clearly asserting his authority over ʿUmar was with respect to ʿUmar's opposition to the treaty at Ḥudaybiyya:

> [For on the day of Ḥudaybiyya,] ʿUmar came up and asked [the Prophet], "Are we not in the right and they in the wrong? And won't those of us who are killed go to paradise while they will go to hell?" [The Prophet] said, "Yes." He [ʿUmar] said, "Then why

> should I compromise our religion for an affair of this world, with us turning back [from a battle], and letting God judge between us [instead]? [The Prophet] said, "Ibn al-Khaṭṭāb, I am the Messenger of God, and God will never ever let me perish!"[37]

Here, the Prophet was going so far as to assert that he was the Messenger of God to convince ʿUmar to abandon his black-and-white thinking. In another example, the Prophet ordered ʿUmar to stop pelting Ethiopians he found playing in the mosque with gravel, as the Prophet himself had been tolerating their play there. The Prophet told ʿUmar, "Let them play!"[38]

THE PROPHET DEFERS TO ʿUMAR?

We have established that the Prophet was well capable of asserting his will over ʿUmar when he deemed it necessary; thus, instances in which the Prophet did back down when faced with ʿUmar's demands stand out. Moreover, now that we have established that the Prophet was not intimidated by ʿUmar and did not always defer to his moral judgment, instances in which the Prophet did let ʿUmar's opinions stand can therefore be more plausibly understood as a result of the content of what ʿUmar was saying. Either the Prophet agreed with ʿUmar in such instances, or he chose not to battle ʿUmar on those occasions. In many if not most of the cases in which the Prophet deferred to ʿUmar's demands and opinions that differed from his own, the issue at hand concerned women.

The picture that al-Bukhārī's *Kitāb al-jāmiʿ al-ṣaḥīḥ* paints of ʿUmar's relations with his own wives is revealing in this regard. ʿUmar's wife calls him "astonishing" (*aʿjab laka*) for adopting a harsher code of conduct toward his wives compared to that of the Prophet. ʿUmar reports:

> Then [once] while I was considering a certain matter, my wife said [to me], "Would that you do such and such." I said to her, "What is [wrong] with you? Why [are you getting into] this? How can you presume to meddle in a matter that I am dealing with?" She said, "How astonishing you are, Ibn al-Khaṭṭāb! You do not want to be talked back to, and yet your own daughter talks back to the Messenger of God [*pbuh*] up to the point that he stays angry the whole day!"[39]

Umm Salama, the Prophet's's wife, goes on to criticize ʿUmar for involving himself in the Prophet's marital affairs. It seems that Umm Salama may have been referring to the *ḥijāb* verse that ʿUmar influenced: "How astonishing you are, Ibn al-Khaṭṭāb! You stick your nose into everything up to the point that you enter into [the affairs] between the Messenger of God [*pbuh*] and his wives!"[40] Here, a woman – the Prophet's wife, no less – is talking back to ʿUmar and reprimanding him for his harshness and for challenging Prophetic authority.

With regard to women, again we have a report of the Prophet himself being "astonished" by ʿUmar's ferocity and harshness. A group of Qurayshī women who were speaking with the Prophet hastily dispersed when they heard of ʿUmar's imminent arrival:

> [One day] ʿUmar asked permission to [come in and talk to] the Messenger of God [*pbuh*]. Some Qurayshī women [happened to be there] with him. They were speaking with him about a raise [in their share of wealth], and their voices were raised. [However,] when ʿUmar asked permission [to come in], they jumped up in a hurry, rushing to veil themselves. The Messenger of God [*pbuh*] admitted ʿUmar, laughing. ʿUmar said, "May God give you laughter in your old age, Messenger of God!" [The Prophet] said, "I am astonished by these women who were just here with me. As soon as they heard your voice, they jumped up to veil themselves!" ʿUmar said, "Oh Messenger of God, you have more right to be feared [than I do]!" Then ʿUmar addressed [the women], "Oh you enemies of your proper selves! Are you afraid of me and not of the Messenger of God [*pbuh*]?" [The women] responded, "You are more severe and more uncouth than the Messenger of God [*pbuh*]."[41]

There are a few themes to mine from this exchange. The first is that the Prophet seems to have found it at most curious, and even amusing, that ʿUmar's (with all that he represented for women) appearance on the scene caused these women to flee, though we have no reason to assume that the fear and apprehension that fuelled the women's response was not real. This is important, for it shows that on this occasion the Prophet did not prioritize the comfort of the women over ʿUmar's impetuous attitude toward him (though the Prophet was clearly predisposed to be gentle with his wives and to other women in his own house). This is evidenced by his letting ʿUmar descend upon the scene with impunity, where he caused discomfort and scolded the women. Second, ʿUmar is represented as viewing respect primarily in terms of fear. The Prophet laughed at the response that ʿUmar's entrance prompted from these women, and ʿUmar interpreted the Prophet's attitude through his own interpretive lens: respect is shown through fear, and these women are not sufficiently afraid of the Prophet, so let me intervene (for reasons we cannot discern, but that are laminal and interesting) and demand respect for him.

WHAT "THE WOMEN" THOUGHT OF ʿUMAR

The uncritical manner in which ʿUmar's influence is received in the scholarly tradition stands in stunning contrast to the reports of these women, who scold ʿUmar, call him uncouth and severe, and compare him unfavourably and sarcastically to the Prophet.[42] Even the Prophet chimes in. This difference in attitude is highly revealing regarding the women who interacted with ʿUmar and the scholars who lauded him and canonized his legal judgments. Each of these two traditions is as authentic as the next, but only one has succeeded in shaping Islamic orthodoxy and silencing these heterodox voices of dispersed and fearful – yet also subversive and resistant – women. Even praying in the mosque was a dangerous activity for women when ʿUmar was around:

> One of ʿUmar's wives used to perform the morning and evening prayers on Friday at the mosque. Someone said to her, "How can you go out, knowing how much ʿUmar [fanatically] loathes it?" She said "[Do you not know] what prevents him forbidding me?" [The person] responded, "The words of the Messenger of God prevent him: Do not prevent the women servants of God from [going to] His mosques.[43]

It is clear that women at the time needed the Prophet's intercession against ʿUmar in order to preserve their way of life. However, I think the evidence suggests that in the final analysis, ʿUmar's persistence in his opinions about the proper role of women was stronger than the Prophet's own gentle disposition toward women.

It is important to note here that *ḥadīth* reports can be thought of as representing the time in which they were compiled. It is possible that these particular compilations of reports speak more to Iraqi gender sensibilities of the time than they do to the actual historical figure of

ʿUmar.[44] For our purposes, from an intra-Muslim perspective, *ḥadīth* collections are routinely considered reliable reports, or at the very least echoes, of the Prophet and his times. Indeed, as we will recall, ʿUmar was central to the revelation of the *ḥijāb* verse. Strangely, the Prophet is represented as passively resisting that verse, as reported by ʿĀʾisha: when the Prophet did not do *(lam yafʿal)* what ʿUmar literally commanded him to do in the imperative form, namely, veil his wives, divine revelation descended to vindicate ʿUmar's views. Kern states that even after this point the Prophet's wives "continued to agitate against the imposition of the veil, [*sic*] after the verse pertaining to it had been revealed."[45] Kern goes on to argue that as a result, ʿUmar solicited yet another Qurʾanic verse (mentioned earlier) to prescribe *ḥijāb* – Q. 66:55, in which the ante is upped and divorce is threatened if the Prophet's wives do not veil. "And [then there was] the verse of Veiling. I said, 'Oh Messenger of God, would that you order your wives to veil [themselves], [since both] the righteous and the profligate speak to them!' Then the verse of Veiling was revealed" (Q. 33:59). "The wives of the Prophet got together in opposition to that. So I told them, 'It is possible that if he divorced you, his Lord could substitute spouses better than you!' Then this verse was revealed [in the same words]" (Q. 66:55).[46] One should note that it could also be that ʿUmar was a useful examplar for Iraqi notions of women's roles, so they took advantage of the traditions associated with him and expanded upon them.

So the question must be asked here: is there a relationship between ʿUmar's sheer persistence on this issue, the Prophet's relative passivity (especially when compared to his willingness to "stand up" to ʿUmar on other issues), and divine revelation? A further question is how this dialogic triad and theme in the tradition is translated into *tafsīr* and *fiqh*, as well as histories – both high culture histories and folk ones, down to the most intimate subjectivity of the modern Muslim.

In fairness, I must include a report in which the Prophet displayed displeasure at the way ʿUmar's son divorced his wife and conveyed that displeasure to ʿUmar. I think it is an open question, however, whether the Prophet was incensed because of the unfair manner in which Ibn ʿUmar's wife was treated, or because the rules of divorce (waiting through the *ʿidda* period) were not observed, thereby threatening the nascent patrilineal order. Here is the report:

> [When] ʿUmar mentioned that [Ibn ʿUmar] divorced his wife while she was menstruating] to the Messenger of God [*pbuh*]

> he became very angry about it. [The Prophet] said, "May he return to her and abstain [from relations] with her, until she becomes pure again [i.e., until she has finished menstruating]. Then [he should wait until] she menstruates [again]. If it is [still] clear for him that he [wants to] divorce her [after this period of time has elapsed], then he may divorce her while she is [in a] pure [state], [as long as he has not had] sexual relations with her. This is the prescribed waiting period that God has commanded."[47]

ʿUMAR'S ATTITUDE TOWARD WOMEN

This history of women's resistance to the veiling verse is basically hidden. Al-Bukhārī's collection serves only to codify and hegemonize the verses and, concomitantly, ʿUmar's authority. The back-history of resistance to those verses is rarely discussed except to show how quickly that resistance was turned back by a Qurʾanic verse preempted by ʿUmar. The following examples provide more basis for the argument that the Prophet's and ʿUmar's wives made various gestures of resistance to ʿUmar – including resistance to the veiling verse. These gestures, which represent an alternative, contrapuntal women's history during this period, of course did not make it into the orthodoxy (canon). Curiously, this hidden history shares a similarly dubious epistemological space as the stoning verse.

The following is ʿUmar's opinion about the women of the *anṣār* (helpers), complaining to Ibn ʿAbbās: "We were the people of Quraysh [who] dominated [*naghlibu*] their women. And when we came to the Anṣār, lo and behold, [they were] a people whose women dominated them [*taghlibuhum nisāʾuhum*]." Reminiscing fondly about the status of women in the Jāhiliyya, ʿUmar was nostalgic for the days when "women did not count at all" (*mā naʿuddu liʾl-nisāʾ shayʾ*;[48] in another version, *mā naʿuddu liʾl-nisāʾ amran*[49]).

On several occasions, ʿUmar seems eager to sacrifice his closest kinship relations with women in order to ingratiate himself further with the Prophet. Al-Tabarī reports that ʿUmar took the drastic step of divorcing all of his wives once he learned that it was not permitted for Muslims to be married to polytheists: "Muḥammad ibn Isḥāq (d. 151/768) also said in his report: Among those who divorced [their un-believing wives] was ʿUmar ibn al-Khaṭṭāb, who divorced his wives Qurayba bint Abī Umayya ibn al-Mughīra … and Umm Kulthūm bint ʿAmr ibn Jarwal al-Khuzāʿiyya, the mother of ʿUbayd Allāh ibn ʿUmar."[50]

Two incidents involving ʿUmar's daughter Ḥafṣa, one of the Prophet's wives, show perhaps most clearly ʿUmar's willingness to forgo his kinship relations with women. The most famous examples of ʿUmar "loving" the Prophet over and above his own daughter are two reports that tell of his reactions when hearing that the Prophet's wives were giving him trouble. Ḥafṣa was reportedly becoming haughty, thinking that the Prophet loved her as he loved ʿĀʾisha:

> ʿUmar began to restrain and warn his daughter not to imitate this pampered lady [ʿĀʾisha]. He would say to her: "What are you compared to ʿĀʾisha and your father compared to her father?" And when one day he heard from his wife that his daughter had behaved pertly towards the Prophet, he went to his daughter to ask if it were true. When she said it was so, he rebuked her, saying: "Daughter, you know that I warn you against the punishment of God and the anger of his Prophet. Do not be deceived by the one who is proud of her beauty and the fact that the Prophet loves her. By God! I know that the Prophet does not love you and if it were not for me, he would have divorced you."

He left Ḥafṣa and in his estimation had put her in her proper place.[51]

The notion that Ḥafṣa could have any sound basis for complaint against the Prophet's favouritism toward his other wives seems immaterial to ʿUmar, who worried only that the Prophet should be upset by his daughter's behaviour. As one can note from the above examples, ʿUmar's attitude toward women hints at a relationship between his vociferous advocacy of the *rajm* verse and an overarching pattern of viewing women as sexual objects, tools of political exchange and expediency, and subjects to be controlled.

CONCLUSIONS

This chapter has shown how Islam's second caliph, ʿUmar ibn al-Khaṭṭāb, has been positioned – at least in the later, medieval interpretive tradition – as the main driver and agent of justification for the legalization of the stoning punishment in Islamic law. There is every reason the punishment should not have achieved hegemonic legal status: not only is it absent from the Qurʾan, but the Qurʾan mandated a different punishment – flogging – for the same crime of *zinā*, or illegal sexual activity (Q. 24:2). Furthermore, to legalize stoning, jurists and exegetes had to wade into at best murky epistemological waters by developing a form of abrogation – abrogating the recitation of a verse without abrogating its legal force – to legalize stoning, the only example to which this form of abrogation is applied. These intellectual acrobatics with abrogation threatened the continuity of the logic of perfect, divine revelation, but this risk was deemed worth taking to legalize stoning. This chapter has attempted to ask why such a risk was taken. We cannot have a definitive answer, but I suggest here that regulating the movement and sexuality of women might have had something to do with it. To support this point, I have pointed out times when ʿUmar is represented as having predicted or pre-empted Qurʾanic verses that limited the movement and appearance of women in public space, urging women to appear "behind a veil" and take *ḥijāb*. These verses are represented as having been revealed explicitly to silence the objections of the Prophet's wives to ʿUmar's opinions. Next, I provided examples of the Prophet standing up to an impetuous ʿUmar on matters in which he wished his opinion to prevail, such as burying hypocrites or allowing children to play near the mosque. Yet the Prophet was silent or acquiescent to ʿUmar's harsher views on women, allowing the latter's opinions on the matter to prevail. I conclude from this that on issues of "gender justice," to use an modern term for the moment, the Prophet was willing to let ʿUmar's less generous stances prevail in the interest, perhaps, of keeping the peace for the sake of "more important" issues. What this points to is not only a hidden history of women's resistance in Islam's formative period to attitudes that restricted them, but also the emergence of a kind of realpolitik that plainly regarded those concerns as unimportant when compared to matters that had to do with consolidating political and social power. These attitudes, which made their way diligently into al-Bukhārī's *ḥadīth* collections, al-Suyūṭī's *tafsīr*, and many other sources, would become calcified in the tradition, setting a pattern of gender norms that have resonated until the present day in Muslim-majority societies.

While this debate might be dismissed by some as water under the bridge, as a history that no longer matters, I argue that this could not be further from the truth, particularly considering the case in Nigeria with which I opened this chapter. In the course of this research I discovered that the stoning punishment was almost never meted out in Islamic courts until the postmodern/postcolonial period. In other words, we are living in an era of explosion of the stoning punishment.

I have laid out the history of the shaky foundations of the stoning punishment in Islam; yet that history can also be applied, if sociologically necessary, to destabilize (again) the stoning punishment in Islamic law. The punishment as written in the books applies to men and women equally; yet the relative political, social, and economic weakness of women around the world – perhaps especially in the contemporary Muslim-majority world – has placed women at particular risk of it. For this reason, and a number of others that are less social and more intellectual, the issue of stoning in Islam should not be closed. Reopening it for the sake of reinterpretation will begin with acknowledging the misogynistic attitudes surrounding its legalization in Islam's earliest sources.

NOTES

I would like to acknowledge the late Shahab Ahmed for giving me much important feedback on a much earlier iteration of this chapter.

1 Ibn Rajab al-Ḥanbalī, *Jāmiʿ al-ʿulūm wa'l-ḥikam*, vol. 2, 124.

2 Eltantawi, *Sharī'ah on Trial.*

3 It is easier to discern why the Twelver Shiʿi tradition would have legalized stoning, though at first glance this fact appears even more mysterious, as the Shiʿi tradition would not accept ʿUmar as a lawgiver. Early Shiʿi *uṣūl al-fiqh* scholars, eager to build their own repository of laws and legal thinking in a Baghdādī society increasingly dominated by Sunnis, were in a position of having to choose their intellectual battles. Since stoning was never functionally meted out, Shiʿi's were in a position to accept the legalization of the punishment while being confident it would not be meted out. See, Eltantawi, "Ṭūsī Did Not 'Opt Out.'"

4 See Burton, *Sources of Islamic Law*, 6–8.

5 Al-Suyūṭī, *Al-Itqān fī ʿulūm al-Qurʾān*, vol. 3, 66.

6 See, for example, Wazārat al-Awqāf, "*Rajm*," vol. 22, 124–5; and Crone and Zimmerman, *Epistle of Salim*, 164, no. 70.

7 See Poucher, "Crimes and Punishment," in *A Dictionary of the Bible*, 520–7; cf. Young, "Stoning and Hand Amputation," 155–6.

8 Al-Bayhaqī, *Al-Sunan al-kubrā*, vol. 7, 87, no. 13282.

9 Ibid.

10 Al-ʿAsqalānī, *Fatḥ al-bārī*, no. 4516. http://library.islamweb.net/newlibrary/display_book.php?bk_no=52&ID=2555&idfrom=8657&idto=8693&bookid=52&startno=14.

11 Al-Haythamī, *Majma' al-zawā'id*, vol. 3, 175, no. 2505.
12 "Then of the drop We created a blood clot, then of the blood clot We created a lump of flesh, then of the lump of flesh We created bones and We clothed the bones with flesh; then We brought him into being as another creation. Blessed is God, the best of all Creators!" Translation from Nasr, *Study Quran*, 852.
13 Al-Suyūṭī, *Tārīkh al-khulafā'*, 88.
14 Al-Ṭabarī, *Tārīkh al-rusul wa'l-mulūk*, 196–7.
15 Hakim, "Conflicting Images," 174.
16 Al-Bayhaqī, *Al-Sunan al-kubrā*, vol. 8, 552.
17 Ibid.
18 Ibid., 177.
19 Hallaq, *Sharī'a*, 97.
20 Burton, *Sources of Islamic Law*, 96.
21 Al-Suyūṭī, *Al-Itqān*, vol. 20, 60.
22 Ibid.
23 Ibid.
24 Ibid., vol. 2, 61.
25 Ibid.
26 Ibid.
27 Ibid., 77.
28 Ibid.
29 It is important to note that there is a rich history in the Islamic tradition of not only opposing the form of abrogation that led to the legalization of the stoning punishment (thus calling the legality of stoning itself into question), but also a tradition of rejecting abrogation altogether. See, for example, al-Saqqā, *Lā Naskh fī al-Qur'ān*.
30 Burton, *Sources of Islamic Law*, 467.
31 Reinhart, "Jurisprudence," 436.
32 Kern, *Riddle of 'Umar ibn al-Khaṭṭāb*.
33 Translation from Nasr et al., *Study Quran*, 527–8.
34 Ibid., 519–20.
35 As quoted by Kern, *Riddle of 'Umar ibn al-Khaṭṭāb*, 33, from *Al-Jāmi' al-Ṣaḥiḥ: Kitāb tafsīr al-Qur'ān*.
36 Ibid.
37 Ibid., 48.
38 Ibid., 43.
39 Ibid., 35.
40 Ibid., 35–6.
41 Ibid., 36.

42 Fatima Mernissi's groundbreaking work on this topic must be acknowledged here. See, for example, *Veil and The Male Elite.*
43 Ibid., 55.
44 See for example Cheikh, *Women, Islam*.
45 Kern, *Riddle of 'Umar ibn al-Khaṭṭāb*, 57.
46 Nasr et al., *Study Qur'an*, verse 65:5, 1390.
47 Ibid., 57.
48 Kern, *Riddle of 'Umar ibn al-Khaṭṭāb*, 140.
49 Ibn Ḥajar, *Fatḥ al-Bārī, Kitāb tafsīr al-Qur'ān, Sūrat al-Taḥrīm*, no. 4629.
50 Kern, *Riddle of 'Umar ibn al-Khaṭṭāb*, 140.
51 Bint al-Shāti', *Wives of the Prophet*, 105.

REFERENCES

'Asqalānī, Aḥmad ibn 'Alī ibn Ḥajar al-. *Fatḥ al-bārī bi-sharḥ ṣaḥīḥ al-Bukhārī*. Ed. Muḥammas Fu'ād 'Abd al-Bāqī, Muḥibb al-Dīn al-Khaṭīb, and Quṣayy Muḥibb al-Dīn al-Khaṭīb. 14 vols. Cairo: Dār al-Rayyān li'l-Turāth, 1986.

Bayhaqī, Aḥmad ibn al-Ḥusayn ibn 'Alī, al-. *Al-Sunan al-kubrā*. Vols 7–8. Beirut: Dār al-Kutub al-'Ilmiyya. 2003.

Bint al-Shāṭi' ['Ā'isha 'Abd al-Raḥmān]. *The Wives of the Prophet*. Translated and with an Introduction by Matti Moosa and Nicholas D. Ranson. Lahore: Sh. Muhammad Ashraf, 1971.

Bukhāri, Muḥammad ibn Ismā'īl. *Kitāb al-jāmi' al-ṣaḥīh*. Ed. L. Krehl and Th.W. Juynboll. 4 vols. Leiden: 1862–1908.

Burton, John. *The Sources of Islamic Law: Islamic Theories of Abrogation*. Edinburgh: Edinburgh University Press, 1990.

Cheikh, Nadia Maria El. *Women, Islam, and 'Abbasid Identity*. Cambridge, MA: Harvard University Press, 2015.

Crone, Patricia, and Fritz Zimmerman. *The Epistle of Sālim ibn Dhakwān*. Oxford: Oxford University Press, 2001.

Eltantawi, Sarah. *Shari'ah on Trial: Northern Nigeria's Islamic Revolution*. Berkeley: University of California Press, 2017.

– "Ṭūsī Did Not 'Opt Out': Shiite Jurisprudence and the Solidification of the Stoning Punishment in the Islamic Legal Tradition." In *"Oceanus Paedagogicis": A Festschrift in Celebration and Honor of Professor Ahmad Mahdavi Damghani's 90th Birthday*, ed. Alireza Korangy, Roy P. Mottahedeh, and William Granara, 312–32. Berlin: De Gruyter, 2016.

Hakim, Avraham. "Conflicting Images of Lawgivers: The Caliph and the Prophet Sunnat 'Umar and Sunnat Muḥammad." In *Method and Theory in the Study of Islamic Origins*, ed. Herbert Berg, 159–77. Leiden: E.J. Brill, 2003.

Hallaq, Wael B. "Context: ʿUmar ibn Al-Khaṭṭab." In *The Blackwell Companion to the Qurʾān*, ed. Andrew Rippen, 218–35. Malden: Blackwell, 2006.

– *Sharīʿa: Theory, Practice, Transformations*. Cambridge: Cambridge University Press 2012.

Haythamī, Nūr al-Dīn ʿAlī ibn Abī Bakr al-. *Majmaʿ al-zawāʾid wa-manbaʿ al-fawāʾid*. Ed. Al-ʿIrāqī and Ibn Ḥajar. Vol. 9. Beirut: Dār al-Kutub al-Islāmiyya, 1994.

Ibn Ḥajar al-ʿAsqalānī, Aḥmad ibn ʿAlī. *Fatḥ al-bārī bi-sharḥ ṣaḥīḥ al-Bukhārī*. 14 vols. Cairo: Dār al-Rayyān li'l-Turāth, 1986.

Ibn Rajab al-Ḥanbalī, Zayn al-Dīn ʿAbd al-Raḥmān ibn Aḥmad. *Jāmiʿ al-ʿulūm wa'l-ḥikam fī sharḥ khamsīn ḥadīthan min jawāmiʿ al-kalim*, ed. Shuʿayb al-Arnaʾūṭ and Ibrāhīm Bājis, Beirut: Muʾassassat al-Risāla, 2001.

Kern, Linda Lee. "The Riddle of ʿUmar ibn al-Khattāb in Bukhārī's Kitāb al-Jāmiʿ aṣ-Sahīh (and the Question of the Routinization of Prophetic Charisma)." PhD diss., Harvard University, 1996.

Mernissi, Fatima. *The Veil and the Male Elite: A Feminist Interpretation of Women's Rights in Islam*. Trans. Mary Jo Lakeland. New York: Basic Books, 1991.

Muqātal ibn Sulaymān. *Tafsīr Muqātil ibn Sulaymān 80-150 [A.]H.* Ed. ʿAbd Allāh Maḥmūd Shiḥāta. 5 vols. Cairo: Al-Hayʾa al-Miṣriyya al-ʿĀmma li'l-Kitāb, 1979.

Nasr, Seyyed Hossein, Caner K. Dagli, Maria Massi Dakake, Joseph E. B. Lumbard, and Mohammed Rustom, eds. *The Study Quran: A New Translation and Commentary*. New York: HarperCollins, 2015.

Poucher, J. "Crimes and Punishment." In *A Dictionary of the Bible*, ed. J. Hastings, 520–7. Edinburgh: T&T Clark, 1898.

Reinhart, Kevin A. "Jurisprudence." In *The Blackwell Companion to the Qurʾān*, ed. Andrew Rippen, 434–49. Malden: Blackwell, 2006.

Saqqā, Aḥmad Ḥijāzī al-. *Lā naskh fī al-Qurʾān*. Cairo: Dār al-Fikr al-ʿArabī, 1978.

Suyūtī, Jalāl al-Dīn ʿAbd al-Raḥmān al-. *Al-Durr al-manthūr fī al-tafsīr bi'l-maʾthūr*. 6 vols. Cairo: Maṭbaʿat al-Anwār al-Muḥammadiyya, 1985.

– *Al-Itqān fī ʿulūm al-Qurʾān*. Ed. Muḥammad Abū al-Faḍl Ibrāhīm. Vol. 3. 3rd ed. Cairo: Dār al-Turāth, 1985.

– *Tārīkh al-khulafāʾ*. Beirut: Dār al-Arqam, 2016.

Ṭabarī, Muḥammad ibn Jarīr al-. *Tārīkh al-rusul wa'l-mulūk* (*History of the Prophets and Kings*), vol. 9: *The Last Years of the Prophet: The Formation of the State, AD 630–32 / AH. 8–11*. Trans. Ismail K. Poonawala. Albany: SUNY Press, 1993.

Wazārat al-Awqāf wa'l-Shu'ūn al-Islāmiyya. "*Rajm*." In *al-Mawsū'a al-fiqhiyya*, vol. 22, 124. 6th ed. Kuwait: Wazārat al-Awqāf wa'l-Shu'ūn al-Islāmiyya, 2008.

Young, Walter. "Stoning and Hand Amputation: The Pre-Islamic Origins of the *ḥadd* Penalties for *zinā* and *sariqa*." Master's thesis, Institute of Islamic Studies at McGill University, Montreal, 2005.

10

Revisiting the Issue of Minor Marriages

Multidisciplinary *Ijtihād* on Contemporary Ethical Problems

Yasmin Amin

I believe that ideas such as absolute correctness, complete accuracy, ultimate truth, etc. are fantasies that should not be allowed in any science or scholarship ... It is the belief in a single truth and being its owner that is the root of all Evil in the world.

Max Born, *Von der Verantwortung des Naturwissenschaftlers*

Child marriage and its repercussions on health, life, and ethics remain a problematic issue worldwide and more so in Islamic countries.[1] According to UNICEF, more than 700 million women alive today were married before their eighteenth birthday.[2] More than one in three (about 245 million) were married before they were fifteen.[3] Nujūd ʿAlī, a Yemenite, was the youngest divorcee in the world at the age of ten.[4] As stated by the UN Population Fund, girls younger than fifteen are five times more likely to die in childbirth than those in their twenties.[5]

The International Centre for Research on Women reports that in Yemen 48.4 percent and in Nigeria 43.3 percent of all girls were married before they were eighteen.[6] Of the twenty countries with the highest rates of child marriage, eighteen are Muslim or majority-Muslim countries. The problems of child marriage are not only medical but also ethical and legal.

In Muslim countries, the practice is sanctioned by a *ḥadīth* (prophetic tradition), especially in *Ṣaḥīḥ al-Bukhārī*, that narrates that ʿĀʾisha was six years old at the time of her marriage to the Prophet and that she was nine years old when the marriage was consummated. However, when we look into Islamic heritage books – history books, *Sīra* works, and biographical dictionaries – a different picture emerges. According to these books, she was at least nineteen years old at the time of her marriage.

This chapter examines the "canonical" rulings, as well as the alternative available historical information, using *ijtihād* (independent reasoning) to challenge the claimed *ijmā'* (consensus) of the rulings on the permissibility of child marriage based on an erroneous *qiyās* (deductive analogy). It also proposes a multidisciplinary approach that combines *'aqlī* (rational) and *naqlī* (transmitted) knowledge. In this chapter, scientific rational knowledge as found in medicine, statistics, linguistics, and contemporary concepts of human rights and the rights of children and of women will be combined with the traditional transmitted and canonized knowledge of *ḥadīth* and its sciences, such as *'ilm al-rijāl* (biographical evaluation), *tafsīr* (exegesis), *fiqh* (jurisprudence), and Islamic ethics. The aim is to call for a decanonization of child marriage by refuting its origins and development, challenging it from within the tradition, and applying the strengths of the sciences to develop a way forward to the future.

IJTIHĀD

The practice of *ijtihād* waxed and waned and has been defined in many ways across Islamic history, yet it has remained a viable method for deriving laws. *Ijtihād* has remained at the heart of intellectual and social transformations, and as Wael Hallaq argues, its doors have never been completely closed.[7] The classical era of *ijtihād*[8] was characterized by great creativity and resourcefulness.[9] The most important sources or principles of *ijtihād* in the classical era are the Qur'an, the *ḥadīth*, *qiyās* (analogy), and *ijmā'* (consensus). Additional sources are *istidlāl* (logic or inferential reasoning), *'adāt* or *'urf* (custom), *istiṣlāḥ* (discerning public good), and *istiḥsān* (juristic preference). All *madhāhib* (schools of thought) agree on the first four, though not all agree on the rest.[10] This period was followed by centuries[11] of mainly *taqlīd* (conformity, following) with limited *ijtihād*, where *fiqh* began to turn inward and interpretation of the interpretations was practised instead of new interpretations being offered.[12]

While Muslims generally view the Qur'an as applicable for all times and all people everywhere,[13] the social, economic, political and ideological conditions are not static but are always changing, with new developments that necessitate seeking legal answers to the processes and requirements of transformation and modernization.[14] *Taḥdīth* (modernization) and *ijtihād* are two concepts belonging to two distinct fields in terms of the subject matter, with differences in terms of objectives and the means used to serve the goals.[15] *Taḥdīth* relates to the social and communal presence and its associated patterns of existence, be they political, economic, legal or intellectual, as well as awareness of emerging events and new knowledge. Briefly put, it is a process related to society.[16] Coupled with *taḥdīth*, *ijtihād* is a religious view of social, economic, and political developments and serves as the legal means for responding to the challenges of transformation and change, and might be complied with at some times but not at others.[17] *Ijtihād* thus provides solutions and answers to developments in Islamic society so that it can cope with the changing requirements,[18] for example, to reconcile Islamic teachings with the demands of advanced clinical medicine or scientific developments, such as biomedical ethics.[19]

The importance of *ijtihād* in these modern debates stems from the possibility that it might provide a new avenue for Islamic Law, one that stays within the bounds of Islamic tradition even while avoiding conformity or blind following without consideration of the changing conditions of contemporary times. Hence, *ijtihād* is a prerequisite for the survival of Islam in today's world. [20] By exercising *ijtihād*, contemporary Muslims can change the rules to suit the needs of their current society.[21] Both modernists and Islamists accept that the appropriate utilization of this legal mechanism will provide Islamic law with fresh interpretations that are suitable for today's world.[22] This chapter looks at the "canonized" rulings on child marriage through the lens of a multidisciplinary *ijtihād,* to determine its applicability.

METHODOLOGY

Al-Alwani argues that *ijtihād* is a precondition for reform because there would be no reform without it and there can be no revival without reform.[23] Resurrecting the *ʿaql* (intellect or rationality) versus *naql* (transmitted knowledge and revelation) discussion that raged in Islamic thought for centuries is not the purpose of this study. On the one hand, *ʿaql* is the first means for establishing the truthfulness of the Qurʾan and the Prophet Muḥammad's message. However, to place *naql* over it would be to undermine the means that led to the acceptance of *naql*. On the other hand, dismissing *naql* by undermining the oral sources, branding them as less reliable or outmoded, would negate centuries of rational and traditional Islamic thought by great luminaries. This chapter proposes a methodology for a new *ijtihād* that balances *ʿaql* and *naql*. The *naqlī* elements in our case are the exegetical works, biographical dictionaries, *ḥadīth* collections, and books of jurisprudence and Islamic Law, or to sum it up, all of the sources used by traditional Muslim scholars. The *ʿaqlī* elements are medical findings, linguistic theories, and statistical data, as well as contemporary human, women's, and children's rights discourses. The definition of rationality usually adopted in the social sciences is drawn from linking it to how an action is received and interpreted in the culture in which it originated, rather than to the intention of the subject of that action or in other words how the interpretation of the *naqlī* elements are perceived by the intellect.[24] Hence, this chapter proposes a multidisciplinary approach combining *ʿaql* and *naql* into a coherent method. This chapter demonstrates the suitability of the suggested methodology for applying and recontextualizing the social practice of child marriage, as well as the canonical rulings on it. Placing the different fields of Islamic Studies together in dialogue is definitely advantageous when it comes to examining the canonized basis of this practice and its centuries of dominance in Islamic thought.

DETERMINING AISHA'S AGE AT HER MARRIAGE: *ḤADĪTH*, *ḤADĪTH* SCIENCES AND HISTORY BOOKS

Al-Bukhāri

This section analyzes the different accounts to determine their historical probability, looking at the collection, arrangement, editing, and modification of the "canonical" sources and the selectivity and preferences of some accounts over others. This approach is often taken to reconstruct the development of thought. This is done cautiously, as historians also recognize that interpretation often reflects the values and concerns of the historian and that revisionism and the reinterpretation of the past is sometimes stimulated by the political agenda of the present.[25] Integrating the *ʿaqlī* with the *naqlī* methodology of *ʿilm al-rijāl* can shed light on the canonization of the account used as precedence for the legality of child marriage in Islamic thought.

Brown argues that the *ṣaḥīḥ* collections of al-Bukhārī and Muslim first emerged as canons of authenticity around the end of the fourth/tenth century.[26] Brown further notes that "the notion of consensus provided the key to authorizing these two works within the expanded boundaries of a widened Sunni Islam,"[27] endowing the *Ṣaḥīḥayn* (al-Bukhārī and Muslim) with a new potential authority within the body of transmission-based scholars.[28] The *Ṣaḥīḥayn* canon was meant to provide jurists with the authority of the Prophet's authentic Sunna in a manageable form, once it had been thoroughly examined by those two scholars, who had come to exemplify the critical accuracy and meticulousness of the *ḥadīth* tradition and were approved by the community's "infallible" consensus.[29] Brown states that "the practical manifestation of the authority of tradition in Sunni scholarship is the notion of consensus, which transforms received opinion among scholars into a direct manifestation of God's authority as deposited in His chosen *Umma*."[30] He further elaborates that: "The primacy of the *Ṣaḥīḥayn* in the Sunni vision of the Prophet's legacy represented both an act of communal consensus and the priorities that the Sunni tradition had set in elaborating the ḥadīth sciences. The Sunni tradition was thus heavily invested in defending the position of the two books as the acme of ḥadīth scholarship."[31] Brown summarizes that loyalty to the canon meant loyalty to the *umma* (community).[32] He also notes that especially in recent times, criticisms of the *Ṣaḥīḥayn* canon met with remarkable hostility.[33] A key observation Brown makes is that "al-Bukhārī and Muslim also became a synecdochic trope for scholars constructing narrative in Islamic history."[34] Having established that the *Ṣaḥīḥayn* canon are the most authoritative body, this section will examine only the traditions in *Ṣaḥīḥ al-Bukhārī*, as it is considered the most authentic text after the Qur'an, ranking even above *Ṣaḥīḥ Muslim*, which comes a close second.[35]

Several traditions in *Ṣaḥīḥ al-Bukhārī* narrate that ʿĀ'isha was six years old at the time of her marriage to the Prophet and nine when the marriage was consummated. These traditions are used mostly as a precedent and basis for permitting child marriage; they also establish the required precedence for *fiqh*. All of the versions are ascribed to ʿĀ'isha herself without being linked to the Prophet, though according to al-Naysabūrī they are *mawqūf* (stopped) as the *ḥadīth* stops at her, considering her a companion; therefore they should not be considered *musnad* (supported).[36] In addition, Ibn Ḥajar defined a *ḥadīth* as having been said by the Prophet only, while a *khabar* or *athar* can be said by anyone else.[37] By those criteria, established by traditional Muslim scholars, these traditions should not even be considered as *aḥadīth*; however, the scope of this chapter does not permit us to delve deeper into this issue; it is, though, an avenue for further research.

Yet it is important to note Brown's view on this: a canon emerges as an attempt to dominate the textual landscape of a religious tradition, and also as a tool for control and exclusion.[38] This is especially apparent in the fact that the entire Muslim community did not consider the *Ṣaḥīḥayn* to be completely authentic or authoritative. For example, the Imāmī Shiʿis did not concur with this view. Brown argues that the consensus "is fundamentally self-centered, invoked and defined by scholars attempting to make their beliefs normative by ascribing them to a wider community."[39] Yet in spite of this flaw, consensus and the concept of an authoritative canon are used not only to exclude those who do not ascribe to them, but also to create common conventions to bridge rifts so as to minimize "sources of contention."[40]

The shortest version in *Ṣaḥīḥ al-Bukhārī* (5133) translates thus: "The Prophet married me when I was six and the marriage was consummated when I was nine years old."[41] This version also notes that it relates to verse Q. 65:4, which will be discussed in the *tafsīr* section.

Another version (3896) narrates how the Prophet married her about two years after Khadīja's death, when she was six, and that the marriage was consummated when she was nine.[42] Yet another version (3894) narrates that she was playing on a swing with her playmates when her mother came to wash her face and then took her to the Prophet's house, where other women dressed her up and told her she was married now. The marriage was consummated when she was nine. Still another version tells us she was playing with dolls in the Prophet's house before the marriage was consummated.[43] There are several other versions, but these will suffice as examples. All versions are narrated and transmitted from ʿĀʾisha by ʿUrwa ibn al-Zubayr and from him by his son Hishām ibn ʿUrwa (d. 146/763).

ʿIlm al-rijāl (Biographical Evaluation, Literally Meaning "Knowledge of Men")

According to a number of *muḥaddithūn* (traditionists), most notably Ibn Ḥajar (852/1449) and al-Dhahabī (748/1348), Hishām ibn ʿUrwa was not a trustworthy narrator in his old age in Iraq. Ibn Ḥajar writes that in his old age he narrated much without knowing what he was narrating.[44] He was called a *mudallis* at worst and excused with bad memory at best. *Mudallis* comes from the root *d-l-s*, which denotes the action of *tadlīs* (concealment) and is described by the verb *dallasa*. This literally refers to a situation in which there is mostly darkness, but with some light, as opposed to pitch-black darkness, and it denotes obfuscation, confusion, and doubt. It is used to define a narrator who narrates from someone he never actually met yet claims to have met. It is also used for someone who narrates something he did not hear and, hence, should not report, and is also used for someone who narrates traditions that are contrary to what other reliable trustworthy sources have reported and, hence, casts doubt on the tradition. *Tadlīs* has three main categories: *tadlīs al-isnād* (hiding of a link in the chain of narration to improve it), *tadlīs al-taswiya* (omission of a narrator anywhere in the chain to remove weak narrators or to hide some defects), and *tadlīs al-shuyūkh* (intentional hiding of one's teacher's identity).

Hishām ibn ʿUrwa lived for most of his life in Medina, where he was considered a trustworthy narrator. In his old age, he left Medina for Iraq, where he was accused of mixing up traditions, particularly the traditions relating to ʿĀ'isha's marriage, which he did not narrate in Medina, but only in Iraq, where his memory started to fail him. In *Ṣaḥīḥ al-Bukhārī*, most of the narrators narrating from Hishām ibn ʿUrwa are Iraqis, suggesting that the narrative indeed originated in Iraq. *Ḥadīth* (3896) is narrated from Hishām by Abū Usāma, Ḥammād ibn Usāma al-Kūfī, al-Kūfī here indicating he was from Kufa, in Iraq. Ibn Ḥajar opines that he perhaps engaged in *tadlīs* at the end of his life and that he narrated *aḥādīth* by others, ascribing them to himself.[45]

Ḥadīth (3894) is narrated by ʿAlī ibn Musshir al-Kūfī, a *qāḍī* (judge) who buried his books and became blind before he died. Ibn Ḥajar classifies him as trustworthy yet also states that he narrated many *gharīb* (scarce, strange) *aḥādīth* after his blindness.[46]

Ḥadīth (5133) is narrated by Sufyān, who could either be Sufyān ibn ʿUyayna al-Kūfī or Sufyān al-Thawrī, both from Kufa and both classified by Ibn Ḥajar as *mudallisīn*.[47] Sufyān ibn ʿUyayna al-Kūfī is accused of engaging in *tadlīs* from trustworthy narrators, ascribing the narration to himself, while Sufyān al-Thawrī is considered *maqbūl* (acceptable).[48] In conclusion, all the narrations about ʿĀ'isha's age in *Ṣaḥīḥ al-Bukhārī* are from Iraq and most of the narrators were considered *mudallisīn* based on the traditionists' own criteria.

Ḥadīth scholars viewed the act of *tadlīs* as *makrūh jiddan* (detestable or abominable), and the resulting narrations were deemed weak. Yet in spite of this, the different versions of this *ḥadīth* not only were canonized but indeed became the precedent and basis for the ruling on child marriages. Furthermore, despite this verdict, Ibn al-Ṣalāḥ al-Shahrazūrī (d. 643/1245) notes that there are traditions found in the *Ṣaḥīḥayn* that often depended on the transmission of a *mudallis*.[49]

Heritage Books

In his book *Life of Muhammad*, Muḥammad ibn Isḥāq (d. 150/767)[50] writes about the *sabiqūn* and *sabiqāt*, who accepted Islam very early on, saying: "After them came Abū ʿUbayda ibn al-Jarrāḥ, al-Arqam ibn Abū al-Arqam, ʿUthman ibn Mazʿūn and his two brothers Qudāma and ʻAbd Allāh, ʿUbayda ibn al-Ḥārith, Saʿīd ibn Zayid and his wife Fāṭima bint al-Khaṭṭāb, Asmāʾ bint Abū Bakr together with her younger sister ʿĀʾisha, in the first year after the first revelation."[51]

The paragraph is quoted without attribution to Ibn Isḥāq in the *Sīra*[52] by Ibn Hishām (d. 218/833). The same list is found in Ibn Kathīr's (d. 774/1373) *al-Sīra al-Nabawiyya* with a different phrasing, namely that ʿĀʾisha was *ṣaghīra* (young).[53] However, if ʿĀʾisha and Asmāʾ adopted Islam together in the first year of the Prophet's mission, as mentioned in several sources,[54] she could not have been nine at the time of consummating her marriage in the second year after *hijra*, because then she could not have been born yet at the time of her accepting Islam.

To become aMuslim, she would have had to understand what she was doing and also be able to articulate the *shahāda*. All the sources agree that the Prophet stayed in Mecca for thirteen years after his call to Prophethood and the first revelation. An example is found in *Tārīkh al-Ṭabarī*, in which al-Ṭabarī states that the Prophet stayed another twelve years in Mecca after the first year.[55] The first year of *al-baʿth* (The call to Prophethood) was fourteen years before the consummation of her marriage, so if the *ḥadīth* about her age is correct, then she was not yet born. However, Ibn Isḥāq and Ibn Hishām wrote their accounts a long time before al-Bukhārī, and considering that a number of later scholars record this statement, the veracity of the *ḥadīth* becomes questionable, more so because the later scholars glossed over the contradiction and did not attempt any reconciliation of the conflicting ages.

MENSTRUAL AGE IN TAFSĪR (EXEGESIS)

Tafsīr (Exegesis)

This section looks at the *naqlī* exegetical genre, its structure, tone, and content, analyzing the different accounts critically. It also ties that genre to the *ʿaqlī* knowledge of medicine, scientific method, and statistics as well as to linguistics. This method tends to disregard cultural and societal influences on the content, as well as those of individual authorship, but tying that content to statistics and etymology overcomes this by determining the extent to which the idea of ʿĀʾisha's age at the time of her marriage dominated Islamic thought. It also shows how that idea's effects shaped readers' understanding. This type of interpretive/qualitative research aims to understand events by unearthing the meanings that scholars attributed to their readings of the sacred texts. The focus is not on discovering laws about causal relationships but rather on understanding how human nature in medieval culture opted for the canonization of this practice.[56]

This section also applies *tafsīr al-Qurʾan bi-l-Qurʾan*[57] to compare related Qurʾanic verses and offer a thematic holistic reading (as opposed to reading certain verses in isolation), as well as to clarify problematic words. It traces the etymology of certain words, given that ideology has a major impact on language. Ideology often points toward matters that contribute to establishing and maintaining social relations of domination and inequality.[58]

As mentioned in the previous section, version 5133 of the tradition refers to verse Q. 65:4[59] of the Qurʾan to argue that since girls can be divorced, it must be permissible for them to marry. This section looks at sixty-three different *tafsīr* works, the earliest by Mujāhid ibn Jabr al-Makhzūmī (d. 104/722) and the most recent by Asʿad Ḥawmad (d. 1432/2010). The appendix lists all of the exegetical works consulted, focusing on the definitions provided by the authors for the words "have not menstruated," for the purpose of showing how the understanding of the words changed and varied. These works cover different schools of thought as well as different sects: they are from Ibāḍī, Zaydī, Twelver Shiʿi, *ummahāt al-tafsīr* (Heritage), Sufi, *Ahl al-Sunna al-Salafiyya*, and *Ahl al-Sunna wa-l-jamāʿa* works as well as contemporary works. The analysis focuses on the relevant part of the verse *al-lāʾī lamm yaḥiḍna* (those who have not menstruated).

The analysis shows that 75 percent of the items in this data set (i.e., forty-seven exegetical works) consider the phrase to mean minor girls, while 37 per cent (twenty-three exegetical works) apply it to both minor girls and grown women (see appendix). The reasons given for the lack of menstruation in grown women vary, from as yet unknown pregnancy, to breastfeeding or a medical condition.

It is interesting to note that al-Hawārī (d. 280/823 or 296/908), who includes both minor girls and grown women, also provides a name, calling such a woman *al-ḍahyā'* or *al-ḍahyā'a*, adding that this is a woman who has never menstruated and remains infertile.[60]

Lisān al-'Arab by Ibn Manzūr, a comprehensive dictionary of the Arabic language, gives two definitions for *al-ḍahyā'* or *al-ḍahyā'a*, stating that in general it refers to a woman who does not menstruate, does not develop breasts, and does not become pregnant and hence is assumed to be infertile. It also states that sometimes these words are also used for pregnant women, who do not menstruate during pregnancy.[61] Given that al-Hawārī's was one of the early exegetical works, and that he provided a name for this condition, we can safely assume that the condition was known, perhaps even fairly common.

Linguistics, Grammar, and Etymology

Fifteen (23 percent) of these *tafsīr* works applying the phrase to minor girls add the word *ba'd* (yet) to emphasize that these girls have not menstruated as yet and to suggest that they eventually will. To name a few examples, that word is used in *Tafsīr irshād al-'aql al-salīm ilā mazāyā al-kitāb al-karīm* by Abū-l Su'ūd, who was a Ḥanafī,[62] as well as in *Tafsīr al-ṣāfī fī tafsīr kalām Allāh al-wāfī* by Fayḍ al-Kāshānī, who was an Imāmī Shi'i.[63]

The Qur'ānic text does not include the word "yet," which is an addition by the *mufassirūn* (exegetes). Furthermore, the verse collectively refers to these three groups of women[64] as *nisā'* (women). Both the first verse in the sura, Q. 65:1,[65] and Q. 65:4 speak of women collectively. These women are all called *nisā'*, without making any distinction such as *jāriya* (girl) or *ṣaghīra* (little girl), which is what the *mufassirūn* call them throughout their exegesis of verse Q. 65:4.

Al-Ṭūsī (d. 460/1015) even specifies this, writing that they are girls under nine years of age.[66] In *Lisān al-'Arab*, *nusi'at al-mar'a* means that her menstruation is late, possibly due to pregnancy. The word *nisā'* is defined as *al-nisā' wa'l niswān* as the plural of *al-mar'a* (woman).[67] So linguistically and etymologically, *nisā'* as a word is tied to menstruation, suggesting that these divorcees or ex-wives had to be old enough to be called women and not *banāt* (girls) or otherwise. Using the word *nisā'* for girls who have not menstruated yet is a reading that reduces the totality (all women) to only a partial (only those who have not menstruated yet), thereby restricting the absolute. Exegetes have used two types of exegetical tools to provide a particular reading and interpretation to emphasize certain perspectives and exclude others. These two tools – *taqyīd al-muṭlaq* (restriction of the totality of persons) and *takhṣīṣ al-ʿām* (assigning particular specifications to generic groups) – restrict the interpretations to specific groups of persons. In our case here, the exegetes restricted the women who had not menstruated (a total generic group) to only minor girls who had not yet menstruated (a small portion of all those who had not menstruated).

The methodology of *tafsīr al-Qur'an bi-l-Qur'an*[68] has been applied historically and by contemporary reformers equally, to argue that the Qur'an, by its own explicit statement, is a clear book that is coherent in all its parts.[69] Applying that, one notices that the Qur'an indeed distinguishes between *nisā'* and *banāt*. There are several places in the Qur'an where the word *banāt* is used to denote young girls[70] – most notably Q.33:59,[71] which clearly distinguishes between them, as the two words, *nisā'* and *banāt*, appear next to each other in the context of a dress code. Moreover, Q. 24:59[72] clearly states that all prepubescent youth are considered *aṭfāl* (children). So how can girls, who are essentially still considered to be *aṭfāl*, as they have neither reached puberty nor menstruated yet, be considered *nisā'* in the exegesis of Q. 65:4?

Furthermore, in grammatical definitions, there is a difference between the words *lam* (not) and *lamma* (not yet). Abū Hilāl al-Ḥasan ibn Mahrān al-ʿAskarī (d. 395/1004) states that according to Sibawayh (d. 148/796), the influential linguist and grammarian of Arabic, *lam* and *lammā* denote two different states.[73] Most grammarians use Q. 49:14[74] as a reference, according to which *lam* is preceded a *ḥukm qāṭiʿ* (categorical rule), emphasizing that an event has not occurred and will not occur; whereas *lammā* means that the act has not occurred up until the manifestation of the statement, here the verse's revelation, with, however, a possibility of a future occurrence eventually.

Considering that in Q. 65:4 the Qur'an says "*al-lā'ī lam yaḥiḍna*" rather than "*al-lā'ī lammā yaḥiḍna,*" this could indicate that it does not refer to prepubescent girls at all, who will eventually experience menstruation, but rather to grown women who do not menstruate, possibly because they suffer from amenorrhea, or because they are pregnant but are not yet certain of it. This also ties in with the fact that in most of the exegetical works mentioned above, the first two groups of women (those who have reached menopause and those who did not menstruate) receive the same ruling with regard to the waiting period after divorce. This means that for both groups, their waiting period after divorce was interpreted as three months. However, logically speaking, the first group of women (menopausal) had already received their ruling about the length of their wait before the other two groups (those who had not menstruated and the pregnant ones). Hence, these two remaining ones should logically receive their ruling, which in the verse is set as a waiting period until they give birth. This combining of the second (those who have not menstruated) and third (pregnant) groups of women naturally implies that those who have not menstruated most likely refers to those women who suspect they are pregnant but are not yet certain. However, linking those who have not menstruated to the menopausal women confuses the issue and obfuscates the fact that there may be a pregnancy that is not yet confirmed, to strengthen the faulty argument that they are to be regarded as prepubescent girls.

Clinical Medicine

In the previous section, al-Hawārī provided a name for a woman who does not menstruate for medical reasons, calling such a woman *al-ḍahyāʾ* or *al-ḍahyāʾa*. Medical books provide a name for this condition, amenorrhoea, dividing it between primary and secondary amenorrhoea. Amenorrhoea is a common problem in contemporary times, affecting 10 percent of women of reproductive age.[75] Primary amenorrhea is defined as the failure to achieve menarche by age fifteen.[76] The age of puberty varies: normally it sets in between ten and fourteen, with amenorrhea being the second main cause for its delay,[77] a function of the woman's general health, body weight, and athletic ability. A chronic illness, low body weight, or hard physical exertion several times weekly can delay menstruation.[78] Primary amenorrhoea has several interrelated causes, such as low weight, undernourishment, excessive physical exertion, and severe anemia, or it can be the result of a genetic abnormality or thyroid disorder.[79] This section has identified the three main causes for primary amenorrhoea; the next sections look at each of these separately and at living conditions in first/seventh century Arabia.

MALNUTRITION

Hormone production is not the only trigger for menstruation. The body needs to have a certain percentage of its weight as fat, the optimum being 14 percent.[80] In normal-weight women, being 10 to 15 percent under ideal body weight is linked to amenorrhea.[81] Given the living conditions in first/seventh-century Arabia, amenorrhoea was likely quite common; this is reflected in the *tafsīr* literature, which provides a name for this condition.

In the canonized narrative of *Ḥadīth al-ifk* (the story of the slander), as reported in *Ṣaḥīḥ al-Bukhārī*, ʿĀʾisha is quoted as saying: "They carried the *hawdaj* (palanquin) and placed it on the camel thinking I was inside. Women at that time were light in weight, and were not corpulent, as they only ate small morsels of food. Hence, the people did not wonder about the light weight of the palanquin."[82]

Several other narrations from *Ṣaḥīḥ al-Bukhārī* speak of austere conditions, such as 6458, where ʿĀʾisha narrates that for one month there was no fire lit in the Prophet's house,[83] and they ate only dates, water, and scraps of meat given to them as charity by their neighbours.[84] There is also 6459, where the period extends to two months and there is no meat at all.[85] In 6451, she narrates that when the Prophet died, there was nothing edible left on her shelf except some barley.[86] Malnutrition could therefore be one of the likely causes of amenorrhoea in first/seventh-century Arabia.

ANEMIA

As mentioned, research suggests that good nutrition brings on puberty and that malnutrition delays it. In undernourished girls, puberty can be delayed several years. Severe food restrictions completely prevent the pubertal process.[87] Anemia, literally meaning "without blood," is present when there is a decrease of either the red blood cells or the haemoglobin, or both.[88] The substance that is necessary for normal blood formation is vitamin B12.[89] A principal cause of anemia is an imbalanced diet and a lack of iron and vitamin B12. A slight deficiency in iron causes anemia characterized by fatigue and weakness, while a chronic deficiency can lead to organ failure.[90] The sources for iron and vitamin B12 are mainly liver, sunflower seeds, nuts, beef, lamb, beans, whole grains, dark leafy vegetables such as spinach, and artichokes, apricots, and prunes. Regarding the diet in first/seventh-century Arabia, the canonical historical sources mention *tharīd* (bread soaked in meat stock with a little vinegar), *talbīna* (a kind of a porridge made from barley with honey), *ihāla* (melted fat), *ʿaṣīda* (cooked wheat flour, sometimes with added butter or honey), and occasional chicken, lamb, or camel meat and dried fish when travelling, as well as *washīqa* or *qadīd* (boiled meat, which is then dried to be taken on travels), pumpkin, dates (eaten plain or mixed with fat or honey), and *ḥalwa* (sweets); none of these are rich in iron or vitamin B12. Yet the sources also mention the Prophet's *zuhd* (asceticism) and his deliberate austerity. Al-Ḥiṣnī (d. 829/1426) emphasized that the Prophet often only had plain barley for a meal and said: "Oh God, let the sustenance of Muḥammad's family be bare subsistence."[91]

To conclude, though anemia had not been discovered at that time, it seems to have been common in Arabia, and likely was the cause of amenorrhea in women, which the exegetes knew about, for they referred to women suffering from it as *al-ḍahyāʾ* or *al-ḍahyāʾa*. So it is highly possible that the group of women mentioned in Q.65:4, – those who had not had their menses – were not necessarily prepubescent little girls, but rather grown women suffering from amenorrhea.

PHYSICAL EXERTION

Research has shown that female professional athletes and ballerinas do not menstruate regularly and generally suffer from late onset of menarche and/or amenorrhea as a result of continuous excessive exercise.[92] Research has also indicated that 43 percent of female athletes in a wide variety of sports suffer from the same,[93] and that for each year of training prior to the expected age of menarche, menstruation may be delayed by an average of four months.[94] Climate in itself is not thought to influence the age of menarche.[95]

Women in first/seventh-century Arabia were carrying heavy water skins back and forth daily, which involved excessive physical exertion. Several traditions in al-Bukhārī's canonized collection corroborate this. For example, 5224, narrated by Asmāʿ bint Abū Bakr, says that she used to work like a slave, daily drawing water from the well, carrying date stones on her head from her husband's land, two-thirds of a *farsakh*[96] from her house, and that she would then would grind the stones to feed his horse. Only after her father sent a servant to look after the horse did she feel that she was manumitted and set free.[97]

Ibn Ḥajar offers several versions of a narration by ʿAlī ibn Abī Ṭālib detailing how Fāṭima used to fetch water in a water skin until her neck suffered, how she carried water daily until it scarred her chest, how she ground the grains using a hand mill, swept the floor, cooked, and did many chores until she was afflicted with great pain.[98]

Asmāʾ and Fāṭima were from the elite of the nascent Muslim community, yet they suffered as a consequence of menial labour, physical exertion, and daily hard work. So it is logical to assume that most women exerted themselves in the same manner and, therefore, that physical exertion was another likely reason for amenorrhoea in women in first/seventh-century Arabia.

FIQH

Child Marriage in Scholarly Deliberations

In Sunni Islam, the four main sources of Islamic law are the Qurʾan, the Prophet's Sunna as recorded in the canonical collections of *Ḥadīth* and *Sīra* works, and reasoning by analogy and by consensus. The next section deals with the jurisprudence and rulings around child marriage. The two previous sections dealt with the Prophet's Sunna and the Qurʾan and showed that the ruling was based on a flawed interpretation as well as on a weak Prophetic tradition. This section looks at how jurists applied both of these faulty readings to approve child marriage, as well as at various conventions, legal maxims, and discussions from *fiqh* works, weighing these against contemporary medicine and science in order to question fundamental conceptual distinctions, contradictions, or oppositions. It also re-evaluates the principles presented in the canonical texts and the meaning and significance of their implications. It studies the ways in which dominance, inequality, and abuses of power are produced by textual readings. In this way, the roots of social inequality will be exposed.[99]

The notion that scholarly consensus amounts to solid legal proof is encountered in almost every work on legal theory.[100] However, as mentioned above, during the process of canonizing the *Ṣaḥīḥayn* of al-Bukhārī and Muslim as completely authentic or authoritative, the Imāmī Shiʿis did not espouse this view. Therefore, there is no complete consensus, but only a Sunni one. Furthermore, there seems to be no *ijmāʿ* whatsoever regarding the permissibility of forced marriage of prepubescent girls. This is understandable, given that no explicit support for child marriage is to be found in the Qur'an.[101] Carolyn Baugh has shown that there is no real *ijmāʿ* about child marriage in the early sources.[102] She explores the consensus on prepubescent marriage throughout the genre of consensus/disagreement and finds that "rather than being a scholarly-wide legal opinion on child marriage, it is little more than a validation of the report of 'Ā'isha," discussed at length above.[103]

In *Ikhtilāf al-Aʾimma al-ʿulamāʾ*, Ibn Hubayra (d. 560/1165) points out that scholars disagree regarding whether a man can force his minor daughter to marry. He reports that Mālik and al-Shāfiʿī opined that a father can force her, but that Mālik excluded the "spinster," who was still unmarried when she reached forty years of age, as well as the divorced daughter who had shared a *khulwa*[104] with her husband yet remained a virgin and managed her own affairs, knew her interests, and dealt with her own expenses. In those two cases the father could not force his daughter to marry.[105] Abū Ḥanīfa opined that the father could not force her at all, while Aḥmad [Ibn Ḥanbal] said that if she had reached nine years of age, she could not be married without her consent.[106] Obviously, the age "nine" is based on ʿĀʾisha's alleged age at her marriage, which, as demonstrated, is questionable.

Al-Sarakhsī (d. around 490/1096), the Ḥanafī jurist known as *Shams al-Aʾimma* (sun of the scholars), cites Q. 4:6,[107] *ḥatta idhā balaghū-l-nikāḥ*, "until they reach marriageable age", opining that they must have reached puberty, because marriage is meant to prevent desire for unlawful intercourse and to lead to procreation, which is not the case with prepubescent children as they can neither procreate nor feel any sexual desire as yet.[108]

Ibn Ḥazm (d. 456/1064), the leading Ẓāhirī scholar, was of the opinion that a father can marry off his young prepubescent virgin daughter without her consent. He further contests *khiyār al-bulūgh,* which literally means "option of puberty." By exercising this right, the minor prepubescent girl can repudiate the marriage contracted on her behalf after experiencing her first menstruation. Ibn Ḥazm refutes that once a girl reaches puberty, she can contest the marriage after her first menstruation. If she is a *thayb* (not a virgin: widowed or divorced), neither the father nor anyone else can force her to marry until she reaches puberty. A virgin or non-virgin daughter who reaches puberty cannot be married without her consent. Any marriage forced on her is *mafsūkh* (invalid, annulled). The non-virgin can marry whomever she chooses even if the father objects.[109]

Al-Sarakhsī contests *khiyār al-bulūgh* once, citing that the Prophet did not give ʿĀʾisha that choice.[110] Yet he allows it on the grounds that the guardian might not want to spend on the girl or is looking to keep her *mahr* (dowry), and he mentions that there is disagreement among the jurists about *khiyār al-bulūgh*.[111]

According to Harald Motzki, the discourse in the "canonical" *fiqh* manuals shows that there are three expressions relating to perceived maturity. The first expression is *ḥattā tuṭīq al-rijāl*, which means that the consummation of the marriage may not take place until the girl is physically fit to engage in sexual intercourse. The second expression is *balaghat*, which refers to reaching sexual maturity with the first menses. The ages of the first two can coincide, though the jurists think that physical fitness for the consummation of the marriage can be reached earlier than sexual maturity.[112] *Rushd* is the intellectual or economic maturity to handle one's own property.[113] When physical maturity does not manifest itself through puberty, majority is accepted to be at the age of fifteen years according to the Ḥanafīs, Shafiʿīs, and Ḥanbalīs, and eighteen years according to the Mālikīs.[114] The jurists consider someone no longer a minor and free to dispose of their property only when both *bulūgh* and *rushd* are fulfilled.[115] It is worth noting that the Qurʾan takes into account an age at which one is still a child (e.g., verses 24:31; 24:58–9) and an age at which one ceases to be a child (e.g., verses 6:152; 12:22; 17:34; 22:5; 28:14, and 40:67) and reaches maturity.[116]

Interestingly, Ibn Ḥazm argues in *al-Muḥallā* that the proof for allowing a father to marry off his minor virgin daughter is the precedent of Abū Bakr marrying ʿĀʾisha to the Prophet when she was six years old. He continues that "this is a well-known matter, so it is needless to provide an *isnād* for it. Whoever claims that this is a *sui generis* [personal or unique case], has not paid attention to Q. 33:21: Everything the Prophet did becomes an example to be followed, unless there is clear textual evidence that this was intended personally and only for him."[117] Needless to say, this precedent may have been built on false premises, as demonstrated earlier. Ibn Ḥazm quotes Q. 33.21 to emulate the Prophet with regard to child marriage, yet here he completely glosses over his refusal to give away Fāṭima in marriage when she was a child, though God's testimony in Q. 68.4[118] of the Prophet's sublime morality supports that he would never choose something harmful. However, when it comes to precedents from his Sunna, his choice for his own daughter is completely ignored by the scholars, even though the traditions about it are also included in the canon.

Both Abū Bakr and ʿUmar ibn al-Khaṭṭāb asked for Fāṭima's hand, and both were refused by the Prophet, who cited her young age as a reason and also that she was not yet mature and was unable to handle marital duties. A report in *Sunan al-Nasāʾī* tells how the Prophet rejected Abū Bakr's proposal because she was too young.[119] The Prophet accepted ʿAlī's proposal later, and Fāṭima was married in Medina when she was eighteen years old.[120] It is inconceivable that the Prophet, characterized as he was by sublime morality in the Qurʾan, would refuse something for his own daughter then allow the same for someone else's daughter.

In this case, the rulings on child marriage reflect the selective "pragmatism" of Islamic political discourse. As Sachedina argues, "the ethical claims that are universal in nature are downplayed in favour of all forms of male dominance in the patriarchal-tribal culture."[121] Even if the legal issues are evaded, the moral ones are significant.

Brown argues that the Sunna, as the lens through which the Qurʾan was understood, controlled how Muslims interpreted the Qurʾanic revelation.[122] Yet when it comes to child marriage, the canonized precedent of ʿĀʾisha's marriage, which as demonstrated is questionable, is invoked even in the exegesis of Q. 65:4, while the Prophet's refusal to marry off his youngest daughter Fāṭima at a young age, which is ethically valuable, is ignored.

Marrying off a girl without her consent goes against the condition of consent for a marriage to be legally valid. The pillars of a valid marriage include *ijāb* (declaration, proposal) and *qubūl* (acceptance/consent).[123] With regard to Mālikīs, Fadel argues: "the fact that Mālikīs allowed such a [physically mature] woman to be married against her will, insofar as they considered her to lack complete legal capacity, can only be described as a major error in legal reasoning. In some sense it is charitable to describe this as a 'mistake' and not attribute it to some other, less benign explanations."[124] Obviously, the same statement can be extended to the other *madhāhib*.

Al-Nawawī (d. 676/1277), in his *Sharḥ Muslim*, wrote that if the husband and guardian agree on something that does not harm the minor, it is done. Aḥmad [Ibn Ḥanbal] and Abū ʿUbayd said that the nine-year-old *tujbar* (was to be forced). Mālik, al-Shāfiʿī, and Abū Ḥanīfa opined that she had to be able to *tuṭīq al-waṭʾ* (endure sexual intercourse), and that this timing varied between girls and was not age dependent.

She perhaps could endure sexual intercourse before reaching the age of nine.[125] However, the concept of marriage *bi'l-jabr* (forced marriage) sets aside the consent of the girl, even though consent is one of the pillars of marriage. Baugh notes that the earliest texts consistently referred to the practice of forced prepubescent marriage as applying equally to boys and girls; this became limited to girls only in later sources, ignoring gender equality and justice.[126]

A famous canonical *ḥadīth* is often quoted with regard to forced marriage: Khansāʾ bint Khidhām al-Anṣāriya said, "My father *ankaḥanī* [married me off] and I did not like this match, so I complained to the Messenger of Allah, who said to me 'then this marriage is invalid.'" Another version, by Sufyān al-Thawrī, who as previously mentioned was regarded as a *mudallis*, narrates that she was a virgin.[127] Ibn Ḥajar concludes the discussion by quoting the Prophet saying *lā tukrihūhunna* (do not force them).[128] Al-Harawī (d. 1014/1606), to reconcile both, concludes that there were two women named Khansāʾ: one was previously married, while the other was a virgin.[129] Al-Sarakhsī, supporting bridal consent, adds that Khansāʾ bint Khidhām al-Anṣāriya said that she accepted what her father arranged for her, but wanted women to know that their fathers have no right to force an unwanted marriage on them.[130]

Ensuring that the minor girl was able to endure intercourse explains why there was no need to set a minimum age. It was the girl's physical appearance as *jasīmah* (plump and buxom) that indicated to the jurists whether the marriage could be consummated without undue harm, regardless of her mental or physical readiness or the development of her internal organs. Interestingly, al-Sarakhsī mentions that a *ḥadīth* tells that in preparation for her marriage, ʿĀʾisha was deliberately fed to gain weight (*samminūha*) and that when she became plump the marriage was consummated.[131] Yet there is nothing in all the various *ḥadīth* versions mentioned about her that suggests that ʿĀʾisha was *jasīmah*; in fact and as mentioned, in *Ḥadīth al-ifk* she herself reports that the palanquin was carried away because they did not notice that she was not inside, suggesting that she was light in weight. This could indicate that this particular tradition may have been forged to support the discussion about when a girl could "endure" physical intercourse; however, this is an avenue for further research and not the subject of this chapter.

Preconditions for the consummation of the marriage set by the jurists were therefore neither the onset of menstruation nor the attainment of sexual maturity. Q.4:6[132] suggests that there is a marriageable age, which al-Ṭabarī in his *Jāmiʿ al-bayān fī tafsīr āy al-Qurʾan* equates with puberty.[133] However, the verse ties the marriageable age to *rushd*, and as previously mentioned, *rushd* is accepted by the Ḥanafīs, Shāfiʿīs, and Ḥanbalīs to be the age of fifteen, while the Mālikīs set it at eighteen. How then can a prepubescent girl be regarded as having attained marriageable age?

With regard to *tuṭīq al-waṭʾ*, feminist scholars have noted that "what is, of course, inescapable here is the weight of the male gaze: by undermining the *sharīʿa* stipulation of a girl's sexual maturity as the minimum requirement for her to be given to the husband who has been contracted for her, male social power worked to lower the age at which a girl was 'ready for men.'"[134]

In addition, despite the discussion that a child marriage should be consummated without undue harm, the *fiqh* manuals discuss possible harm and punishments for it. For example, Ibn Qudāma (d. 620/1223) in *al-Mughnī* writes: "Whoever has intercourse with his wife, who is a minor, and causes her to tear or rip, has to pay a third of the *diyya*" (*diyya*: plural *diyyāt*; in Islamic law, the financial compensation paid to the victim or heirs of a victim in cases of murder or bodily harm). Ibn Qudāma continues:

> A rip means the tearing of the perineum [area between the anus and the scrotum or vulva], though it is farfetched as the walls are strong and would not tear from intercourse. There are two aspects to this issue, the first being the necessity of a guarantee, or a security and the second being the outcome. As for the first, a guarantee is necessary for the small and thin girl, who is not able to endure intercourse, but not for the grown one who can bear it, which was also Abū Ḥanīfa's view.[135]

Shāfiʿī opined: "A guarantee is necessary for all, because it is a felony ... If the husband performed sexual intercourse deliberately knowing that she cannot endure it, he has to pay a monetary compensation."[136] This allusion to possible harm indicates that the jurists knew it was possible and that it had to have happened before, necessitating the need to provide rulings. According to modern medicine, neither the perennium's tear nor its strength nor the unlikelihood that it would tear from intercourse, as Ibn Qudāma argued, is correct, as will be discussed in the section about fistula.

In addition, the expression *tuṭīq al-waṭʾ* or *tuṭīqu-l-rijāl* is ethically offensive, for it prevents the girl from experiencing sexual pleasure by turning a potentially pleasurable experience into an exercise of endurance. There is no celibacy in Islam, which considers sexual pleasure to be *ṣadaqa*, a gift from God that should be enjoyed with gratitude.[137] For both genders, sexual pleasure and gratification is emphasized over the duty to procreate. Kolig argues that "creating the perfect society is one of Islam's main goals and the assumption is that sexually fulfilled people make better and more committed societal members, as long as sexuality does not lead to socially disruptive behaviour."[138]

The Qurʾan allows sexual pleasure. It views sex not simply as a means for procreation, but as a natural urge and a comfort for both partners (Q. 2:187). There is no restriction on sexual positions (Q. 2:223), and men are supposed to ascertain that their partner is satisfied.[139] Sexual manuals[140] were written to address problems, provide tips, and offer advice on how to use perfume and cosmetics for seduction and how to please one's spouse. They also emphasized cleanliness.[141] The Sunna supports and encourages female sexual interests, and several prophetic traditions say that "your wife has a right over you."[142] Furthermore, classical jurists mentioned that a husband should refrain from sexual acts that his wife finds vulgar, disagreeable, or offensive.[143] They also argued that women have as much right to sexual fulfillment as their husbands. Foreplay, kissing, *ghunj* (sexually explicit talk or noises), and after-play are subjects the Prophet mentioned in his traditions, setting an example for the men of his community.[144] Islam permits women and men to seek sexual pleasure within a lawful marriage. The Prophet's example teaches that sexual pleasure does not come naturally, but that pleasure should be savoured and refined, and that intercourse should not be hurried, rushed, or animalistic, lest intercourse provide release without satisfaction.[145] Hence, reducing this act to one of mere endurance or "suffering through" on the part of a child is more than reprehensible, for it robs her of a gift granted to her by God and abuses her inexperience and trust.

Maqāṣid

In Islam, the concept of justice is at the core of a number of jurisprudential, legal, and philosophical doctrines.[146] *Maqāṣid* have been defined as the divine intents and moral concepts on which Islamic law is based. Traditionally the *maqāṣid* have been divided into three levels:

ḍarūriyyāt (necessities), *ḥājiyyāt* (needs), and *taḥsīniyyāt* (luxuries). Necessities are considered essential for human life and are further classified into what preserves one's faith, life, intellect, progeny, and property. Preserving one's offspring necessitates marriage as a first step, and hence the rulings on marriage in general and on child marriage in particular should be in the spirit of preserving the rest of the *maqāṣid*, namely mind and life, which include health.

Contemporary medical research has shown that child marriage affects more than just young brides; their children too are at higher risk for illness and early death. Adolescent mothers have a 35 to 55 percent higher risk than older women for delivering infants preterm and of low birthweight, and the mortality rate for infants born to mothers younger than twenty is 73 percent higher than for those born to older mothers.[147]

Kamali argues that

> the desire to rejuvenate the dynamism of Islamic thought can be better served through *maqāṣid*-oriented *ijtihād*. Equipped with a credible methodology to ensure the proximity and nexus of *maqāṣid* with the scriptural guidelines of Islam, *maqāṣid*-oriented *ijtihād* can provide a promising prospect for the advancement of a fresh genre of Islamic legal thought in conjunction with new and unprecedented developments ... [and can be] a bridge between the *uṣūl al-fiqh* and *maqāṣid*.[148]

There is no consensus regarding what *maqāṣid* covers. Ibn Ashur prioritized *maqāṣid* that are concerned with the *umma* (nation) over those concerned with individuals, while Rashīd Riḍa included reform and women's rights in his theory of *maqāṣid* and Yūsuf al-Qaraḍāwī incorporated human dignity and rights in his theory.[149] These are expansions, and the *maqāṣid*-oriented *ijtihād* allowed them to respond to timely issues and to develop practical answers for reform and renewal.

Current scholarship has introduced new conceptions and classifications of *maqāṣid* by considering new dimensions and the scope of rulings they cover. Contemporary classifications divide *maqāṣid* into three levels: general,[150] specific,[151] and partial.[152] As the most recent division includes the welfare of children in the specific *maqāṣid*, the issue of child marriage should definitely be revisited. Contemporary research has concluded that the mortality rate for children under five can be 28 percent higher for those born to mothers under twenty than for those born to older mothers.[153] A child born to a teen mother is twice as likely to die before the age of one as the child of a woman in her twenties, if they survive the low-birthweight and/or premature birth.[154] Muslim jurists should re-evaluate their "canonized" permission of child marriage by simply looking at the consequences.

Maṣlaḥa

The *maqāṣid* are not the only concept looking to preserve human life with all it entails. *Maṣlaḥa* is not one of the traditional four sources of *sharīʿa*, yet it has become the most important legal concept for contemporary practice. Contemporary jurists use *maṣlaḥa* as a vital vehicle for legal change.[155] *Maṣlaḥa* literally means the well-being, welfare, and social wealth of a person or a community. In her detailed work *Maṣlaḥa and the Purpose of the Law*, Opwis notes that *maṣlaḥa* suggests more than "public interest" and "social good," which are the most common translations. Careful to convey the specific sense in which *maṣlaḥa* is understood in classical legal discourse, Opwis writes: "*Maṣlaḥa*, although not mentioned in the Qurʾan, has become synonymous with God's purpose in revealing His law to humankind. The purpose of the divine law is understood as attaining the well-being (*maṣlaḥa*) of humanity in all their mundane and otherworldly affairs."[156] In Islamic jurisprudence, all acts are evaluated in terms of their consequences and whether they are *maṣāliḥ* (benefits/social goods) or *mafāsid* (detriments/social evils).[157]

Al-Ghazālī stated that marriage has five main purposes: bearing children, satisfying the sexual drive, establishing a household and a family, companionship, and providing for women in a humane manner.[158] Al-Shāṭibī (790/1388) adds the enjoyment of the beauty and good qualities of one's wife, avoidance of falling into sinful illicit sexual conduct as embodied in the concept of *iḥṣān* (chastity of the married spouses), peace of mind, and cooperation with one's wife on both material and spiritual matters.[159] An important concept of marriage, discussed at length in *fiqh*, is the issue of *kafāʾa* (suitability or compatibility) of the man and woman. In Islamic law, the term *kafāʾa* refers to equivalence in social status, fortune, profession, and religious status of the bride and groom, or some of these. The Mālikī school, however, limits it to simply religion and physical condition; thus, it is defined as *tadayyun* (piety) and the absence of physical defects.[160]

Unfortunately, the scope of this chapter does not permit an extended foray into discussion of suitability.[161] However, when talking about suitability, it seems that it was not considered when child marriage was involved, for a child is not suitable for any marital responsibilities, be they mental, physical, sexual, or otherwise. The father or guardian of the child may be willing to marry his daughter off for economic or financial reasons, such as debt, poverty, or even greed.[162] This raises an important question, as posed by Fadel: "If the guardian is not acting to protect his own interests, whose interests is he representing?"[163] Islamic law may grant the guardian the legal right to treat a minor however he wishes, but does the guardian have the moral right to do so? Leaman asks: "Even if parents are allowed to kill their children, they did after all produce them, are they morally allowed to do so?"[164]

Opwis argues that the driving force behind the emergence of the concept of *maṣlaḥa* in Islamic legal theory seems to have been the political and theological quest to achieve legitimate legal change.[165] However, the analysis and identification of *maṣlaḥa* must be made with serious consideration so as to ensure that it is an authentic and not just an apparent *maṣlaḥa*. Kamrava argues that *maṣlaḥa* must be beneficial to the entire population or society and not just to one group, class, or individual, and that it must not contradict or conflict with an authentic text from the Qur'an or the Sunna.[166] What is viewed as an interest at one point in time can later be viewed as the opposite, and vice versa. Real interests in one period may become clear harms in later periods, without retrogressively extending their present legal judgment to their previous status.[167] So when considering an interest or a benefit, it is imperative not to lose sight of other interests, especially the ones that are more important in value and scope. With regard to child marriage, the question that arises is whose interests and benefits are being considered? What is the benefit to the female child in getting married, losing her childhood, being burdened with responsibilities she is not ready for, facing possible harm to her body and health, and suffering injury, and all of that without her consent?

Dar'u-l-mafāsid

An examination of verses Q. 22:78[168] and Q. 3:104[169] and of numerous canonical *aḥadīth* shows that *sharī'a* was revealed with the principal objective of providing benefit and preventing harm to mankind. To support this and to regulate human life, *al-qawā'id al-fiqhiyya*

(Islamic legal maxims) were established as a later development in Islamic legal thought.[170] Some of these are *la ḍarar wa-la ḍirār* (neither harming nor counter-harming), *'adam jawāz taklīf mā lā yuṭāq* (not obliging anything that goes beyond someone's capability), *raf' al-ḥaraj* (elimination of hardship from Islamic obligations), and *dar' - al-mafāsid muqaddam 'alā jalb al-maṣāliḥ* (giving the avoidance of [real] dangers priority over [imaginary] benefits).

However true these maxims sound, *dar'u-l-mafāsid* has often been used to argue for child marriage, in terms of concern for the potential future immorality of minor females and to protect them from what would lead to their ruin, spiritual and otherwise, as well as to prevent the corruption of society. Welchman argues that controlling the sexual conduct of a daughter, be it before her marriage or through the father arranging that marriage when he deems it appropriate, was the expected role of the father as guardian.[171] Abou El Fadl has noted that "puritanical Salafism often invokes concepts of *al-maṣāliḥ wa'l-mafāsid al-'āmma* [public interest or public harms] in the context of gender relations, especially the purported interest in protecting the society from the sexual allures of women."[172] Many contemporary scholars have pointed out that the juristic principle of *dar' al-mafāsid muqaddam 'alā jalb al-maṣāliḥ* (averting causes of corruption has precedence over bringing about that which has benefit) has been regularly invoked to curb not only women's rights but also the rights of minorities.[173] Al-Shāṭibī includes other concepts that could influence the outcome of a ruling, such as *ḥiyal* (legal trickery), which entails the manipulation of legal concepts.[174] It is a form of *ḥiyal* that such concepts are still used falsely to permit child marriage, even when medicine and science have shown how much *mafāsid* (harm) it can cause – see the section on fistula below.

Lā ḍarar wa lā ḍirār

A canonical tradition says: *lā ḍarar wa lā ḍirār* (let there be no harm or reciprocating harm). In his commentary, al-'Uthaymīn defines *ḍarar* first as harm to the body, then financial harm, then harm to one's progeny and possessions; he follows this with an explanation of the differences, stating that *ḍarar* happens unintentionally, whereas *ḍirār* is inflicted intentionally.[175] Luqman reads this prophetic tradition as a prohibition of harm and injury and as a call for the elimination of hardship.[176] Ibn 'Abd al-Barr (d. 463/1071) in his *Tamhīd* makes an interesting distinction between the two words: *ḍarar* is harm inflicted on another from which the perpetrator derives benefit, while *ḍirār* is harm inflicted on another from which no one benefits.[177]

As will be demonstrated later in this chapter, the harm that comes to the child-bride is definitely great, regardless of the benefit derived for the bride's husband or father. If the father and husband do not know that the bride cannot endure intercourse and harm results, then that would be unintentional, yet selfish, and definitely *ḍarar*. It is shocking that this maxim has not been invoked with regard to child marriage.

Fistula

Worldwide, at least two million women suffer from fistula. An estimated fifty to a hundred thousand new cases occur each year.[178] Contrary to Ibn Qudāma's opinion in *al-Mughnī*, that the perennial walls are strong and would not tear from intercourse,[179] current research has shown that in consensual intercourse, with preliminary stimulation and consequent lubrication, injuries are rarely seen. However, in young and inexperienced and often unwilling girls, injuries may occur, varying from minimal trauma to extensive lacerations, because there is a clear disproportion between a grown man's penis size and the size of a child's vagina.[180] Additionally, during the first sexual intercourse, the hymen is stretched and torn and a small amount of bleeding results; occasionally more bleeding and rupture occurs. The most frequently encountered fistulae lie between the vagina and the bladder (vesicovaginal fistula) or between the vagina and rectum (rectovaginal fistula).[181] Vesicovaginal fistula often results from sexual activity, often forceful, with girls whose vulvas and reproductive systems are not yet fully formed.[182] Traumatic fistula results from forceful penetration, violent intercourse, an immature vagina, and when physical growth is incomplete.[183]

Obstetric fistula is a childbirth complication after obstructed labour when the tissues between the vagina and the bladder or rectum are damaged from continuous pressure by the baby's head stuck in the birth canal. The result is a hole through which the affected woman continuously leaks urine or faeces or sometimes both.[184] Girls aged ten to fifteen are especially vulnerable, because their pelvic bones are not ready for childbearing and delivery; their risk for fistula is as high as 88 percent.[185] Girls between ten and fourteen are five times more likely than women twenty to twenty-four to die in pregnancy and childbirth.[186] Children who deliver children are at a significantly higher risk for debilitating illness and even death. Women and girls living with fistula are often ostracized and isolated, mainly because of their foul odour. Young wives who develop obstetric fistulae are frequently abandoned by their husbands and families.[187]

Islam emphasizes cleanliness especially regarding prayer, so any affected female is considered unclean and can no longer pray, though when her condition comes to be regarded as incurable, resumption of prayer is permitted.[188] With all of these harmful side effects, how can child marriage and the resulting child pregnancies not be considered a major *ḍarar* (harm) or a great *mafsada*, which should be avoided or prohibited rather than permitted?

HUMAN RIGHTS AND RIGHTS OF WOMEN AND CHILDREN

In Muslim writings on the relationship between Islamic and international human rights, a wide range of opinions have been adopted. They range between two extremes, from the assertion that international human rights are fully compatible with Islam to the claim that human rights are the products of an alien Western culture, representing values that are incompatible with Islam. The compromise position is that Islam accepts many, but not all, aspects of international human rights or that it endorses human rights with certain reservations and qualifications.[189] For example, a significant number of Muslim countries originally acceded with reservations to CEDAW.[190] These reservations state that any provision of the convention that contradicts *sharīʿa* shall not be applicable. Many Muslim States have noted their reservations, citing possible contradictions with Islam.[191] Sachedina notes that "the critical area of Islamic heritage that holds essential keys to reassert the absolute human rights of women based on their inherent dignity and moral worth similar to men is located in the ethical-theological doctrines."[192] It has been shown that Islamic juridical rulings reflect and maintain male dominance; hence, there has been little progress in challenging the dominant religious discourse based on these rulings, according to which women and minorities remain in need of *wilāya* (guardianship) and continue to be viewed as incompetent minors, however mature and competent they might be.

Globally, the incidence of child marriage is at 40.3 percent.[193] In many places where child marriage is most prevalent, religion and tradition wield a powerful influence over communities.[194] Child marriage is defined by UNICEF[195] as marrying before the age of eighteen. UNICEF estimated in 2014 that 140 million girls would be married off early in the next decade – that is, nearly 40,000 girls every day.[196]

As has been demonstrated, when a girl is married under the age of eighteen, it profoundly affects her life and health, leading to health complications, compromised psychological well-being, and a lack of participation in the community and society at large.[197] Girls' offspring are at increased risk for premature birth and death as neonates, infants, or children. Child marriage is one of the earliest and most pervasive forms of gender-based violence.[198] Sexual abuse is defined as the involvement of dependent, developmentally immature children and adolescents in sexual activities they do not truly comprehend and to which they are unable to give informed consent.[199] Any child below the age of consent may be deemed to have been sexually abused when a sexually mature person has engaged or permitted the engagement of that child in any activity of a sexual nature, which is intended to lead to the sexual gratification of the sexually mature person.[200] In spite of international agreements and national laws, child marriage affects millions worldwide. Child marriage is a human rights violation that prevents girls from obtaining an education, enjoying optimal health, maturing, and ultimately choosing their own partners.[201]

In the context of the ongoing debate about the hidden political agenda of international human rights and the need to convince Muslim communities to support the moral universality of human rights, it is more advisable that the protection of women's dignity as human persons be approached from the theological perspective of moral agency of autonomous human beings endowed with equal capabilities to advance their lives. Child marriage is a harmful traditional cultural practice, a human rights violation, and a public health challenge.

CONCLUSION

Limiting the practice of child marriage, particularly of girls, has long been a concern of social reformers, feminists, and women's rights activists, and is given weight in international bodies such as the various organizations of the UN.[202] Muslim reformers have focused on the physical and mental health risks of early marriage for girls and very young women and issues of their consent to marriage, as well as the loss or at least substantial limitation of their opportunities for education and work.[203] Despite widespread condemnation of the practice, child marriage persists and is at times defended in the name of tradition or even Islam.[204] Islam requires both men and women to voluntarily consent to marriage.[205] Given children's limited ability to reach well-informed consent for marriage, this lack of maturity could be used as an argument not to allow child marriage at all. One could legitimately argue that child marriage should be avoided; however, one should also be aware that legal prohibition of child marriage would not be enough to change existing cultural patterns and undo centuries of practice.

Rulings about child marriage in Islamic law were based on the precedent of ʿĀʾisha's marriage, though the canonized *ḥadīth* setting her age at six/nine is questionable, as demonstrated, and contradicts historical information found in the heritage books. Motzki argued that it is conceivable that the authors of the first *Ḥadīth* collections made mistakes, subjectively assessed information, missed information, or turned a blind eye when a problematic narrator was found in the chain of narration, when they deemed the tradition acceptable.[206] Furthermore, those authors based their conclusions on a faulty interpretation of Q. 65:4 as explained, rendering two of the four sources of the legislation of child marriage defective and the resulting *qiyās* erroneous. Canons and authoritative books in *ḥadīth* and *fiqh* are susceptible to interpretation and at times even contradict one another, as demonstrated. Abou El Fadl argues that "there is a serious problem with arguing that God intended to lock the epistemology of the seventh century into the immutable text of the Qurʾan, and then intended to hold Muslims hostage to this epistemological framework for all ages to come,"[207] which would limit the effectiveness of the Divine text and would undermine the notion that the Qurʾan is suitable for all people at all times.

Child marriage, as discussed, is a model of male authority and female submission that contradicts two Islamic notions of justice and equity, as well as contemporary notions of human rights, and cannot be justified on religious grounds; therefore a "decanonization" of this patriarchal interpretation that ultimately found its way into exegetical texts and laws should be considered. Respect for past precedents that were canonized in authoritative books and sources of Islamic law should not prevent future generations of Muslims from amending or setting aside prior interpretations and understandings of Islamic law that no longer respond to the changed realities of Muslim communities. Khaled Abou El Fadl wrote: "I do not accept a consensus that permits an error to prevail. The consensus of one generation does not bind another, and an immoral unanimity is immoral all the same."[208]

APPENDIX

The following is a list of *tafsīr* (exegetical) works consulted and the definitions of the word *lamm yaḥiḍna* (have not menstruated) given there.

#	Title	Author	Death date	Definition
1	*Tafsīr Mujāhid*	Mujāhid ibn Jabr al-Makhzūmī	104/722	No details
2	*Tafsīr Muqātil*	Muqātil ibn Sulaymān	150/767	*Jāriya* (girl) who has not menstruated yet
3	*Tafsīr kitāb Allāh al-ʿazīz*	Hūd ibn Muḥakkam al-Hawwārī	280/823 or 296/908	Grown women who do not menstruate or the *ḍahyā'* (Ammenoraic)
4	*Tafsīr al-Qur'ān*	ʿAlī ibn Ibrāhīm al-Qummī	307/919	No details
5	*Jāmiʿ al-bayān ʿan ta'wīl āy al-Qur'ān*	Abū Jaʿfar Muḥammad ibn Jarīr al-Ṭabarī	310/923	Those who have not menstruated yet
6	*Ta'wīlāt al-Qur'ān*	Abū Manṣūr Muḥammad ibn Muḥammad ibn Maḥmūd al-Samarḳandī, often referred to as al-Māturīdī	333/944	*Saghīrāt* (little girls)
7	*Al-Tafsīr al-kabīr*	Abū al-Qāsim Sulaymān ibn Ayyūb ibn Muṭayyir al-Lakhmī al-Ṭabarānī	360/971	*Saghīrāt*
8	*Baḥr al-ʿulūm*	Abū al-Layth Naṣr ibn Muḥammad. ibn Aḥmad ibn Ibrāhīm al-Samarqandī	373/983	Grown women who do not menstruate
9	*Tafsīr al-hidāya ila bulūgh al-nihāya*	Abū Ṭālib Muḥammad ibn ʿAlī ibn ʿAṭiyya al-Ḥārithī al-ʿAjamī al-Makkī	386/996	Women who do not menstruate due to a medical condition
10	*Tafsīr al-Qur'an al-ʿazīz*	Ibn Abī Zamanayn, Abū ʿAbd Allāh Muḥammad ibn ʿAbd Allāh ibn ʿĪsā al-Murrī,	399/1009	Woman or minor girl who is not pregnant
11	*Al-Kashf wa'l-bayān ʿan tafsīr al-Qur'ān*	Abū Isḥāq Aḥmad ibn Muḥammad ibn Ibrāhīm al-Nīsābūrī al-Thaʿlabī	427/1035	*Saghīrāt* and grown women with menstrual problems
12	*Al-Nukat wa'l-ʿuyūn*	Abū al-Ḥasan ʿAlī ibn Muḥammad ibn Ḥabīb al-Māwardī	450/1058	*Saghīrāt*
13	*Al-Tibyān fī tafsīr al-Qur'ān*	Abū Jaʿfar Muḥammad ibn al-Ḥasan ibn ʿAlī al-Ṭūsī	459–460/1066-7	Not yet nine years old and other minors and those who suffer from menstrual problems

#	Title	Author	Death date	Definition
14	*Laṭā'if al-ishārāt*	Abū al-Qāsim ʿAbd al-Karīm ibn Hawāzin al-Qushayrī	465/1072	No details
15	*Al-Wajīz fī maʿānī al-Qur'ān al-ʿazīz*	Abū al-Ḥasan ʿAlī ibn Aḥmad ibn Muḥammad ibn ʿAlī ibn Mattūya al-Mattūyī al-Wāḥidī	468/1076	*Saghīrāt*
16	*Maʿālim al-tanzīl*	Abū Muḥammad al-Ḥusayn ibn Masʿūd ibn Muḥammad al-Farrā' al- Baghawī	516/1122	*Saghīrāt* and young women who have menstrual problems
17	*Al-Kashshāf ʿan ḥaqā'iq ghawāmiḍ al-tanzīl wa-ʿuyūn al-aqāwīl fī wujūh al-ta'wīl*	Jār Allāh Abū al-Qāsim Maḥmūd ibn ʿUmar al-Zamakhsharī	538/1144	*Saghīrāt*
18	*Majmaʿ al-bayān fī tafsīr al-Qur'ān*	Abū ʿAlī Faḍl ibn Faḍl ibn Ḥasan al-Ṭabarsī (or al-Ṭabrisī)	548/1153	Those who have not menstruated yet
19	*Tafsīr al-Jīlānī*	ʿAbd al-Qādir al-Jīlānī	561/1166	Those who have not menstruated because they are too young or have medical problems
20	*Zād al-masīr fī ʿilm al-tafsīr*	Abu al-Faraj ʿAbd al-Raḥmān ibn ʿAlī ibn Muḥammad ibn al-Jawzī	597/1200	*Saghīrāt* and those who reached menstrual age but have not menstruated
21	*Al-Muḥarrar al-wajīz fī tafsīr al-kitāb al-ʿazīz*	Abū Muḥammad ʿAbd al-Ḥaqq ibn Ghālib ibn ʿAbd al-Raḥmān ibn ʿAṭiyya	546/1151	No details
22	*Mafātīḥ al-ghayb or Kitāb al-tafsīr al-kabīr*	Fakhr al-Dīn Abū ʿAbd Allāh Muḥammad ibn ʿUmar al-Rāzī	606/1210	*Saghīrāt* who have not menstruated yet
23	*Tafsīr al-Qur'ān*	Muḥyi al-Dīn Abū ʿAbd Allāh Muḥammad ibn ʿAlī ibn Muḥammad ibn al-ʿArabī	638/1240	No details
24	*Tafsīr al-Qur'an*	Abū Muḥammad ʿIzz al-Dīn ʿAbd al-ʿAzīz ibn ʿAbd al-Salām	660/1262	No details
25	*Rumūz al-kunūz fī tafsīr al-kitāb al-ʿazīz*	Abū Muḥammad ʿAbd al-Razzāq ibn Rizq Allāh al-Rasʿanī	661/1263	*Saghīrāt*

#	*Title*	*Author*	*Death date*	*Definition*
26	*Al-Jāmiʿ li-aḥkām al-Qur'ān wa'l-mubayyin li-mā taḍammana min al-sunna wa-āyāt al-furqān*	Abū ʿAbd Allāh Muḥammad ibn Aḥmad ibn Abī Bakr ibn Faraj al-Qurṭubī	671/1272	*Saghīrāt*
27	*Anwār al-tanzīl wa-asrār al-ta'wīl*	Nāṣir al-Dīn Abū al-Khayr ʿAbd Allāh ibn ʿUmar ibn Muḥammad ibn ʿAlī al-Bayḍāwī	685/1286	No details
28	*Madārik al-tanzīl wa ḥaqā'iq al-ta'wīl*	Ḥāfiẓ al-Dīn Abū al-Barakāt ʿAbd Allāh ibn Aḥmad ibn Maḥmūd al-Nasafī	710/1310	*Saghīrāt*
29	*Lubāb al-ta'wīl fī maʿānī al-tanzīl*	ʿAlī ibn Muḥammad al-Baghdādī	725/1324	*Saghīrāt* and those who reached menstrual age but failed to menstruate
30	*Kitāb al-tashīl li-ʿulūm al-tanzīl*	Abū ʿAbd Allāh Muḥammad ibn Muḥammad ibn Aḥmad ibn Juzayy al-Kalbī al-Gharnāṭī	741/1340	*Saghīrāt* who have not menstruated yet and young women with medical problems causing the lack of menstruation
31	*Tafsīr al-baḥr al-muḥīṭ*	Athīr al-Dīn Abū Ḥayyān Muḥammad ibn Yūsuf ibn ʿAlī al-Andalusī	745/1344	*Saghīrāt* who have not menstruated yet because of their young age and the *ḍahyā'*
32	*Tafsīr al-nahr al-mād min al-baḥr al-muḥīṭ*	Athīr al-Dīn Abū Ḥayyān Muḥammad ibn Yūsuf ibn ʿAlī al-Andalusī	745/1344	*Saghīrāt* who have not menstruated yet because of their young age and the *ḍahyā'*
33	*Al-Durr al-maṣūn*	Aḥmad ibn Yūsuf ibn Muḥammad al-Samīn al-Ḥalabī	756/1355	No details
34	*Ṭafsīr Ibn Kathīr*	ʿImād al-Dīn Ismāʿīl ibn ʿUmar ibn Kathīr	774/1373	*Saghīrāt*
35	*Tafsīr al-Qur'ān*	Maj_d al-Dīn Abū al-Ṭāhir Muḥammad ibn Yaʿqūb ibn Muḥammad ibn Ibrāhīm al-Shīrāzī al-Fīrūzābādī	817/1415	*Saghīrāt*
36	*Tafsīr gharā'ib al-Qur'ān wa-raghā'ib al-furqān*	Niẓām al-Aʿraj Niẓām al-Dīn Ḥasan ibn Muḥammad ibn al-Ḥusayn al-Nīsābūrī	~ 827/1424	*Saghīrāt*

#	*Title*	*Author*	*Death date*	*Definition*
37	*Al-Jawāhir al-ḥisān fī tafsīr al-Qur'ān*	ʿAbd al-Raḥmān ibn Muḥammad ibn Makhlūf al-Jazā'irī al-Thaʿālibī	873/1468	No details
38	*Al-Lubāb fī ʿulūm al-kitāb*	ʿUmar ibn ʿAlī ibn ʿĀdil al-Dimashqī	880/1476	*Saghīrāt* and those with medical conditions preventing menstruation
39	*Naẓm al-durar fī tanāsub al-āyāt wa'l-suwar*	Burhān al-Dīn Ibrāhīm ibn ʿUmar ibn Ḥasan al-Baqqāʿī	885/1480	*Saghīrāt* and those with medical conditions preventing menstruation
40	*Tafsīr al-Jalālayn*	Jalāl al-Dīn al-Maḥallī and Jalāl al-Dīn al- Suyūṭī	911/1505	*Saghīrāt*
41	*Al-Durr al-manthūr fī al-tafsīr bi'l-ma'thūr*	Jalāl al-Dīn Abū al-Faḍl ʿAbd al-Raḥmān ibn Abī Bakr ibn Muḥammad al- Suyūṭī	911/1505	*Jāriyāt* who are too young to menstruate and those with medical conditions that prevent menstruation
42	*Irshād al-ʿaql al-salīm ilā mazāyā al-Qur'ān al-karīm*	Abū al-Suʿūd Muḥammad ibn Muḥammad ibn Muṣṭafā al-ʿImādī	982/1574	*Saghīrāt* who have not menstruated yet due to their young age
43	*Tafsīr al-Aʿqam*	Aḥmad ʿAlī Muḥammad ʿAlī al-Aʿqam al-Ānisī al-Zaydī	1107/1695?	*Saghīrāt*
44	*Al-Ṣāfī fī tafsīr kalām Allāh al-wāfī*	Al-Fayḍ al-Kāshānī Muḥammad Muḥsin ibn Murtaḍā	1091/1680	Those who have not menstruated yet
45	*Kitāb al-burhān fī tafsīr al-Qur'ān*	Hāshim ibn Sulaymān al-Ḥusaynī al-Baḥrānī	1107/1695–6	Those who do not menstruate
46	*Rūḥ al-bayān fī tafsīr al-Qur'ān*	Ismāʿīl Ḥaqqī al-Khalwatī al-Brūsawī or al-Uskudārī	1137/1725	*Saghīrāt* and women with medical conditions
47	*Al-Baḥr al-madīd fī tafsīr al-Qur'an*	Abū al-ʿAbbās Aḥmad ibn Muḥammad ibn al-Mahdī ibn ʿAj_ība	1224/1809	*Saghīrāt*
48	*Ḥāshiyat al-Ṣāwī ʿala tafsīr al-Jalālayn*	Aḥmad ibn Muḥammad al-Ṣāwī	1241/1826	*Saghīrāt* who have not menstruated as they have not reached puberty and young women who are breastfeeding or whose menstruation stopped
49	*Fatḥ al-qadīr*	Muḥammad ibn ʿAlī ibn Muḥammad al-Shawkānī	1255/1839	*Saghīrāt*
50	*Ruḥ al-maʿānī fī tafsīr al-Qur'ān al-ʿaẓīm*	Shihāb al-Dīn Abū al Thanā' Maḥmūd al-Ālūsī	1270/1854	Those who have not menstruated because of their young age

#	Title	Author	Death date	Definition
51	*Bayān al-saʿāda fī maqāmāt al-ʿibāda*	Sulṭān Muḥammad al-Janābidhī Sulṭān Alī Shāh	1327/1909	Those who have not menstruated yet though they have reached the menstrual age
52	*Al-Tafsīr al-lughawī fī maḥāsin al-taʾwīl*	Muḥammad Jamāl al-Dīn al-Qāsimī	1332/1914	*Saghīrāt*
53	*Hīmyān al-zād ilā dār al-maʿād*	Muḥammad ibn Yūsuf al-Wahbī al-Ibāḍī	1332/1914	*Saghīrāt* who have not menstruated yet and young women with medical problems
54	*Aysar al-tafāsīr*	Abū Bakr Jābir ibn Mūsā ibn ʿAbd al-Qādir Jazāʾirī	1339/1921	Those who do not menstruate either for being too young or too old
55	*Tafsīr āyāt al-aḥkām min al-Qurʾān*	Muḥammad ibn ʿAlī al-Ṣābūnī	1349/1931	*Saghīrāt* who have not menstruated yet
56	*Taysīr al-Karīm al-Raḥmān fī tafsīr kalām al-Mannān*	ʿAbd al-Raḥmān ibn Nāṣir al-Saʿdī	1376/1957	*Saghīrāt* who have not menstruated yet and young women with medical problems
57	*Tafsīr al-taḥrīr wa'l-tanwīr*	Muḥammad al-Ṭāhir Ibn ʿĀshūr	1393/1973	No details
58	*Aḍwāʾ al-bayān fī īḍāḥ al-Qurʾān bi'l-Qurʾān*	Muḥammad al-Amīn ibn Muḥammad al-Mukhtār ibn ʿAbd al-Qādir al-Shanqīṭī	1393/1973	No details
59	*Al-Mīzān fī tafsīr al-Qurʾān*	Muḥammad Ḥusayn al-Ṭabāṭabāʾī	1401/1981	Those who have reached menstrual age but have not menstruated
60	*Taysīr al-tafsīr*	Ibrāhīm al-Qaṭṭān	1404/1984	*Saghīrāt*
61	*Tafsīr al-Shaʿrāwī*	Muḥammad Mutawallī al-Shaʿrāwī	1419/1998	*Saghīrāt* who have not menstruated yet
62	*Tafsīr al-wasīṭ li'l-Qurʾān al-karīm*	Muḥammad Sayyid Ṭanṭāwī	1431/2010	No details
63	*Aysar al-tafāsīr*	Asʿad Ḥawmad	1432/2010	*Saghīrāt*

NOTES

All translations from Arabic, unless explicitly stated, are the author's.

1 Child marriage is also common in the southern United States, with the highest incidences being in West Virginia, Texas, Nevada, Oklahoma, Arkansas, California, Tennessee, and North Carolina. See for example Syrett, *American Child Bride*.

2 UNICEF, *Ending Child Marriage*.

3 Ibid.

4 See for example Nujud Ali, *I am Nujud*, trans. Linda Coverdale (Portland: Broadway Books, 2010)..

5 UNFPA, *When Pregnancy Harms*.

6 ICRW, *Child Marriage around the World*.

7 See, for example, Hallaq, "Was the Gate of Ijtihad Closed?," 129–41.

8 Khan and Ramadan define it as being between 11/632 and 261/875.

9 Khan and Ramadan, *Contemporary Ijtihad*, 14.

10 Ibid., 36.

11 Khan and Ramadan define it as being between 271/875 and 1292/1875.

12 Khan and Ramadan, *Contemporary Ijtihad*, 39.

13 Nouryeh, *Art of Narrative*, 98.

14 Al-ʿAlawī, *al-Ijtihād wa'l-taḥdīth*, 17.

15 Ibid., 15.

16 Ibid.

17 Ibid., 17.

18 Ibid., 16.

19 Haykel, *Revival and Reform*, 79.

20 Vikør, *Development of Ijtihad*.

21 Syed, *Position of Women*, 41.

22 Hasan, "Introduction," 30.

23 Al-Alwani, *Ijtihad*, 20.

24 Pizzorno, "Rationality and Recognition," 164.

25 Della Porta and Keating, "How Many Approaches," 25.

26 Brown, *Canonization*, 154.

27 Ibid., 203

28 Ibid., 206.

29 Ibid., 301.

30 Ibid., 329

31 Ibid., 278.

32 Ibid., 359.

33 Ibid., 300.

34 Ibid., 349
35 Al-Qastillānī, *Irshād al-sārī*, vol. 1, 29.
36 Al-Naysābūrī, *Ma'rifat 'ulūm al-ḥadīth*, 146.
37 Ibn Ḥajar, *Nuzhat al-naẓar*, 35.
38 Brown, *Canonization*, 371.
39 Ibid., 203–4.
40 Ibid., 371.
41 Al-Bukhārī, *Ṣaḥīḥ al-Bukhārī*, no. 1309.
42 Ibid., no. 954.
43 Ibid.
44 Ibn Ḥajar, *Ṭabaqāt al-mudallisīn*, 26.
45 Ibid., 30.
46 Ibn Ḥajar, *Kitāb tahdhīb al-tahdhīb*, 705.
47 Ibn Ḥajar, *Ṭabaqāt al-mudallisīn*, 32.
48 Ibn Ḥajar, *Kitāb tahdhīb al-tahdhīb*, 349.
49 Ibn al-Ṣalāḥ, *Ma'rifat anwā' 'ilm al-ḥadīth*, 323.
50 It is noteworthy that Ibn Isḥāq died 106 years before al-Bukhārī.
51 Ibn Isḥāq, *Life of Muḥammad*, vol. 1, 106.
52 Ibn Hishām, *al-Sīra al-nabawiyya*, vol. 1, 200.
53 Ibn Kathīr, *al-Bidāya wa'l-nihāya*, vol. 1, 32.
54 See also Ibn Hishām's *al-Sīrah al-nabawiyya*.
55 Al-Ṭabarī, *Ta'rīkh al-Ṭabarī*, vol. 1, 230.
56 Della Porta and Keating, "How Many Approaches," 26.
57 Interpreting the Qur'an by its own context, or by means of other Qur'anic verses rather than by means of extraneous material.
58 O'Keeffe. "*Media*," 68.
59 [Q. 65:4] "And [as for] those of your women who have despaired of menstruation, if you have a doubt, their prescribed time shall be three months, and of those too who have not had their courses; and [as for] the pregnant women, their prescribed time is that they lay down their burden; and whoever is careful of (his duty to) Allah He will make easy for him his affair."
60 http://www.altafsir.com/Tafasir.asp?tMadhNo=0&tTafsirNo=48&tSoraNo=65&tAyahNo=4&tDisplay=yes&UserProfile=0&LanguageId=1.
61 http://www.baheth.info/all.jsp?term=%D8%B6%D9%87%D9%8A%D8%A7%D8%A1.
62 http://www.altafsir.com/Tafasir.asp?tMadhNo=0&tTafsirNo=28&tSoraNo=65&tAyahNo=4&tDisplay=yes&UserProfile=0&LanguageId=1.
63 http://www.altafsir.com/Tafasir.asp?tMadhNo=4&tTafsirNo=41&tSoraNo=65&tAyahNo=4&tDisplay=yes&UserProfile=0&LanguageId=1.

64 The menopausal, those who have not menstruated as well as the pregnant women.

65 [Q. 65:1] "O Prophet, when you [Muslims] divorce women, divorce them for [the commencement of] their waiting period and keep count of the waiting period, and fear Allah, your Lord. Do not turn them out of their [husbands'] houses, nor should they [themselves] leave [during that period] unless they are committing a clear immorality. And those are the limits [set by] Allah. And whoever transgresses the limits of Allah has certainly wronged himself. You know not; perhaps Allah will bring about after that a [different] matter."

66 http://www.altafsir.com/Tafasir.asp?tMadhNo=4&tTafsirNo=39&tSoraNo=65&tAyahNo=4&tDisplay=yes&Page=2&Size=1&LanguageId=1.

67 http://www.baheth.info/all.jsp?term=%D9%86%D8%B3%D8%A7%D8%A1

68 Interpreting the Qur'an by its own context, or by means of other Qur'anic verses, rather than by means of extraneous material.

69 Hoffman, "Qur'anic Interpretation," 90.

70 See, for example, Q. 4:23; 6:100; 11:79; 15:71; 16:57; 37:149; 37:153; 43:16; and 52:39.

71 [Q. 33:59] "O Prophet, tell your wives and your daughters and the women of the believers to bring down over themselves [part] of their outer garments. That is more suitable that they will be known and not be abused. And ever is Allah Forgiving and Merciful."

72 Q 24:59 "And when the children among you reach puberty, let them ask permission [at all times] as those before them have done. Thus does Allah make clear to you His verses; and Allah is Knowing and Wise."

73 Al-ʿAskarī, *Muʿjam al-furūq al-lughawiyya*, 467.

74 [Q. 49:14] "The dwellers of the desert say: We believe. Say: You do not believe, but say: We submit; and faith has not yet entered into your hearts; and if you obey Allah and His Apostle, He will not diminish aught of your deeds; surely Allah is Forgiving, Merciful."

75 Santoro and Neal-Perry, *Amenorrhea*, v.

76 De Souza and Toombs, "Amenorrhea Associated," 104.

77 Hurst and Marshburn and Hurst, *Disorders of Menstruation*, 33.

78 Dewhurst, *Female Puberty*, 120.

79 Scrambler and Scrambler, *Menstrual Disorders*, 6.

80 Jackson, "Nutritional Concerns," 409.

81 Polotsky and Santoro, "Role of Body Weight," 127.

82 Al-Bukhārī, *Ṣaḥīḥ al-Bukhārī*, no. 1016.

83 Meaning that they did not cook.
84 Al-Bukhārī, *Ṣaḥīḥ al-Bukhārī*, no. 1608.
85 Ibid.
86 Ibid., 1606.
87 Fern and Warren, *Menstrual Cycle*, 80.
88 Roby, "Pernicious Anemia," 581.
89 Conley, "Anemias," 958.
90 See, for example, Vieth and Lane, "Anemia," 613–28; Bridges and Pearson, *Anemias.*
91 Al-Ḥiṣnī, *al-Mu'mināt wa-siyar al-sālikāt*, 16.
92 Dewhurst, *Female Puberty*, 31.
93 De Souza and Toombs, "Amenorrhea," 103.
94 Fern, Jewelewicz, and Warren, *Menstrual Cycle*, 148.
95 Dewhurst, *Female Puberty*, 33.
96 A *farsakh* is between 4 and 6 kilometres.
97 Al-Bukhārī, *Ṣaḥīḥ al-Bukhārī*, no. 1331.
98 Ibn Ḥajar, *Fatḥ al-bārī*, 119.
99 Van Dijk. "Critical Discourse Analysis," 352.
100 Lucas, "Abu Bakr b. al-Mundhir," 356.
101 Kamali, *Law in Afghanistan*, 125.
102 Baugh, "An Exploration of the Juristic Consensus."
103 Ibid., 53.
104 A man and a woman alone together.
105 Ibn Hubayra, *Ikhtilāf al-a'imma al-'ulamā'*, vol. 2, 123.
106 Ibid.
107 [Q. 4.6] "And test the orphans until they attain marriageable age [puberty]; then if you find in them maturity of intellect, make over to them their property, and do not consume it extravagantly and hastily, lest they attain to full age; and whoever is rich, let him abstain altogether, and whoever is poor, let him eat reasonably; then when you make over to them their property, call witnesses in their presence; and Allah is enough as a Reckoner."
108 Al-Sarakhsī, *Kitāb al-mabsūṭ*, vol. 4, 212.
109 Ibn Ḥazm, *al-Muḥallā*, vol. 9, 460.
110 Al-Sarakhsī, *Kitāb al-mabsūṭ*, vol. 4, 213.
111 Ibid., 217.
112 Motzki, "Child-Marriage," 135.
113 Ibid.
114 Giladi, *Children of Islam*, 116.
115 Motzki, "Child-Marriage," 136.

116 Baugh, "Exploration," 68.
117 Ibn Ḥazm, *al-Muḥallā*, 459-60.
118 [Q. 68.4] "And indeed, you are of a great moral character."
119 *Sunan al-Nasāʾī: Kitāb al-nikāḥ, bāb tazawwuj al-marʾa mithlahā fī al-sinn*, 412.
120 Talhami, *Historical Dictionary of Women*, 124.
121 Sachedina, *Islam and the Challenge of Human Rights*, 119.
122 Brown, *Hadith*, 150.
123 Ali, *Marriage and Divorce*, 82.
124 Fadel, "Reinterpreting the Guardian's Role," 12.
125 Al-Nawawī, *al-Minhāj fī sharḥ ṣaḥīḥ Muslim*, vol. 9, 206.
126 Baugh, "Exploration," 40.
127 Ibn Ḥajar, *Fatḥ al-bārī*, 462-3.
128 Ibid.
129 Al-Harawī, *Mirqāt al-mafātīḥ*, 267–8.
130 Al-Sarakhsī, *Kitāb al-mabsūṭ*, vol. 5, 12.
131 Ibid., 222.
132 [Q. 4.6] "And test the orphans until they attain marriageable age; then if you find in them maturity of intellect, make over to them their property, and do not consume it extravagantly and hastily, lest they attain to full age; and whoever is rich, let him abstain altogether, and whoever is poor, let him eat reasonably; then when you make over to them their property, call witnesses in their presence; and Allah is enough as a Reckoner."
133 http://www.altafsir.com/Tafasir.asp?tMadhNo=0&tTafsirNo=1&tSoraNo=4&tAyahNo=6&tDisplay=yes&UserProfile=0&LanguageId=1.
134 Joseph et al. *Encyclopedia of Women*, vol. 3, 57.
135 Ibn Qudāma, *Al-Mughnī*, vol. 12, 169–72.
136 Ibid.
137 Kolig, *Conservative Islam*, 153.
138 Ibid.
139 Al-Tijānī, *Tuḥfat al-ʿarūs*, 113–14. See also Q. 2:223: "engage in foreplay in preparation for yourselves" (*qaddimū li-anfusikum*).
140 See, for example, *Irshād al-labīb īlā muʿasharāt al-ḥabīb* by Aḥmad ibn Muḥammad ibn ʿAlī al-Yamanī; *Nuzhat al-albāb fīmā lā yūjad fī kitāb* by Aḥmad ibn Yūsuf al-Tīfāshī; *al-Rawḍ al-ʿāṭir fī nuzhat al-khāṭir* by ʿUmar ibn Muḥammad al-Nafzāwī; and *al-īḍāḥ fī ʿilm al-nikāḥ* and *Shaqāʾiq al-utrunj fī raqāʾiq al-ghunj* by Jalāl al-Dīn al-Suyūtī, who wrote more than eleven such manuals.
141 Amin, "Sexuality," 245.
142 Al-Bukhārī, *Saḥīḥ al-Bukhārī*, no. 1326.

143 See for example, *Tuḥfat al-ʿarūs wa-mutʿat al-nufūs* by Muḥammad ibn Aḥmad Tijānī; *Rawḍat al-muḥibbīn wa-nuzhat al-mushtāqīn* by Ibn Qayyim al-Jawzīyya; *al-Qiyān* by Abūal-Faraj al-Iṣbahānī; *Rashf al-zulāl min al-siḥr al-ḥalāl* by Jalāl al-Dīn al-Suyuṭī; *Jughrāfiyā al-maladhdhāt* by Ibrāhīm Maḥmūd; and *Nuzhat al-albāb fīmā lā yūjadu fī kitāb* by Aḥmad ibn Yūsuf al-Tīfāshī.

144 Bouhdiba, *Sexuality in Islam*, 127.

145 Sanjakdar, "Sacred Pleasure," 104.

146 Souaiaia, *Contesting Justice*, 1.

147 Nour, "Health Consequences," 1647.

148 Kamali, *Maqāṣid al-Sharīʿah*, 87.

149 Auda, *Maqasid al-Shariah*, 5.

150 These *maqāṣid* are observed throughout the body of the Islamic law, such as the necessities and needs and newly proposed *maqāṣid*, such as "justice" and "facilitation."

151 These *maqāṣid* are observed throughout a certain "chapter" of Islamic law, such as the welfare of children in family law, preventing criminals in criminal law, and preventing monopoly in financial transactions law.

152 These *maqāṣid* are the "intents" behind specific scripts or rulings, such as the intent of discovering the truth in seeking a certain number of witnesses in certain court cases, the intent of alleviating difficulty in allowing an ill and fasting person to break his/her fasting, and the intent of feeding the poor in banning Muslims from storing meat during Eid days.

153 Bicego and Ahmad, *Infant and Child Mortality*.

154 Bhabha, *Human Rights and Adolescence*, 297.

155 Amanat, *Shari'a: Islamic law*, 17.

156 Opwis, *Maslaḥa and the Purpose*, 2.

157 Foltz, Denny, and Baharuddin, *Islam and Ecology*, 194.

158 Rispler-Chaim, *Disability in Islamic Law*, 46.

159 Ibid.

160 Fadel, "Reinterpreting the Guardian's Role," 14–15.

161 For more on the topic see Farhat J. Ziadeh, "Equality (*Kafāʾah*) in the Muslim Law of Marriage," *American Journal of Comparative Law* 6, no. 4 (1957): 503–17.

162 Motzki, "Child Marriage," 138.

163 Fadel, "Reinterpreting the Guardian's Role," 18.

164 Leaman, *Controversies*, 118.

165 Opwis, *Maṣlaḥa and the Purpose*, 28.

166 Kamrava, *New Voices of Islam*, 76.

167 Meiloud, "Conflict," 86.

168 [Q. 22:78] And strive hard in [the way of] Allah, [such] a striving a is due to Him; He has chosen you and has not laid upon you an hardship in religion; the faith of your father Ibrahim; He named you Muslims before and in this, that the Apostle may be a bearer of witness to you, and you may be bearers of witness to the people; therefore keep up prayer and pay the poor-rate and hold fast by Allah; He is your Guardian; how excellent the Guardian and how excellent the Helper!
169 [Q. 3:104] "And let there be [arising] from you a nation inviting to [all that is] good, enjoining what is right and forbidding what is wrong, and those will be the successful."
170 Abu-Rabi', *Blackwell Companion*, 265.
171 Welchman, *Women and Muslim Family Laws*, 64.
172 Abou El Fadl, *Reasoning with God*, 258.
173 Daftary, *Intellectual Traditions in Islam*, 169.
174 Dien, *Islamic Law*, 62.
175 Al-'Uthaymīn, *Sharḥ al-arba'īn al-nawawiyya*, 353.
176 Zakariyah, *Legal Maxims*, 158.
177 Ibid., 160.
178 UNFPA, *Campaign to End Fistula*, 5.
179 Ibn Qudāma, *al-Mughnī*, vol. 12, 169–72.
180 Aggrawal, *Forensic Medicine and Toxicology*, 359.
181 Oats and Abraham, *Llewellyn-Jones Fundamentals*, 319.
182 Eltantawi, "Between Strict Constructionist Shariah," 98.
183 Lindert and Levav, *Violence and Mental Health*, 214.
184 Talley, *Saving Face*, 182.
185 UNICEF, *Fistula in Niamey, Niger*.
186 Bhabha, *Human Rights and Adolescence*, 297.
187 Wond and Özel, *Fistulae*, 331.
188 Zacharin, *Obstetric Fistula*, 137.
189 Shah, *Women, the Koran*, 3.
190 CEDAW is the Convention on the Elimination of All Forms of Discrimination against Women.
191 Bydoon, *Reservations on the "Convention,"* 51.
192 Sachedina, *Islam and the Challenge*, 119.
193 Nguyen and Wodon, , "Global and Regional," 8.
194 Walker, "Engaging Islamic Opinion Leaders," 53.
195 UNICEF.
196 IMF and World Bank, *Global Monitoring Report 2015/2016*, 155.
197 Wodon, *Child-marriage, Family Law*, 1.
198 McCleary-Sills et al., "Child Marriage," 70.

199 Glaser and Frosh, *Child Sexual Abuse*, 5.
200 Ibid.
201 Nour, "Health Consequences," 1644.
202 Welchman, *Women and Muslim Family Laws*, 65.
203 Ibid., 66.
204 Joseph et al., *Encyclopedia of Women*, vol. 3, 58.
205 Nasir, *The Status of Women*, 31.
206 Motzki, *Wie glaubwürdig sind die Hadithe?*, 15.
207 Abou El Fadl, *Epistemology of the Truth*, 4.
208 Abou El Fadl, *The Search for Beauty*, 116.

REFERENCES

Primary Sources

ʿAskarī, Abū Hilāl al-Ḥasan ibn Mahrān al-. *Muʿjam al-furūq al-lughawiyya.* Qum: Muʾassasat al-Nashr al-Islāmī Qum, 1991.

Bukhārī, Abū ʿAbd Allāh Muḥammad ibn Ismāʿīl al-. *Ṣaḥīḥ al-Bukhārī.* Damascus: Dār Ibn Kathīr, 2002.

Harawī, ʿAlī ibn Sulṭān Muḥammad al-Qārī al-. *Mirqāt al-mafātīḥ: sharḥ mishkāt al-maṣābīḥ.* Vol. 6. 12 vols. Beirut: Dār al-Kutub al-ʿIlmīyya, 2001.

Ibn al-Ṣalāḥ, Abū ʿAmr ʿUthmān ibn ʿAbd al-Raḥmān al-Shahrazūrī. *Maʿrifat anwāʿ ʿulūm al-ḥadīth.* Ed. ʿAbd al-Laṭīf al-Hamīm and Māhir Yāsīn al-Faḥl. Beirut: Dār al-Kutub al-ʿIlmiyya, 2002.

Ibn al-Ḥajjāj al-Qushayrī, Muslim. *Ṣaḥīḥ Muslim.* Riyadh: Dār Ṭība li'l-Nashr wa'l-Tawzīʿ, 2006.

Ibn Ḥajar al-ʿAsqalānī, Aḥmad ibn ʿAlī. *Kitāb tahdhīb al-tahdhīb.* Cairo: Dār al-Kitāb al-Islamī, 1909.

– *Nuzhat al-naẓar fī tawḍīḥ Nukhbat al-fikar.* Cairo: al-Maktab al-Islāmī li-Iḥyā' al-Turāth, 2005.

– *Ṭabaqāt al-mudallisīn.* Ed. ʿĀṣim ibn ʿAbd Allāh al-Qaryūṭī. Amman: Maktabat al-Manār, 1983.

Ibn Ḥazm, Abū Muḥammad ʿAlī ibn Aḥmad ibn Saʿīd. *Al-Muḥallā bi'l-āthār.* Vol. 9. 11 vols. Cairo: Idārat al-Ṭibāʿa al-Munīriyya, 1933.

Ibn Hishām al-Maʿāfirī, Abū Muḥammad ʿAbd al-Malik. *Al-Sīra al-nabawiyya.* Cairo: Dār al-Khayr li'l Ṭibāʿa wa'l Nashr wa'l Tawzīʿ, 1992.

Ibn Hubayra al-Shaybānī, ʿAwn al-Dīn Abū al-Muzzafar Yaḥyā ibn Hubayra. *Ikhtilāf al-aʾimma al-ʿulamāʾ.* Vol. 2. 2 vols. Beirut: Dār al-Kutub al-ʿIlmiyya, 2002.

Ibn Isḥāq, Muḥammad. *Life of Muḥammad, translation of Ibn Isḥāq's Sīrat Rasūl Allah with an Introduction and Notes by A. Guillaume.* Oxford: Oxford University Press, 1955.

Ibn Kathīr al-Dimashqī, 'Imād al-Dīn Ismā'īl ibn 'Umar. *Al-Bidāya wa'l-nihāya.* Beirut: Maktabat al-Ma'ārif, 1966.

Ibn Qudāma, Muwaffaq al-Dīn 'Abd Allāh ibn Aḥmad. *Al-Mughnī.* 10 vols. Riyadh: Dār 'Ālam al-Kutub, 1997.Nasā'ī, Abū 'Abd al-Raḥmān ibn Shu'ayb al-. *Ṣaḥīḥ sunan al-Nasā'ī.* Ed. Muḥammad Nāṣir al-Dīn al-Albānī. Vol. 2. 3 vols. Riyadh: Maktabat al-Ma'ārif li'l-Nashr wa'l-Tawzī', 1998.

Naysābūrī, Abū 'Abd Allāh Muḥammad ibn 'Abd Allāh al-Ḥākim al-. *Ma'rifat 'ulūm al-ḥadīth wa-kammiyyat ajnāsih.* Beirut: Dār Ibn Ḥazm, 2003.

Qastillānī, Shihāb al-Dīn Aḥmad ibn Muḥammad al-. *Irshād al-sārī ilā sharḥ ṣaḥīḥ al-Bukhārī.* Cairo: al-Maṭba'a al-Kubrā al-Amīriyya, 1323/1905.

Sarakhsī, Muḥammad ibn Aḥmad al-. *Kitāb al-mabsūṭ.* 21 vols. Beirut: Dār al-Ma'rifa, n.d.

Ṭabarī, Abū Ja'far Muḥammad ibn Jarīr al-. *Ta'rīkh al-Ṭabarī.* Beirut: Manshūrāt Mu'assassat al-A'lamī li'l-Maṭbū'āt, 1998.

Tijānī, Muḥammad Aḥmad *al-.Tuḥfat al 'Arūs wa-mut'at al nufūs*, London: Riad al Rayyes Books Ltd., 1992.

Medical Sources

Aggrawal, Anil. *Forensic Medicine and Toxicology for Ayurveda.* New Delhi: Avichal, 2016.

Bicego, G. and O. B. Ahmad. *Infant and Child Mortality.* Demographic and Health Surveys, Comparative Report no. 20. Calverton: Macro International Inc., 1996.

Bridges, Kenneth R., and Howard A. Pearson, eds. *Anemias and Other Red Cell Disorders.* New York: McGraw-Hill Medical, 2008.

Conley, Lockard. "The Anemias." *American Journal of Nursing* 52, no. 8 (1952): 957–9.

Dewhurst, Sir John. *Female Puberty and Its Abnormalities.* Edinburgh: Churchill Livingstone, 1984.

Fern, Michel, Raphael Jewelewicz, and Michelle Warren. *The Menstrual Cycle – Physiology, Reproductive Disorders, and Infertility.* Oxford: Oxford University Press, 1993.

Jackson, Catherine G. Tatzin. "Nutritional Concerns of Female Recreational Athletes." In *Nutritional Concerns of Women*, ed. Dorothy Klimis-Zacas and Ira Wolinsky, 397–418. London: CRC Press, 2003.

Lindert, Jutta and Itshak Levav. *Violence and Mental Health: Its Manifold Faces*. Dordrecht: Springer, 2015.

Marshburn, Paul B., and Bradley S. Hurst, eds. *Disorders of Menstruation*. Hoboken: Wiley-Blackwell, 2011.

McCleary-Sills, Jennifer, Lucia Hanmer, Jennifer Parsons, and Jeni Klugman. "Child Marriage: A Critical Barrier to Girls' Schooling and Gender Equality in Education." *Review of Faith and International Affairs* 13, no. 3 (2015): 69–80.

Nour, Nawal M. "Health Consequences of Child Marriage in Africa." *Emerging Infectious Diseases Journal* 12, no. 11 (2006): 1644–9.

Nguyen, Minh Cong, and Quentin Wodon. "Global and Regional Trends in Child Marriage." *Review of Faith and International Affairs* 13, no. 3 (2015): 6–11.

Oats, Jeremy, and Suzanne Abraham. *Llewellyn-Jones Fundamentals of Obstetrics and Gynaecology*. New York: Elsevier, 2016.

Polotsky, Alex J., and Nanette Santoro. "The Role of Body Weight in Menstrual Disturbances and Amenorrhea." In *Amenorrhea: A Case-Based, Clinical Guide*, ed. Nanette F. Santoro and Genevieve Neal-Perry, 127–40. New York: Humana Press, 2010.

Roby, Joseph. "Pernicious Anemia." *American Journal of Nursing* 17, no. 7 (1917): 579–83.

Santoro, Nanette F., and Genevieve Neal-Perry, eds. *Amenorrhea: A Case-Based, Clinical Guide*. New York: Humana Press, 2010.

Scrambler, Annette, and Graham Scrambler. *Menstrual Disorders*. Tavistock: Routledge, 1993.

Souza, M.J. De, and R.J. Toombs. "Amenorrhea Associated with the Female Athlete Triad: Etiology, Diagnosis, and Treatment." In *Amenorrhea: A Case-Based, Clinical Guide*, ed. Nanette F. Santoro and Genevieve Neal-Perry, 101–26. New York: Humana Press, 2010.

Vieth, Julie T., and David R. Lane. "Anemia." In *Hematology/Oncology Emergencies*, ed. John C. Perkins, Jonathan E. Davis and Sanjay Arora, 613–28. Philadelphia: Elsevier, 2014.

Wodon, Quentin. "Child Marriage, Family Law, and Religion: An Introduction to the Fall 2015 Issue." *Review of Faith and International Affairs* 13, no. 3 (2015): 1–5.

Wond, Micheline, and Begüm Özel. "Fistulae." In *Management of Common Problems in Obstetrics and Gynecology*, ed. T. Murphy Goodwin, Martin N. Montoro, Laila Muderspach, Richard Paulson, and Subir Roy, 328–33. New York: John Wiley and Sons, 2010.

Zacharin, Robert F. *Obstetric Fistula*. Vienna: Springer, 1988.

Secondary Sources

Abou El Fadl, Khaled. "The Epistemology of the Truth in Modern Islam." *Philosophy and Social Criticism* 41, nos. 4–5 (2015): 473–86.

– *Reasoning with God: Reclaiming Shari'ah in the Modern Age*. Lanham: Rowman and Littlefield, 2014.

– *The Search for Beauty in Islam: A Conference of the Books*. Lanham: Rowman and Littlefield, 2006.

Abu-Rabi', Ibrahim M. 2006. *The Blackwell Companion to Contemporary Islamic Thought*. Malden, MA; Oxford: Blackwell.

'Ạlawī, Sa'īd Binsa'īd al-. *Al-Ijtihād wa'l-tahḍīth: dirāsa fī uṣūl al-fikr al-salafī fī al-Maghrib*. Malta: Markaz Dirāsāt al-'Ālam al-Islāmī, 1992.

Alwani, Taha Jabir al-. *Ijtihad*. London: International Institute of Islamic Thought, 1993.

Amanat, Abbas. 2007. *Shari'a: Islamic Law in the Contemporary Context*. Translated by Frank Griffel. Stanford: Stanford University Press.

Amin, Yasmin. "Sexuality." In *The Oxford Encyclopedia of Philosophy, Science, and Technology in Islam*, ed. Ibrahim Kalin, 244–6. Oxford: Oxford University Press, 2014.

Auda, Jasser. *Maqasid al-Shariah as Philosophy of Islamic Law: A Systems Approach*. London: International Institute of Islamic Thought, 2007.

Baugh, Carolyn. "An Exploration of the Juristic Consensus (*ijmā'*) on Compulsion in the Marriages of Minors." *Comparative Islamic Studies* 5, no. 1 (2009): 33–92.

Bhabha, Jacqueline. *Human Rights and Adolescence*. Philadelphia: University of Pennsylvania Press, 2014.

Born, Max. *Von der Verantwortung des Naturwissenschaftlers. Gesammelte Vorträge*. München: Nymphenburger Verlagshandlung, 1965.

Bouhdiba, Abdelwahab. *Sexuality in Islam*. London: Routledge and Kegan Paul, 1985.

Brown, Jonathan A.C. *The Canonization of al-Bukhārī and Muslim – The Formation and Function of the Sunnī Ḥadīth Canon*. Leiden: E.J. Brill, 2007.

– *Hadith – Muhammad's Legacy in the Medieval and Modern World*. Oxford: Oneworld, 2009.

Bydoon, Maysa. "Reservations on the 'Convention on the Elimination of All Forms of Discrimination against Women (CEDAW)' Based on Islam and Its Practical Application in Jordan: Legal Perspectives." *Arab Law Quarterly* 25 (2011): 51–69.

Daftary, Farhad. *Intellectual Traditions in Islam*. London: I.B. Tauris in association with the Institute of Ismaili Studies, 2000.

Della Porta, Donatella, and Michael Keating. "How Many Approaches in the Social Sciences? An Epistemological Introduction." In *Approaches and Methodologies in the Social Sciences – A Pluralist Perspective*, ed. Della Porta and Keating, 19–39. Cambridge: Cambridge University Press, 2008.

Dien, Mawil Izzi. *Islamic Law: From Historical Foundations to Contemporary Practice*. Edinburgh: Edinburgh University Press, 2004.

Eltantawi, Sarah. "Between Strict Constructionist Shariah and Protecting Young Girls in Nigeria: The Case of Child Marriage (*ijbār*)." In *Women's Rights and Religious Law: Domestic and International Perspectives*, ed. Fareda Banda and Lisa Fishbayn Joffe, 91–107. London: Routledge, 2016.

Fadel, Mohammad. "Reinterpreting the Guardian's Role in the Islamic Contract of Marriage: The Case of the Maliki School." *Journal of Islamic Law* 3 (1998): 1–26.

Foltz, Richard, Frederick Mathewson Denny, and Azizan Haji Baharuddin. *Islam and Ecology: A Bestowed Trust*. Cambridge, MA: Center for the Study of World Religions, Harvard Divinity School, 2003.

Giladi, Avner. *Children of Islam: Concepts of Childhood in Medieval Muslim Society*. New York: St. Martin's Press, 1992.

Glaser, Danya, and Stephen Frosh. *Child Sexual Abuse*. London: Macmillan, 1993.

Hallaq, Wael B. "Was the Gate of Ijtihad Closed?" *International Journal of Middle East Studies* 16, no. 1 (1984): 3–41.

Hasan, Aznan. "An Introduction to Collective Ijtihad (Ijtihad Jama'i): Concept and Applications." *American Journal of Islamic Social Sciences* 20 (2003): 26–46.

Haykel, Bernard. *Revival and Reform in Islam: The Legacy of Muhammad al-Shawkānī*. Cambridge: Cambridge University Press, 2003.

Hoffman, Valerie J. "Qur'anic Interpretation and Modesty Norms for Women." In *The Shaping of an American Islamic Discourse: A Memorial to Fazlur Rahman*, ed. Earle H. Waugh and Frederick M. Denny, 89–117. Atlanta: Scholars' Press, 1998.

International Center for Research on Women (ICRW). *Child Marriage around the World*. Washington, DC: ICRW, 2006.

International Monetary Fund and World Bank. *Global Monitoring Report 2015/2016: Development Goals in an Era of Demographic Change*.

Washington, DC: International Bank for Reconstruction and Development, the World Bank, 2016.

Joseph, Suad, Afsaneh Najmabadi, et al . *Encyclopedia of Women & Islamic Cultures*, vol. 3: *Family, Body, Sexuality, and Health*. Leiden: E.J. Brill, 2006.

Kamali, Mohammad Hashim. *Law in Afghanistan: A Study of the Constitutions, Matrimonial Law, and the Judiciary*. Leiden: E.J. Brill, 1985.

– *Maqāṣid al-Sharīáh, ijtihad, and Civilisational Renewal*. London: International Institute of Islamic Thought, 2012.

Kamrava, Mehran. *The New Voices of Islam: Rethinking Politics and Modernity – A Reader*. Berkeley: University of California Press, 2007.

Khan, Liaquat Ali, and Hisham M. Ramadan. *Contemporary Ijtihad: Limits and Controversies*. Edinburgh: Edinburgh University Press, 2011.

Kolig, Erich. *Conservative Islam: A Cultural Anthropology*. Lanham: Lexington Books, 2012.

Leaman, Oliver. *Controversies in Contemporary Islam*. Abingdon: Routledge, 2014.

Lucas, Scott C. "Abu Bakr b. al-Mundhir, Amputation, and the Art of Ijtihād." *International Journal of Middle East Studies* 39 (2007): 351–68.

Meiloud, Ahmed. "A Conflict between Divine Texts and Human Legal Needs?" *Islamic Africa* 7 (2016): 81–9.

Motzki, Harald. "Child Marriage in Seventeenth-Century Palestine." In *Islamic Legal Interpretation: Muftis and Their Fatwas*, ed. Muhammad Khalid Masud, Brinkley Messick, and David S. Powers, 129–40. Cambridge, MA: Harvard University Press, 1996.

– *Wie glaubwürdig sind die Hadithe? Die klassische islamische Hadith-Kritik im Licht moderner Wissenschaft*. Wiesbaden: Springer Verlag, 2014.

Nasir, Jamal J. *The Status of Women under Islamic Law*. Leiden and Boston: E.J. Brill, 2009.

Nouryeh, Christopher. *The Art of Narrative in the Holy Qur'ān: A Literary Appreciation of a Sacred Text*. Lewiston: Edwin Mellen Press, 2008.

O'Keeffe, Anne. "The Media." In *The Routledge Handbook of Applied Linguistics*, ed. James Simpson, 67–80. Abingdon: Routledge, 2011.

Opwis, Felicitas. *Maslaḥa and the Purpose of the Law: Islamic Discourse on Legal Change from 4th/10th Century to 8th/14th Century*. Leiden: E.J. Brill, 2010.

Pizzorno, Alessandro. "Rationality and Recognition." In *Approaches and Methodologies in the Social Sciences – A Pluralist Perspective*, ed. Donatella Della Porta and Michael Keating, 162–74. Cambridge: Cambridge University Press, 2008.

Rispler-Chaim, Vardit. *Disability In Islamic Law.* Dordrecht: Springer Verlag, 2007.

Sachedina, Abdulaziz. *Islam and the Challenge of Human Rights.* Oxford: Oxford University Press, 2009.

Sanjakdar, Fida. "Sacred Pleasure: Exploring Dimensions of Sexual Pleasure and Desire from an Islamic Perspective." In *The Politics of Pleasure in Sexuality Education: Pleasure Bound*, ed. Louisa Allen, Mary Louise Rasmussen and Kathleen Quinlivan, 95–114. New York: Routledge, 2014.

Shah, Niaz A. *Women, the Koran, and International Human Rights Law: The Experience of Pakistan.* Leiden: Nijhoff, 2006.

Souaiaia, Ahmed E. *Contesting Justice: Women, Islam, Law, and Society.* Albany: SUNY Press, 2010.

Syed, Mohammad Ali. *The Position of Women in Islam: A Progressive View.* Albany: SUNY Press, 2004.

Syrett, Nicholas L. *American Child Bride: A History of Minors and Marriage in the United States.* Chapel Hill: University of North Carolina Press, 2016.

Talley, Heather Laine. *Saving Face: Disfigurement and the Politics of Appearance.* New York: NYU Press, 2014.

United Nations Population Fund (UNFPA). *Campaign to End Fistula.* Annual Report. New York: 2008.

– *When Pregnancy Harms: Obstetric Fistula.* New York: 2012.

United Nations Children's Fund (UNICEF). *Ending Child Marriage: Progress and Prospects.* New York: 2014.

– *Fistula in Niamey, Niger.* New York: 1998.

'Uthaymīn, Muḥammad ibn Ṣāliḥ al-. *Sharḥ al-arbaʿīn al-nawawiyya.* Unaizah: Dār al-Thurayā li-l-nashr, 2004.

Van Dijk, Teun A. "Critical Discourse Analysis." In *The Handbook of Discourse Analysis*, ed. Deborah Schiffrin, Deborah Tannen, and Heidi Ehernberger Hamilton, 352–71. Malden: Blackwell, 2001.

Vikør, S. Knut. "The Development of Ijtihad and Islamic Reform, 1750–1850." Paper presented at the Third Nordic Conference on Middle Eastern Studies, Joensuu, Finland, 19–22 June 1995. https://org.uib.no/smi/paj/Vikor.html.

Walker, Judith-Ann. "Engaging Islamic Opinion Leaders on Child Marriage: Preliminary Results from Pilot Projects in Nigeria." *Review of Faith and International Affairs* 13, no. 3 (2015): 48–58.
Welchman, Lynn. *Women and Muslim Family Laws in Arab States: A Comparative Overview of Textual Development And Advocacy.* Amsterdam: Amsterdam University Press, 2007.
Zakariyah, Luqman. *Legal Maxims in Islamic Criminal Law: Theory and Applications.* Leiden and Boston: Brill Nijhoff, 2015.
Ziadeh, Farhat J. "Equality (Kafā'ah) in the Muslim Law of Marriage." *Journal of Comparative Law* 6, no. 4 (1957): 503–17.

Conclusion

Yasmin Amin

The Qur'an is written in straight lines between two covers. It does not speak by itself; however, men speak for it.

'Alī ibn Abī Ṭālib

This quote is 'Alī ibn Abī Ṭālib's famous response to the Khawārij when they objected to his acceptance of arbitration at the Battle of Ṣiffīn, crying out *"No rule but God's"* at what they perceived to be a false interpretation of the Qur'an. Perhaps 'Alī ibn Abī Ṭālib was the first to raise this awareness, which the chapters in this volume all try to explain. The central issue discussed in the chapters here is the "power of texts." Yet none of the chapters reject any texts; rather, rejection is directed at the uncontested authority of some texts and at human deficiencies in understanding, interpreting, and explaining the ultimate text, the Qur'an.

Contesting some of the authoritative, canonized texts and rulings on the basis of their unjust consequences not only implicitly argues for their "decanonization" but also argues for the rights of different interpretations to exist as a parallel discourse, as noted in Thomas Bauer's book *Die Kultur der Ambiguität* (The Culture of Ambiguity). Bauer argues that today, intolerance in Islam has replaced a long history of tolerance that allowed different discourses to exist in parallel. That tolerance ended around the mid-nineteenth century, as a consequence of Western rigidity and perceived cultural superiority, as well as colonialism. In his third chapter, Bauers highlights the various discourses and interpretations with regard to Qur'anic exegesis that existed side by side, uncontested. Contrary to the expected, these discourses were tolerated, for the Qur'an itself is an allegorical, multilayered text[1] that is open to different interpretations.[2] He quotes Abū al-Khayr Shams al-Dīn Muḥammad ibn Yūsuf al-Jazarī (d. 833/1429), who likened the Qur'an to a bottomless, endless ocean whose shores one never reaches and that never stops flowing;[3] this underscores the point that the Qur'an alone is sacred, yet its different interpretations are not, which in turn opens the door for different opinions, readings, and interpretations.

Decanonization of the established religious tradition often goes hand in hand with the formation of newer and more flexible canons. These, according to H.M. Vos, answer to no other criteria than the religious well-being of the subjects,[4] which is precisely one of the central tenets of this volume. By providing new interpretations that are ethical, gender-conscious, and just, it is possible to construct a new, flexible canon, one that allows believing women agency and participation.

Since the days of Malak Ḥifnī Nāṣif (d. 1918) and May Ziyāda (d. 1941), women scholars, reformists, feminists, and activists have often been silenced, ridiculed, and fought against. The accusation that women lack methodological expertise compared to methodologically sophisticated traditionally male, Muslim scholars has arisen repeatedly over the decades. A case in point is Nazira Zeineddine (d. 1976), who wrote her first book *al-Sufūr wa'l-ḥijāb* (Unveiling and Veiling) in 1928, in which she contested the veil being mandatory, as well as seclusion of and discrimination against women. Much as we have done in this volume, Zeineddine applied the same methodologies used by the traditional male scholars, offering evidence from various holy and canonized texts to contest existing interpretations and offer new ones. She also emphasized the importance of using reason and applying one's intellect, both strongly encouraged by Islam as "the Qur'an invites to reflect upon its meaning in contemporary contexts and to draw reasonable prescriptive rules consistent with its entirety."[5] Zeineddine advised members of the Muslim community to use reason and their own judgment to distinguish between what was moral and ethical and what was not. Like all of the contributors to this volume, she contextualized Qur'anic verses that male clergy and scholars had long interpreted in a misogynistic way, and argued that the Qur'an was not sexist. However, its exclusively male interpreters were, with the expected result that many clerics banned her book.

Today, there are numerous women scholars, many of them Muslim, who specialize in Islamic and Islam-related subjects; however, too often they are still opposed, ridiculed, silenced, and overlooked despite their valuable contributions. In her Al-Faruqi Memorial Lecture, "Muslim Scholars, Islamic Studies, and the Gendered Academy," given at the annual American Academy of Religion in 2017, Kecia Ali demonstrated the gender bias and what she termed as the "politics of citation" in the academy.[6] She presented examples showing how male scholars rarely engage with women's scholarship and even fail to cite it. Her first example was a study of modern Muslim intellectuals that named only three women, none of them Muslim, in an index citing 240 individuals. Her second touched on two books about Black American Muslim thought and identity, which failed to mention Amina Wadud, the African American Muslim thinker who has had a significant global impact. Lastly, she mentioned a book about Muslim reform in which only four Muslim women were named, all from the first/seventh-century community around the Prophet, and all but one from Muḥammad's own household.[7] "Ali asserted that the widespread tendency to frame the findings of Islamic Gender Studies and its emerging canon as 'common sense' highlights the devaluation of women's scholarly (and other) work."[8]

Women scholars and reformers, who are critical of misogynistic readings, are often critiqued very harshly, yet those critiques must not be confused with the critics, because even when the critics are rejected or dismissed, their critique may still be valid and constructive. Furthermore, women scholars even critique themselves. For example, Aysha Hidayatullah's *Feminist Edges of the Qur'an* critiques Islamic feminist hermeneutics and exegesis. Although critique is helpful and identifies valuable questions, one thing about Muslim women's scholarship remains clear, namely its importance as a tool for positive change.

Hegemonic and misogynistic practices are constantly open to subversion and reconfiguration.[9] Steven Snow argues that while the male scholarly "elites" do not necessarily generate the myths that justify their control, they certainly are willing and able to exploit them. Moreover, they are clearly adept at perpetrating deceptions through well-funded propaganda.[10] While women scholars refute deceptions with facts and strong arguments, as demonstrated in this collection, the task of changing these controls is much harder.

One such myth is the *ijmāʿ* (consensus) perpetuated by male scholars and theologians. In fact, there is no real consensus at all. There is no *ijmāʿ* on the definition of *ijmāʿ* itself, on whose it is, on whether it is one of the entire community or only its clerics, on the competence of the constituent members, on the period covered, on the scope of its subject matter, on the source of its authority, on whether matters of creed and dogma fall within its scope, on whether it must be on the basis of positive expression or whether it can be based on the silence of some, and finally, once a so-called consensus is reached, on whether it can be modified in the future based on new evidence or not.[11]

Muḥammad ʿAbduh (d. 1905), the former Grand Mufti of Egypt, a jurist, religious scholar, and reformer, much like Nazira Zeineddine was a strong advocate of the role of reason and the right of independent reasoning. With all the different opinions about *ijmāʿ*, he viewed it as much less dogmatic than the traditional scholars did and as more of a consensus of reason that could reasonably be presumed to be free from error rather than an affirmation of absolute infallibility.[12] Abduh also gave future generations the right to reinterpret the law in the context of their changing lived realities and circumstances, thus restoring the dynamic relationship between reason and consensus.[13]

The aim of this volume has not been to deconstruct or destroy, but to constructively critique, so as to create an atmosphere in which criticism and skepticism can be applied to restore dynamism and to effectively subvert. But what do we mean by subversion? There is no single universally accepted definition of subversion.[14] The Latin root *subvertere* means "to turn from below," and in this collection we understand it as "to turn from within," given that all the chapters work from within the Islamic tradition, using not only the same sources, but also the same methodologies applied by the classical traditional male scholars. Acts of subversion are a powerful way to protest injustice. In this book the term refers to a process that identifies unjust and gender-biased attitudes and preferences that need to be contradicted or reversed, and that questions and re-examines the established order to bring about positive, gender-conscious, and just change.

According to Vos, undisputed authority is difficult to uphold and each process of contextualization is perceived as suspect or even subversive.[15] He adds: "The authority of the canon is already at stake whenever one begins to harbour doubt concerning the internal non-contradiction and consistency of the canon, or whenever one begins to attach a greater value and significance to certain sections of the canon over other sections."[16] This is precisely what happened with certain interpretations that have become more authoritative than others, leading to the exclusion of some. It is also what all the chapters in this collection have done: contextualize, and point out the internal contradictions and inconsistencies inherent in the canon.

Gender is an important factor in the composition, formation, and maintenance of a canon, yet because literacy was generally a privilege of scholars, theologians, and jurists, who were almost exclusively male, it also empowered the male elite.[17] Some have tended toward a problematic approach to their concept of gender, implying that women somehow possess a threatening sexuality, while men do not. This explains the extent to which modern concepts of sexuality are historically situated, political, and cultural.[18] In that context, and much like what Mohammad Omar Farooq intends, the aim is to emphasize how the understanding of the Qur'an and the Prophetic legacy has been clouded by the "interpretive constructs emanating from fallible humans."[19] Farooq calls for the implementation of a value-oriented approach taken from the Qur'an and the life of the Prophet to determine Muslim understanding of the *sharīʿa* and of daily life.[20] This collection is calling for the same thing. Modern challenges, while respectful of the knowledge accumulated over the centuries, require a fresh understanding based on an objective and untainted comprehension of the foundational sources, and a return to broader Islamic values and principles such as justice and equity, as well as the inclusion of contemporary and scientific knowledge.

Vos writes that decanonization can come about in different ways, with at least two variations. The first is decanonization as a result of the dismantling of the canon. He cites the example of the historical analysis of the Bible, which, according to him, "has led to the decomposition and destruction (viz. deconstruction) of that which once was considered to form a unity and that such a process of decanonization can develop under the surface, almost accidentally, as a result of believing Christians."[21] He further argues that the search for the essence of the canonicity of the canon cannot obscure the fact that the canon as such has by then already lost its canonicity. The second process of decanonization occurs when the Holy Scripture is hardly ever read and thus ceases to play the role of a directive and standard in people's daily lives. Vos concludes that this process can occur without the canon's truth or unity ever being disputed.[22]

Vos works within a different religious tradition (i.e., biblical). The challenges of borrowing terms and concepts from Christianity and applying them to Islam were noted in the introduction to this volume.

So the conclusion here uses his theories to help make analogies that explain this volume's aims. In this volume, much like in Vos's argument about the first decanonization process, the chapters provide a theologically grounded discourse of mainly believing women, challenging certain interpretations of the sacred text – however, not the actual text itself or its status as divine revelation. These challenges are intended to deconstruct that which once was considered to form a unity by showing its inconsistencies and subjectivities as well as the effects of its authors' various contexts (political, ideological, sectarian, historical, etc.), which are completely separate from the actual Qur'anic text and its divine status. In addition, the chapters challenge the uses and abuses of *aḥādīth* (Prophetic traditions) to bolster subjective rulings and discriminatory laws that serve existing power structures and augment prevailing hierarchies, thereby showing a disconnect with the Prophet as a role model as well as with the Prophetic legacy. And finally, the chapters draw a line between divine *sharīʿa* and man-made Islamic law, which have long been bestowed an erroneously sacred status and have, as well, long been conflated to silence any critics. These challenges aim at restoring the Qur'anic and Prophetic values, spirit, and principles. As Farooq argues: "A society's real character is a reflection of its values and principles. A legal system and environment also reflect the values and principles that a given society upholds."[23]

The contributors to this volume read the sacred text in order to distil the directives and standards that were obscured as a result of the immense historical and historiographical problems to which the Muslim canon gave rise and which, as Al-Azmeh has noted, have not been studied thoroughly.[24] Al-Azmeh argues "that one could arguably construct variant and highly divergent narratives and histories from the same sources. What modern scholarship does not note often enough or with much consequence is the fact that the traditional Arabic sources cite many varieties of traditions that not only disturb the standard narrative, but could potentially subvert it."[25] This is the subversion this collection has hoped to achieve: to challenge the standard traditional canonized narrative, provide different ones, and (hopefully) eventually decanonize some of the misogynistic accounts. This collection hopes to affect a positive change through a critical gaze, and a creative and constructive intellectual rejuvenation, as well as moral and ethical clarity, in order to ensure a dynamic problem-solving and a value-oriented approach.

The introduction to this volume divided the essays into three parts according to their subject matter and the three aspects of canonization: texts, figures, and laws. This conclusion regroups the chapters in terms of how they address and challenge the canon, deconstruct existing interpretations to provide a new flexible canon, and point out internal inconsistencies and contradictions to subvert and call for decanonization and change.

Omaima Abou-Bakr and Mulki Al-Sharmani's "Islamic Feminist *Tafsīr* and Qur'anic Ethics: Rereading Divorce Verses," Nevin Reda's "*Tafsīr*, Tradition, and Methodological Contestations: The Case of Polygamy," and Asma Afsaruddin's "Reading the Qur'an through a Gendered, Egalitarian Lens: Revisiting the Concept of *Wilāya* in Q. 9:71" all demonstrate the internal inconsistency of classical exegesis and its hesitant steps toward ethical directives. They contest the restriction of interpretation to a limited number of possibilities that all favour a perceived male privilege. They all provide new interpretations as possible kernels for a new, more flexible canon favouring social justice, especially for vulnerable members of the community in important matters, such as divorce, marriage, and guardianship. All three demonstrate how the classical interpretations were shaped more by certain cultural and historical contexts than by systematic and consistent attention to Qur'anic ethics, and thus failed to meet the criteria of justice and egalitarianism. Therefore, those interpretations should lose their canonical status so that the equal partnership of men and women inherent in the Qur'an can be restored, hopefully leading to change and reform.

Vos's argument that each process of contextualization is subversive is especially apparent in Amira Abou Taleb's "Constructing the Image of the Model Muslim Woman: Gender Discourse in Ibn Sa'd's *Kitāb al-ṭabaqāt al-kubrā*" and Doris Decker's "The Love of Prophet Muḥammad for the Jewish woman Rayḥāna bint Zayd: Transformation and Continuity of Gender Conceptions in Classical Islamic Historiography and *Aḥādīth*-Literature." These two chapters illustrate the immense historical and historiographical problems of the sources, reflecting how the authors' political, geographical, sectarian, and ideological positions led them to manipulate the portrayal of historical persons and events to bring about certain behaviours and restrictions. The chapters' historicization and conceptualization of the content also reveals the classical authors' problematic approaches to gender and their implicit accusation that women somehow possess a much more threatening sexuality than men, which must be curtailed and controlled.

The topic of perceived female threatening sexuality is also discussed in Amina Inloes's "How Did Eve Get Married? Two Twelver Shi'i *Ḥadīth* Reports" and Hoda El Saadi's "*Fiqh* Rulings and Gendering the Public Space: The Discrepancy between Written Formality and Daily Reality"; however, these two chapters also provide a different "counter-narrative," which again highlights the internal inconsistencies, contradictions, and discrepancies within the canon. By juxtaposing the legal with the spiritual, and the legal rulings with the lived reality, respectively, these two chapters demonstrate that subversion and contestation of the harsh interpretations and rules did not remain theoretical or desirable, but were actively implemented. Reading the subtexts of *aḥadīth* and rulings and comparing them to the Qur'an and to one another allows for more nuanced discussions and sheds light on the historical developments and contexts, raising serious doubts concerning the internal consistency of the canon.

Aisha Geissinger's "Female Figures, Marginality, and Qur'anic Exegesis in Ibn al-Jawzī's *Ṣifat al-ṣafwa*" validates the argument about literacy being generally conceived of as a privilege of scholars, theologians, and jurists, who were almost exclusively male; this empowered the male elite by reducing the representations of female figures with any degree of interpretive authority to very few, with limited details about their knowledge. The various portrayals, enhancing some while downplaying others, serve to shape and frame them as exceptional rather than normative; in this way they serve somewhat as propaganda tools to bolster the myths justifying male scholars' control, thereby deceptively marginalizing women.

Sarah Eltantawi's "Mysterious Legislation: 'Umar ibn al-Khaṭṭāb's Role in the Legalization of the Stoning Punishment in the Sunni Islamic Tradition" and Yasmin Amin's "Child Marriages Revisited" highlight extra-Qur'anic sources that contributed to legal rulings as well as their disregard of the Qur'an and the Prophetic legacy, placing these sources above both, thereby transgressing against two of the established four sources agreed upon for the formulation of legal rulings. The legalization of the stoning punishment through epistemological contortions, and the legalization of forced child marriage, contradict and even reverse the Qur'an's justice and egalitarianism, as well as its protection of vulnerable members of the community, in order to consolidate men's political and social power. The juxtaposition of a more lenient and gender-just Prophet with the harsh, almost women-unfriendly ʿUmar, and the contrast of the Prophet's alleged marriage to a child bride with his refusal to marry off his own young daughter, undermine the elusive mythical consensus, illustrating that authoritative interpretations can be challenged from within the sources. Applying and simultaneously critiquing the traditional methodologies used by the classical scholars provides a different reading that undermines the permissibility of both stoning and child marriage. Eltantawi's chapter also reinforces Bauer's point about intolerance being a result of Western inflexibility and colonialism, for the stoning punishment was almost never meted out in an Islamic court until the postmodern/postcolonial period.

This collection demonstrates the subjectivity and biases inherent in certain interpretations and the erosion of the Qur'an's egalitarian and gender-just spirit. The Qur'an was effectively placed second to extra-Qur'anic sources through the manipulation of history and historical individuals across the ages. This book offers a thoughtful, deliberate, constructive critique of canonization, often subverting classical methodologies to provide more ethical and egalitarian interpretations that remain true to the Qur'an and the Prophetic legacy, rather than the understanding of fallible humans. As a discourse, it also has an important spiritual and theological dimension: its social-justice–oriented activism is an expression of spirituality and an act of worship aiming at righting the wrongs and injustices accorded women through wrongful interpretations in the name of God. It thus contributes to women's (and men's) spirituality and the healing of souls, enhancing their experience of what it means to be human.

NOTES

1 See, for example, Q. 3.7, "He it is Who has revealed the Book to you; some of its verses are decisive, they are the basis of the Book, and others are allegorical; then as for those in whose hearts there is perversity they follow the part of it which is allegorical, seeking to mislead and seeking to give it (their own) interpretation. but none knows its interpretation except Allah, and those who are firmly rooted in knowledge say: We believe in it, it is all from our Lord; and none do mind except those having understanding."

2 Bauer, *Die Kultur der Ambiguität*, 46.

3 Ibid., 116.
4 Vos, "The Canon as a Straitjacket," 375.
5 Ramadan and Khan, *Contemporary Ijtihad*, 21.
6 IIT, "Dr. Kecia Ali."
7 Ali, Al-Faruqi Memorial Lecture.
8 IIIT, Dr. Kecia Ali.
9 Hayes, *Reading the French Enlightenment*, 67.
10 Snow, *Bourgeois Ideology and Education*, 57.
11 Farooq, *Toward Our Reformation*, 160.
12 DeLong-Bas and Esposito, *Women in Muslim Family Law*, 149.
13 Ibid.
14 Spjut, "Defining Subversion."
15 Vos, "The Canon as a Straitjacket," 375.
16 Ibid., 362.
17 Goody, "Canonization in Oral and Literature Cultures," 13.
18 Carr, "The Song of Songs as a Process," 178.
19 Farooq. *Toward Our Reformation*, viii.
20 Ibid., xi.
21 Vos, "The Canon as a Straitjacket," 363.
22 Ibid.
23 Farooq, *Toward Our Reformation*, 63–4.
24 Al-Azmeh, "The Muslim Canon from Late Antiquity," 193.
25 Ibid., 194.

REFERENCES

Al-Azmeh, A. "The Muslim Canon from Late Antiquity to the Era of Modenism." In *Canonization and Decanonization: Papers Presented to the International Conference of the Leiden Institute for the Study of Religions (LISOR), held at Leiden 9–10 January 1997*, ed. Arie van der Kooij and Karel van der Toorn, 191-228. Leiden: E.J. Brill, 1998.

Al-Azmeh, Aziz. *The Times of History: Universal Topics in Islamic Historiography*. Budapest: Central European University Press, 2007.

Ali, Kecia. *Al-Faruqi Memorial Lecture: Muslim Scholars, Islamic Studies, and the Gendered Academy*. Video. Boston: IIIT, 19 November 19, 2017. https://www.youtube.com/watch?v=ai5XF-bP3KE.

Bauer, Thomas. *Die Kultur der Ambiguität. Eine andere Geschichte des Islams*. Berlin: Verlag der Weltreligionen/Suhrkamp, 2011.

Carr, D.M. "The Song of Songs as a Microcosm of the Canonization and Decanonization Process." In *Canonization and Decanonization: Papers*

Presented to the International Conference of the Leiden Institute for the Study of Religions (LISOR), held at Leiden 9–10 January 1997, ed. Arie van der Kooij and Karel van der Toorn, 173–90. Leiden: E.J. Brill.

Cooke, Miriam. *Nazira Zeineddine: A Pioneer of Islamic Feminism.* Oxford: Oneworld, 2010.

DeLong-Bas, John, L. Esposito, and J. Natana. *Women in Muslim Family Law.* Syracuse: Syracuse University Press, 2001.

Farooq, Mohammad Omar. *Toward Our Reformation: From Legalism to Value-Oriented Islamic Law and Jurisprudence.* Herndon: International Institute of Islamic Thought, 2011.

Goody, J. "Canonization in Oral and Literature Cultures." In *Canonization and Decanonization: Papers Presented to the International Conference of the Leiden Institute for the Study of Religions (LISOR), held at Leiden 9–10 January 1997*, ed. Arie van der Kooij and Karel van der Toorn, 3–16. Leiden: Brill, 1998.

Hayes, Julie Candler. *Reading the French Enlightenment: System and Subversion.* Cambridge: Cambridge University Press, 2006.

Hidayatullah, Aysha A. *Feminist Edges of the Qur'an.* New York: Oxford University Press, 2014.

International Institute of Islamic Thought (IIIT). "Dr. Kecia Ali: Muslim Scholars, Islamic Studies, and the Gendered Academy." Herndon, Virginia, 27 November 2017. https://www.iiit.org/news/dr-kecia-ali-muslim-scholars-islamic-studies-and-the-gendered-academy.

Snow, Steven G. *Bourgeois Ideology and Education: Subversion through Pedagogy.* New York: Routledge, 2018.

Spjut, R.J. "Defining Subversion." *British Journal of Law and Society* 6, no. 2 (1979): 254–61.

Ṭabarī, Abūi Ja'far Muḥammad ibn Jarīr al-. *Tārīkh al-Ṭabarī: tārīkh al-rusul wa'l-mulūk li-Abī Ja'far Muḥammad ibn Jarīr al-Ṭabarī.* Beirut: Dār Ṣādir, 2008.

van der Kooij, Arie,and Karel van der Toorn, eds. *Canonization and Decanonization: Papers Presented to the International Conference of the Leiden Institute for the Study of Religions (LISOR), held at Leiden 9–10 January 1997.* Leiden: Brill, 1998.

Vos, H.M. "The Canon as a Straitjacket." In *Canonization and Decanonization: Papers Presented to the International Conference of the Leiden Institute for the Study of Religions (LISOR), held at Leiden 9–10 January 1997*, ed. Arie van der Kooij and Karel van der Toorn, 351–70. Leiden: E.J. Brill, 1998.

Contributors

OMAIMA ABOU-BAKR is professor of English and comparative literature at Cairo University; a founding member of the Women and Memory forum; and board member and researcher in the global organization Musawah. She specializes in medieval Sufi poetry and comparative topics in medieval English and Arabic literature. Her research interests also include women's mysticism and female spirituality in Christianity and Islam, feminist theology, Muslim women's history, and gender issues in Islamic discourses. Publications include an edited reader that contains translations into Arabic of foundational articles in Christian feminist theology and Islamic feminist research: *al-niswiyya wa'l-dirāsāt al-dīniyya: Feminism and Religious Studies* (2012) and two edited volumes of collected articles; in English: *Feminist and Islamic Perspectives: New Horizons of Knowledge and Reform*, in Arabic: *al-Niswiyya wa'l-manẓūr al-Islāmī* (2013).

AMIRA ABOU-TALEB is adjunct professor in the Department of Arabic and Islamic Civilization at the American University in Cairo. Her most popular course is titled "Beauty and Reason in Arab/Islamic Civilization," which she designed and has taught since 2013. Her current research project explores the historical interpretations of the ethical and moral message of the Qur'an and their impact on modern-day gender relations. She is currently working on Musawah's new research initiative, Building Egalitarian Ethics and Jurisprudence of Muslim Marriages.

ASMA AFSARUDDIN is professor of Islamic studies in the Hamilton Lugar School of Global and International Studies at Indiana University,

Bloomington. She is the author and editor of eight books, including *Jihad: What Everyone Needs to Know* (Oxford University Press, forthcoming); *Contemporary Issues in Islam* (Edinburgh University Press, 2015); the award-winning *Striving in the Path of God: Jihad and Martyrdom in Islamic Thought* (Oxford University Press, 2013), which is being translated into Bahasa Indonesian; and *The First Muslims: History and Memory* (OneWorld, 2008), which has been translated into Turkish and Bahasa Malay. Her research has been funded, among others, by the Harry Frank Guggenheim Foundation and the Carnegie Corporation of New York, which named her a Carnegie Scholar in 2005. Dr Afsaruddin is a founding member of the Women's Islamic Initiative in Spirituality and Equality (WISE) Shura Council.

MULKI AL-SHARMANI is senior lecturer at the Faculty of Theology, University of Helsinki, Finland, and a member of the knowledge-building working group at Musawah. Dr Al-Sharmani researches and writes on contemporary Muslim family law and Islamic jurisprudence; Islamic interpretive tradition and Islamic feminist hermeneutics; Muslim marriage norms and practices in Egypt and Finland; and migration and transnational Muslim families. She is the author of *Gender Justice and Legal Reform in Egypt: Navigating Muslim Family Law* (American University in Cairo Press, 2017); the co-editor of *Men in Charge? Rethinking Authority in Muslim Legal Tradition,* with Ziba Mir-Hosseini and Jana Rumminger (OneWord, 2015); and the co-editor of *Wellbeing of Transnational Muslim Families: Marriage, Law, and Gender,* with Marja Tiilikainen and Sanna Mustasaari (Routledge, 2019).

YASMIN AMIN is finalizing a PhD in Islamic studies at the University of Exeter's Institute of Arab and Islamic Studies, researching "Humour and Laughter in the Ḥadīth." She obtained a postgraduate diploma in Islamic studies in 2006 and an MA in Islamic studies in 2010, both from the American University in Cairo. Her research covers various aspects of gender issues, early Muslim society and culture, and the original texts of Islamic history, law, and Ḥadīth. She is cotranslator of *The Sorrowful Muslim's Guide* and the author of the forthcoming *Musnad Umm Salama and the Factors Affecting Its Evolution.*

DORIS DECKER is research assistant at the Department of Comparative Studies in Culture and Religion at the University of Marburg, Germany.

Her PhD dissertation, published as "Frauen als Trägerinnen religiösen Wissens. Konzeptionen von Frauenbildern in frühislamischen Überlieferungen bis zum 9. Jahrhundert," focused on the depiction of women in early Islamic sources. Her main research areas are the religious history of Islam, early Islamic history and literature, sexuality and religion, and gender-related topics. Studies and research took her to Syria, Egypt, Jordan, and Lebanon. Her postdoctoral project deals with gender and sexuality in modern Shiʿi Islam, using the example of the works of Grand Ayatollah al-Sayyid Muḥammad Ḥusayn Faḍl Allāh.

HODA EL-SAADI is adjunct professor in the Department of Arabic and Islamic Civilization at the American University in Cairo and a cofounder of the Women and Memory forum. She has published several papers on women's work in premodern Muslim societies, including "Gulf Women and The Economy: Pre-Oil Gulf States" in *Gulf Women*, edited by Amira Sonbol (Qatar: Bloomsbury Qatar Foundation, 2012), "Islamic Feminism in Egypt: Between Acceptance and Rejection," in *Arab Feminism: Gender Equality in the Middle East*, edited by Jean Maqdisi, Rafif Sidawy, and Noha Bayoumi (London: IB Tauris, 2014), and *Questions and Answers about Gender and Feminism* [Cards] (Cairo: Women and Memory Forum, 2016) with Aya Sami. Dr El-Saadi is currently working on Musawah's Building Egalitarian Ethics and Jurisprudence of Muslim Marriages project.

SARAH ELTANTAWI is associate professor of modern Islam at Fordham University in New York City. She is the author of *Shariʿah on Trial: Northern Nigeria's Islamic Revolution* (University of California Press, 2017) and has published on issues ranging from Shiʿi jurisprudence on the stoning punishment in Islam to the revolution in Egypt. She frequently contributes to public discourse on issues concerning Islam, Muslims, and Middle East affairs. She earned her MA in Middle Eastern studies and PhD in the study of religion from Harvard University.

AISHA GEISSINGER is associate professor in the Religion Program at Carleton University in Ottawa, Canada. Geissinger's research is located at the intersection of the study of the Qur'an and the history of its exegesis (*tafsir*), the *ḥadīth* literature, and gender. Her recent publications on these areas include: *Gender and Muslim Constructions of Exegetical Authority: A Rereading of the Classical Genre of Qur'an Commentary* (Leiden and Boston: Brill, 2015), and "No, a Woman Did Not 'Edit the Qur'an': Towards a Methodologically Coherent Approach to a Tradition Portraying a Woman and Written Quranic Materials," *Journal of the American Academy of Religion*, 85, no. 2 (2017): 416–45.

WAFYA HAMOUDA specializes in translation studies. She received her BA in education with high honours from Tanta University in 2000. She received her PhD from Newcastle University in 2014 with a dissertation titled "Anaphora Resolution for Arabic Machine Translation: A Case of Nafs" and is currently a lecturer at the Faculty of Education, Tanta University. She has presented on various topics at several international conferences, for example at the Discovering Babel workshop at Oxford in 2011.

AMINA INLOES is lecturer at the Islamic College in London, UK. She completed her PhD at the University of Exeter on the subject of Shiʿi *ḥadīth* about women in pre-Islamic sacred history. Her research interests include narrative in Islam and esoteric Shiʿi theology, and her publications include articles on Shiʿi history and *ḥadīth* as well as *Women in Shiʿism – Ancient Stories, Modern Ideologies* (Gorgias Press, 2019).

NEVIN REDA is assistant professor of Muslim studies at Emmanuel College of Victoria University in the University of Toronto. Her research interests include the poetics and hermeneutics of qurʾanic narrative structure, Hebrew Bible, and Qurʾan, spiritually integrative approaches to the Qurʾan, Islamic ethical-legal theory (*uṣūl al-fiqh*), Islamic political theory, and Islamic feminist hermeneutics. Her most recent publication is *The al-Baqara Crescendo: Understanding the Qurʾan's Style, Narrative, Structure, and Running Themes* (Montreal and Kingston: McGill-Queen's University Press, 2017). Dr Reda is a founding member of the Women's Islamic Initiative in Spirituality and Equality (WISE) Shura Council and is currently working with Musawah on the organization's new research initiative: Building Egalitarian Ethics and Jurisprudence of Muslim Marriages.

Index

banāt, 324
Banū Qurayẓa. *See* Qurayẓa tribe
al-Baqīʿ, 219, 233
Barlas, Asma 27–9, 116
Barsbay, Ashraf, 275, 278
Basra, 154–5, 158–9, 165–6, 227, 243, 245
Battle of the Camel, 184, 191
bayʿa, 182, 193, 195. *See also* ʿAqaba pledge
al-Bayḍāwī, ʿAbd Allāh ibn ʿUmar, 112, 114, 346
al-Bayhaqī, Abū Bakr, 162, 211, 235–7, 241, 247, 293
Belsey, Catherine, 180
Boisliveau, Sylvie, 6
Brown, Jonathan, 7, 9, 69, 77, 247, 318–19, 331
al-Bukhārī, 7, 15–6, 112, 246, 291–3, 300, 302, 306, 308, 314, 317–21, 326–8

canon, 4–9, 365–73; in biographical literature, 12, 14, 179–81, 201–2, 209–12, 222, 224, 229, 238, 240–3; in *fiqh* and lawmaking, 15–16, 24, 57, 79, 210, 264, 289, 304, 306, 315–17, 322, 330, 336, 342–3; in ḥadīth, 12, 15, 128–31, 135, 317–19, 321, 326–8, 331–2, 337–8, 342; kanòn, 6; in Qur'an exegesis, 11, 13, 23–4, 57, 68–9, 74, 77–9, 90–1, 101–2, 119–20
Christians, 8, 80, 130, 138, 236, 239, 369
concubine, 188, 216, 226, 228–32, 234–8, 241
consensus. *See ijmāʿ*
Cooperson, Michael, 197
Cornell, Rkia, 153–5, 166
corruption. *See fasād*

al-ḍaḥyāʾ, 323, 325, 327, 344, 346
Damascus, 164, 244, 248, 267
daraja, 43–4
al-Dārānī, Abū Sulaymān, 163–4
ḍarar, 338–40
ḍarūriyyāt, 32, 335
al-Dāwūdī, 155
al-Dhahabī, 319
Dhū al-Nūn, 151, 156–7
dirʿ, 185
diyya, 333
Draz, Muhammad, 11, 34–5, 47, 51

El Cheikh, Nadia Maria, 198
El-Shamsy, Ahmed, 7, 69
Eve, 12, 87, 103, 127–39, 141–5, 372
exegesis. *See tafsīr*
exegetical traditions. *See āthār*

Fadel, Mohammad, 331, 337
al-Farābī, 31
fasād, 265
Fāṭima bint Muḥammad, 88, 127, 137, 141, 144, 146, 328, 330–1
Fāṭima of Nishapur, 151, 156–9, 161, 169
fidya, 110
fiqh, 7, 10–12, 14–15, 29, 31–2, 104, 180, 188, 191, 196, 210, 243, 245, 261–5, 270–3, 277–80, 290, 299, 305, 315, 318, 328, 330, 333, 335–6, 342, 372
fistula, 333, 338–40
fitna, 158, 184, 265
Foucault, Michel, 180